ARTIFICIAL INTELLIGENCE QUESTION BANK

(For CLASS IX)
(Based on CBSE Syllabus Code 417)

S P Verma

www.bpbonline.com

FIRST EDITION 2022

REPRINT 2023

ISBN: 978-81-943344-0-8

Distributors:

BPB PUBLICATIONS
20, Ansari Road, Darya Ganj
New Delhi-110002
Ph: 23254990/23254991

DECCAN AGENCIES
4-3-329, Bank Street,
Hyderabad-500195
Ph: 24756967/24756400

MICRO MEDIA
Shop No. 5, Mahendra Chambers,
150 DN Rd. Next to Capital Cinema,
V.T. (C.S.T.) Station, MUMBAI-400 001
Ph: 22078296/22078297

BPB BOOK CENTRE
376 Old Lajpat Rai Market,
Delhi-110006
Ph: 23861747

Published by Manish Jain for BPB Publications, 20 Ansari Road, Darya Ganj, New Delhi-110002 and Printed by him at Manipal Technologies Limited, Manipal

www.bpbonline.com

Dedicated to

In the Fond Memory

Of

Late Dr UVS Verma ji

(Elder brother),

Late Mrs Raj Rani Verma ji

(Bhabhi)

and

Late Mr Vijay Kumar Verma ji

(Younger brother)

About the Author

S P Verma, M.Sc; M.Ed; PGCPM has been working in the field of education since last 35 years. As a seasoned educationist, teacher trainer, career counsellor, academic auditor, motivator, mentor, author and editor, he has authored 55 school books, 6 research papers, 10 research articles, more than 70 articles on careers and edited more than 200 educational products. More than 20k educators (teachers and principals) attended his training sessions across the country. More than 200k students were career counselled and inspired to take right career plan by him.

Formerly holding the positions like Principal, Kendriya Vidyalaya Sangathan, New Delhi; Regional Director, Teacher Sity, New Delhi; Regional Director, iDC, New Delhi; and Director (School Trg), Vidya Institute of Training and Development, VKP, Meerut; he is now serving as Director (Trg and Innovation), GEM Foundatiions, Bengaluru. Besides Associate Life Member of Computer Society of India (CSI), he is associated with a number of professional bodies as Life Member, like Vigyan Parishad, Allahabad; Hindi Vigyan Sahitya Parishad, BARC, Mumbai; InSc, Bengaluru, PTAI, New Delhi, etc.

Acknowledgements

I would like to acknowledge the contributions of all the educationists (teachers and principals), professionals, and reviewers, who provided their feedback and suggestions on the MS of this book. Especially, I am grateful to **Mr. Pavnesh Kumar**, Former Controller of Examinations, CBSE; **Dr DK Sharma**, Dean (School of Engineering and Technolgy), IIMT University, Meerut; **Prof. RC Singh**, Controller of Examinations, Sharda University, Greater Noida; **Mr. Akshay Sharma**, B.Tech., ONGC, Mehsana and **Mrs. Shweta Agrawal**, MCA for their specific suggestions.

It's my proud privilege to put on record my sincere gratitude to my publisher **M/s BPB Publications**, New Delhi, for accepting my vision and plan of writing AI Resource books for classes IX to XII (Question Bank) and Coding books for classes VI to VIII and providing me the opportunity for the same. The initial interaction with **Mr. Manish Jain**, CEO, and **Mr. Varun Jain**, Director was fruitful in making a long-term association and bonding. I am grateful to them and the entire team of BPB Publications for bringing out these publications in a short span of time.

I am grateful to my well-wishers namely **Mr. RL Jamuda**, Former Commissioner KVS; **Dr. MM Swami**, Former Deputy Commisioner, KVS; **Mr VK Gupta,** Former Deputy Commissioner, KVS; **Mr. DK Saini**, Former Deputy Commissioner, KVS; **Mr NK Verma**, AGM, BHEL HQ; **Mr AK Verma**, CEO, Eduwix, New Delhi; **Mr AK Pattnaik**, Senior GM (Academic), Kalorex Group of Institutions, Ahmedabad; **Prof MC Bansal, Pr SP Sharma, Prof GL Mittal, Mr YP Sharma, Mr Vipin Agrawal; Mr. Matin Ahmed, Mr. NK Giri, Mr NK Bansal** and **Mr SC Sharma** for their constant support, help and motivation to do something good to the society.

I am touched by the love, patience and tolerance shown, during the completion of this project, by my family members- **Mrs. Rekha Verma** (Life Partner), **Sqn Ldr Anuj Verma** (Son), Dearest **Atharv** (Grandson) and **Mrs. Shelja Sharma**, B.Tech. (Daughter in Law). I am grateful to them as well as to all my friends and relatives supporting me in all the creative tasks.

While preparing the manuscript of this book, I have gone through a number of books and different websites. I am grateful to all those authors, contributors, editors, freelancers whose articles are read and used in one or another way in this book. And last but not least, I am indebted to God for keeping my brain alive and my health sound even at the time of the Covid Pandemic so that He could get completed this task through me.

— S P Verma

Preface

It is a matter of great pleasure and satisfaction to put the first edition of **"Artificial Intelligence Question Bank (for class IX)"** before the enthusiastic learners. Artificial intelligence is getting more attention in the world day by day. It is touching almost all fields related to the development of the human-beings. AI based Technology using coding and its applications is changing at a very fast rate influencing day-to-day life positively. AI and coding are nowadays applied in almost all fields, be it education, transport management, air traffic control, medicine manufacturing, space research, customer care, pandemic control, or entertainment.

After understanding the importance and demand of AI, the Govt of India, through CBSE, has launched Skills Development subjects from class VIII onwards, including Coding, Artificial Intelligence, Data Science, etc. CBSE has introduced ***'Artificial Intelligence'*** as a skill subject in classes IX-XII to simplify the AI learning experience. It is an attempt to nurture design thinking, logical flow of ideas and apply this across all the disciplines.

This resource book is written according to the latest examination guidelines and syllabus of AI issued by CBSE. The main objective of writing this series of books for classes IX to XII is to provide test items on technical knowledge with all examination aspects of AI. Thus, the learners will become fully competent to face the challenges of living in an AI-based applications-equipped futuristic society and to face the exams boldly to get shining success. Moreover, emphasis on the development of 21st Century Life Skills through a variety of test items is laid down.

The resource book contains nine chapters and Solved and Unsolved Sample Papers. The salient features of the book are as follows:

- It is based on the syllabus and guidelines issued by CBSE.
- Simple, easy, and understandable language is used to clarify the content through a variety of test items.
- Each unit is divided into four sections, viz Unit in Brief, CBSE/NCERT Section, Solved Exercises, and Unsolved Exercises.
- It explains the concepts of each unit in lucid language in the form of **"Unit In Brief"**.
- **'CBSE/NCERT Section'** contains all solved questions appeared in CBSE/NCERT textbook and/manual.
- **'Solved Exercises'** section provides all sorts of the test items including MCQs, Fill in the Blanks, True/False Type, Statements Based Questions, Assertion Reason Type Questions, VSAQs, SAQs, LAQs, and HOTS Questions related to the content of the unit.
- **"Competency Based Questions"** are incorporated in all units for enhancing and evaluating competencies among learners as per NEP 2020.
- **'Unsolved Questions'** section provides additional unsolved questions for practice.
- **Solved Sample Papers**, and **Unsolved Papers for Term 1 and Term 2 are provided.**
- Each book incorporates a pictorial setup in presenting the content by using tables, charts, graphs, pictures, photographs, etc.

I am sure that the sincere efforts put in by the author and publication team will be well received by the dynamic, dedicated and passionate teachers, and energetic learners. The author and the publisher will appreciate all sorts of feedback from the readers to improve the quality of the content.

Dated 05 Sept. 2021

SP Verma
E-mail: spv1962@gmail.com

Coloured Images

Please follow the link to download the
Coloured Images of the book:

https://rebrand.ly/ec5d3f

We have code bundles from our rich catalogue of books and videos available at **https://github.com/bpbpublications**. Check them out!

Errata

We take immense pride in our work at BPB Publications and follow best practices to ensure the accuracy of our content to provide with an indulging reading experience to our subscribers. Our readers are our mirrors, and we use their inputs to reflect and improve upon human errors, if any, that may have occurred during the publishing processes involved. To let us maintain the quality and help us reach out to any readers who might be having difficulties due to any unforeseen errors, please write to us at :

errata@bpbonline.com

Your support, suggestions and feedbacks are highly appreciated by the BPB Publications' Family.

Piracy

If you come across any illegal copies of our works in any form on the internet, we would be grateful if you would provide us with the location address or website name. Please contact us at **business@bpbonline.com** with a link to the material.

If you are interested in becoming an author

If there is a topic that you have expertise in, and you are interested in either writing or contributing to a book, please visit **www.bpbonline.com**. We have worked with thousands of developers and tech professionals, just like you, to help them share their insights with the global tech community. You can make a general application, apply for a specific hot topic that we are recruiting an author for, or submit your own idea.

Reviews

Please leave a review. Once you have read and used this book, why not leave a review on the site that you purchased it from? Potential readers can then see and use your unbiased opinion to make purchase decisions. We at BPB can understand what you think about our products, and our authors can see your feedback on their book. Thank you!

For more information about BPB, please visit **www.bpbonline.com**.

Table of Contents

Syllabus

ARTIFICIAL INTELLIGENCE (SUBJECT CODE 417)
Class IX (Session 2021-22)
Total Marks: 100 (Theory-50 + Practical-50)

	TERM	UNITS	NO. OF HOURS for Theory and Practical	MAX. MARKS for Theory and Practical
PART A	**Employability Skills**			
	Term I	Unit 1: Communication Skills-I	10	5
		Unit 2: Self-Management Skills-I	10	
		Unit 3: ICT Skills-I	10	
	Term II	Unit 4: Entrepreneurial Skills-I	15	5
		Unit 5: Green Skills-I	05	
		Total	**50**	**10**
PART B	**Subject Specific Skills**			**Marks**
	Term I	Unit 1: Introduction to Artificial Intelligence (AI)		10
		Unit 2: AI Project Cycle		10
	Term II	Unit 3: Neural Network		5
		Unit 4: Introduction to Python		15
		Total		**40**
PART C		**Practical Work:** • Unit 4: Introduction to Python		20
		Practical Examination		10
		Viva Voce		5
		Total		**35**
PART D		Project Work/ Field Visit/ Practical File/ Student Portfolio		10
		Viva Voce		5
		Total		**15**
		GRAND TOTAL	**200**	**100**

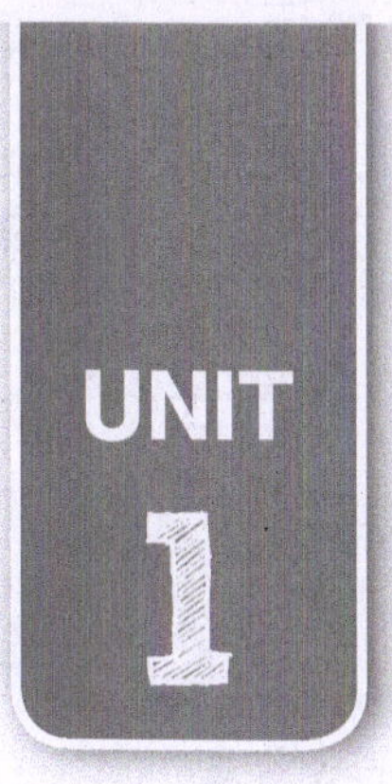

UNIT 1 Communication Skills – I

1.1 UNIT IN BRIEF

- The word 'Communication' has been derived from the Latin word 'commūnicāre,' which means 'common.'
- Communication is defined as a process of exchanging information, knowledge, feelings, thoughts, or attitude between at least two persons.
- Communication may occur between one person to another person, one person to many persons, or many persons to one person.
- Communication is the 'sharing' of information, knowledge, feelings, or attitude between two or more individuals or within a group to reach a common understanding.
- Communication skills are those skills that are required to speak and write properly and effectively.

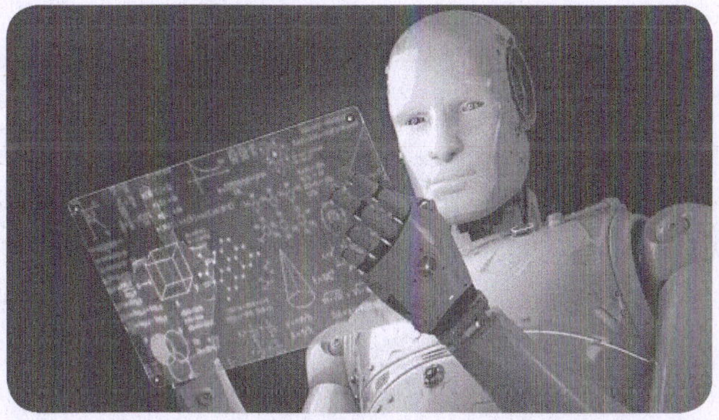

Figure 1.1

- There are three types of communications-verbal, non-verbal and visual communication.
- Verbal communication use linguistics to convey the message/information/feelings.
- Non-verbal communication uses other forms like tactile, auditory, kinaesthetic channels to transmit knowledge.
- In visual communication, information/ideas/feelings are communicated by using visuals.
- Five types of visual communication (Objects, Models, Photographs, Graphs, Maps) are used.
- In verbal communication, the use of sounds and words is done to express oneself, especially in contrast to using gestures or mannerisms (non-verbal communication). It enables us to share the knowledge, thoughts, information, or feelings with others by using the words in such a manner that the other person(s) may understand it well.

- If we understand the components/elements required to make verbal communication effective, then it is easier for us to communicate verbally effectively.
- Speaking fast conveys an excited or agitated feel. Speaking in a low tone can send a steady, reliable feeling.
- Voice volume may range from a whisper to a scream and everything in between. A very low voice can represent that you are shy or something you do not want to be overheard, that you are depressed, or you are mischievous.
- It is essential to use appropriate language, i.e., the language which can be easily understood by the receiver(s). In modern world, more than 6000 languages are spoken.
- Vocabulary reflects how comfortable you are with your wordy style. It helps in the usage of suitable words in different contexts. Using correct words at the right time tells the wisdom of the speaker.
- Non-verbal communication is the non-linguistic transmission of information through visual, auditory, tactile, and kinaesthetic channels. Thus, it enables us to share our thoughts with other persons by using any other method than using words.
- Grammar is defined as 'the set of rules for how words in a language are converted into phrases and phrases into sentences, and so on'.
- Listening is an essential component of the communication process and to respond appropriately to communication. Listening removes a lot of misunderstandings.
- Non-verbal communication or non-word communication is an act of exchanging thoughts, feelings, postures, opinions, or information without the use of words. Thus, in the type of communication, gestures, sign language, facial expression, and body language are used.
- Smile is a powerful expression that transmits Happiness, Friendliness, Warmth, and Liking.
- There may be two types of feedback-positive Feedback and Negative Feedback. For effective Feedback, a person should have a goal, take action to achieve the goal, and receive goal-related information.
- Feedback plays an important role in communication as it conveys both the source/sender and the receiver how the message is being interpreted.
- Visual communication is the transmission of ideas, information, and knowledge in the forms that can be seen. It is also known as graphic communication.
- There are many types of facial expressions, but happiness, anger, sadness, and fear are considered universal facial expressions.
- 'A picture is worth more than one thousand words' is an old proverb, which clearly defines the importance of visuals in the process of communication. Graphs, charts, etc., are used to convey specific information, while road signals convey a particular meaning.
- When the message sent is understood correctly by the receiver, it is known as effective communication.
- Communication is a two-way process.
- Effective communication is regarded as the key to success in all spheres of life.

- Perspectives are defined as the ideas, views, or fixed ways of thinking, which may affect our communication.
- Visual perception is defined as the ability to see and interpret (analyse and give meaning to) the visual information that surrounds us.
- Forms of Visual Communication include Public Signs, Visual Symbols, Charts and Graphs, Tables, Maps, Diagrams, etc.
- Visual perceptual skills involve the ability to organise and interpret information correctly.
- When our positive or negative past experiences affect our communication or alter our full potential for communicating, then we need to be aware.
- Prejudices are due to cultural differences and personal preferences or experiences. Not all prejudices involve a negative characteristic.
- There are five main types of writing, namely expository, descriptive, narrative, persuasive, and creative.
- Writing skills filter our knowledge and intelligence to the point of value.
- For communicating in writing, one must know about the basic writing skills and should try the development of these writing skills.
- Persuasive writing explains the opinion of the writer and attempts to influence the reader.

Figure 1.2

- The narrative is the writing in which the author tells a story.
- In descriptive writing, imagery and specific details are incorporated in writing.
- A phrase is defined as a group of words that are used together to give a specific meaning.
- A phrase does not have a full verb, and it may be short or long, but it does not include the subject.
- A noun phrase may be a single noun or a group of words built around a single noun.
- A group of words that gives the complete meaning of the ideas is called a sentence.
- A sentence should be grammatically correct.
- There are four main types of sentences.
- Command or imperative sentence commands or make requests.

- Exclamatory sentences express emotion using an exclamatory mark (!).
- Writing skills are treated essential for effective communication and professional growth.
- Essential elements for writing effectively include reading, comprehension, transcription, sentence construction, content knowledge, planning, and self-regulation.
- Parts of speech in English grammar include noun, pronoun, verb, adjective, adverb, preposition, conjunction, and interjection.
- Two types of articles-definite and indefinite, are used.
- Four elements for paragraph writing are unity, order, coherence, or completeness.

1.2 CBSE/NCERT SECTION (SOLVED CBSE/NCERT EXERCISES)

1.2.1 Multiple Choice Questions

Read the questions carefully and circle the letter (a), (b), (c), or (d) that best answer the question.

1. What is the purpose of communication?
   a) Inform (tell someone about something)
   b) Influence (get someone to do something you want)
   c) Share thoughts, ideas, feelings
   d) All of the above
2. Which of the following methods is used to receive information from the sender through a letter?
   a) Listening b) Speaking c) Reading d) Writing
3. How do you receive information on the phone?
   a) Listening b) Speaking c) Reading d) Writing
4. Choose the correct example of oral communication.
   a) Reports b) Newspapers
   c) Face-to-face conversation d) Notes
5. When we communicate verbally, we should use _______.
   a) difficult words b) simple words
   c) confusing words d) abbreviations
6. Why do we send emails?
   a) To reach on time b) To share documents and files
   c) To talk to each other d) To meet each other
7. Which of these is a positive (good) facial expression?
   a) Staring hard b) Nodding while listening
   c) Wrinkled forehead d) Looking away from the speaker

8. What does an upright (straight) body posture convey/ show?
   a) Shyness b) Fear Procedure c) Confidence d) Intelligence
9. Which of these is not an appropriate non-verbal communication at work?
   a) Putting an arm around a co-worker's shoulder
   b) Shaking hands firmly
   c) Looking at the speaker with a smile
   d) Standing with an upright posture
10. When you are preparing for a presentation, you should ________________.
    a) focus on the objectives of the presentation
    b) practice your speech in front of a mirror or friend
    c) do rehearsals to time your presentation of slides
    d) All of the above
11. What is a sentence?
    a) A group of ideas that form a complete paragraph
    b) A group of words that communicate a complete thought
    c) A set of rules that we must follow to write correctly
    d) A set of words that contains all the basic punctuation marks
12. Which of these sentences does not use uppercase letters correctly?
    a) I am Hungry. b) Divya and Sunil are reading.
    c) The bucket is full of water. d) She lives in Delhi.
13. Which of these sentences is punctuated correctly?
    a) Where are you going:
    b) I have a pen, a notebook, and a pencil?
    c) I am so happy to see you!
    d) This is Abdul's house.
14. Identify the subject in the sentence, "The children played football."
    a) The children b) Children played
    c) Played d) Football
15. Identify the object in the sentence, "The children played football."
    a) The children b) Children played
    c) Played d) Football
16. Which of these sentences has both indirect and direct objects?
    a) I am watching TV. b) She bought a blue pen.
    c) The girls played cricket. d) He wrote his sister a letter.

17. Which of these sentences is in passive voice?
    a) They are watching a movie.
    b) The clock was repaired by Raju.
    c) He is sleeping in the room.
    d) My pet dog bit the postman.
18. What is phonetics?
    a) It is the study of how we write words in English.
    b) It is the study of how people understand sentences.
    c) It is the study of how many words the English language has.
    d) It is the study of the sounds we make when we speak.
19. What are the different types of sounds used in English pronunciation?
    a) Vowel sounds
    b) Diphthong sounds
    c) Consonant sounds
    d) All of the above
20. You say 'Good Morning' when it is ______________.
    a) 11 am
    b) 9 am
    c) 8 am
    d) All (a), (b) and (c)
21. You may say 'Hi' when you meet ______________.
    a) your teacher in class
    b) a senior in the office
    c) your Principal
    d) your friends at a shop
22. You say 'Good Afternoon' when it is ______________.
    a) 10 am
    b) 11.59 am
    c) 6 pm
    d) 1 pm
23. You say 'Good Evening' when it is ______________.
    a) 11 am
    b) 9 am
    c) 2 pm
    d) 7 pm
24. A postal code is ______________.
    a) a group of numbers or letters used to identify a government building.
    b) A code is used to indicate the door number of a house.
    c) A group of numbers or letters is used by the post office to identify a region.
    d) a code used to identify different post offices
25. Raju is the class monitor. He wants to know why Ramesh is coming late every day. Which of the following is a question that Raju can ask Ramesh?
    a) Do you come on time?
    b) Are you late?
    c) Why are you late every day?
    d) Will it not be easier to complete your work if you come on time?

26. If you have not understood a task given to you, which question should you ask?
    a) Where are the reports of this task?
    b) Can you repeat the instructions for this task?
    c) Can you give me an example of this task?
    d) Why are you doing this task?
27. Sheela does not have time, so she decides to delay a task. Which question should he ask before ignoring the task?
    a) What is this task?
    b) When does this task need to be completed?
    c) Is this task important?
    d) No need to ask any question.
28. Renuka is joining a new school. Which of the following questions will help her become comfortable with her new classmates?
    a) How long have you been studying here?
    b) Would you like to share my lunch?
    c) What do you all do in your free time?
    d) All the options are correct.
29. What are close-ended questions?
    a) Questions that can have any answer
    b) Questions that do not have answers
    c) Questions with yes/no answers
    d) Questions that have many answers
30. Which of these are open-ended questions?
    a) Where do you live?
    b) Are you hungry?
    c) How do you feel?
    d) Did you meet him?
31. Which of these are not question words?
    a) What
    b) Want
    c) Which
    d) How
32. Which of these is the correct way to convert the sentence "You are studying" into a question?
    a) You are studying?
    b) Studying you are?
    c) Are you studying?
    d) Studying are you?

ANSWERS									
1. (d)	2. (d)	3. (a)	4. (c)	5. (b)	6. (b)	7. (b)	8. (c)	9. (a)	10. (d)
11. (b)	12. (a)	13. (d)	14. (a)	15. (d)	16. (d)	17. (b)	18. (d)	19. (d)	20. (d)
21. (d)	22. (d)	23. (d)	24. (d)	25. (d)	26. (b)	27. (c)	28. (d)	29. (c)	30. (c)
31. (b)	32. (c)								

1.2.2 Match the columns

Column A: Communication Barriers	Column B: Examples
(i) Language	A. Trying to read a book when somebody else is watching TV in the same room.
(ii) Emotional	B. In some cultures, wearing shoes and walking inside the kitchen is considered rude and disrespectful.
(iii) Environmental	C. Talking in Hindi when others know only Tamil.
(iv) Cultural	D. Parent is not talking to the child.

ANSWERS			
(i) (C)	(ii) (D)	(iii) (A)	(iv) (B)

1.2.3 Fill in the blanks

1. Use the following words to complete the form given below:

   football and swimming, seven-years-old, Hassan, Yasmin, in Bengaluru.

   (a) My first name is ______________.

   (b) My surname is __________.

   (c) I am _________.

   (d) I live __________.

   (e) I like __________.

ANSWERS	
(a) My first name is Yasmin.	(b) My surname is Hassan.
(c) I am seven years-old.	(d) I live in Bengaluru.
(e) I like football and swimming.	

2. Fill correct nouns and verbs from the box to fill in the blanks given below:

   girl, girls, boy, milk, dog, skipping, riding, running, studying, drinking, barking

   a. The ______________ is ____________________.

   b. The ______________ is ____________________.

   c. The ______________ is ____________________.

   d. The ______________ are ____________________.

   e. Raju is ______________ ________________.

   f. The ______________ is _________________.

ANSWERS		
a. The dog is barking.	b. The girl is running.	c. The boy is riding.
d. The girls are skipping.	e. Raju is drinking milk.	f. The boy is running.

3. Put a (×) mark against the actions below which are incorrect for demonstrating the use of non-verbal communication otherwise put (√) mark.

Actions	Correct (√) / Incorrect (x) use of non-verbal communication
Laughing during formal communication	
Scratching head	
Smiling when speaking to a friend	
Nodding when you agree with something	
Standing straight	
Yawning while listening	
Sitting straight	
Maintaining eye contact while speaking	
Biting nails	
Firm handshake	
Clenching jaws	
Looking away when someone is speaking to you	
Intense stare	

Answer:

Actions	Correct (√) / Incorrect (x) use of non-verbal communication
Laughing during formal communication	X
Scratching head	X
Smiling when speaking to a friend	√
Nodding when you agree with something	√
Standing straight	√
Yawning while listening	X
Sitting straight	√
Maintaining eye contact while speaking	√
Biting nails	X
Firm handshake	X
Clenching jaws	X
Looking away when someone is speaking to you	X
Intense stare	X

1.2.4 Short Answer Type Questions

1. Select the noun, pronoun, adjective, verb, and adverb in these sentences.

   a) Sanjay plays football every day.

   b) Divya gave him new books.

   c) I opened the red box carefully.

Ans. a) Noun-Sanjay, football; Verb-plays; adverb-everyday

b) Noun-Divya, books; Pronoun-him; Verb-gave; Adjective-new

c) Noun- box; Pronoun-I; Verb-opened; Adjective-red; Adverb-carefully

2. Write down the different types of verbal communication. Give an example for each type.

Ans. In verbal communication, the use of sounds and words is done to express oneself, especially in contrast to using gestures or mannerisms (non-verbal communication). It enables us to share the knowledge, thoughts, information, or feelings with others by using the words in such a manner that the other person(s) may understand it well.

Verbal communication is of four types:

(i) **Intrapersonal verbal communications:** This form of communication is quite private and restricted to ourselves. It includes the silent conversation we have with ourselves, wherein we juggle roles between the sender and receiver for processing our thoughts. When a person is sitting in "Dhyan" (meditation), he/she may use this type of communication.

(ii) **Interpersonal verbal communication:** This form of communication takes place between two individuals and is thus a one-on-one conversation. In this case, the two individuals involved will exchange their roles of sender and receiver to communicate more openly.

(iii) **Small group communication**: This type of communication may take place only when there are more than two persons involved. Here, in the group number of persons will be small so that every group member may communicate. For example, a teacher in the class, 4-6 students participating in group discussion, process conferences, board meetings, team meetings, etc.

(iv) **Public Communication:** This form of communication takes place where one individual address a large gathering of people. For example, election campaigns, public speeches by a leader, public meetings, etc.

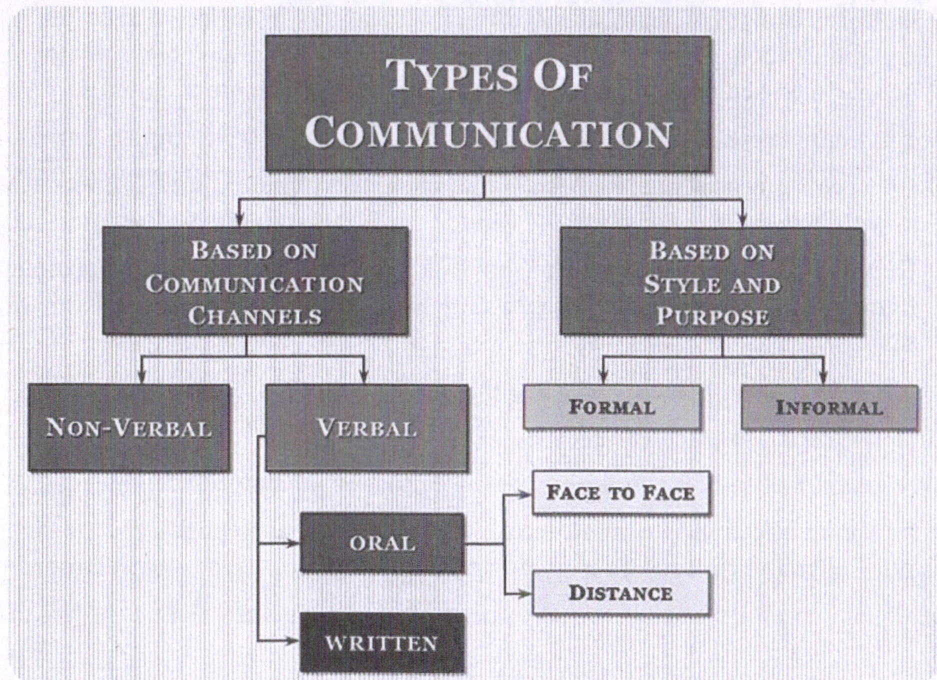

Figure 1.3

3. Write down the seven factors affecting perspectives in communication.

Ans. The following seven factors affect perspectives in communication:

i. **Language**: When someone uses incorrect words and unfamiliar language, then language can act as a barrier to communication. For example, language can act as a communication barrier when an Indian who only knows Hindi and Japanese who have knowledge of the Japanese language only want to interact with each other.

ii. **Prejudice**: It is pre-decided ideas such as thinking, "No one in my class likes me," which may stop a student from communicating openly in the class.

iii. **Visual Perception**: Visual perception is defined as the brain's ability to make sense of what we see through our eyes. For example, completing a partially drawn picture with visual perception, whereas it may be something else.

iv. **Past Experience**: Sometimes our experience stops us from understanding or communicating clearly. For example, "This milkman cheated me last time. Let me be careful". or "I scored low marks in my Maths exam, so I am scared to ask and answer questions in the class."

v. **Feelings/ emotions**: Our feelings and emotions like lack of interest or not trusting the other person may affect communication. For example, "I am not feeling well, so I don't want to talk to you."

vi. **Environment**: Noise or disturbance in the environment may make communication difficult. For example, I was talking to a friend at a function where loud music was played by the band/orchestra.

vii. **Culture**: It signs which have a different meaning in different cultures may affect communication. For example, showing a thumb may mean 'good job' done for some people in one culture, but it may be insulting to others in other cultures.

4. Give an example of the following: (a) Clear communication (b) Complete communication.

Ans. (a) **Clear communication**: Ramesh is making a telephonic call to his friend Naman and asked, "When are you visiting our home?" and Naman replied- "Today at 7.00 pm".

(b) **Complete communication**: The above clear communication will be completed when Ramesh gets the Feedback by confirming his arrival time. The conversation maybe like this:

Ramesh- "Ok, Have you said today at 7.00 pm?"

Naman- "Yes, it is confirmed today at 7.00 pm."

5. Give examples of any four common signs used for visual communication.

Ans. Visual communication is a broad term that includes signs, typography, drawing, graphic design, illustration, industrial design, advertising, animation, color, and electronic resources.

Some Common Signs used in visual communication are given below:

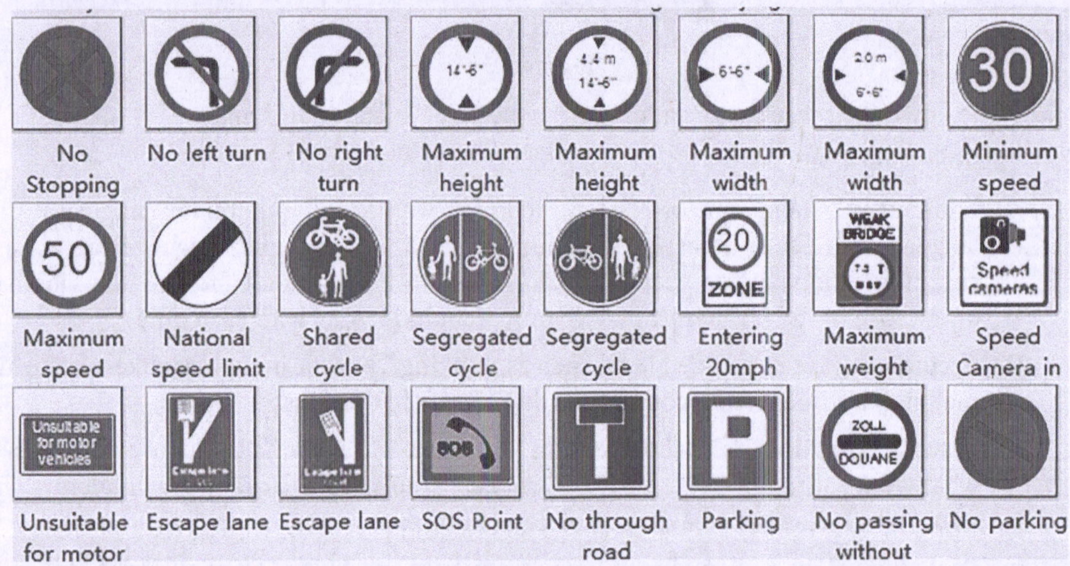

Figure 1.4

6. Identify the conjunctions and prepositions (Remember, conjunctions join two sentences while prepositions help answer the words 'where', 'when' and 'how'.). Choose the conjunctions and prepositions from the box given below.

Under, And, In, At, Or, Up

Ans. Conjunctions: and, or

Prepositions: under. In, at, up

7. Write one sentence of each type—statement, question, exclamatory, and order.

Ans. Statement: Lucknow is the capital of Uttar Pradesh.

Question: Where are you going now?

Exclamatory: Great job!

Order: Come here.

8. Which is your favourite festival? Write two paragraphs about your favourite festival. Each paragraph should have a minimum of four sentences. Make sure you follow all the rules about the sentences and paragraphs you have learnt.

Ans. Indians celebrate a number of festivals each year. In almost all months, we celebrate one or another festival related to our religion or culture. Festivals unite society to enhance mutual bonding. Celebrating festivals spreads Happiness.

I like the Diwali celebration very much. Diwali is also called the 'Festival of Lights. The lighting of earthen Diyas and candles all around the home, worshipping the Laxmi Ganesha for good health and wealth, and bursting crackers are the main rituals of this festival. Family members and friends exchange heartfelt gifts during Diwali. A special and grand feast hvaing delicious food and varieties of sweets is the special attraction of the occasion.

9. Write two to three lines you would use to introduce yourself.

Ans. Hello friends! I am Vikram Soni. I live in Jaipur in Rajasthan. I study in class IX in St Francis World school. I want to become a fighter pilot.

10. Re-arrange the words to form questions.

a. she/like/sing?/Does/to

b. waiting/What/are/you/for?

c. play/like/football?/Do/ you/to

d. fighting?/they/are/Why

Ans. a. Does she like to sing?

b. What are you waiting for?

c. Do you like to play football?

d. Why are they fighting?

11. Make a note of five questions your friends asked you. How many open-ended questions were? Make a list of five close-ended questions you asked other people in one day.

Ans. My friends asked me the following questions:

i. How are you?

ii. Have you completed the homework?

iii. How do you come to school?

iv. From where have you purchased this shirt?

v. Why are you not participating in the school fest?

Out of these five questions, only two questions are open-ended questions (iii & v).

I have asked the following close-ended questions from other persons:

i. What is your name?

ii. Where do you live?

iii. In which class do you study?

iv. Which sweet do you like the most?

v. What is your favourite colour?

1.3 SOLVED EXERCISES

1.3.1 Multiple Choice Questions

Tick (√) the correct option.

1. Which of the following is not related to the 7Cs of communication?

   a) Concreteness b) Cleverness
   c) Clarity d) Completeness

2. Which is a barrier to communication?

   a) Cultural b) Emotional
   c) Gender d) All of the above

3. Which of the following examples is not Positive Feedback?

   a) Excellent job!
   b) I noticed you completed the work very nicely.
   c) I appreciate you for accepting that project.
   d) You take a long to reply to emails!

4. Which word act as an adjective in this sentence?

   Sanjana gave him a new book.

   a) Sanjana b) gave c) new d) book

5. Which of the following sentences is punctuated correctly?

   a) She is so happy to see him!
   b) This is Aman's house?
   c) Where are we going?
   d) Indresh has a pen, a notebook, a rubber, and a pencil.

6. Which of the following is not a correct function of verbal communication?

   a) It hinders the maintenance of relationships.
   b) It helps us define reality.
   c) It can be used to reward and punish.
   d) It helps to organise complex ideas and experiences into meaningful categories.

7. The important factors of communication is/are:

   a) Content b) Process c) Context d) All of these

8. Which is a facial expression?

   a) Happiness b) Anger c) Pain d) All of these

9. Why should one prefer emails over other methods?

   a) To share documents and files with one or more persons within seconds.

   b) To keep a record of communication.

   c) To talk to each other in real-time.

   d) To communicate with many people simultaneously.

10. Which of the following is a type of writing?

    a) Descriptive b) Depository c) Narrative d) Persuasive

11. Which of the following examples is not a phrase?

    a) Once in a blue moon b) A red fox jumped.

    c) In the car d) Running water

12. Which of the following actions is not required for effective writing skills?

    a) Explain the contents in clear language

    b) Use simple language

    c) Use passive voice to strengthen the writing

    d) Use good grammar and correct punctuation

13. Consider the following phrases:

    i. Plants need carbon dioxide and water.

    ii. Who ate the last samosa?

    iii. All passengers with valid tickets can board flight no AIR 8401 now.

    iv. They have been working since 7 am.

    v. Nithya Chandran has nice ideas.

    Examples of Noun phrases are:

    a) (ii) only b) (iii) (iv) only

    c) (ii) (iii) only d) (i) (iv) (v) only

14. An example of oral communication is:

    a) Phone call b) Blogs c) email d) Letters

15. What refers to explaining things in a brief yet comprehensive manner?

    a) Concreteness b) Clarity c) Conciseness d) Correctness

16. What is about avoiding the use of complex words, sentences, and confusing language?

    a) Clarity b) Accuracy c) Fluency d) Punctuation

17. Which of these is an example(s) of negative Feedback?

    a) I do not like to tell you this, but your communication skills are poor.

    b) Rama! You can't improve your drawing.

c) This is a good drawing, but you can do better.

d) None of the above

18. Which is not an element of the communication cycle?

a) Sender b) Receiver c) Messenger d) Channel

19. What is the most significant benefit of using effective communication techniques?

a) It makes us famous. b) It improves our relationships.

c) It helps us earn more money. d) All of the above

20. An example of positive Feedback is:

a) Yogita! You are mostly doing it the wrong way.

b) Wonderful! You have improved this machine.

c) I noticed your non-dedication towards the assignment.

d) All of these

21. A smile and a nod is an example of:

a) Verbal Communication b) Non-verbal Communication

c) Oral Communication d) Written Communication

22. Which barrier does occur due to some inherent traits or the frame of mind of the communicator?

a) Internal b) External c) Emotional d) Cultural

23. An upright (straight) body posture conveys:

a) Confidence b) Professionalism c) Pride d) Humility

24. Which is not a form of non-verbal communication?

a) Facial expressions b) Hand gestures

c) Oral expressions d) Eye contact

25. Which form of communication is known as extremely private communication?

a) Interpersonal b) Intrapersonal

c) Small group d) None of the above

26. Which is an appropriate non-verbal communication at the workplace?

a) Tilting head a bit to listen b) Sitting straight

c) Talking at moderate speed d) All the above

27. ____________ is the final component in the process of communication as it defines the response given by the receiver to the sender.

a) Feedback b) Notice c) Response d) Request

28. Which of the following words does refer to a word or phrase that expresses a strong emotion?

a) Interjection b) Conjunction c) Verb d) Preposition

29. Which of the following components is an effective component of good Feedback?

a) Direct and honest
b) Detailed and time taking
c) Specific
d) Non-specific

30. The information provided in the communication should be:

a) Incomplete
b) Complete
c) Short and Neat
d) None of these

31. Why should one prefer emails over other methods?

a) To communicate with many people simultaneously.
b) To talk to each other in real-time.
c) To keep a record of communication.
d) To share documents and files with one or more persons.

32. Which parts of speech do refer to a word that exhibits the relationship of a noun, pronoun, or noun phrase to another word?

a) Adverb
b) Interjection
c) Preposition
d) Conjunction

33. By which action can senders not send their messages?

a) Gestures
b) Reading
c) Speaking
d) Writing

34. What is used to keep our record of the communication for future reference?

a) Spoken words
b) Written words
c) Hand movements
d) Symbols

35. The information that the sender wishes to convey is called:

a) Noise
b) Feedback
c) Message
d) Communication barrier

36. Which refers to the situation or environment in which the message is delivered?

a) Process
b) Content
c) Context
d) All of the above

37. Which type of communication brings personal warmth and friendliness between the sender and receiver?

a) Written Communication
b) Visual Communication
c) Oral Communication
d) None of these

38. Effective communication results in:

a) Building trust
b) Reducing misunderstandings
c) Resolving conflicts
d) All of these

39. Which mode of communication is used to convey a message consisting of spoken words?

a) Oral Communication
b) Visual Communication
c) Written Communication
d) Non-verbal Communication

40. Communication is required:

a) At no time b) Sometimes c) Frequently d) At all times

41. During communication, the sender should be:

a) Polite b) Unruly
c) Rude d) None of these

42. Which process is related to sharing information between two or more people?

a) Communication b) Description
c) Transition d) Transcription

43. The ____________ the response, the more effective it is the communication cycle.

a) Clear b) Slower c) Quicker d) Vague

44. The information provided in the communication should be:

a) Complete b) Incomplete
c) Short and Neat d) None of these

45. Which factor(s) should be considered while a medium of communication is selected?

a) Timing
b) Nature of the interaction
c) Distance between the sender and the receiver
d) None of these

46. What is given in the descriptive Feedback in the form of written comments or verbal conversations?

a) General rules b) General guidance
c) Specific information d) None of these

47. Which refers to communication that is believable and credible in order to create trust between the communicators?

a) Completeness b) Conciseness
c) Concreteness d) None of the above

48. The goal(s) of effective communication is/are:

a) Creating understanding b) Changing attitude
c) Sharing information d) All of these

49. Considering the feelings and points of view of the target group is good, but it is important to treat the audience in a friendly and ____________ manner.

a) Hasty b) Courteous c) Virtual d) Anxious

50. The important aspect/s of writing skills is/are:
    a) Using correct grammar
    b) Selecting the right words
    c) They are forming easy, simple, and understandable sentences.
    d) All of the above
51. Consider the following examples of sentences:
    i. Chandrika sings a beautiful bhajan.
    ii. Go there.
    iii. Where are you moving to?
    iv. Subhash Chandra Bose is known as Netaji.
    v. Don't pack up that item.
    vi. Ahmedabad is famous for the Sabarmati ashram.

    Examples of imperative sentences are:
    a) (i) only
    b) (iii) (iv) only
    c) (ii) (v) only
    d) (iii) (vi) only
52. ____________ is defined as a set of marks that help us separate parts of a sentence and explain its meaning.
    a) Punctuation
    b) Grammar
    c) Predicate
    d) Conjunction
53. Which of the following is not a disadvantage of verbal communication?
    a) More chances of misunderstanding
    b) Absence of the permanent record
    c) Distortion of the meaning of words used
    d) Suitable for the lengthy message
54. Which of the following factors does not affect 'Effective Communication'?
    a) Emotional Barriers
    b) Perceptual Barriers
    c) Physiological Barriers
    d) Cultural Barriers
55. Which of the following is not required for public speaking?
    a) Prepare
    b) Practice
    c) Perform
    d) Defame
56. Which of the following is mismatched?
    a) Message: It is the information that the sender wishes to send.
    b) Decoding: This is the method of how the sender chooses to bring the message into a form appropriate for posting it.
    c) Channel: This means the medium by which the message is sent.
    d) Feedback: The receiver's response to the message.

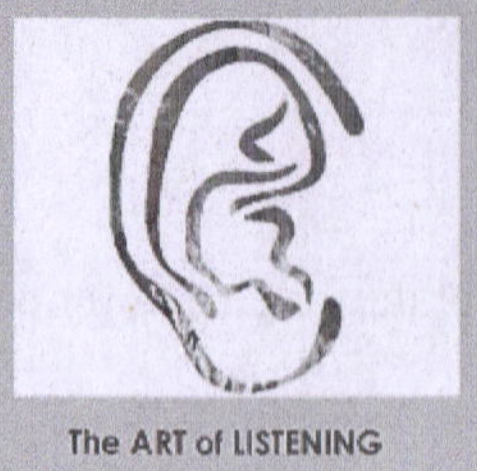

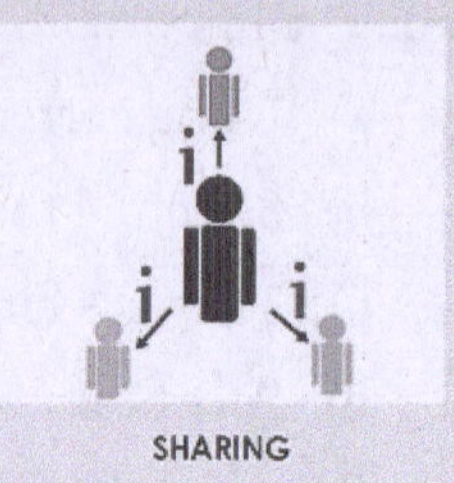

WHY VISUAL
COMMUNICATION

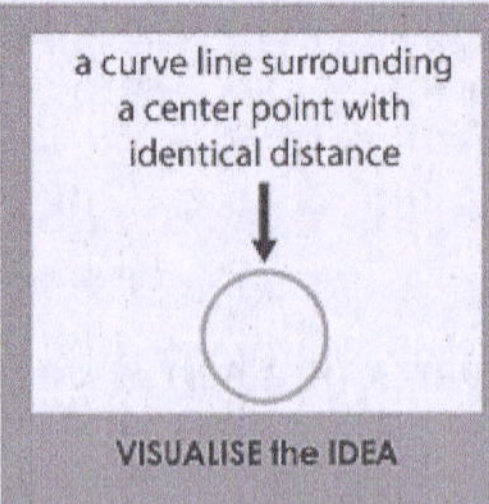

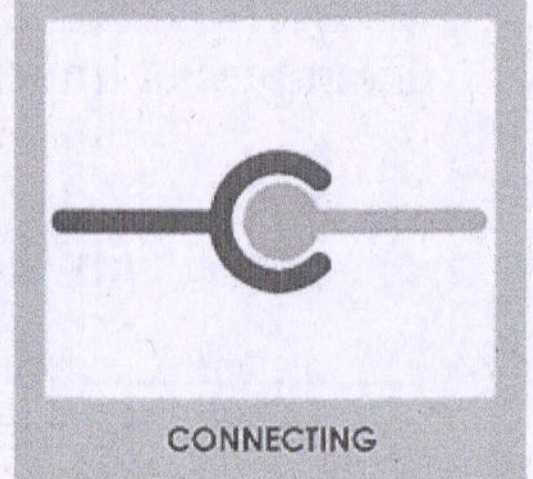

Figure 1.5

ANSWERS									
1. (b)	2. (d)	3. (d)	4. (c)	5. (c)	6. (a)	7. (d)	8. (d)	9. (b)	10. (a)
11. (b)	12. (c)	13. (c)	14. (a)	15. (b)	16. (a)	17. (b)	18. (c)	19. (b)	20. (b)
21. (b)	22. (a)	23. (a)	24. (c)	25. (b)	26. (d)	27. (a)	28. (a)	29. (c)	30. (b)
31. (d)	32. (c)	33. (b)	34. (b)	35. (c)	36. (c)	37. (c)	38. (d)	39. (a)	40. (d)
41. (a)	42. (a)	43. (c)	44. (a)	45. (b)	46. (c)	47. (c)	48. (d)	49. (b)	50. (d)
51. (c)	52. (a)	53. (d)	54. (c)	55. (d)	56. (b)				

1.3.2 Fill in the blanks

1. ____________ is a process of sharing information between two or more people to reach a common understanding.
2. A ____________ is anything that prevents us from receiving and understanding the messages others use to convey their information, ideas and thoughts.
3. The position of the body when standing, sitting, or working is called ____________.
4. ____________ are the verbs used along with a main verb to convey additional information, such as time and mood.
5. The other parts of spoken language (besides words), tone, rate, loudness, etc., is called ____________.
6. ____________ is a sudden cry or remark expressing surprise, emotion, or pain.

7. ____________ is a name that describes someone's position or job.
8. If Amit is a member of the school Cricket team and has a totally different viewpoint from his teammates on the topic of organising a training programme, then he has a ____________ barrier.
9. Not stating instructions clearly on notice is an example of ____________ barrier.
10. Neha has her own private cabin to work in her office, and she is not willing to meet her teammates face to face. Then, it is an indication of a ____________ barrier.
11. When Sonika is overcome by her own feelings and unable to communicate well, it means that she has an ____________ barrier.
12. If Sneha thinks that she is more intelligent than others and is superior in knowledge, then she has a ____________ barrier.
13. LS Khumman is using slang or words that are used within his own social group. This is an example of a ____________ barrier.
14. Not understanding the customs or traditions of a speaker could mean there is a ____________ barrier.
15. Speech, vocabulary, rhythm, tone, and pitch are some of the factors that enhance ____________ communication.

ANSWERS			
1. Communication	2. communication barrier	3. Posture	
4. Auxiliary verbs	5. Paralanguage	6. Exclamation	7. Title
8. conceptual	9. language	10. Physical	11. Emotional
12. Attitudinal	13. Cultural	14. Cultural	15. oral

1.3.3 True/ False Type Questions

1. Encoding deals with how the sender wishes to communicate the message.
2. Press conferences, board meetings, and teleconferences are examples of Large-Group Communication.
3. Perspectives are defined as the ideas, views, or fixed ways of thinking, which may affect our communication.
4. Negative Feedback can enhance a student's confidence, self-awareness, and enthusiasm for learning.
5. Forms of Visual Communication include Public Signs, Visual Symbols, Charts and Graphs, Tables, Maps, Diagrams, etc.
6. Visual perceptual skills involve the ability to organise and interpret information correctly.
7. Visual perception is defined as the ability to see and interpret (analyse and give meaning to) the visual information that surrounds us.
8. Specific Feedback provides a direction for the students to identify the steps taken to fulfil their goals.
9. Effective communication does not enhance our confidence.
10. Written communication means communicating through written words.

11. The Communication process enlists the steps users to take to comprehend each other properly.
12. Encoding refers to how the receiver interprets the message and translates it into thoughts.
13. Descriptive Feedback reduces the gap between the present level of performance and the learning goal.
14. The effectiveness of a communication cycle depends on how long it takes for Feedback to be received by the initial sender.
15. Right Feedback given at the right time may lead the communicators towards their desired goal.

Figure 1.6

ANSWERS						
1. T	2. F(small-group)	3. T	4. F (Positive Feedback)	5. T	6. T	7. T
8. T	9. F	10. T	11. T	12. F (Decoding)	13. T	14. T
15. T						

1.3.4 Matching Type Question

(I) Match the items of column A with those of column B correctly.

Column A	Column B
i. Sender	(a) The means by which the information is sent.
ii. Receiver	(b) The information that the sender wants to convey.
iii. Message	(c) The receiver's acknowledgment and response to the message
iv. Channel	(d) The person to whom the message is sent.
v. Feedback	(e) The person beginning the communication.

(II) Match the items of column A with those of column B correctly.

Column A (Type of sentence)	Column B (Example)
i. Assertive	(a) Sugandha is not studying well.
ii. Interrogative	(b) Wow! You have done well.
iii. Exclamatory	(c) Rakesh is eating an apple.
iv. Negative	(d) Who is going to address the meeting?

ANSWERS				
I. i. (e)	ii. (d)	iii. (b)	iv. (a)	v. (c)
II. i. (c)	ii. (d)	iii. (b)	iv. (a)	

1.3.5 Statements Based Questions

1. Statement 1: Prejudices are due to cultural differences and personal preferences or experience.

   Statement 2: There are five main types of writing, namely expository, descriptive, narrative, persuasive, and creative.

   a) Statement 1 is correct, but statement 2 is incorrect.

   b) Statement 1 is incorrect, but statement 2 is correct.

   c) Both the statements are correct.

   d) Both the statements are incorrect.

2. Statement 1: Narrative writing states the opinion of the writer and attempts to influence the reader.

   Statement 2: Persuasive writing is the writing in which the author tells a story.

   a) Statement 1 is correct, but statement 2 is incorrect.

   b) Statement 1 is incorrect, but statement 2 is correct.

   c) Both the statements are correct.

   d) Both the statements are incorrect.

3. Statement 1: Verbal communication is an act of exchanging thoughts, feelings, postures, opinions, or information without the use of words.

   Statement 2: Smile is a powerful expression that transmits Happiness, Friendliness, Warmth, and Liking.

   a) Statement 1 is correct, but statement 2 is incorrect.

   b) Statement 1 is incorrect, but statement 2 is correct.

   c) Both the statements are correct.

   d) Both the statements are incorrect.

4. Statement 1: A phrase is defined as a group of words that are used together to give a specific meaning.

   Statement 2: A phrase has a full verb, and it may be short or long, but it does not include the subject.

   a) Statement 1 is correct, but statement 2 is incorrect.

   b) Statement 1 is incorrect, but statement 2 is correct.

   c) Both the statements are correct.

   d) Both the statements are incorrect.

5. Statement 1: Verbal communication is the transmission of ideas, information, and knowledge in the forms that can be seen.

   Statement 2: There are many types of facial expressions, but Happiness, anger, sadness, and fear are considered universal facial expressions.

   a) Statement 1 is correct, but statement 2 is incorrect.

   b) Statement 1 is incorrect, but statement 2 is correct.

   c) Both the statements are correct.

   d) Both the statements are incorrect.

6. Statement 1: Communication is a two-way process.

   Statement 2: Forms of Visual Communication include Public Signs, Visual Symbols, Chart and Graph, Tables, Maps, Diagrams, etc.

   a) Statement 1 is correct, but statement 2 is incorrect.

   b) Statement 1 is incorrect, but statement 2 is correct.

   c) Both the statements are correct.

   d) Both the statements are incorrect.

7. Statement 1: A picture is worth more than one thousand words is an old proverb, which clearly defines the importance of visuals in the process of communication.

   Statement 2: Graphs, charts, etc., are used to convey specific information while road signals convey a particular meaning.

   a) Statement 1 is correct, but statement 2 is incorrect.

   b) Statement 1 is incorrect, but statement 2 is correct.

   c) Both the statements are correct.

   d) Both the statements are incorrect.

8. Statement 1: Communication may occur between one person to another person, one person to many persons, or many persons to one person.

   Statement 2: It is not essential to use appropriate language, i.e., the language which can be easily understood by the receiver(s).

   a) Statement 1 is correct, but statement 2 is incorrect.

   b) Statement 1 is incorrect, but statement 2 is correct.

   c) Both the statements are correct.

   d) Both the statements are incorrect.

9. Statement 1: For effective Feedback, a person should not have a goal and take action to receive goal-related information.

   Statement 2: There may be two types of feedback-positive Feedback and Negative Feedback.

   a) Statement 1 is correct, but statement 2 is incorrect.

   b) Statement 1 is incorrect, but statement 2 is correct.

   c) Both the statements are correct.

   d) Both the statements are incorrect.

10. Statement 1: Grammar reflects how comfortable you are with your wordy style.

    Statement 2: Vocabulary is defined as the set of rules for how words in a language are converted into phrases and phrases into sentences, and so on.

    a) Statement 1 is correct, but statement 2 is incorrect.

    b) Statement 1 is incorrect, but statement 2 is correct.

    c) Both the statements are correct.

    d) Both the statements are incorrect.

ANSWERS									
1. (c)	2. (d)	3. (b)	4. (a)	5. (b)	6. (c)	7. (c)	8. (a)	9. (b)	10. (d)

1.3.6 Assertion Reason Type Questions

1. Assertion (A): Listening is an essential component of the communication process and to respond appropriately to communication.

   Reason(R): Listening removes a lot of misunderstandings.

   a) Both A and R are correct, and R is the correct reason for A.

   b) Both A and R are correct, and R is not the correct reason for A.

   c) A is correct, but R is incorrect.

   d) A is incorrect, but R is correct.

2. Assertion (A): A pronoun phrase can be a single noun or a group of words built around a single noun.

   Reason(R): A group of words that gives the complete meaning of the ideas is called a sentence.

   a) Both A and R are correct, and R is the correct reason for A.

   b) Both A and R are correct, and R is not the correct reason for A.

   c) A is correct, but R is incorrect.

   d) A is incorrect, but R is correct.

3. Assertion (A): Communication is the 'sharing' of information, knowledge, feelings, or attitude between two or more individuals or within a group to reach a common understanding.

   Reason(R): Communication skills are those skills that are required to speak and write properly and effectively.

   a) Both A and R are correct, and R is the correct reason for A.

   b) Both A and R are correct, and R is not the correct reason for A.

   c) A is correct, but R is incorrect.

   d) A is incorrect, but R is correct.

4. Assertion (A): Feedback plays an important role in communication.

   Reason(R): Feedback conveys both the source/sender and the receiver, how their message is being interpreted.

a) Both A and R are correct, and R is the correct reason for A.
b) Both A and R are correct, and R is not the correct reason for A.
c) A is correct, but R is incorrect.
d) A is incorrect, but R is correct.

5. Assertion (A): Speaking slowly conveys an excited or agitated feel.
   Reason(R): Voice volume may range from a whisper to a scream and everything in between.
   a) Both A and R are correct, and R is the correct reason for A.
   b) Both A and R are correct, and R is not the correct reason for A.
   c) A is correct, but R is incorrect.
   d) A is incorrect, but R is correct.
6. Assertion (A): Effective communication is not regarded as the key to success in all spheres of life.
   Reason(R): Perspectives are defined as the ideas, views, or fixed ways of thinking, which may affect our communication.
   a) Both A and R are correct, and R is the correct reason for A.
   b) Both A and R are correct, and R is not the correct reason for A.
   c) A is correct, but R is incorrect.
   d) A is incorrect, but R is correct.
7. Assertion (A): It is easier for us to communicate verbally effectively.
   Reason(R): We understand the components/elements required to make verbal communication effective.
   a) Both A and R are correct, and R is the correct reason for A.
   b) Both A and R are correct, and R is not the correct reason for A.
   c) A is correct, but R is incorrect.
   d) A is incorrect, but R is correct.
8. Assertion (A): Visual perception is defined as the ability to see and interpret (analyse and give meaning to) the visual information that surrounds us.
   Reason(R): Visual perceptual skills involve the ability to organise and interpret information correctly.
   a) Both A and R are correct, and R is the correct reason for A.
   b) Both A and R are correct, and R is not the correct reason for A.
   c) A is correct, but R is incorrect.
   d) A is incorrect, but R is correct.
9. Assertion (A): Non-verbal communication is the non-linguistic transmission of information through visual, auditory, tactile, and kinaesthetic channels.
   Reason(R): Non-verbal communication enables us to share our thoughts with other persons by using any other method than using words.
   a) Both A and R are correct, and R is the correct reason for A.
   b) Both A and R are correct, and R is not the correct reason for A.

c) A is correct, but R is incorrect.

d) A is incorrect, but R is correct.

10. Assertion (A): In verbal communication, the use of sounds and words is done to express oneself, especially in contrast to using gestures or mannerisms (non-verbal communication).

Reason(R): Visual communication enables us to share knowledge, thoughts, information, or feelings with others by using the words in such a manner that the other person(s) may understand them well.

a) Both A and R are correct, and R is the correct reason for A.

b) Both A and R are correct, and R is not the correct reason for A.

c) A is correct, but R is incorrect.

d) A is incorrect, but R is correct.

ANSWERS									
1. (a)	2. (d)	3. (b)	4. (a)	5. (d)	6. (c)	7. (a)	8. (b)	9. (a)	10. (c)

1.3.7 Competency-Based Questions

1. Suppose Sujata, CEO of Disha Advertising Agency was explaining the importance of a type of communication as below:

   i. It helps in re-enforcing oral communication.

   ii. It classifies the meaning of the discussion.

   iii. It supports the information and has a stronger impact than words.

   iv. It can be understood by both illiterate and literate people.

   v. It is universal and easy to remember.

   She was talking about:

   a) Verbal communication
   b) Visual communication
   c) Non-verbal communication
   d) None of the above

2. Suppose Neetika is talking about the advantages of a type of communication as follows:

   i. Quick and flexible

   ii. Understanding, clarity, and transparency

   iii. Immediate Feedback

   iv. An effective tool for motivation

   v. An effective tool for group communication / public address

   vi. Synergy and mutual creativity

   She is talking about:

   a) Verbal communication
   b) Non-verbal communication
   c) Visual communication
   d) None of the above

3. A German group visited Vedika AI Pvt Ltd. The Indian team of the company communicated with the German group using different prompts like body movements, gestures, facial expressions, symbols, images, signals charts, and soon to express sentiments, attitudes, or information. This type of communication is called:

a) Visual Communication b) Verbal Communication
c) Non-verbal Communication d) None of the above

4. Consider the following limitations/disadvantages:
   i. It is more expensive.
   ii. More time and effort are required to produce them.
   iii. It has limited scope.
   iv. Complete and detailed information is not conveyed.
   v. Sometimes there may be a design issue.

   These limitations are related to:

   a) Verbal Communication b) Non-verbal Communication
   c) Visual Communication d) All of the above

5. Suppose Bipul Kalita belongs to Assam and he has a friend AK Panduranga from Maharashtra. Both have ethnic, religious, and social differences that can often create misunderstandings during communication. These differences can also affect one's perception and create confusion in getting a message correctly. This type of communication barrier is known as:

   a) Attitudinal barriers b) Perceptual barriers
   c) Linguistic barriers d) Cultural barriers

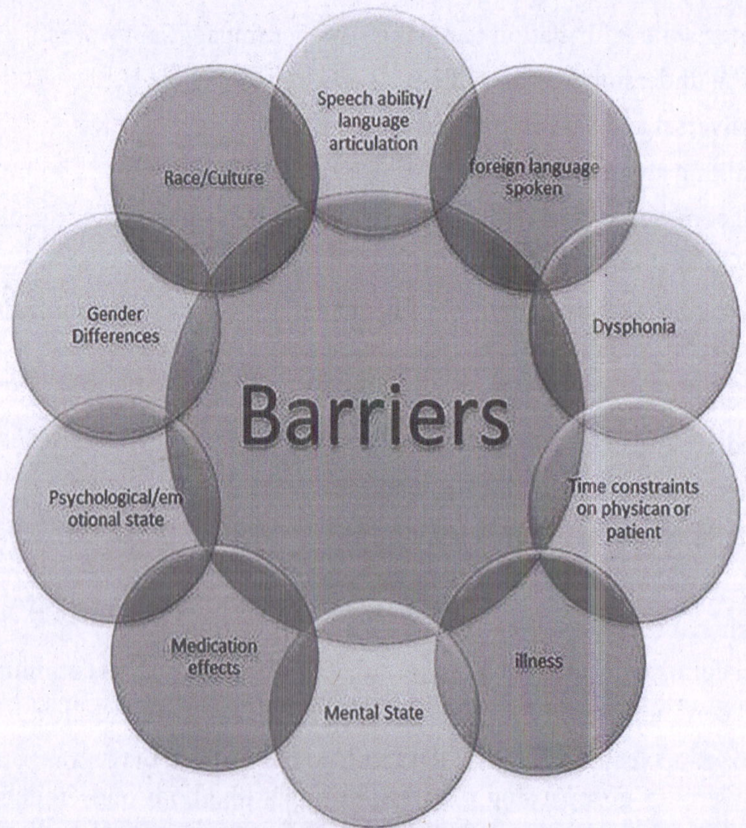

Figure 1.7

ANSWERS				
1. (b)	2. (a)	3. (c)	4. (c)	5. (d)

1.3.8 VSA

1. How is communication regarded as a two-way process?

Ans. Communication is a two-way process because, in this process, the exchange of information, knowledge, feelings, thoughts, or attitude takes place between at least two persons.

2. Why is it essential to use appropriate language in communication?

Ans. It is essential to use appropriate language, i.e., the language which can be easily understood by the receiver(s). In the world, more than 6000 languages are spoken.

3. Define Feedback.

Ans. Feedback is the response that a receiver gives after the message is received.

4. How is Feedback given?

Ans. Feedback may be provided verbally or in written form. Feedback may be specific or non-specific.

5. What is descriptive Feedback?

Ans. Descriptive Feedback gives detailed input, while general Feedback is not so important.

6. Which term is used for the set of rules for how words in a language are converted into phrases and phrases into sentences, and so on?

Ans. Grammar.

7. What is used during Non-verbal communication or non-word communication?

Ans. In non-verbal communication, gestures, sign language, facial expression, and body language are used.

8. What are the main two types of Feedback?

Ans. There may be two types of feedback-positive Feedback and Negative Feedback.

9. Why is visual communication known as graphic communication?

Ans. Visual communication is the transmission of ideas, information, and knowledge in the forms that can be seen, and hence, it is known as graphic communication.

10. Which facial expressions are considered universal facial expressions?

Ans. Happiness, anger, sadness, and fear are considered universal facial expressions.

11. What is necessary for communication to become effective?

Ans. When the message sent is understood correctly by the receiver, it is known as effective communication.

12. What are the forms of visual communication?

Ans. Forms of Visual Communication include Public Signs, Visual Symbols, charts and Graphs, Tables, maps, diagrams, etc.

13. What is the origin of prejudices?

Ans. Prejudices are due to cultural differences and personal preferences or experiences.

14. What are the five main types of writing?

Ans. Expository, descriptive, narrative, persuasive, and creative.

15. Define persuasive writing.

Ans. Persuasive writing explains the opinion of the writer and attempts to influence the reader.

16. Why is there a misunderstanding during communication?

Ans. When the message does not come across as intended, and noise leads to miscommunication, then there may be misunderstandings during communication.

17. What is concreteness in communication?

Ans. The message should be supported by factual material such as data and figures.

18. Define communication.

Ans. Communication is the process of sharing information, ideas, altitude, and/ feelings between two or more people.

19. What do you mean by communication barriers?

Ans. A communication barrier is defined as an obstacle that prevents the receiver from receiving and understanding the message sent by a sender.

20. Why is Feedback necessary in communication?

Ans. To improve the quality of communication, Feedback is necessary.

21. Define visual communication.

Ans. The conversion of ideas and information in forms that can be seen through the eye is termed visual communication.

22. What are the three basic types of communication?

Ans. Three basic types of communication are verbal, non-verbal, and visual communication.

23. Define effective communication.

Ans. Effective communication implies that the transmitted content has been received and understood well by the receiver.

24. What is reduced ineffective communication?

Ans. Effective communication reduces misunderstandings.

25. Define verbal communication.

Ans. Sounds and words to express by someone, especially in contrast to using gestures or mannerisms (non-verbal communication), are used in verbal communication.

26. Define paragraph.

Ans. In a paragraph, a group of sentences dealing with a single topic is used. Thus, a paragraph is a series of sentences that are organised and coherent and are all related to a single topic.

27. Define a Sentence.

Ans. A group of words giving complete meaning to the ideas is called a sentence. A sentence should be grammatically correct.

28. What is used in verbal communication to convey the message?

Ans. Verbal communication use linguistics to convey the message/information/feelings.

29. What are the two primary mediums of verbal communication?

Ans. Oral Communication and Written Communication.

30. When is Non-verbal communication used?

Ans. Non-verbal communication occurs in the absence of any oral or composing words.

31. Mention the main purpose of specific Feedback.

Ans. Specific Feedback helps to improve the thought process.

32. What is achieved through specific Feedback?

Ans. Specific Feedback provides a detailed analysis /information about something particular relating to a task or the individual's performance.

33. Why is non-specific Feedback considered not good?

Ans. Non-specific Feedback provides a vague response to the receiver.

34. Define internal barrier?

Ans. Internal barriers occur due to some inherent traits or the frame of mind of any of the communicators.

35. Define external barriers?

Ans. External barriers occur due to the factors which are outside our body and mind. We have no control over them.

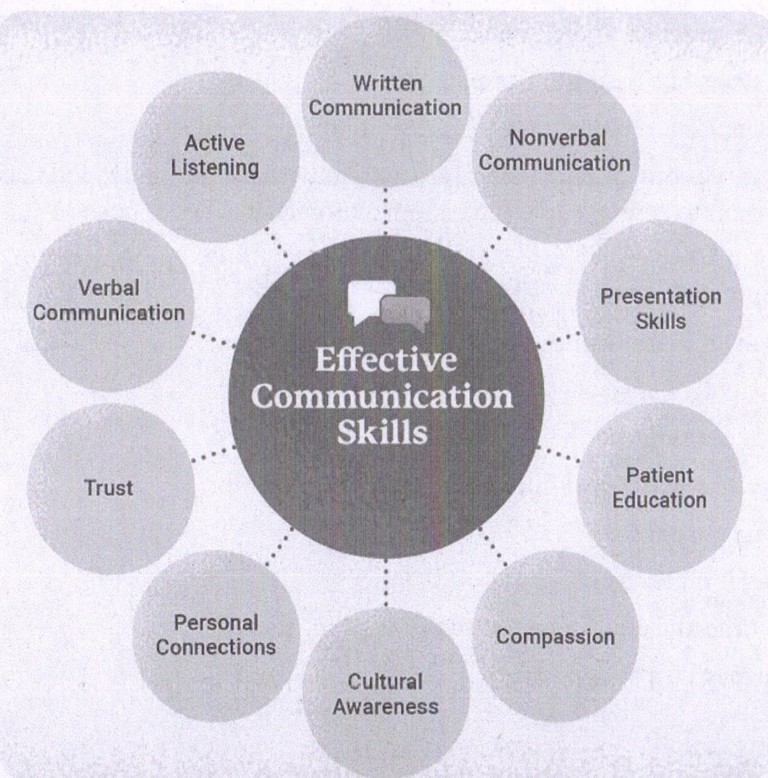

Figure 1.8

1.3.9 Short Answer Type Questions

1. Enlist the factors responsible for enhancing oral communication.

Ans. Speech, vocabulary, rhythm, tone, and pitch are some of the factors that enhance oral communication.

2. What points are to be taken care to plan for effective public speaking?

Ans. The following points are to be taken care of:

i. Think and research about your topic
ii. Think about what your listeners need to know about the topic
iii. Think about the best way to make your listeners understand your topic
iv. Write what you plan to say

3. Enlist various tools and techniques for improving non-verbal communication.

Ans. The following are the list of tools and techniques used for non-verbal communication:

i. Use good eye contact.
ii. Pay attention to non-verbal signals.
iii. Pay attention to your tone of voice while speaking.
iv. Use correct signals to make communication more meaningful.
v. Be aware that signals can be misread.
vi. Look for incongruent behaviours.
vii. Practice, practice, and practice.

4. Give two types of Visual Communication.

Ans. Two types of visual communication are as follows:

(i) Objects: Various kinds of objects are used for visual communication to clear the concept. If we want to convey something about a mobile, it is better to show it.
(ii) Models: Various types of models in place of living things are used in visual communication.

5. Mention any six disadvantages of visual communication.

Ans. Six disadvantages of visual communication are as follows:

i. Visual communication has limited scope.
ii. Complete and detailed information is not conveyed.
iii. It is more expensive.
iv. Storing is quite costly.
v. More time and effort are required to produce them.
vi. There may be a design issue.

6. Enlist the types of Feedback.

Ans. There are different types of feedbacks, as mentioned below:

i. Positive Feedback
ii. Negative Feedback
iii. Deliberate positive Feedback
iv. Deliberate negative Feedback
v. Immediate Feedback
vi. Delayed Feedback
vii. No feedback

7. Explain Perspectives in Communication.

Ans. Perspectives are defined as ideas, views, or fixed ways of thinking. These may affect our communication. People communicate with their own 'filter' through which they see the world, the person they are communicating with, and the situation or topic they are communicating about. These filters mean that they don't always start with the same perspective as the person they are communicating with.

8. How do our feelings affect communication?

Ans. Our feelings may affect the communication with other persons in two ways:

Firstly, it simply refers to the way that we feel on a particular day; if we feel well, we'll communicate in a good way, and if we are not feeling well, we'll communicate in another way.

Secondly, it refers to our feelings and association with a particular person. When we genuinely like some person, the way we communicate is going to reflect it. If we dislike someone, it will be reflected in the way of communication also.

9. Enumerate the essential skills needed for written expressions.

Ans. The skills required for written expressions are as follows:

i. Reading comprehension
ii. Sentence construction
iii. Planning, revising, and editing
iv. Transcription
v. Genre and content knowledge
vi. Self-regulation

10. Why is Feedback important?

Ans. Feedback is important due to the following reasons:

i. It makes communication meaningful.
ii. It tells whether the communication is making sense or not.
iii. It completes the communication cycle.

iv. It is the basis for measuring the effectiveness of communication.

v. It generates new ideas and helps to remove misinterpretation.

vi. It builds relationships and helps with networking.

11. Explain 'Intrapersonal Communication Barriers'.

Ans. Several factors present in the individual sometimes put a hurdle in the process of communication, both in sending and receiving the message. These barriers are within our control. Our attitude, beliefs, prejudices, experiences, cultural background, socio-economic conditions, etc., are the main elements of this barrier. Rituals, pastimes, genes closeness, etc., are ways in which people keep throwing away from each other.

12. What do you mean by 'Environmental Communication Barriers'? Explain with suitable examples.

Ans. There are many environmental barriers in communication, including external noise, time, physical distance, space, climate, and place. External noise is the main environmental barrier in communication because it makes it difficult or impossible for people to hear one another. If the temperature is too high or too low, or strong wind is blowing, it will also act as a barrier in communication (climatic condition).

13. Why do we need communication skills?

Ans. Communication skills are required to speak effectively with a variety of people whilst good eye contact demonstrates a varied vocabulary. Therefore, communication allows us to express ourselves through auditory means such as speaking, singing, and sometimes the tone of voice, and non-verbal, physical means such as body language, sign language, touch, eye contact, or the use of writing with a literate person.

14. Enlist seven elements of the communication cycle.

Ans. The communication cycle comprises seven elements: sender, message, encoding, communication channel, receiver, decoding, and Feedback.

15. What will happen when a message is not understood clearly by the receiver?

Ans. When a message is not understood clearly, then it may lead to communication gaps, causing confusion and misunderstanding between the sender and receiver.

16. What are the factors responsible for causing barriers?

Ans. The factors that cause barriers related to the message being conveyed include lengthy messages, language problems, intonation issues, or the non-verbal communication used.

17. What are the factors that influence internal barriers?

Ans. Factors influencing internal barriers include intense emotions, poor listening skills, prejudice, different viewpoints, or different cultural backgrounds.

18. What are the factors that cause non-effective communication?

Ans. Factors like noise, cultural differences, different time zones and distance, faulty communication equipment or technologies, etc., are responsible for non-effective communication.

19. What are the main goals of effective communication?

Ans. The main goals of effective communication are to establish trust and understanding, change behaviour, and acquire information.

20. What are the three important points to be considered in communication?

Ans. Content, process, and context.

21. What are the seven principles of communication?

Ans. The principles of communication are based on the 7 C's-Clear, Concise, Concrete, Correct, Coherent, Complete, and Courteous.

22. What are the essential elements for writing?

Ans. Essential elements for persuasive writing include reading comprehension, transcription, sentence construction, content knowledge, planning, and self-regulation.

23. What are the elements for paragraph writing?

Ans. Elements for paragraph writing are unity, order, coherence, and completeness.

24. What is the purpose of Feedback?

Ans. Feedback is mainly required to continue the process of active communication. It can be effective only when it is heard, interpreted, and accepted.

25. Explain descriptive Feedback.

Ans. Descriptive Feedback is defined as the specific information in the form of written comments or verbal communications that help the sender understand what he/she needs to do in order to improve communication. It can be taken in the form of checklists/evaluations through standard rubrics. Therefore, descriptive Feedback is specific information in the form of written comments or verbal conversations. It strengthens communication. For providing descriptive Feedback, listening to the message properly by the receiver is a must. Age, qualification, religion, region, etc., of the receiver, is also important to get the correct Feedback.

26. Differentiate between specific and non-specific Feedback.

Ans.

Specific Feedback	Non-specific Feedback
i. Specific Feedback provides a detailed analysis or specific information on a particular topic.	i. General Feedback is termed non-specific Feedback. It may be vague.
ii. Specific Feedback helps in modifying the behaviour or thinking for the purpose of learning by influencing the thought process.	ii. Non-specific Feedback is not so helpful in modifying the behaviour or thinking process.

Figure 1.9

27. What are the techniques to hone active listening skills?

Ans. The following five-step approach may be used:

i. Acknowledge the other person's ideas, thoughts, or feedings

ii. Paraphrase the other person's words to ensure understanding.

iii. Ask questions without judging.

iv. Summarize and classify what you hear.

v. Offer your opinion if it is required.

28. Define the phrase and give two examples of it.

Ans. A group of words that are used together is called a 'Phrase.' A phrase does not contain a full verb. A phrase may be short or long, but it does not include the subject.

Examples,

i. A black rose

ii. A white cat

iii. At the bus station

iv. Very beautiful flower

v. Complete communication.

29. Give two examples of Gestures.

Ans. (a) Raising a hand for greeting or to say goodbye.

(b) Pointing the finger at someone.

30. Define and illustrate small group communication.

Ans. Small group communication is a type of communication that can take place where there are more than two persons involved. Here in the group number of persons will be small so that each and every group member may communicate. For example, a teacher in the class, 4-6 students are participating in group discussion, process conferences, board meetings team meetings.

1.3.10 Long Answer Type Questions

1. Explain components of effective verbal communication.

Ans. The following are the basic elements for effective verbal communication.

i. **Listening:** It is an important component of the hearing process and to respond properly in communication. Listening is the key to success and removes a lot of misunderstandings.

ii. **Language**: It matters a lot. Use of appropriate language is must. In our world more than 6000 languages are spoken.

iii. **Voice Tone**: Voice tone is very basic, and it can come into play every when you are not uttering words. Even when you are making a laugh, your voice tone modifies how it is likely to be interpreted.

iv. **Voice Speed:** Speaking too fast can convey an excited or agitated feel. Speaking slightly slower can convey a steady, reliable feel.

v. **Vocabulary:** It reflects how comfortable you are with your wordy language. It helps in the usage of suitable words in different contexts. Using the correct words as per the requirements of the situation is required.

vi. **Voice Volume**: Volume of voice may vary from a whisper to a scream and everything in between. A very cool and quiet voice can represent that you are shy, something you don't want to be overheard, that you are depressed, or you are mischievous. A very loud voice may express great joy. A humorous voice demonstrates a lively atmosphere.

vii. **Grammar**: Grammar is defined as the set of rules for how words connect into phrases and phrases into sentences, and so on. Using grammatically correct sentences is preferred for effective communication.

viii. **Learned Awareness**: It is your awareness about your surroundings including the latest events in the world because it gives you the confidence to communicate effectively.

ix. **Subject knowledge**: Your expertise in the chosen area like arts, science, commerce, etc., will enhance the effectiveness of communication.

2. Explain the SMCR Model of Communication with the help of an example.

Ans. Communication is a two-way process. It means that a minimum of two persons is required during communication. There may be one-to-one communication (between two persons) or one to many communication (one is speaking, and many persons are listening like in a class, the teacher is speaking, and children are listening); or many to one communication (many persons are speaking to one person like crowed is saying something to an individual leader).

A communication message or piece of information is sent or communicated through a channel (or medium) by a sender to the receiver. This is called the SMCR (Sender/Source-Message- Channel -Receiver) model of communication.

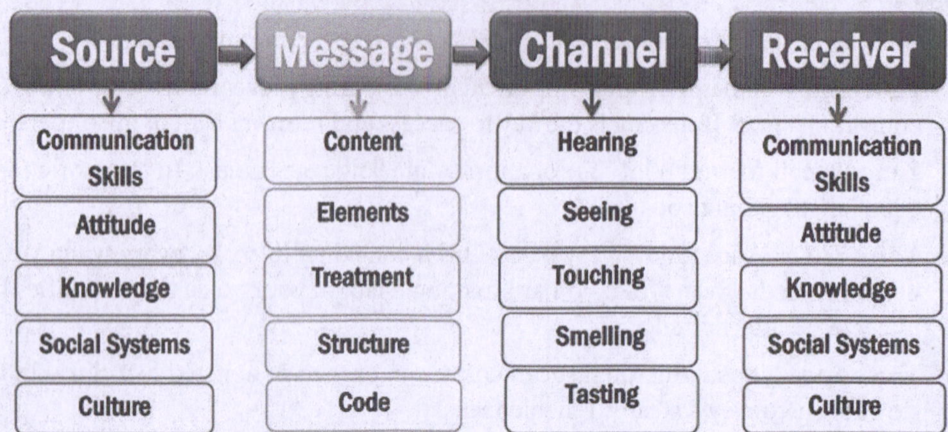

Figure 1.10 SMCR Model of communication

For example, suppose Sangeeta wants to communicate a piece of information to his friend Niharika; she may choose the channel of speaking or writing. Five senses of human beings are used as channels. Here, Sangeeta will be the sender, and Niharika will be the receiver.

3. Enlist the main advantages of verbal communication.

Ans. Verbal communication has the following advantages:

i. Quick and flexible
ii. Time-saving
iii. Immediate Feedback
iv. Economical
v. Synergy and mutual creativity
vi. Developing better relationship
vii. An effective tool for motivation
viii. An effective tool for group communication / public address
ix. Understanding, clarity, and transparency

4. Enumerate disadvantages of verbal communication.

Ans. Verbal communication has the following disadvantages:

i. Verbal communication uses written or spoken words, and hence sometimes, the meanings of the words used can be confusing and difficult to understand.
ii. Distortion of the meaning of words used
iii. Not suitable for the lengthy message
iv. No legal validity
v. Cultural differences may create problems.
vi. Absence of the permanent record

vii. Confused speech may be a disturbing element.

viii. More chances of misunderstanding

5. Discuss the strategy for mastering verbal communication.

Ans. Three steps strategy for mastering verbal communication is used as discussed below:

(a) Prepare:

(i) Think and research about your topic.

(ii) Think about what the listeners need to know about the topic.

(iii) Think about the best way to make the listeners understand your topic.

(iv) Write what you plan to say.

(b) Practice

(i) Practice by yourself first, talk in front of a mirror.

(ii) Speak clearly, loudly, and with appropriate speed (neither very fast nor very slow).

(iii) Talk in front of family members and friends, and ask them what they think about your way of expression.

(c) Perform

(i) Take a deep breath in case you are feeling nervous.

(ii) Have confidence in yourself and start speaking confidently.

(iii) Speak slowly and clearly but in a loud voice.

(iv) Have voice modulation and make eye contact with the audience.

6. Explain the various types of non-verbal communication.

Ans. Various types of non-verbal communications relying on various non-verbal means, like physical movements, tasks, colours, signs, symbols, signals, charts, etc., are used to express feelings, attitudes, and information.

i. Body Language: It includes biting nails, washing hair, etc.

ii. Eye Contact: It helps regulate the flow of communication.

iii. Facial expressions: It conveys what someone is feeling.

iv. Gestures: These are the movements of the arms, legs, hands, and head.

v. Touch: It conveys the feelings (good touch, bad touch).

vi. Symbols: These are used to represent an idea, a physical entity, or a process.

vii. Humour: It makes the atmosphere lively.

viii. Silence: It converts both positive and negative message.

ix. Proximity: Maintain a comfortable distance for interaction, keeping in mind the cultural differences.

x. Posture and body orientation: Messages are conveyed by the way you walk, talk, stay, and sit.

xi. Personal appearance: Your costume/dress conveys about you.

xii. Chromatics: It uses colours for communication.

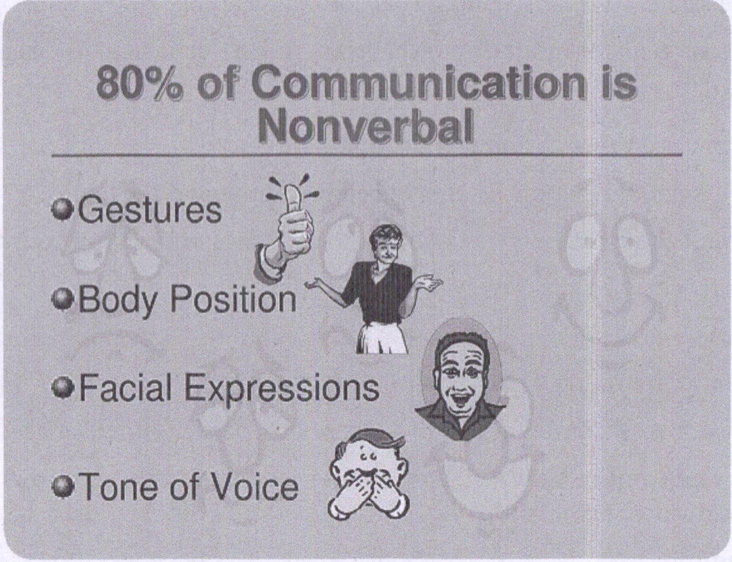

Figure 1.11

7. Explain five types of visual communication.

Ans. There are five types of visual communication:

i. Objects: Various types of objects are used for visual communication to clear the concept. If we want to convey something about an apple, it is better to show it.

ii. Models: Various types of models in place of living things are used in visual communication.

iii. Photographs: The main advantage of using photographs is to clear all points or to explain minute details too. For example, pictures of slum areas can give an accurate description of the slum areas and their problems.

iv. Graphs: These are used to convey statistical data in an understandable manner. There are various types of graphs, like line graphs, bar graphs, pie charts, etc.

v. Maps: Maps are used to understand geographical concepts in a better way. It can be used to show the locations of an item in a city/country.

8. What are the limitations/disadvantages of visual communication?

Ans. Visual communication has the following limitations/disadvantages:

i. It is more expensive.

ii. Storing is quite costly.

iii. More time and effort are required to produce them.

iv. Sometimes visuals are not easy to understand.

v. Visual communication has limited scope.

vi. Complete and detailed information is not conveyed.

vii. Sometimes there may be a design issue.

viii. It is prone to misunderstandable /misinterpretation.

9. Discuss the ways and means to improve communication skills.

Ans. The following ways are suggested to improve the communication skills:

i. **Use correct language/words**: Use correct words to speak clearly. Don't mumble. Use the appropriate words after observing the audience and their cultures.

ii. **Keep the flow:** When you are very fast in speaking, people will perceive you as nervous and unsure of yourself; however, being very slow may be boring. So, be careful in keeping the voice-speed medium.

iii. **Use correct pronunciation of the words**: Improve your competency through your vocabulary and use correct pronunciation of words.

iv. **Make eye contact**: Look into one of the listener's eyes and then move to the other.

v. **Use gestures**: Use gestures to make your whole body talk. Use smaller gestures for individuals and a small group, and use larger gestures for the larger group.

vi. **Animate the voice**: Avoid a monotonous voice. Use dynamics, and your pitch should rise and lower. Voice volume should be soft and loud enough to be listened to properly.

vii. **Develop the voice**: Keep doing exercises to lower the pitch of your voice to make it your own identity.

viii. **Use appropriate pitch and voice volume**: Use a voice volume that is appropriate for the setting. Speak more softly if you are alone and close. Speak louder if you are speaking to larger group or across larger spaces.

ix. **Don't send mixed messages:** Make your words, gestures, facial expressions, tone, and message match. Avoid a mixed message. If you want to deliver a positive or negative message, make sure that your words, facial expressions, and tone match the message.

10. Explain the seven elements of the communication cycle.

Ans. The communication cycle has mainly seven elements:

i. **Sender:** This is a person who starts communication.

ii. **Message**: This is the information that the sender wants to send or share.

iii. **Encoding:** This is how the sender chooses to send the message into a form appropriate for sending.

iv. **Channel**: This means by which medium the message is sent.

v. **Receiver:** The person who receives the message

vi. **Decoding**: This is how the receiver interprets and understands the message.

vii. **Feedback**: The receiver's response to the message.

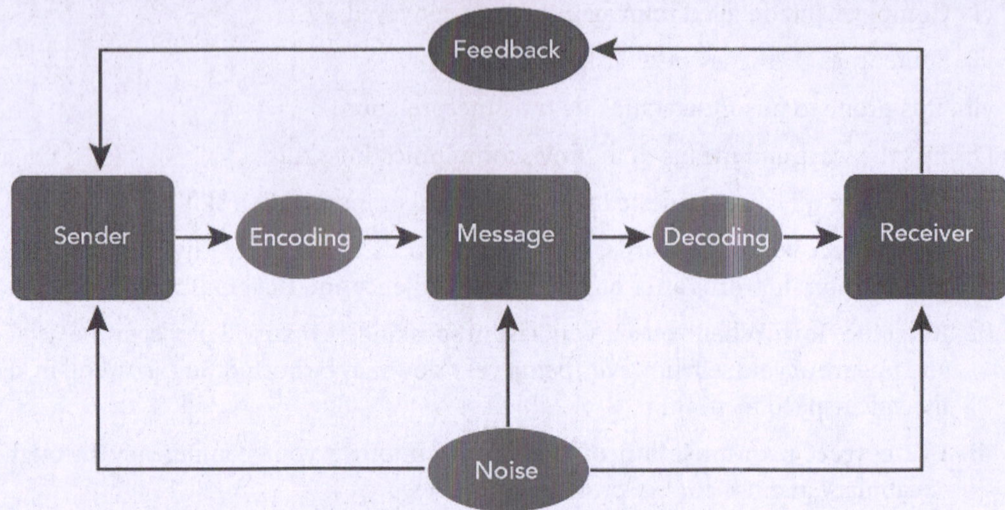

Figure 1.12 Communication Cycle

In the communication cycle, there may be some barriers, which are sometimes known as noise.

11. Explain various types of communication barriers.

Ans. Mainly, communication barriers have the following types.

i. **Physical Barriers:** Physical barriers separate people from each other by marking territories. These barriers can often be seen in the workplace, where offices and closed doors stop communication. Physical barriers can stop a person from being comfortable communicating with a person whom he/she does not come face to face with often.

ii. **Language Barriers:** When a person is not familiar with the language used by another person in communication, misinterpretation will occur. The accents and dialect (use of words) of people belonging to different cultures/places differ even if their language is the same and may become barriers to communication. For example, the abbreviation "LOL" used in social media is used for Lots of Love and Laugh Out Loud. If a person says LOL, the second person can interpret the meaning in any way he wants.

iii. **Gender Barriers**: There are distinct differences between the communication patterns in a man and those in a woman. Variations may exist among masculine and feminine styles of communication. While women often emphasize politeness, empathy, and rapport building, male communication is often more direct and to the point. This means that a man may talk in a linear, logical, and compartmentalized way, which are the features of left-brain thinking, while a woman talks more freely, mixing logic and emotion, features of both sides of the brain. If someone meshes these two styles without awareness, then it could become a barrier.

iv. **Attitudinal Barriers:** As those behaviours or perceptions that are divisive in nature lead to nagging doubt, disagreement, or even overt conflict, they all interfere with and undermine communication. These are barriers that distance one from others. These are visible through withdrawal, meaningless rituals that keep one devoid of real contact, superficial activities, etc.

v. **Perceptual Barriers**:People tend to interpret messages from their own points of view or ideologies. Without thinking, one might only view a message from his or her own mindset rather than looking at it from another viewpoint. Different world views can create misunderstanding. The main problem in communicating with others is that all persons see the world differently.

vi. **Cultural Barriers**: Ethnic, religious, and social differences can often create misunderstandings during communication. These differences can also affect one's perception and create confusion in getting a message correctly.

vii. **Emotional Barriers**: When someone is consumed with emotion, then he/she will have difficulty understanding the message communicated well. Emotions like fear, hostility, anger, love, empathy, etc., make it hard to hear outside one's own self. The roots of the emotional mistrust of others lay in our childhood and infancy when we were taught by our parents to be careful about what we say to others. People must have been often warned- "Mind your P's and Q's." "Don't speak until you're spoken to." That's why many people hold back from communicating their thoughts and feelings to others. While some caution may be wise in some relationships, excessive fear of what others might think of us can stop our development as effective communicators.

12. Discuss the various methods to overcome barriers to communication.

Ans. The following are some methods to overcome barriers to communication:

i. **Use simple language**: Simple and easy language is to be used during communication.

ii. **Stay open-minded for Questions and Answers**: To communicate effectively, one needs to be open-minded and willing to ask and answer questions that may seem frustrating sometimes. Be helpful in the problem-solving process of others.

iii. **Stereotyping:** We often form stereotypes about those whom we know the least. Once our mental sets are created, all our transactions are affected by their sets, preventing us from effective listening.

iv. **Practice listening**: Listen to the speaker carefully is required to understand him/her and the message.

v. **Keep the Message Short:** Communicate to the point and keep messages short, succinct, and packed with only the information a person needs to do his job.

vi. **Communicate as per need:** Noise and distractions can up the communication process at all levels. So, communicate what is necessary or needed.

vii. **Be respectful to others' opinions**: Show respect to the opinions expressed by other people.

viii. **Remain Aware of Cultural Differences**: Various words in different cultures have different meanings. We must be careful in using these types of words. Using the correct words as per the culture should be encouraged while communicating with a group of people.

ix. **Avoid Slang**: Slang and casual language can be fun with friends, but with elders and co-workers, it can create a significant barrier to effective communications. Slang differs significantly across generations and cultures. Slang can cause confusion, and it can be a source of frustration.

x. **Not listening as a status or gender issue**: Some persons in positions listen less to those who are lower in a hierarchy. How well do the parents listen to their children or the juniors in age or experience? If a woman employee is speaking, are men employees as attentive as they would be when a male colleague speaks up?

13. Explain the 7Cs of communication.

Ans. The 7Cs of communication are also termed the seven principles of communication, which ensure effective communication.

i. **Clarity:** Clear and simple language is characterized by explicitness, short sentences, and concrete words. Avoid fuzzy language.

ii. **Correctness**: We correct language free from grammatical errors and stylists' lapses. The use of correct language increases trustworthiness.

iii. **Concreteness**: The message should be supported by factual material such as data and figures.

iv. **Conciseness:** Clear and concise message with facts should be preferred in place of a long message to avoid confusion. In addition to the above, sometimes the following 7Cs are also called.

v. **Coherent:** While communicating with the target group, it is important to relate it to the target group and be involved. Factors playing a role here are professional knowledge, level of education, age, interest, etc.

vi. **Courtesy**: In addition to understanding the feelings and opinions of the target group, it is also important to address the audience in a friendly manner. Use the terms and phrases that show respect and regards to the receiver(s).

vii. **Completeness**: The message for communication must be complete and geared to the receiver's perception of the world. It should be based on facts, and a complex message is to be explained.

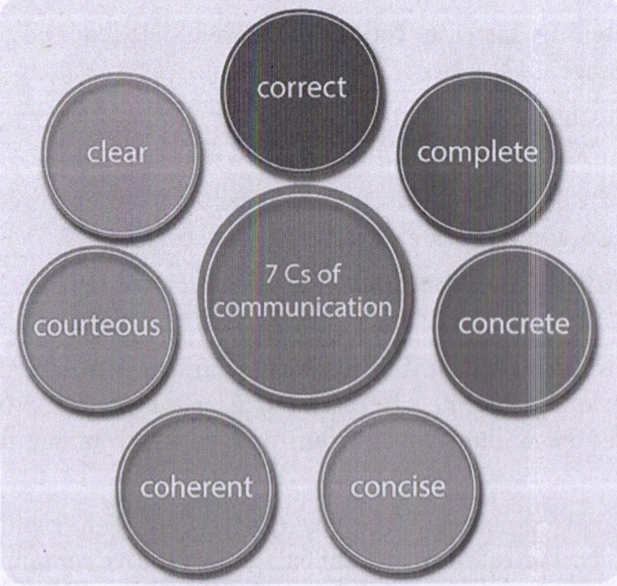

Figure 1.13

14. Discuss the steps for writing a paragraph.

Ans. The following steps are to be followed in writing a paragraph:

i. **Topic Sentence:** The first sentence of the paragraph is termed 'Topic Sentence.' It should be a general statement by introducing the overall idea without giving detail. It should be indented. The topic sentence is also termed as the "main idea" of the paragraph.

ii. **Body Sentences:** The body of the paragraph contains sentences that follow the topic sentences. Here, the additional details are provided to give a clear, coherent idea of what the paragraph is about. Insert facts, make arguments, and analyse the issue in the body sentences.

iii. **Conclusion:** The final sentence should sum up all of the information found mainly in the topic and body sentences. By this point, we should have made our case. This is where connections are made. Think of the conclusion sentence as the reverse of the topic sentence; the final statement should be general but sum up the entire paragraph.

iv. **Coherent Details:** All three elements: topic sentence, body sentences, and conclusion, should be presented in a clear and concise manner. The details in your paragraph should be clear enough so that a reader follows what you've written and understands it.

15. Explain the elements essential for paragraph writing.

Ans. There are four essential elements for paragraph writing, namely unity, order, coherence, and completeness.

i. **Unity:** Unity in a sentence starts with the subject phrase. Every sentence has one individual, managing concept that is indicated in its subject phrase. A sentence is specific around this main concept, with the assisting phrases offering details and conversation. For creating a good subject phrase, think about the style and all the details to be made.

ii. **Order**: Order represents the way in which the phrases are arranged. Whether you choose the date order, the order of importance, or another reasonable demonstration of detail, a solid sentence always has a certain organisation. In a well-ordered sentence, people follow along easily with the design you've established. Order helps people understand the indicating and avoid misunderstandings.

iii. **Coherence**: Coherence is the quality that makes the writing understandable. Sentences within a paragraph need to be connected to each other, and they should work together as a whole. One method to achieve coherency is to use transition words, which create bridges from one sentence to the next. Moreover, in writing a paragraph, using a consistent verb tense is an important ingredient for coherency.

iv. **Completeness**: Completeness means that an expression is well-developed. When all words clearly and properly assist the significant idea, then the expression is complete. When there are not enough words or enough information to confirm the dissertation, then the expression is partial. The last sentence of expression should sum up the significant idea by strengthening the topic.

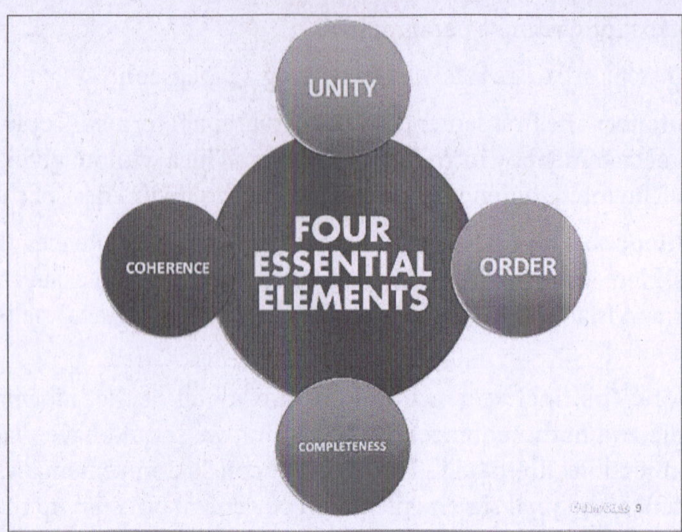

Figure 1.14

1.3.11 HOTS QUESTIONS

1. What is the main purpose of verbal communication?

Ans. Verbal communication helps us to think, maintain relationships, define reality, and organise complex ideas and experiences into meaningful experiences.

2. How do non-verbal communications occur?

Ans. Non-verbal communication uses different non-verbal prompts like body movements, gestures, facial expressions, symbols, images, signals charts, and soon to express sentiments, attitudes, or information.

3. Why are communication skills needed?

Ans. Communication skills are needed basically for three reasons:

i. **Inform**: You may be required to inform facts or information with someone. For example, informing the IPL timetable to a friend.

ii. **Influence:** You may require to influence or change someone's attitude in an indirect manner. For example, negotiating the price of an item with a shopkeeper to reduce it or helping a friend to overcome stress due to an exam or any other reason.

iii. **Express feelings**: Talking about your feelings is required to express them freely. For example, sharing the excitement about doing well in the exams, sharing your feelings with your parents and friends.

4. Which three parts of communication are considered important and why?

Ans. Communication has three important parts, as follows:

(i) **Transmitting**: The sender transmits the message through one medium or other.

(ii) **Listening**: The receiver listens or understands the message.

(iii) **Feedback:** The process in which the receiver conveys his/ her understanding of the message to the sender in the form of Feedback completes the communication cycle.

Without these three parts, no communication is considered complete. That's why these are important.

5. How are 'Attitudinal Barriers' creating misunderstanding during communication?

Ans. As the behaviours or perceptions that are divisive in nature lead to nagging doubt, disagreement, or even overt conflict, they all interfere with and undermine communication. These are barriers that distance one from others. These are visible through withdrawal, meaningless rituals that keep one devoid of real contact, superficial activities, etc. These barriers create misunderstandings during communication.

1.4 PRACTICE QUESTIONS

1. Define the cultural barrier.
2. Define non-verbal communication.
3. Define a sentence.
4. What are the elements of communication?
5. Illustrate different types of communication barriers.
6. Give an example of a language barrier.
7. What do you mean by the article?
8. What are indefinite articles?
9. What are the different types of sentences?
10. Define paragraph.
11. Define and give examples of non-verbal communication.
12. What do you mean by visual communication?
13. What are the advantages of visual communication?
14. What are the different types of non-verbal communication?
15. Explain the SMCR model of communication?
16. What are the different methods of communication?
17. Explain the components of verbal communication.
18. Discuss the use of punctuation.
19. Discuss the barriers to communications.
20. Why is effective communication required? Explain.
21. Discuss the importance of Feedback in communication.
22. What are the principles of communication?
23. Discuss the importance of the use of correct phrases and sentences in communication.
24. Describe the elements of paragraph writing.
25. Mention the advantages of visual communication?
26. Discuss the advantages and disadvantages of verbal communication.

27. What do you mean by punctuation?
28. What are the different types of sentences?
29. What are the elements of paragraph writing?
30. What are the different types of sentences?
31. Give examples of various types of articles.

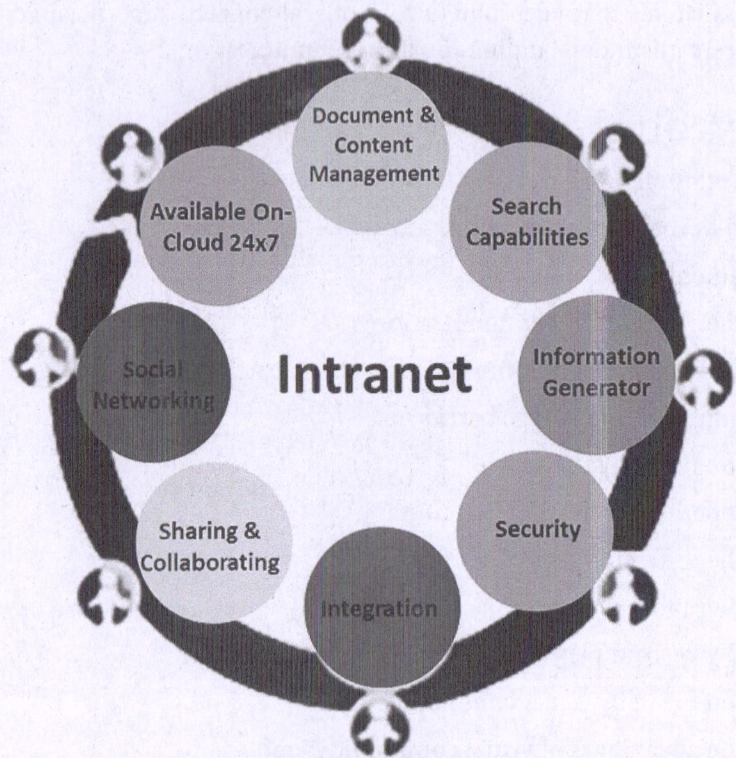

Figure 1.15

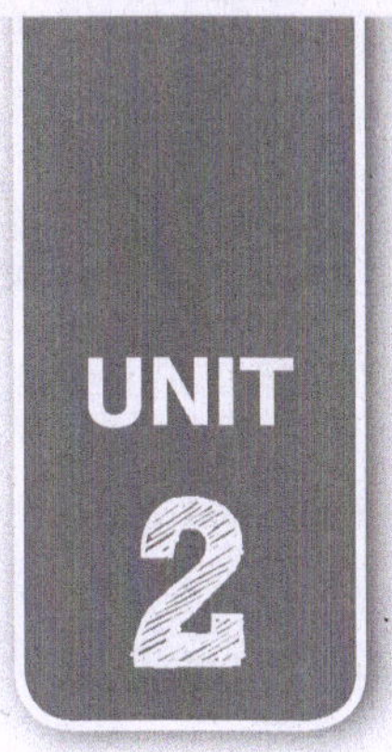

Self-Management Skills – I

2.1 UNIT IN BRIEF

- The ability to control your behaviour, discipline, etc., is called self-control. It is defined as the ability to regulate one's emotions, thoughts, and behaviour in the face of temptations and impulses.
- Dressing in a proper way for school, friend's place or playground creates a good and favourable impression.
- Expressing certainty or affirmation, even in tough situations, is termed positive thinking. Positive thinking may also be defined as a mental and emotional attitude that focuses on the bright side of life first and expects positive results.
- General neatness, appropriate dressing, grooming, apt verbal and non-verbal communication are the main components of a good personality.
- Independent working means a situation/condition when an individual is assigned a task(s) and he/she takes ownership and doesn't require constant supervision or assistance for completing that task(s).
- It is important to know the self because only then you can measure your strengths and weaknesses.

Figure 2.1

- Knowing what he does well or not so well in an issue will help him in converting his weaknesses into strengths and strengths into exceptional performance. The strength and weakness analysis helps you in this process.
- People with strong self-management skills are capable of doing different activities effectively, including managing their time-management, focusing on their tasks, cooperating with others in school and at home, and performing better in their studies.

- Planning realistic goals to be accomplished within a set timeframe is termed goal setting. It is a process for thinking about your ideal future and for motivating yourself to convert your vision into reality. Stress refers to a state of psychological tension and discomfort originating from unforeseen, difficult, confusing, and challenging situations.
- Real belief and trust of an individual in one's own judgment, capabilities, and worthiness is self-confidence.
- Self-confidence is a sense of trusting one's own abilities and self.
- Self-management is about preparing for the future, owning your present, and taking care of what you do, as well as learning how you could do better next time.
- Self-management is defined as the ability to regulate one's emotions, thoughts, and behaviour effectively in different situations.
- Self-management skills are also known as self-control or self-regulation. Self-control skills are important as these characteristics contribute to a better work environment for oneself and others in the workplace.
- Self-management skills are helpful in setting goals and achieving them with bright success.
- Self-management skills include self-awareness, self-confidence, self-control, problem-solving skills, time management, goal setting, stress management, personal hygiene and grooming, teamwork, etc.
- Self-management skills play an essential role in one's life to regulate one's emotions, thoughts, and behaviour effectively in different situations to achieve success.
- Strength and weakness analysis means knowing our inner strengths, hidden talents, skills, and even weaknesses.
- Strengths are what we do well and are good at. Each person has some strengths.
- Stress management is the managing of stress to avoid its negative impact on the physical and mental health of an individual.
- The ability to regulate one's thoughts, emotions, and behaviour effectively in different situations is known as self-management skills.
- The concept of self-esteem is commonly used as self-assurance in one's judgment, ability, power, etc.
- The process of doing tasks on your own without any external motivation is termed self-motivation. Self-motivation is also defined as a force that drives you to do things.
- The process of understanding a problem and finding a solution using a step-by-step method is called problem-solving skill.
- Weaknesses are also known as 'areas of improvement,' and these are the areas where we do not do well and are not good at.
- When one believes in oneself that one can do any task that is given to him/he and is not scared of taking risks, it is termed as self-confidence.

✦ Working together with different types of people to accomplish shared goals is called teamwork. Teamwork is defined as a collaborative effort of any group to achieve a common goal or to complete a task in an effective and efficient way.

Figure 2.2

2.2 CBSE/NCERT SECTION (SOLVED CBSE/NCERT EXERCISES)

2.2.1 Multiple Choice Questions

1. Which of the following qualities is not a self-management skill?
   a) Problem-solving
   b) Bargaining
   c) Understanding self
   d) Confidence building
2. Grooming is a term that is associated with:
   a) time management
   b) problem-solving
   c) neat and clean appearance
   d) self-management
3. What steps should one take to build confidence?
   a) Set goals in life
   b) Appreciate oneself for all the achievements
   c) Always think positively
   d) Talk to people who are confident
4. Which of the following qualities is a quality of a self-confident person?
   a) Patient
   b) Compassionate
   c) Committed
   d) Passionate
5. Which is the best way to start our day positively?
   a) Thinking about all that can go wrong.
   b) Thinking about the difficult test you will face during the day.
   c) Thinking about all your accomplishment so far and feel good about them.
   d) Thinking about the traffic on the road and feel stressed.

6. Rahul gets feedback on his project work from his teacher. Which of these options demonstrates a positive attitude in this situation?
   a) Rahul tells others that the teacher is wrong.
   b) Rahul ignores the feedback.
   c) Rahul takes the feedback but does not use it.
   d) Rahul learns from the feedback and makes his project work better.
7. What can you do to get rid of negative thoughts/ feelings?
   a) Meditate to calm down and feel positive.
   b) Ignore them and move on in life.
   c) Act based on negative thoughts or feelings.
   d) Talk to a friend and share all the negative feelings.
8. Do you think people living in hill stations should skip taking a bath for many days?
   a) No, irrespective of the climate, one should take a bath regularly.
   b) Yes, not taking a bath for many days is acceptable for people staying in a cold climate.
   c) Yes, when they wipe themselves with a wet cloth, then it is fine.
   d) None of the above
9. Radha wants to grow her hair, and she applies a lot of hair oil. She does not wash her hair for days, and sometimes it smells bad too. What would be your suggestion to her?
   a) She can leave the oil in her hair; after all, it helps her hair to grow.
   b) She can leave it on at night and wash her hair every day before leaving home.
   c) She should not apply the oil at all.
   d) She can apply the oil and pour a little water on her hair before leaving home to reduce the smell.
10. Dressing and grooming are important because they help us to look ____________.
   a) smart
   b) untidy
   c) shabby
   d) All of the above

ANSWERS									
1. (b)	2. (c)	3. (c)	4. (c)	5. (c)	6. (d)	7. (a)	8. (a)	9. (b)	10. (a)

2.2.2 Short Answer Type Questions

1. Write a short note on the factors influencing self-management.

Ans. Self-management skills are also known as self-control or self-regulation. Self-control skills are important as these characteristics contribute to a better work environment for oneself and others in the workplace. Various factors that influence self-management skills include physical factors, social factors, emotional factors, cultural factors, etc.

2. List any 05 self-management skills.

Ans. Self-management skills include:

i. Self-confidence,

ii. Persistence

iii. Patience

iv. Resilience

v. Perceptiveness

vi. Emotional regulation

vii. Self-motivating

viii. Setting and working towards personal and academic goals

3. What are the factors that affect self-confidence?

Ans. The following factors affect the self-confidence of people:

i. Social Factors: Interactions with family and social environment, like friends, relatives, teachers, and media, influences the self-confidence of individuals. The development of confidence in self is a process that results from the experiences of individuals while interacting with others.

ii. Cultural factors: These comprise of values, beliefs, and customs. Indians give much importance to family values, believe in the philosophy of "Vasudev Kutumbhkam" .

iii. Physical factors: These factors include self-efficacy, physical activity, and social physique anxiety, which are found to be influencing the self-confidence of individuals. Physical activity is directly related to self-confidence. Physical self-efficacy refers to the physical potential to complete a specific task. Social physique anxiety is a concern amongst individuals about the perceived evaluation of one's physical self by society.

4. List three things you will do for personal grooming in each of CARE, WASH, and AVOID to keep clean.

Ans. **(a) CARE:**

i. Brush the teeth twice a day.

ii. Cut the nails every week.

iii. Keep the hair free of dandruff.

iv. Rub oil/cream to take care of the skin.

(b) WASH:

i. Take a bath every day.

ii. Wash the hands with soap frequently.

iii. Wash the feet often.

iv. Wash the clothes regularly.

v. Wash the hair at least every second day.

(c) AVOID:

i. Blow the nose/cough into a handkerchief to avoid spreading germs.

ii. Keep the feet dry and change your socks every day.

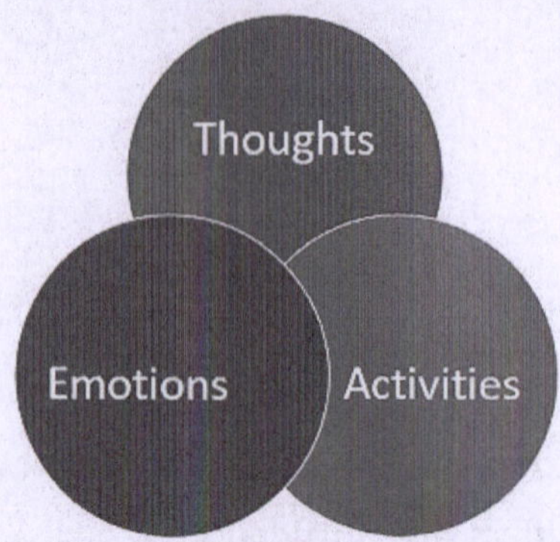

Figure 2.3

2.3 SOLVED EXERCISES

2.3.1 Multiple Choice Questions

Choose the correct option out of the four options given for each question.

1. The ability to regulate one's thoughts, emotions, and behaviour effectively in different situations is known as ____________ skills.

   a) Self-awareness b) Self-management

   c) Self-regulation d) Self-confidence

2. Real belief and trust of an individual in one's own judgment, capabilities, and worthiness is termed ____________.

   a) Self-aware b) Teamwork

   c) Self-motivated d) Self -confidence

3. Suppose Srijit is more confident in handling problems affecting their lives, tends to rely less on others, easily makes decisions, and is emotionally independent. He represents:

   a) Independent people b) Confident people

   c) Stressed people d) Democratic people

4. Which of the following is termed the "wear and tear" that the human body experiences?

   a) Stress b) Eustress

   c) Motivation d) Self-awareness

5. Consider the following examples and choose the examples of strengths.

   i. I am not good at creative articles and stories.

   ii. I have a fear of the water.

   iii. I play cricket very well.

iv. I am good at speaking Hindi and Marathi.

v. I find it challenging to solve Maths problems.

vi. I am good at writing in Gujarati.

a) (ii) (iiii) (iv) b) (iv) (v) (vi) c) (iii) (iv) (vi) d) All of them

6. General neatness, appropriate dressing, grooming, apt verbal and non-verbal communication are the main components of a good ____________.

   a) Locality b) Personality c) Confidence d) Looking

7. Which of the following statements does not exhibit an example of weaknesses?

   a) I have a fear of swimming in a pond.

   b) I am wonderful at cricket.

   c) I would like to speak French fluently.

   d) I do not like to lose in any indoor game.

8. Suppose Tina possesses the skills like self-motivation, organisational skills, multitasking ability, discipline, communication skills, and resourcefulness and works independently. Which of the following is the key skill in order to work independently?

   a) Self-awareness b) Self-motivation

   c) Self-regulation d) All of the above

9. While vacationing with family and friends, one is able to:

   a) Deepen social relations b) Break the monotonousness of life

   c) Admire nature's beauty d) All of these

10. Which statement related to an independent person is incorrect?

    a) He/she tends to rely more on others.

    b) He/she is resourceful.

    c) He/she is wholly responsible for the outcome of the task which he has undertaken.

    d) He/she is self-aware.

11. What makes Rehan complete his studies without others cheering him?

    a) Self-confidence b) Self-motivation

    c) Communication d) Self-esteem

12. Expressing certainty or affirmation, even in tough situations, is termed ____________.

    a) Positive thinking b) Negative thinking

    c) Creativity d) Critical thinking

13. Suppose Nikita Sharma works hard to get the 'Best Anchor' award at the annual sports day function. What type of motivation is this?

    a) Internal b) External

    c) Both internal and external d) None of the above

14. Meditation brings a sense of:
    a) Depression
    b) Anxiety
    c) Self-awareness
    d) Stress
15. Which of the following is the key skill for becoming an independent person?
    a) Self-awareness
    b) Self-regulation
    c) Self-motivation
    d) All of these
16. Which of the following options provides the people with the energy and motivation to achieve the goals?
    a) Stress
    b) Eustress
    c) Distress
    d) Anxiety
17. Which of the following words is a stressor?
    a) Dangerous
    b) Useless fellow
    c) Irrelevant
    d) All of these
18. Suppose Gauransh studies in class IX, and he is aware of his personality, including his strengths, weaknesses, thoughts, beliefs, emotions, and motivations. Which of the following skills does he possess?
    a) Communication skills
    b) Empathy
    c) Self-awareness
    d) Critical Thinking
19. Which of the following statements related to self-regulation is correct?
    a) Self-regulation helps people to cope with strong feelings.
    b) Self-regulation makes people more independent.
    c) Self-regulation helps people to behave in socially acceptable ways.
    d) None of these
20. Which factor does create a chaotic atmosphere in a person's life leading to 'stress'?
    a) Pressure from family and society
    b) Endless greed
    c) Achieving our goals
    d) All of these
21. Which element is not used to keep a person motivated?
    a) Personal drive to achieve goals
    b) Initiative or readiness to act on opportunities
    c) Being aware of the personality
    d) Commitment to personal or organisational goals
22. The factor(s) that may bring about negative changes in a person suffering from stress is/are:
    a) Peer pressure
    b) Threat
    c) Financial loss
    d) All of these

23. A person who is wholly responsible for the outcome of the task which he has undertaken is called:
    a) Resourceful person
    b) Independent person
    c) Self-motivated person
    d) Confident person
24. Stress management is helpful for:
    a) Focus and complete tasks on time.
    b) Be more energetic
    c) Be able to spend quality time with your friends and family.
    d) All the above
25. Which of the following skills is more important than others in getting success in a professional career?
    a) Intelligence Quotient (IQ)
    b) Emotional and social skills
    c) Communication skills
    d) None of the above
26. Self-management is helpful in:
    a) Nurturing good habits
    b) Overcoming challenges and difficulties to reach goals
    c) In avoiding stress and providing time and opportunities to get involved in fun activities.
    d) All of the above
27. Which of the following is not included in self-management skills?
    a) Resilience
    b) Perceptiveness
    c) Perception
    d) Emotional regulation

ANSWERS									
1. (b)	2. (d)	3. (a)	4. (a)	5. (c)	6. (b)	7. (b)	8. (d)	9. (d)	10. (a)
11. (b)	12. (a)	13. (a)	14. (c)	15. (d)	16. (b)	17. (d)	18. (c)	19. (b)	20. (d)
21. (c)	22. (d)	23. (b)	24. (d)	25. (b)	26. (d)	27. (c)			

2.3.2 Fill in the blanks

1. ____________ skills include self-confidence, persistence, patience, resilience, perceptiveness, emotional regulation, motivating oneself, and setting and working towards personal and academic goals.
2. There are two types of awareness-____________ self-awareness and internal self-awareness.
3. Yoga helps in relieving ____________ and uplifting our mood.
4. ____________ includes a pool of techniques that assist individuals in eradicating anxiety and negative thoughts and work on their well-being.
5. ____________ referred to an automatic response of the nervous system to any threat, challenge, or Problem.

6. Stress can make you feel hot due to a rise in ____________.
7. ____________ may also be defined as a mental and emotional attitude that focuses on the bright side of life first and expects positive results.
8. ____________ means being aware of the personality, including your strengths, weaknesses, thoughts, beliefs, emotions, and motivations.
9. Systematic efforts to direct thoughts, feelings, actions to attain the required success in the assigned task is termed ____________.
10. ____________ people are likely to be more confident in handling problems affecting their lives.
11. Planning concrete goals to be accomplished within a set timeframe is termed as ____________.
12. Self-management skills are also known as ____________ or self-regulation skills.
13. Stress-causing agents are known as ____________.
14. ____________ is a natural and inexpensive way that provides immunity to stress.
15. The force within someone that drives him to do things is called ____________.

Figure 2.4

ANSWERS			
1. Self-management	2. External	3. stress	4. Stress management
5. Stress	6. blood pressure	7. Positive thinking	
8. Self-awareness	9. self-regulation	10. Independent	11. goal setting.
12. self-control	13. stressors.	14. Meditation	15. Self-motivation

2.3.3 True or False

1. Goal setting is defined as a process for thinking about your ideal future and for motivating yourself to convert your vision into reality.
2. Stress refers to a state of psychological tension and discomfort originating from unforeseen, difficult, confusing, and challenging situations.

3. Stress Management covers all the tools that are available to deal with chronic stress, which could otherwise prove to be a lethal disease.
4. The ability to regulate one's thoughts, emotions, and behaviour effectively in different situations is known as self-awareness skills.
5. The process of doing tasks on your own without any external motivation is termed self-control.
6. Teamwork is defined as a collaborative effort of any group to achieve a common goal or to complete a task in an effective and efficient manner.
7. Expressing certainty or affirmation, even in tough situations, is termed positive thinking.
8. The important thing about stress is that it cannot be managed.
9. Working together with people to accomplish shared goals is called empathy.
10. Our body is equipped with a natural 'fight or flight response, in which it reacts spontaneously to protect itself from any unfavourable situation.
11. Nature walk induces the basic qualities of living in harmony, peace, and cooperation.
12. The first step for a positive outlook is having a long-term goal and short-term goals.
13. Stress is a charged-up internal condition of our body in response to some repulsive external or internal situations.
14. Stress can be viewed as a disease that affects people of all age groups.
15. Self-confidence involves being able to control reactions to emotions like frustration or excitement.

ANSWERS
1. (T) 2. T 3. (T) 4. F (self-management skills) 5. F (self-motivation)
6. (T) 7. (T) 8. F 9. F (Teamwork) 10. (T) 11. (??) 12. (T) 13. (F) 14. (T)
15. F (self-regulation)

2.3.4 Matching type

(I) Match the items of column A with those of Column B correctly.

Column A	**Column B**
(i) Emotional awareness	(a) Ability to regulate one's own emotions
(ii) Harnessing emotions	(b) Ability to identify and name one's own emotions.
(iii) Managing emotions	(c) Ability to apply emotions to tasks like thinking and problem-solving.

ANSWERS
(I) (i)-b (ii)-c (iii)-a

2.3.5 Statements Based Questions

1. Statement 1: Strengths are what we do well and are good at.

Statement 2: Weaknesses are also known as 'areas of improvement,' and these are the areas where we do not do well and are not good at.

a) Statement 1 is correct, but statement 2 is incorrect.

b) Statement 1 is incorrect, but statement 2 is correct.

c) Both the statements are correct.

d) Both the statements are incorrect.

2. Statement 1: Stress may be defined as a reaction to any external stimuli that trigger changes in one's personality.

   Statement 2: The process of understanding a problem and finding a solution using a step-by-step method is called decision-making skill.

   a) Statement 1 is correct, but statement 2 is incorrect.

   b) Statement 1 is incorrect, but statement 2 is correct.

   c) Both the statements are correct.

   d) Both the statements are incorrect.

3. Statement 1: Knowing what he does well or not so well in an issue will help him in converting his weaknesses into strengths and strengths into exceptional performance.

   Statement 2: Self-confidence is about preparing for the future, owning your present, and taking care of what you do, as well as learning how you could do better next time.

   a) Statement 1 is correct, but statement 2 is incorrect.

   b) Statement 1 is incorrect, but statement 2 is correct.

   c) Both the statements are correct.

   d) Both the statements are incorrect.

4. Statement 1: Setting realistic goals with proper time management will produce less stress.

   Statement 2: Stress means pressure, tensions, worries, and problems of life, affecting the balance in life.

   a) Statement 1 is correct, but statement 2 is incorrect.

   b) Statement 1 is incorrect, but statement 2 is correct.

   c) Both the statements are correct.

   d) Both the statements are incorrect.

5. Statement 1: It is not important to know the self because only then you can measure your strengths and weaknesses.

   Statement 2: Yoga does not help in relieving stress and uplifting our mood.

   a) Statement 1 is correct, but statement 2 is incorrect.

   b) Statement 1 is incorrect, but statement 2 is correct.

   c) Both the statements are correct.

   d) Both the statements are incorrect.

6. Statement 1: Self-confidence is not required for completing all tasks.

   Statement 2: Self-control involves being able to control reactions to emotions like frustration or excitement.

   a) Statement 1 is correct, but statement 2 is incorrect.
   b) Statement 1 is incorrect, but statement 2 is correct.
   c) Both the statements are correct.
   d) Both the statements are incorrect.

7. Statement 1: Stress management techniques may include physical exercise, yoga, meditation, spending time with friends and family, talking, etc.

   Statement 2: Common responses to stress may be aches and pains, energy levels and sleep, feelings, and other emotional signs.

   a) Statement 1 is correct, but statement 2 is incorrect.
   b) Statement 1 is incorrect, but statement 2 is correct.
   c) Both the statements are correct.
   d) Both the statements are incorrect.

8. Statement 1: Intrinsic motivation refers to the behaviour of a person that is driven by the desire to achieve some type of external reward, including money, power, and good grades.

   Statement 2: External self-awareness represents how clearly one sees one's own values, passions, aspirations, thoughts, feelings, behaviours, strengths, weaknesses, and their impact on others.

   a) Statement 1 is correct, but statement 2 is incorrect.
   b) Statement 1 is incorrect, but statement 2 is correct.
   c) Both the statements are correct.
   d) Both the statements are incorrect.

9. Statement 1: The ability to control your behaviour, discipline, etc., is called self-esteem.

   Statement 2: When one believes in oneself that one can do any task that is given to him/he and is not scared of taking risks, it is termed as self-confidence.

   a) Statement 1 is correct, but statement 2 is incorrect.
   b) Statement 1 is incorrect, but statement 2 is correct.
   c) Both the statements are correct.
   d) Both the statements are incorrect.

10. Statement 1: Realistic belief and trust of an individual in one's own judgment, capabilities, and worthiness is self-awareness.

    Statement 2: The concept of self-control is commonly used as self-assurance in one's judgment, ability, power, etc.

    a) Statement 1 is correct, but statement 2 is incorrect.
    b) Statement 1 is incorrect, but statement 2 is correct.

c) Both the statements are correct.

d) Both the statements are incorrect.

ANSWERS									
1. (c)	2. (a)	3. (a)	4. (c)	5. (d)	6. (b)	7. (c)	8. (b)	9. (b)	10. (d)

2.3.6 Assertion Reason Type Questions

1. Assertion (A): Self-control or self-regulation skills are important in one's life.

   Reason(R): Self-control skills contribute to a better work environment for oneself and others in the workplace.

   a) Both A and R are correct, and R is the correct reason for A.

   b) Both A and R are correct, and R is not the correct reason for A.

   c) A is correct, but R is incorrect.

   d) A is incorrect, but R is correct.

2. Assertion (A): Dressing in a proper way for school, friend's place or playground creates a good and favourable impression.

   Reason(R): Independent working means a situation/condition when an individual is assigned some task(s), he/she takes ownership and doesn't require constant supervision or assistance to complete that task(s).

   a) Both A and R are correct, and R is the correct reason for A.

   b) Both A and R are correct, and R is not the correct reason for A.

   c) A is correct, but R is incorrect.

   d) A is incorrect, but R is correct.

3. Assertion (A): Stress is always useful, helping us to accomplish great things.

   Reason(R): The most important thing about stress is that it can be managed.

   a) Both A and R are correct, and R is the correct reason for A.

   b) Both A and R are correct, and R is not the correct reason for A.

   c) A is correct, but R is incorrect.

   d) A is incorrect, but R is correct.

4. Assertion (A): The process of doing tasks on your own without any external motivation is termed self-motivation.

   Reason(R): The process of understanding a problem and finding a solution using a step-by-step method is called problem-solving skill.

   a) Both A and R are correct, and R is the correct reason for A.

   b) Both A and R are correct, and R is not the correct reason for A.

   c) A is correct, but R is incorrect.

   d) A is incorrect, but R is correct.

5. Assertion (A): Expressing certainty or affirmation, even in tough situations, is termed as positive thinking.

   Reason(R): General neatness, grooming, appropriate dressing, apt verbal and non-verbal communication are the main components of a good personality.

   a) Both A and R are correct, and R is the correct reason for A.
   b) Both A and R are correct, and R is not the correct reason for A.
   c) A is correct, but R is incorrect.
   d) A is incorrect, but R is correct.

6. Assertion (A): Stress management includes a set of techniques that assist individuals in eradicating anxiety and negative thoughts and work on their well-being.

   Reason(R): Regular practice of Yoga increases stress, anxiety, and depression.

   a) Both A and R are correct, and R is the correct reason for A.
   b) Both A and R are correct, and R is not the correct reason for A.
   c) A is correct, but R is incorrect.
   d) A is incorrect, but R is correct.

7. Assertion (A): Eustress may have a positive impact on people.

   Reason(R): Eustress provides us with the energy and motivation to achieve our goals.

   a) Both A and R are correct, and R is the correct reason for A.
   b) Both A and R are correct, and R is not the correct reason for A.
   c) A is correct, but R is incorrect.
   d) A is incorrect, but R is correct.

8. Assertion (A): De-stressors are factors that have an adverse effect on the physical, emotional, behavioural, and mental health of a human being.

   Reason(R): Vacation with friends and family can be a refreshing experience that can help in relieving stress.

   a) Both A and R are correct, and R is the correct reason for A.
   b) Both A and R are correct, and R is not the correct reason for A.
   c) A is correct, but R is incorrect.
   d) A is incorrect, but R is correct.

9. Assertion (A): Doing exercise acts as a stress reliever.

   Reason(R): Doing exercise helps to release endorphins (chemicals in the brain that act as natural painkillers) and eradicate insomnia.

   a) Both A and R are correct, and R is the correct reason for A.
   b) Both A and R are correct, and R is not the correct reason for A.
   c) A is correct, but R is incorrect.
   d) A is incorrect, but R is correct.

10. Assertion (A): Our body is equipped with a natural 'fight or flight response, in which it reacts spontaneously to protect itself from any unfavourable situation.

    Reason(R): Stress management is the managing of stress to avoid its negative impact on the physical and mental health of an individual.

    a) Both A and R are correct, and R is the correct reason for A.

    b) Both A and R are correct, and R is not the correct reason for A.

    c) A is correct, but R is incorrect.

    d) A is incorrect, but R is correct.

ANSWERS									
1. (a)	2. (b)	3. (d)	4. (b)	5. (b)	6. (c)	7. (a)	8. (d)	9. (a)	10. (b)

2.3.7 Competency-Based Questions

1. Suppose Mudit won first prize at Inter-School Taekwondo Tournament. Now, he is more focused on getting the first prize at the National level Tournament. Which type of motivation does Mudit have?

    a) Internal

    b) External

    c) Intermediate

    d) Both internal and external

2. Suppose Suneeti has the ability to control her behaviour, discipline, etc. She has the ability to regulate her emotions, thoughts, and behaviour in the face of temptations and impulses. Which skills are possessed by her?

    a) Self-awareness

    b) Self-control

    c) Self-confidence

    d) Empathy

3. Suppose Vivek Verma studies in class IX and has a force that drives him to do things. He is the master of the process of doing tasks on his own without any external motivation. He possesses:

    a) Self-motivation skills

    b) Self-awareness skills

    c) Self -confidence

    d) Problem-solving skills

4. Suppose Aparna Medhi is comfortable in working together with people to accomplish shared goals. She is always interested in a collaborative effort of a group to achieve a common goal or to complete a task in an effective and efficient way. Which skills are possessed by her?

    a) Self-motivation skills

    b) Self-awareness skills

    c) Self -confidence

    d) Teamwork

5. Suppose Ekta Srinivasan, Creative Director, Disha Ad Agency, possesses the following qualities:

Figure 2.5

i. Self- belief
ii. Hard work
iii. Positive attitude
iv. Commitment

She is:

a) Self-aware
b) Self-motivated
c) Self-confident
d) Self-regulated

ANSWERS
1. (b) 2. (b) 3. (a) 4. (d) 5. (c)

2.3.8 VSA

1. Define preening.

Ans. Personal grooming or preening is the art of cleaning, grooming, and maintaining parts of the body.

2. Define self-control.

Ans. The ability to control your behaviour, discipline, etc., is called self-control. It is the ability to regulate one's emotions, thoughts, and behaviour in the face of temptations and impulses.

3. What is self-confidence?

Ans. When one believes in oneself that one can do any task that is given to him/he and is not scared of taking risks, it is termed as self-confidence.

4. Define Problem-solving skills.

Ans. The process of understanding a problem and finding a solution using a step-by-step method is called problem-solving skill.

5. What do you mean by Self-motivation?

Ans. The process of doing tasks on your own without any external motivation is termed self-motivation. Self-motivation is also defined as a force that drives you to do things.

6. What do you mean by personal hygiene and grooming?

Ans. Keeping oneself clean, healthy, and smart is termed as personal hygiene and grooming.

7. What is positive thinking?

Ans. Expressing certainty or affirmation, even in tough situations, is termed positive thinking. Positive thinking may also be defined as a mental and emotional attitude that focuses on the bright side of life first and expects positive results.

8. Define time management.

Ans. Achieving tasks on time and according to the plan is termed time management. In other words, time management is defined as the way that one organises and plans how long one spends on a specific activity. It may seem a good suggestion to dedicate precious time to learn time management instead of using it for doing your work to get enormous benefits.

9. What do you mean by goal setting?

Ans. Planning realistic goals to be accomplished within a set timeframe is termed goal setting. It is a process for thinking about your ideal future and for motivating yourself to convert your vision into reality.

10. What is stress management?

Ans. Stress refers to a state of psychological tension and discomfort originating from unforeseen, difficult, confusing, and challenging situations. Stress management is the managing of stress to avoid its negative impact on the physical and mental health of an individual.

11. What do you mean by independent working?

Ans. Independent working means a situation/condition when an individual is assigned some task(s) and he/she takes ownership and doesn't require constant supervision or assistance to complete that task(s).

12. Which skill is required to lead a happy and successful life?

Ans. Self-management skills.

13. Define self-awareness.

Ans. Self-awareness is understanding the causes of your own behaviour.

14. What is the right step towards true self-management?

Ans. Taking responsibility for the actions is the right step towards true self-management.

15. What is stress?

Ans. Stress means pressure, tensions, worries, and problems of life, affecting the balance in life.

16. Why is stress management required?

Ans. Stress management is required to lead a peaceful and meaningful life.

17. What are stress-causing agents called?

Ans. Stress-causing agents are known as stressors.

18. What are the common responses to stress?

Ans. Common responses to stress may be aches and pains, energy levels and sleep, feelings, and other emotional signs.

19. What are the main stress management techniques?

Ans. Stress management techniques may include physical exercise, yoga, meditation, spending time with friends and family, talking, etc.

20. What is the main advantage of setting realistic goals?

Ans. Setting realistic goals with proper time management will produce less stress.

21. What is eustress?

Ans. Stress may have a positive impact on people. It can sometimes be useful, helping us to accomplish great things. This is known as 'eustress.'

22. What is the main benefit of yoga and meditation with respect to stress?

Ans. Regular practice of yoga and meditation reduces stress, anxiety, and depression.

23. What do you mean by independent people?

Ans. Independent people are likely to be more confident in handling problems affecting their lives, tend to rely less on others, easily make decisions, and are emotionally stable.

24. What skills are required to work independently?

Ans. In order to work independently, a person must possess certain skills, like-self-motivation, organisational skills, multitasking ability, discipline, communication skills, and resourcefulness.

25. What do you mean by self-awareness?

Ans. Self-awareness means being aware of the personality, including your strengths, weaknesses, thoughts, beliefs, emotions, and motivations.

26. Mention the types of self-awareness.

Ans. There are two types of awareness-External self-awareness and Internal self-awareness.

27. What is external self-awareness?

Ans. External self-awareness requires understanding how other people perceive us.

28. Define internal self-awareness.

Ans. Internal self-awareness represents how clearly one sees one's own values, passions, aspirations, thoughts, feelings, behaviours, strengths, weaknesses, and their impact on others.

29. What is the main purpose of self-motivation?

Ans. Self-motivation drives a person to attempt and accomplish tasks.

30. What are the keys to getting the most out of your day?

Ans. Proper planning and time management are the two keys to getting the most out of your day.

Figure 2.6

2.3.9 Short Answer Type Questions

1. What is the importance of self-management skills?

Ans. People with strong self-management skills are capable of doing different activities effectively, including managing their time, focusing on their tasks, cooperating with others in school and at home, and performing better in their studies.

2. How is self-management useful in leading a successful life?

Ans. Self-management involves understanding oneself, understanding one's interests and abilities, having a positive attitude, and grooming oneself to develop self-confidence.

Self-management is helpful in:

i. Nurturing good habits
ii. Overcoming bad habits
iii. Reaching your goals
iv. Overcoming challenges and difficulties
v. In avoiding stress and providing time and opportunities to get involved in fun activities.

3. What is the impact of positive thinking in life?

Ans. A person having a positive thinking mentality anticipates happiness, health, and success and believes that he/she can overcome all obstacles and difficulties. That's why he/she may find solutions to all problems in life.

4. What do you mean by understanding the self?

Ans. Understanding the self means understanding things like who you are, what you like, what you do not like, what are your beliefs and prejudices, what are your opinions, what is your attitude and background, what you do well, and what do you not do well. It is important to know the self because only then you can measure your strengths and weaknesses.

5. Give some examples of strengths.

Ans. Strengths are what we do well and are good at. Each person has some strengths.

Examples of Strengths:

i. I am good at mathematics.

ii. I am sincere.

iii. I am good at understanding other people's emotions.

iv. I am a hard-working person.

v. I am confident in dealing with strangers while keeping myself safe from any harm.

vi. I am helpful to my colleagues and elders.

vii. I play football very well.

6. How can you identify your strengths?

Ans. For identifying your strengths, sit silently, and take the following steps:

i. Find some time to think about what you do well.

ii. Think and list down the things that you are always good at.

iii. Think about what others appreciate about you.

7. Give some examples of weaknesses.

Ans. Weaknesses are also known as 'areas of improvement,' and these are the areas where we do not do well and are not good at. Everyone has some weaknesses too.

Examples of weaknesses:

i. I am not good at a particular subject.

ii. I am unable to resist junk food when my friends suggest it.

iii. I am not comfortable facing the crowd

iv. I am not well in spoken English

v. I would like to learn more about computers.

vi. I am unable to manage my emotions

8. How can you identify your weakness?

Ans. For identifying your weakness, sit silently and take the following steps:

i. List out the areas where you struggle and what you find difficult to do.

ii. Look at the feedback you receive from other persons.

iii. Remain open to feedback and accept your weaknesses without feeling small about them.

iv. Think of it as an area of improvement.

9. What are the environmental forces for students?

Ans. Special attention is required to respond to the environmental forces. The environmental forces for students can be the class schedule, assignments, competitions, exams, different students and their behaviour, etc.

10. What are the qualities that are owned by self-confident people?

Ans. Real belief and trust of an individual in one's own judgment, capabilities, and worthiness is self-confidence.

Self-confident people have the following qualities:

i. Self-belief

ii. Hard work

iii. Positive attitude

iv. Commitment

11. Enlist some factors that decrease self-confidence.

Ans. Given below are some factors that decrease self-confidence. Avoid them.

i. When we think we cannot do a particular work.

ii. When we keep thinking of our past mistakes and feel bad about them, instead of learning from them.

iii. When we expect to be successful at the first attempt itself and do not try again.

iv. When we are surrounded by people who have a negative attitude, which is reflected in their speech.

12. Differentiate between interests and abilities.

Ans. Interests are the things or activities that you enjoy doing. Whereas ability is an acquired or natural capacity that enables an individual to perform a particular job or task with considerable proficiency. Interests may include:

i. Activities you like to do at school and in your free time that make you feel happy.

ii. Activities you are curious and interested in or would do even if no one asks you to do it.

iii. Activities you want to participate in after learning or would like to do in the future.

13. What are the fundamentals of being independent?

Ans. The fundamentals of being independent are the ability to work on your own, with minimal direction, confidence, self-awareness, self-motivation, and self-regulation.

14. What are the various disease-causing factors caused by stress?

Ans. Stress may cause disease-causing factors, like headaches, upset stomach, rashes, insomnia, ulcers, high blood pressure, heart diseases, and stroke, etc.

15. What are the general causes of stress?

Ans. The cause of stress is highly individual. It depends upon the personality, general outlook on life, problem-solving abilities, and social support system. Many different things cause stress, physical to emotional.

16. Why is Stress Management needed?

Ans. Stress management refers to deal stress using a variety of techniques and psychotherapies for improving everyday functioning. Learning and practicing the techniques for stress management is necessary to lead a happy and meaningful life. Stress management is required to achieve the desired success.

17. Differentiate between abilities and skills.

Ans. The capacity to perform a task is called ability, while a skill is the ability to perform a task with perfection. Abilities can be converted into skills by practicing them.

18. Which abilities are owned by a person capable of working independently?

Ans. Working independent means that one has the following abilities:

i. Self-awareness (knowing self-knowing strengths, weaknesses, likes, dislikes, etc.).

ii. Self-motivating and self-monitoring

iii. Searching for different options as requirement

iv. Planning according to the need and requirements

v. Doing the work as per your plan without any fear.

vi. Learning through the mistakes and not looking for excuses or blame game

vii. Empowering yourself by overcoming the negative thoughts and feelings

19. Differentiate between Interests and Abilities (Strengths).

Ans. The difference between interests and abilities is given below:

Interests	Abilities
(i) Things or activities that you like to do in your free time that make you happy.	(i) The capacity to perform a task is called ability.
(ii) Things or activities you are curious about or would do even if no one asked you to do it.	(ii) It enables you to perform a particular job or task with considerable proficiency.
(iii) Things or activities you want to learn or would like to do in the future.	(iii) There will be no choice available.

20. When is someone called a self-motivated person?

Ans. When any person has the ability to move ahead after identifying effective methods, planning, and making a decision on his own, it is called that he/she is a self-motivated person.

21. Enlist the elements of self-motivation.

Ans. The following are the elements playing an important role in self-motivation:

i. Positive attitude

ii. Commitment to goals

iii. Personal drive to achieve

iv. Initiative (ability to take advantage of opportunities when they occur)

v. Optimism (ability to look on the bright side of any situation)

22. Define time management.

Ans. Time management is defined as the ability to plan and control how the time is spent well to do all the desired things. In other words, time management is utilizing the available time with a mission to complete the assigned jobs effectively.

23. Explain the importance of Time Management.

Ans. Time management is important as it helps people to:

i. Make a daily timetable.

ii. Complete tasks on time.

iii. Submit homework and assignments on time.

iv. Make a time guess for completion of some work/assignment.

v. Not waste time on unproductive works.

24. What are the tips for Practicing for Effective Time Management? Explain.

Ans. The following tips may be used for effective time management:

i. Avoid delay or postponing any planned activity.

ii. Organise your work, room, and school desk.

iii. Develop a 'NO DISTURBANCE ZONE' to sit and complete important tasks.

iv. Use waiting time productively.

v. Prepare a 'To-do' list and prioritize the tasks at hand.

vi. Replace useless activities with productive activities.

Figure 2.7

2.3.10 Long Answer Type Questions

1. Enlist some examples of interests.

Ans. Some examples of interests:

i. I enjoy working in a group of people.

ii. I love to make new friends.

iii. I feel comfortable meeting new people.

iv. I like to listen to people who have thoughts different than mine.

v. I like to send reports about the problems in my area to the authorities in Municipality/ Panchayat.

vi. I like responding to people enthusiastically.

vii. I like organising events.

viii. I want to resolve conflicts between people.

ix. I like working with tools.

x. I enjoy making new things with my own hands.

xi. I like to move around a lot.

xii. I like to use gestures, postures, and non-verbal cues when I communicate.

xiii. I like to learn by doing.

2. Give some examples of abilities.

Ans. Some examples of abilities are as follows:

i. I am good at organising events.

ii. I am a good listener.

iii. I make new friends quickly.

iv. I plan my activities for the day.

v. I keep my things in order.

vi. I see the logic in things that happen around me.

vii. I am physically active.

viii. I am good in drawing.

ix. I have a sense of keeping balance and coordination.

x. I can assemble various parts of an instrument or machine by following instructions.

xi. I work well with tools.

xii. I can work with a group of people.

xiii. I can resolve problems between friends.

xiv. I am good at athletics/sports.

xv. I use a lot of gestures and postures, and non-verbal cues to communicate.

xvi. I can make things using my hands.

3. Explain the positive results of self-management in day-to-day life.

Ans. The following are the positive results of self-management:

i. It guides individuals for self-monitoring their conduct and behaviour. Students, once they become aware that they are responsible for their behaviour, they become pro-active.

ii. It prepares an individual to complete the task independently.

iii. It instils ownership of the task and the consequences amongst individuals.

iv. Self-management makes individuals realize through self-realisation that they need to do course correction by themselves when they do not get desired goals. Once the goals are achieved as desired, it also motivates individuals.

v. It helps in setting individual goals.

vi. It directs evaluation of objective resetting, performance, and enhances self-esteem.

vii. It enhances Self – reinforcement of positive behaviour

viii. Self-management reinforces the appropriate behaviour of students as per the time, situation, and people involved.

ix. It motivates individuals to take up the right things and refrains from getting indulged in negative things, keeping long-term consequences in focus.

x. It enforces self-learning for goal achievement.

xi. Self-reliance is enhanced.

4. What are the factors that help in building self-confidence?

Ans. The following factors help in building self-confidence:

i. **Physical factors**: These factors include self-efficacy, physical activity, and social physique anxiety, which are found to be influencing the self-confidence of individuals. Physical activity is directly related to self-confidence. Physical self-efficacy refers to the physical potential to complete a given task.

ii. **Social factors**: Interactions with family and social environment, like friends, relatives, teachers, and media, influence the self-confidence of individuals. The development of confidence in self is a process that results from the experiences of individuals while interacting with others. Interacting with positive people brings a fresh and progressive perspective to life. Some people have positively handled these situations and interacting with them shall help boost confidence.

iii. **Cultural factors**: These comprise of values, beliefs, and customs. Indians prefer the importance to family values, believe in the philosophy of "Vasudev Kutumbhkam."

5. Explain the skills and qualities included in self-management skills.

Ans. Self-management skills include the following skills and qualities:

i. **Self-awareness:** This includes knowing yourself as an individual – your values, likes, dislikes, strengths, hobbies, interests, and weaknesses. Thus, self-awareness is the ability to take an honest look at your life without attachment to it being right or wrong. Self-awareness is one of the important components of emotional intelligence (EI). Daniel Goleman defined self-awareness as being made up of emotional awareness, accurate self-assessment, and self-confidence. Self-awareness may also be defined as the accurate appraisal and understanding of one's abilities and preferences and the implications for the behaviour and their impact on others.

ii. **Self-control:** Ability to control your behaviour, discipline, etc. It is the ability to regulate one's thoughts, emotions, and behaviour in the face of temptations and impulses.

iii. **Self-confidence**: When you believe in yourself that you can do any task that is given to you and are not scared of taking risks, it is termed as self-confidence. The concept of self-esteem is commonly used as self-assurance in one's judgment, ability, power, etc.

iv. **Problem-solving**: The process of understanding a problem and finding a solution using a step-by-step method is called problem-solving skill.

v. **Self-motivation**: The process of doing tasks on your own without any external motivation is termed self-motivation. Self-motivation is also defined as a force that drives you to do things.

vi. **Personal hygiene and grooming:** Keeping oneself clean, healthy, and smart is termed as personal hygiene and grooming. Personal hygiene involves the practices performed by an individual to care for one's bodily health and well-being through cleanliness. Personal grooming or preening is the art of cleaning, grooming, and maintaining parts of the body.

vii. **Positive thinking**: Expressing certainty or affirmation, even in tough situations, is termed positive thinking. Positive thinking may be defined as a mental and emotional attitude that focuses on the bright side of life first and expects positive results. A person having a positive thinking mentality anticipates happiness, health, and success and believes that he/she can overcome any obstacle and difficulty.

viii. **Teamwork:** Working together with people to accomplish shared goals is called teamwork. Teamwork is a collaborative effort of a group to achieve a common goal or to complete a task in an effective and efficient manner.

ix. **Time management**: Achieving tasks on time and according to the plan is termed time management. Thus, time management is defined as the way that one organises and plans how long one spends on a specific activity. It may seem a good suggestion to dedicate precious time to learn time management instead of using it for doing your work to get enormous benefits.

x. **Goal setting:** Planning concrete goals to be accomplished within a set timeframe is termed goal setting. It is a process for thinking about your ideal future and for motivating yourself to convert your vision into reality.

xi. **Stress Management**: Stress refers to a state of psychological tension and discomfort originating from unforeseen, difficult, confusing, and challenging situations. Stress management is the managing of stress to avoid its negative impact on the physical and mental health of an individual.

xii. **Independent Working:** This means when an individual is assigned some task(s)and he/she takes ownership and doesn't require constant supervision or assistance to complete that task(s).

xiii. **Personality management**: General neatness, appropriate dressing, grooming, apt verbal and non-verbal communication are components of a good personality. Dressing in a proper way for school, friend's place or playground creates a good and favourable impression.

6. Explain the various tips/methods used to build self-confidence.

Ans. The mind is like fertile land; if you do not plant good thoughts there, weeds are bound to grow.

i. **Thinking positively**: Positive thinking brings the brain to a peaceful stage and increases productivity. When individuals start thinking positively, he/she feels happy from within, and his/her self-confidence boosts up.

ii. **Staying happy with small things**: Being thankful for people and the world instills confidence in individuals.

iii. **Removal of negative thoughts**: Going away from negative thoughts takes an individual closer to a peaceful and positive mind. To get rid of negative thoughts, one needs to involve oneself in an activity like taking a walk, draw, singing, dance, chatting, watching, reading, or talking to someone.

iv. **Staying clean, hygienic and smart**: Personal hygiene is very important to a confident person. Keeping hair, fingers, teeth, body, and skin clean and well maintained is an easy and effective way to be the best.

v. **Chatting with positive people**

7. Explain Common Responses to Stress.

Ans. Some common responses to stress are given below:

(a) Aches and Pains

i. Headache,

ii. Backache,

iii. Neckache,

iv. Stomach-ache,

v. Tight muscles,

vi. Clenched jaws, etc.

(b) Energy Level and Sleep

i. Feeling tired without a good reason

ii. Trouble sleeping

(c) Feelings

i. Anger

ii. Anxiety

iii. Tense

iv. Depression

v. Helplessness

vi. Out of Control

(d) Other Emotional Signs

i. Easily irritated

ii. Impatient

iii. Forgetful

8. What are the healthy habits to be inculcating for managing stress? Discuss.

Ans. The following healthy habits may be nurtured for the protection of harmful effects of stress:

i. Spend time with family and friends.

ii. Give up bad habits.

iii. Remember to laugh a lot.

iv. Engage in daily physical activity (walking/swimming/biking/dancing, etc.)

v. Embrace the things you are able to change

vi. Slow down - try to pace instead of race

vii. Get enough sleep

viii. Practice giving back by doing some volunteering work

ix. Try not to worry

x. Have a positive approach towards life

xi. Get organised-have a good timetable.

9. Explain the seven necessary skills required to work independently.

Ans. The following seven skills are required for working independently.

i. Decision-making skills to know what to do and to plan and decide the action plan by keeping in mind the final outcome.

ii. Discipline to keep on the right track for successful completion of a task.

iii. Communication skills to better connect with other people to get their help or support.

iv. Flexibility to adapt your work to suit other people who work with you or for you.

v. Negotiation skills to accommodate other ideas for the benefit in a larger context.

vi. Multitasking skills to perform many tasks at a time to meet the time schedule of the project.

vii. Analytic skills to see the positive and negative aspects of every situation or action and to handle the rejection.

Figure 2.8

10. Explain four types of self-awareness.

Ans. There are four types of self-awareness:

i. **Self-Awareness of Your Strengths**: Every person has more than 80 qualities, but one may not be 100% perfect or outstanding in all abilities. Everyone has some outstanding qualities. Sit in a calm position and list out your strengths, i.e., the best qualities you have.

ii. **Self-awareness about Your Weakness**: You may have some qualities for which you want improvement. These may be called weaknesses. Some of them may be lack of self-confidence, low self-esteem, not speaking fluently in a language, fear of the face of the crowd, etc.

iii. **Self-awareness about Your Dark side**: Some of your weaknesses and the dark side of your life may be brought out into the light by your family or friends. Talk to them.

iv. **Self-awareness about Your Emotional Triggers**: Emotional balance is required in life. We have so many emotions. Emotional stability is achieved by having a positive attitude towards life.

11. Enlist the steps to keep yourself Self-Motivated.

Ans. The following steps are needed to keep oneself self-motivated:

i. Keep learning

ii. Know yourself

iii. Help others

iv. Start simple and keep motivators around your work area.

v. Keep Good company of positive and like-minded people.

vi. Have a positive attitude

vii. Stop thinking, just do.

viii. Track your programs

12. Enlist the methods/techniques for building Self-motivation

Ans. The following methods and techniques may be used to build self-motivation:

i. Write down your goals and reasons for their selection.

ii. Set a large and specific goal. Small goals will follow it.

iii. Stay loyal to your goals and work towards achieving them, even in a difficult time.

iv. Be empathetic and focus on the positive.

v. Remember your successes, not failures.

vi. Monitor yourself and keep faith in yourself.

vii. Remember to have fun.

viii. Make use of your creativity in your projects.

2.3.11 HOTS Questions

1. Why is personal hygiene and grooming required?

Ans. Personal hygiene involves the practices performed by an individual to care for one's bodily health and well-being through cleanliness. It is required for cleaning and maintaining the parts of the body.

2. Why are the skills of teamwork required?

Ans. Working together with people to accomplish shared goals is called teamwork. Teamwork is defined as a collaborative effort of any group to achieve a common goal or to complete a task in an effective and efficient way, and teamwork is required at every phase of life.

3. What are the main components of Personality management?

Ans. General neatness, appropriate dressing, grooming, apt verbal and non-verbal communication are the main components of a good personality.

4. How is Working Independently useful?

Ans. Some of the benefits of working independently are given below:

i. It ensures creativity.
ii. It ensures greater learning.
iii. Individuals become assets to the organisation, groups, and nation.
iv. It enhances the feeling of empowerment and responsibility among individuals.
v. It provides flexibility to define and choose the working hours and working mechanism.
vi. Failure and success of the assignments/tasks/projects are accounted for by individuals.
vii. It enhances the satisfaction level amongst individuals.

2.4 PRACTICE QUESTIONS

1. What do you mean by self-management?
2. What is self-analysis?
3. Define self-confidence.
4. Define qualities/abilities.
5. What is grooming?
6. Which factors do affect the self-confidence building of an individual?
7. Write a short note on the importance of self-management.
8. What are the qualities of a self-confident person?
9. What are the factors that decrease self-confidence?
10. Why is personal hygiene important?
11. Differentiate between interests and abilities.
12. Discuss the self-management skills.
13. How is positive thinking initiated in oneself?
14. What steps will you take for your personal hygiene and cleanliness?
15. What steps can be taken to avoid infection from the coronavirus?
16. What are self-regulation skills?
17. Define positive thinking.
18. What are the factors influencing self-management?
19. List any six self-management skills.
20. Mention five interests/ hobbies and five abilities possessed by you.

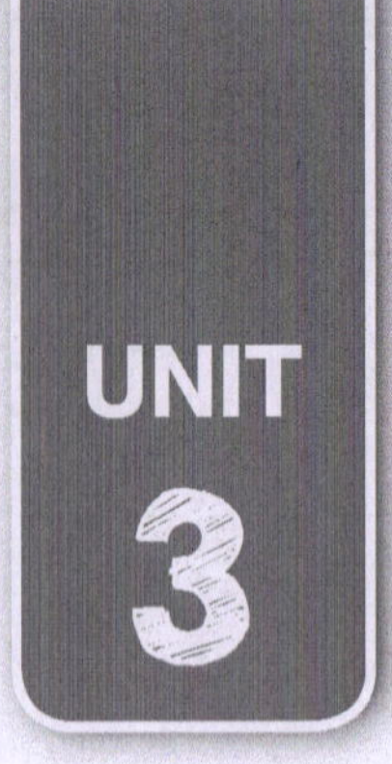

Basic ICT Skills

3.1 UNIT IN BRIEF

- The impact of ICT can be seen in every sphere of life. The digital form of information is the information when it is stored and recorded on electronic devices.
- ICT is generally used to represent a more comprehensive list of all components that are related to computer and digital technologies.
- The list of ICT components is exhaustive that is growing continuously. Some components of ICT are computers, smartphones, digital TVs, and robots.
- Information and Communication Technology includes a diverse set of technological tools and resources that are used to communicate, create, disseminate, store, and manage data.
- ICT includes computers, the internet, broadcasting technologies (radio and television), and telephony.

Figure 3.1

- A computer system is defined as a programmable machine designed to store and retrieve information by performing arithmetic and logical operations to produce meaningful results in the desired format.
- In a laptop, all three units of a computer, input, processing, and output, are combined into one device.
- An input device like a keyboard is used to enter information into the computer.
- Output devices like monitors bring information from the computer to the user.

- Central Processing Unit (CPU) processes information received from the keyboard and gives the output to the monitor or the printer.
- There are three parts of CPU: Control Unit, Processing Unit, Memory Unit.
- There are two types of memory: RAM and ROM.
- CDs, DVDs, PD, external hard disk, etc., are used as storage devices.
- A computer system consists of two main parts: the hardware and the software.
- The physical parts that can be seen and touched are called the hardware. Hardware is the machinery part of a computer and has a keyboard, monitor, CPU, etc.
- The software that we cannot see is the programs that make the hardware work the way we want.
- In digital technology, translation of information is done into binary form (zero or one), whereas each bit represents two distinct amplitudes. While in analog technology, data is translated into electric pulses of varying magnitude.
- Informatics is the branch of science that deals with the design, realisation, evaluation, use, and maintenance of information processing systems (hardware, software), organisational and human aspects, and the industrial, commercial, governmental, and political implications of these.
- Everyone needs to acquire ICT skills. ICT skills help us to communicate well, run our business properly, and stay connected with our beloved family members and friends.
- Social media refers to different online communications channels that are dedicated to community-based input, interaction, content-sharing, and collaboration.
- A blog is a website that is maintained by an individual. Any person who creates and maintains the blog is known as the blogger.
- A web page is defined as a document present on a computer connected to the internet.
- Electronic mail or email is a quick method of sending messages or files, or images to persons using the internet.
- Files containing audios, videos, documents, spreadsheets, etc., can be sent along with the email as attachments.
- All the physical components of a computer system are termed hardware.
- Registers are the temporary storage areas found in the CPU of modern computers.
- Software is a set of computer programs that perform a particular task.
- The operating system is a master control program that runs the computer.
- The system software is defined as a set of one or more programs designed to control the operation of a computer system.
- The program translated into machine code is called the object program.
- Application software is a computer program that is designed to perform a specific type of work.
- A utility program is used to perform maintenance work on an order or the components of the computer.

- The elementary unit of computer memory is called a bit. A group of 4 bits is termed as a nibble, and a group of 8 bits is known as a byte.
- The minimum space that is required to store one character is called one byte.
- A plotter is a device that is used to print large size engineering and architectural drawing on paper or a polyester film.
- It is a temporary memory. When a power supply is switched off, the information stored in RAM is lost, so it is also known as volatile memory.
- The content of the ROM is not lost when the power supply is switched off. That is why ROM is called non-volatile memory.
- Alphanumeric keys are the keys that are used to type alphabets, numbers, and special symbols like $, %, @, etc.
- Special keys such as Shift, Fn, Ctrl, Alt, etc., are used for carrying special functions.
- A numeric keypad is used to enter numbers quickly and is located to the right of the keyboard.
- The primary storage is also called primary memory. It is directly accessible by the CPU.
- All information in a computer is kept stored in the form of files. Different types of files are used to store different types of information.

Figure 3.2

3.2 CBSE /NCERT SECTION (SOLVED CBSE/NCERT EXERCISES)

3.2.1 Multiple Choice Questions

1. What is a short-range wireless communication technology known as :

   a) Wi-Fi b) Internet c) Bluetooth d) PS

2. Which part of the home screen is visible on all pages?

   a) Status bar b) Main icon area c) Dock d) Clock

3. What does GPS stand for?

   a) Global Positioning System b) Global Payment System
   c) Global Program System d) Global Pointing System

4. What is the term used when you press and hold the left mouse key and move the mouse around?

   a) Highlighting b) Dragging c) Selecting d) Moving

5. Which one of the following shortcut keys is used to paste a file? Tick mark the correct answer.

   a) Ctrl + C b) Ctrl + P c) Ctrl + V d) Ctrl + X

6. Which of the following is a valid file extension for Notepad file?

   a) .jpg b) .doc c) .text d) .txt

7. Which key do you use to copy something?

   a) Ctrl+X b) Ctrl+C c) Ctrl+Z d) Ctrl+T

8. To connect to the Internet, the computer has to be connected to the ____________.

   a) Internet Society b) Internet Architecture

   c) Internet Service Provider d) Large Area Network

9. What is the Internet?

   a) Phone connections b) Collection of computer networks

   c) Network of computers in an office d) None of the above

10. Here are the steps to sign in to your Gmail account.

    (i) Type username (ii) Go to www.gmail.com

    (iii) Click Sign in (iv) Type password

    Choose the option with the correct order.

    a) i > ii > iv > iii b) ii > i > iii > iv

    c) ii> i > iv > iii d) ii > iii > i > iv

11. Which one of the following statements is false?

    a) You need to create an account before you can send an email.

    b) You should sign out of your account when you are not using the computer.

    c) You do not need an Internet connection to use your Gmail account.

    d) You must not share your password with others.

12. Which of the following is an email service?

    a) WhatsApp b) WeChat c) Gmail d) Facebook

13. What do you type in the "To" field?

    a) The topic of the email

    b) The main message of the email

    c) Email address of the person to whom you want to send a copy of the email

    d) Email address of the person you are sending the mail to

14. You want to send an email message to your friend Sushil. In which order will you perform the given steps to write and send an email to him?
    (i) Type Sushil's email address, subject, and message
    (ii) Click on the Compose button
    (iii) Click Send
    (iv) Open your email account.

    a) (iv)>(ii)>(i)>(iii) b) (iv)>(i)>(ii)>(iii)
    c) (iv)>(i)>(iii)>(ii) d) (iii)>(i)>(ii)>(iv)
15. What do I need to get information from the World Wide Web?
    a) Computer b) Browser
    c) Internet Connection d) All of the above
16. Which of the following is a web browser?
    a) Internet b) Chrome c) Windows d) None of the above

ANSWERS									
1. (a)	2. (a)	3. (a)	4. (c)	5. (c)	6. (d)	7. (b)	8. (c)	9. (b)	10. (c)
11. (c)	12. (c)	13. (d)	14. (a)	15. (d)	16. (b)				

3.2.2 Fill in the blanks

1. In "To:" section ____________ is typed for sending a message through e-mail.
2. The Attach button in email often has a ____________ as its symbol.
3. In the ____________ section of the e-mail, the topic of the mail is written.
4. After typing the message in the main body of the email, you need to click on ____________ button to send the email.

ANSWERS			
1. email address of the receiver	2. Paper clip icon	3. compose email	4. send

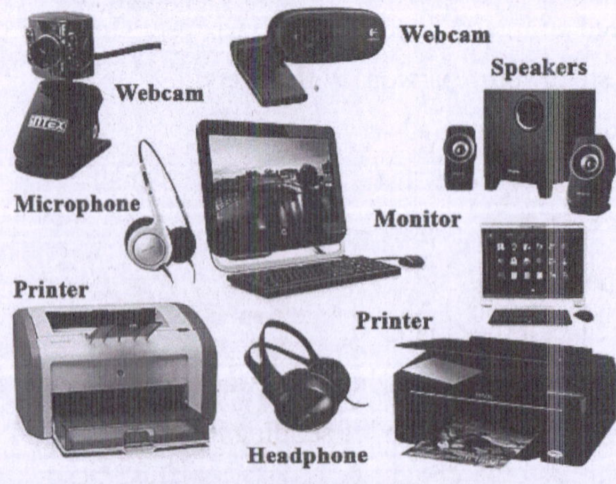

Figure 3.3

3.2.3 State whether the following statements are True or False

1. The full form of ICT is Information Commuting Technology.
2. Live sports and news can only be shown using ICT.
3. By choosing the "Reply" option, the email address of the sender of the original message will appear in the "To" field.
4. Email is an electronic message transmitted over the internet or computer network from one user to another.
5. You can forward the email by clicking on the delete icon.
6. Email cannot be sent to more than one person at a time.
7. Email is an electronic message sent over the internet or a computer network.
8. Pictures, videos, audio files, and spreadsheet files cannot be attached with an email.

ANSWERS							
1. F	2. F	3. T	4. T	5. F	6. F	7. T	8. F

3.2.4 Short Answer Type Questions

1. Give any two uses of ICT at home.

Ans. ICT can contribute to universal access to education, equity in education, quality learning, and teaching to students at home. ICT is also helpful for elders in texting messages, gathering information on various topics, etc.

2. What are the emerging skills in ICT?

Ans. The emerging fields in ICT are as follows:

i. Email Management and Setup
ii. Coding/programming
iii. Search Engine Research
iv. Social Media Management
v. Data Management and Queries

3. What are the key skills one should possess to use ICT?

Ans. Basic Operation of ICT Hardware, like printers, scanners, smartphones, tablets, and projectors. Safe Internet Usage, like using search engines for research information or updating your social media accounts.

4. Write any two differences between a smartphone and a tablet.

Ans. (i) Smartphones are more portable than a tablet.

(ii) Smartphones can be used more frequently and in more places as compared to a tablet.

(iii) The attention span of using a smartphone can be shorter than the use of an average tablet.

5. Describe the functions of at least five types of keys.

Ans. The functions of the five types of keys are as follows:

i. **Function keys**: Keys labelled from F1 to F12 are function keys and are used to perform specific functions. These functions differ from program to program. For example, the function of the F1 key in most programs is to get help on that program. Some keyboards may have fewer function keys.

ii. **Control keys:** These are special control keys that perform special functions depending on when and where they are used, like Control (Ctrl), Shift, Spacebar, Alt, Caps Lock, Tab, etc

iii. **Enter key:** The key is labelled either Enter or Return. By using Enter or the Return key, a new line is started. In some programs, this key is used to send commands and to confirm a task on a computer.

iv. **Punctuation keys**: These keys include keys for punctuation marks, such as a colon (:), semicolon (;), full stop (.), question mark (?), single quotation marks (' '), double quotation marks (" "), etc.

v. **Navigation keys**: Navigation keys include the keys, like the arrow keys, HOME, END, PAGE UP, and PAGE DOWN, etc. These keys are used to move up or down, right or left in a document.

6. Describe the functions of a mouse.

Ans. A mouse allows the user to execute a variety of commands via the mouse buttons and wheel. When we move the mouse on a flat surface, a pointer on the computer display moves in a corresponding direction. Besides moving the pointer, a mouse can be used to execute computer commands using mouse gestures. Common mouse gestures include point, click, right-click, double-click, drag, right-drag, rotate the wheel, and press wheel.

7. Write a short note on the uses of the internet

Ans. The uses of the internet are as follows:

i. Searching information on anything across the globe on a real-time basis.

ii. Communicate, collaborate with others.

iii. Telecommute with others from home.

iv. Do banking transactions.

v. Download files from a remote.

vi. Get educated and entertained.

8. List the steps to search for information using a web browser.

Ans. To serach the information on the various websites, we need an Internet Browser that is an application or a software program on our computer or laptop which helps us visit various websites. Examples of browsers include Google Chrome, Mozilla Firefox, Internet Explorer, etc.

For searching for information, follow the steps given below:

i. Open an Internet browser

ii. Type the topic on which you want information in the search box and hit the Enter key.

iii. The search results having the required information will be displayed.

iv. Select and click the shown information for details.

9. What characters should the password have in an email address to make it more secure?

Ans. Letters (uppercase and lowercase both), numbers, and special characters

10. Which of the following units make up the CPU? Choose and tick all the correct options.

(a) Processing Unit
(b) Input Unit
(c) Memory Unit
(d) Control Unit
(e) Output Unit

Ans. (a) (c) and (d)

11. Which of the following are the names of ports in a computer? Choose and tick all the correct options.

(a) HDMI
(b) Input
(c) VGA
(d) USB
(e) Ethernet

Ans. (a),(c), (d) and (e)

12. There is a talent contest in your town. For participating in the audition, you have to send a recording of a song. What would you connect to your computer to record your song?

(a) Keyboard
(b) Microphone
(c) Scanner
(d) Mouse

Ans. (b)

13. Write the purpose of the I/O devices

Input/Output device	Purpose
Mic/microphone	
Scanner	
Camera	
Barcode Reader	
Printer	
Speaker	

Ans.

Input/Output device	Purpose
Mic/microphone	Input device for entering voice
Scanner	Input device for entering images of pics/text pages
Camera	Input device for taking pictures
Barcode Reader	Input device for reading barcode printed on books /items
Printer	Output device to get print out of pages
Speaker	Output device for getting sound

14. Which of the following functions are performed using a mouse. Choose and tick all the correct options.

(a) Turn on computer
(b) Typing
(c) Right click
(d) Drag and Drop an Icon

Ans. (c) and (d)

15. Rearrange the steps for starting a computer in the correct sequence.
    (a) Desktop appears after login ( )
    (b) Login screen appears ( )
    (c) Power on Self-Test (POST) starts ( )
    (d) Operating system starts ( )
    (e) Welcome screen appears ( )

Ans. The sequence of events will be as follows:
    (a) Desktop appears after login (5)
    (b) Login screen appears (4)
    (c) Power on Self-Test (POST) starts (1)
    (d) Operating system starts (2)
    (e) Welcome screen appears (3)

3.3 SOLVED EXERCISES

3.3.1 Multiple Choice Questions

Choose the correct option out of the four given options for each question.

1. Which of the following is not part of the CPU?
   a) Arithmetic and Logic Unit (ALU)
   b) Control Unit (CU)
   c) Main Memory Unit
   d) Keyboard
2. Which part of the CPU do the calculations and comparisons?
   a) Arithmetic and Logic Unit (ALU)
   b) Control Unit (CU)
   c) Main Memory Unit
   d) Keyboard
3. A computer system comprises:
   a) Computer hardware
   b) Computer software
   c) Both a and b
   d) None of the above
4. The content of the ____________ is not lost when the power supply is switched off, and hence, it is called non-volatile memory.
   a) RAM b) ROM c) COD d) PD
5. Which of the following software is used in mobiles?
   a) Microsoft Windows,
   b) Ubuntu,
   c) Mac OS,
   d) All of the above
6. Which software/program is used to perform maintenance work?
   a) Compiler Assembler Interpreter
   b) Utility Software
   c) Application Software
   d) General Purpose
7. Which of the following software is called the 'Master Control Program'?
   a) System Software
   b) Operating System
   c) Language Processors
   d) Compiler Assembler Interpreter

8. What is the full form of CUI?
   a) Clever User Interface
   b) Common User Interface
   c) Character User Interface
   d) Create User Interface
9. The minimum space required to store one character is:
   a) One byte
   b) Two bytes
   c) Eight bytes
   d) Sixteen bytes
10. By right-clicking on a folder icon, which folder operation cannot be performed?
    a) Renaming folder
    b) Deleting folder
    c) Copying folder
    d) Entering data in the folder
11. Which of the following extensions is a valid file extension for a picture file?
    a) .jpg
    b) .doc
    c) .text
    d) .txt
12. Which part of the computer has a television-like shape?
    a) Keyboard
    b) Mouse
    c) Monitor
    d) System Unit
13. What are McAfee and Quick Heal?
    a) Hardware
    b) Antivirus
    c) Software
    d) Web browser
14. What shortcut keys are used to copy something in a document?
    a) Ctrl+x
    b) Ctrl+p
    c) Ctrl+c
    d) Ctrl+d
15. Which of the following is a punctuation key?
    a) Single/double quotation marks are a key
    b) F1 key
    c) Caps Lock key
    d) PgDn key
16. Which method is required to keep a computer cool?
    a) Keep the device unplugged when not in use.
    b) Do not cover a laptop with a cloth or blanket.
    c) Make sure that the computer's CPU fan is working.
    d) All of the above
17. What must you do to ensure secure online transactions?
    a) Use antivirus
    b) Do not use pirated software
    c) A transaction with the credit/debit card on safe websites only.
    d) Lock the computer
18. Which of the functions is not performed by an OS?
    a) It organises s the structure of the files and directories on a computer.
    b) It ruptures the software resources of the computer.
    c) It allows the user to create, copy, move, and delete files.
    d) It manages the computer memory and keeps track of memory space.

19. Which of the following functions is related to OS?
    a) It tracks the amount of disk space used by a specific file.
    b) It schedules resources among users.
    c) It organises data for secure and rapid access.
    d) All the above.
20. Which of the following software is not an Operating System?
    a) DOS b) Excel c) Unix d) Linux
21. Which shortcut key is used to cut/delete a file?
    a) Ctrl + w b) Ctrl + c c) Ctrl + x d) Ctrl + d
22. Which of the mouse buttons is used to drag an item?
    a) Left mouse button b) Right mouse button
    c) Both a and b d) Scroll button
23. Which of the following keys enables us to take a screenshot of the computer screen?
    a) Esc key b) Print Screen key (PrtScr)
    c) Backspace key d) Insert key
24. Which of the following is not a Navigation key?
    a) HOME b) Tab c) END d) PAGE UP
25. Which of the following keys enables us to type a letter in uppercase?
    a) Page Dn key b) Caps Lock key c) Fn key d) Home key
26. Which of the following is not a source of a computer virus?
    a) CD and PD b) Typing through Keyboard
    c) Email attachments d) Downloading files
27. Which of the following steps is essential for maintaining a keyboard?
    a) Blow dust and other small particles by using a blower.
    b) Turn the keyboard upside down in the air, and shake it to remove any foreign material.
    c) Use a dilute solution of soap and water and a non-abrasive cloth to remove stains from the keycaps.
    d) All of these.
28. What are unwanted bulk emails, or unwanted commercial emails, or junk mail named?
    a) Blog b) Spam
    c) Attachments d) Malware
29. Where are deleted files and folders moved to?
    a) Desktop b) Recycle Bin c) My Computer d) Favourites
30. CAD stands for:
    a) Common-Aided Demo b) Computer-Aided Depot
    c) Computer-Aided Design d) Computer Allowed Departure

31. How can an antivirus protect the device?

    a) It can backup data.
    b) It can protect it from over-heating.
    c) It can prevent data from getting corrupt.
    d) It can increase its performance.

32. What is the term used for the action when you press and hold the left mouse key and move the mouse around?

    a) Selecting
    b) Moving
    c) Dragging
    d) Highlighting

33. Which of the following is not a function of an OS?

    a) It shares hardware among users.
    b) It manages all the devices of the computer.
    c) It facilitates parallel operations.
    d) It facilitates input/output.

34. Which component is not related to the Windows desktop?

    a) Virus
    b) Wallpaper
    c) Icons
    d) Taskbar

35. Which of the following keys is not a command key?

    a) Home
    b) Insert (INS)
    c) Delete (DEL)
    d) Backspace

36. Which file extension is used for Linux files?

    a) .sql
    b) .tar
    c) .xml
    d) .exe

37. Which component is not a part of a computer hardware?

    a) Monitor
    b) Mouse
    c) Keyboard
    d) Windows

38. ____________ is a small electronic device that is used to move, select, and open items on the computer screen.

    a) Mouse
    b) Monitor
    c) Printer
    d) PD

39. What should a strong password consist of?

    a) Only letters
    b) Both numbers and special characters
    c) Name of a person
    d) Letters, numbers, and special characters

40. What is the name given to Keys from F1 to F12?

    a) Numeric keys
    b) Function keys
    c) Shift key
    d) Cursor Control keys

41. Which function is not performed by using a mouse?

    a) Hover
    b) Turn on
    c) Right click
    d) Drag and Drop

42. Which of the following is not a secondary memory?

    a) CD
    b) DVD
    c) RAM
    d) PD

43. Which of the following device is not included in peripheral devices?
    a) Input devices b) Output devices
    c) Storage devices d) CPU
44. Which of the following is not a mobile operating system?
    a) Android b) Symbian c) Linux d) iOS

Figure 3.4

ANSWERS									
1. (d)	2. (a)	3. (c)	4. (b)	5. (d)	6. (b)	7. (b)	8. (c)	9. (a)	10. (d)
11. (a)	12. (c)	13. (b)	14. (c)	15. (a)	16. (d)	17. (c)	18. (b)	19. (d)	20. (b)
21. (c)	22. (c)	23. (a)	24. (b)	25. (b)	26. (b)	27. (a)	28. (b)	29. (b)	30. (c)
31. (c)	32. (c)	33. (a)	34. (a)	35. (a)	36. (b)	37. (d)	38. (a)	39. (d)	40. (b)
41. (b)	42. (c)	43. (d)	44. (c)						

3.3.2 Fill in the blanks

1. The ____________ form of information is the information when it is stored and recorded on electronic devices..
2. A ____________ is an application that is used to access or retrieve information or resources from the internet.
3. A website is regarded as a collection of related ____________ linked to each other by hyperlinks.
4. The Web pages are stored on a computer, which is called a ____________.
5. Files containing audios, videos, documents, spreadsheets, etc., can be sent along with the ____________ as attachments.

6. ____________ represents a mode of communication in which a user can send electronic messages to other users through the internet.
7. The impact of ____________ can be seen in every sphere of life.
8. An ____________ acts as an interface between hardware and software.
9. ____________ button has a cross (x) symbol.
10. The word ____________ is derived from a real-life table-top where you may find files, Notepad, pen stand, clock, calculator, etc.
11. ____________ software is General-purpose software.
12. ____________ feature helps to prevent spam messages from being delivered to your inbox.
13. ____________ refers to different online communications channels that are dedicated to community-based input, interaction, content-sharing, and collaboration.
14. A ____________ is defined as a website or part of a website containing the thoughts and ideas of a user.
15. ____________ is the branch of science that deals with the design, realisation, evaluation, use, and maintenance of information processing systems (hardware, software), organisational and human aspects, and the industrial, commercial, governmental, and political implications of these.

ANSWERS				
1. digital	2. Web browser	3. web pages	4. Server	5. email
6. Electronic mail (Email)		7. ICT	8. operating system	9. Close
10. Desktop	11. Presentation	12. Filter	13. The Social media	
14. blog	15. Informatics			

3.3.3 True or False

1. ICT is generally used to represent a more comprehensive list of all components that are related to computer and digital technologies.
2. A blog is a website that is maintained by an individual, and any person who creates and maintains the blog is known as the blogger.
3. All virus programs do not cause harm to data or programs.
4. WhatsApp is a free mobile app that is used for exchanging text messages, sharing images or videos, and making free voice/video calling.
5. Facebook is a platform on the internet that allows users to share different news items. Also, it enables them to vote for these items.
6. Digital India is a campaign launched by the Government of India for providing government services to citizens electronically.
7. A folder is like a container that can store similar types of files.
8. A web page is defined as a document present on a computer connected to the internet.
9. The virus infects or destroys data in the computer with permission or knowledge.

10. Antivirus software is a computer program designed to identify, prevent, and remove viruses from a computer.
11. The worst ever MS-DOS virus was called Michelangelo that worked in the background and created duplicate copies to spread itself.
12. A computer virus may be defined as a program or a set of programs that do not disrupt the normal operation of a computer.
13. VIRUS stands for Vital Information Resources Under Seize.
14. Electronic mail or email is a slow method of sending messages or files, or images to persons using the internet.
15. The list of ICT components is exhaustive that is growing continuously. Some components of ICT are computers, smartphones, digital TVs, and robots.

ANSWERS								
1. T	2. T	3. F	4. T	5. F	6. T	7. T	8. T	9. F (without)
10. T	11. T	12. F	13. T	14. F (fast)		15. T		

3.3.4 Matching type

(I) Match the action with the correct meaning.

Column A (Action)	Column B (Meaning)
(i) Drag Move	(a) Touch surface for an extended period of time
(ii) Flick	(b) Touch the surface with two fingers and bring them closer together.
(iii) Pinch	(c) Quickly brush the surface with a fingertip.
(iv) Press	(d) Fingertip over the surface without losing contact them apart

(II) Match the items of column A with those of column B correctly.

Column A (Sector)	Column B (ICT used for)
(i) Agriculture:	(a) Training and development programmes
(ii) Banking and Finance	(b) Research activities, development, and training
(iii) Beauty and Wellness	(c) Training programmes, record maintenance

(III) Match the extension with correct description of file

Column A (Extension)	Column B (Description of file)
(i) .ods	(a) audio file
(ii) .xls	(b) Microsoft Excel file
(iii) .aif	(c) CD audio track file
(iv) .cda	(d) AIF audio file
(v) .mp3	(e) OpenOffice Calc spreadsheet file

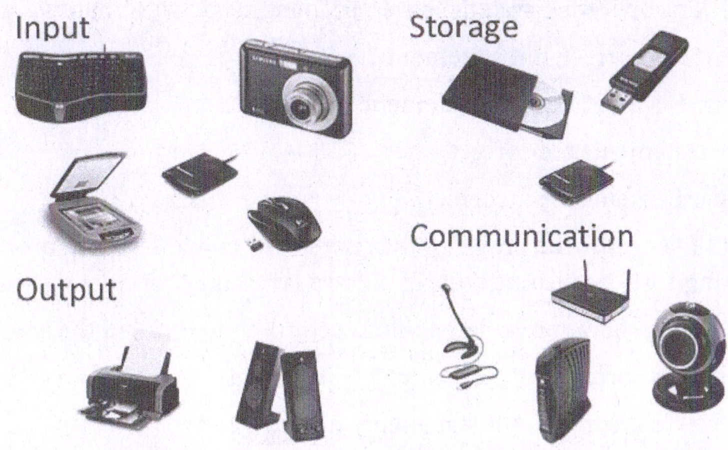

Figure 3.5

ANSWERS				
(I) (i) d	(ii) c	(iii) b	(iv) e	(iv) a
(II) (i) c	(ii) b	(iii) a		
(III) (i) e	(ii) b	(iii) d	(iv) c	(v) a

3.3.5 Statements Based Questions

1. Statement 1: Registers are the temporary storage areas found in the CPU of modern computers.

   Statement 2 The elementary unit of computer memory is called a bit while group of 4 bits is termed as a nibble, and a group of 8 bits is known as a byte.

   a) Statement 1 is correct, but statement 2 is incorrect.

   b) Statement 1 is incorrect, but statement 2 is correct.

   c) Both the statements are correct.

   d) Both the statements are incorrect.

2. Statement 1: An operating system is the second program that gets loaded into computer memory.

   Statement 2: Antivirus software is a computer program designed to identify, prevent, and remove viruses from a computer.

   a) Statement 1 is correct, but statement 2 is incorrect.

   b) Statement 1 is incorrect, but statement 2 is correct.

   c) Both the statements are correct.

   d) Both the statements are incorrect.

3. Statement 1: A antivirus program is used to perform maintenance work on an order or the components of the computer.

   Statement 2: The operating system acts as an interface between hardware and software.

   a) Statement 1 is correct, but statement 2 is incorrect.
   b) Statement 1 is incorrect, but statement 2 is correct.
   c) Both the statements are correct.
   d) Both the statements are incorrect.

4. Statement 1: The translator program that is used to convert source programs written in a high-level language to machine code is called a language processor.

   Statement 2: The program translated into machine code is called the source code.

   a) Statement 1 is correct, but statement 2 is incorrect.
   b) Statement 1 is incorrect, but statement 2 is correct.
   c) Both the statements are correct.
   d) Both the statements are incorrect.

5. Statement 1: In digital technology, data is translated into electric pulses of varying magnitude.

   Statement 2: In analog technology, translation of information is done into binary form (zero or one), whereas each bit represents two distinct amplitudes.

   a) Statement 1 is correct, but statement 2 is incorrect.
   b) Statement 1 is incorrect, but statement 2 is correct.
   c) Both the statements are correct.
   d) Both the statements are incorrect.

6. Statement 1: Numeric keys such as Shift, Fn, Ctrl, Alt, etc., are used for carrying special functions.

   Statement 2: Special keypad is used to enter numbers quickly and is located to the right of the keyboard.

   a) Statement 1 is correct, but statement 2 is incorrect.
   b) Statement 1 is incorrect, but statement 2 is correct.
   c) Both the statements are correct.
   d) Both the statements are incorrect.

7. Statement 1: Information and Communication Technology includes a diverse set of technological tools and resources that are used to communicate, create, disseminate, store, and manage data.

   Statement 2: ICT includes computers, the internet, broadcasting technologies (radio and television), and telephony.

   a) Statement 1 is correct, but statement 2 is incorrect.
   b) Statement 1 is incorrect, but statement 2 is correct.

c) Both the statements are correct.
d) Both the statements are incorrect.

8. Statement 1: Utility software is a computer program that is designed to perform a certain type of work.

   Statement 2: Alphanumeric keys are the keys that are used to type alphabets, numbers, and special symbols like $, %, @, etc.

   a) Statement 1 is correct, but statement 2 is incorrect.
   b) Statement 1 is incorrect, but statement 2 is correct.
   c) Both the statements are correct.
   d) Both the statements are incorrect.

9. Statement 1: Files containing audios, videos, documents, spreadsheets, etc., can be sent along with the email as attachments.

   Statement 2: All the physical components of a computer system are termed a software.

   a) Statement 1 is correct, but statement 2 is incorrect.
   b) Statement 1 is incorrect, but statement 2 is correct.
   c) Both the statements are correct.
   d) Both the statements are incorrect.

10. Statement 1: Electronic mail or email is a quick method of sending messages or files, or images to persons using the internet.

    Statement 2: A blog is a website that is maintained by an individual. Any person who creates and maintains the blog is known as the blogger.

    a) Statement 1 is correct, but statement 2 is incorrect.
    b) Statement 1 is incorrect, but statement 2 is correct.
    c) Both the statements are correct.
    d) Both the statements are incorrect.

ANSWERS									
1. (c)	2. (b)	3. (b)	4. (a)	5. (d)	6. (d)	7. (c)	8. (b)	9. (a)	10. (c)

3.3.6 Assertion Reason Type Questions

1. Assertion (A): Everyone needs to acquire ICT skills.

   Reason(R): ICT skills help us to communicate well, run our business properly, and stay connected with our beloved family members and friends.

   a) Both A and R are correct, and R is the correct reason for A.
   b) Both A and R are correct, and R is not the correct reason for A.
   c) A is correct, but R is incorrect.
   d) A is incorrect, but R is correct.

2. Assertion (A): In a hierarchical file system, the files are organised into folders and sub-folders in a tree-like structure.

   Reason(R): A web page is defined as a document present on a computer connected to the internet.

   a) Both A and R are correct, and R is the correct reason for A.

   b) Both A and R are correct, and R is not the correct reason for A.

   c) A is correct, but R is incorrect.

   d) A is incorrect, but R is correct.

3. Assertion (A): VIRUS (Vital Information Resources Under Seize) is dangerous.

   Reason(R): A computer virus is a program or a set of programs that disrupt the normal operation of a computer.

   a) Both A and R are correct, and R is the correct reason for A.

   b) Both A and R are correct, and R is not the correct reason for A.

   c) A is correct, but R is incorrect.

   d) A is incorrect, but R is correct.

4. Assertion (A): The minimum space that is required to store one character is called one bit.

   Reason(R): A plotter is a device that is used to print large size engineering and architectural drawing on paper or a polyester film.

   a) Both A and R are correct, and R is the correct reason for A.

   b) Both A and R are correct, and R is not the correct reason for A.

   c) A is correct, but R is incorrect.

   d) A is incorrect, but R is correct.

5. Assertion (A): Software is a set of computer programs that perform a particular task.

   Reason(R): The operating system is a master control program that runs the computer.

   a) Both A and R are correct, and R is the correct reason for A.

   b) Both A and R are correct, and R is not the correct reason for A.

   c) A is correct, but R is incorrect.

   d) A is incorrect, but R is correct.

6. Assertion (A): RAM is a temporary memory/volatile memory.

   Reason(R): When a power supply is switched off, the information stored in RAM is lost.

   a) Both A and R are correct, and R is the correct reason for A.

   b) Both A and R are correct, and R is not the correct reason for A.

   c) A is correct, but R is incorrect.

   d) A is incorrect, but R is correct.

7. Assertion (A): An operating system is a set of programs that control a computer.

   Reason(R): Basic computer operations are controlled by operating systems.

   a) Both A and R are correct, and R is the correct reason for A.

   b) Both A and R are correct, and R is not the correct reason for A.

   c) A is correct, but R is incorrect.

   d) A is incorrect, but R is correct.

8. Assertion (A): The primary storage is also called primary memory.

   Reason(R): The primary storage is directly accessible by the CPU.

   a) Both A and R are correct, and R is the correct reason for A.

   b) Both A and R are correct, and R is not the correct reason for A.

   c) A is correct, but R is incorrect.

   d) A is incorrect, but R is correct.

9. Assertion (A): Briefly touching the surface with a fingertip is called tap.

   Reason(R): Tapping does not activate a control or select an item.

   a) Both A and R are correct, and R is the correct reason for A.

   b) Both A and R are correct, and R is not the correct reason for A.

   c) A is correct, but R is incorrect.

   d) A is incorrect, but R is correct.

10. Assertion (A): Operating systems and language processors come under the category of system software.

    Reason(R): The system software is a set of one or more programs designed to control the operation of a computer system.

    a) Both A and R are correct, and R is the correct reason for A.

    b) Both A and R are correct, and R is not the correct reason for A.

    c) A is correct, but R is incorrect.

    d) A is incorrect, but R is correct.

ANSWERS									
1. (a)	2. (b)	3. (a)	4. (d)	5. (b)	6. (a)	7. (b)	8. (a)	9. (c)	10. (a)

3.3.7 Competency-Based Questions

1. Consider the following software:

   i. Norton 360 Antivirus Plus

   ii. McAfee Total Protection

   iii. Kaspersky Antivirus Protection

   iv. Quick Heal Total Security

   v. Firefox

   vi. Safari

The antivirus software is:

a) (i) (ii) (v) only
b) (i) (iv) (v) only
c) (i) (ii) (iii) (iv) only
d) (iii) (iv) (v) (vi) only

2. Consider the following programs:
   i. Google chrome
   ii. Opera
   iii. Firefox
   iv. Internet explorer
   v. Safari

   Which of the following is a web browser?

   a) (i) (ii) only
   b) (i) (iv) (v) only
   c) (ii) (iii) (iv) (v) only
   d) (i) (ii) (iii) (iv) (v)

3. Which one of the following is not malware?

   a) Virus
   b) OS
   c) Trojan horse
   d) Worm

4. Consider the following functions:
   i. It implements the user interface.
   ii. It keeps track of the status of the device, whether it is busy or not.
   iii. It makes users capable of sharing data among themselves.
   iv. It prevents users from interfering with one another.
   v. It facilitates making errors.

   Which functions are performed by an OS?

   a) (ii) (iii) (iv)
   b) (iii) (iv) (v)
   c) (v) (iv) (iii) (ii)
   d) All of these

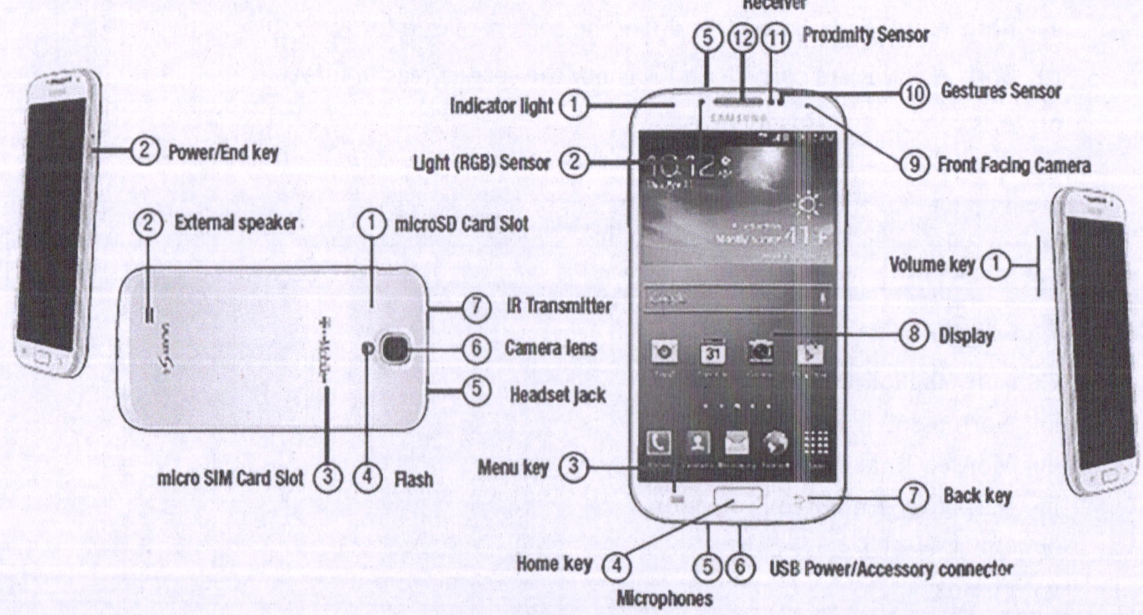

Figure 3.6

ANSWERS			
1. (c)	2. (d)	3. (b)	4. (c)

3.3.8 VSA

1. Define Plotters.

Ans. A plotter is a device that is used to print large size engineering and architectural drawing on paper or a polyester film.

2. What is Bluetooth?

Ans. Bluetooth is a short-range wireless technology that is used to connect one device with other devices within 30 feet. Once connected, you can transfer messages and songs.

3. Define Wi-Fi.

Ans. Wi-Fi is a wireless network technology device used to connect the smartphone to the local area network and to connect to the internet for connecting social media and anything to do which requires the internet.

4. What is Cellular network connectivity?

Ans. Cellular network connectivity app is used to provide the network through which users can make calls.

5. What is the Global Positioning System app?

Ans. GPS app is used for navigation (direction finding) system and used to navigate, find direction, and maps to specific locations.

6. Which devices are used for entering data into the computer?

Ans. Input devices are used for entering data or instructions into the computer.

7. Give two examples of input devices.

Ans. Keyboard, mouse, and scanner

8. What is the main function of a scanner?

Ans. Scanners are another important hardware device that is used to convert a picture or text of a book or page into a digital form.

9. What are the two types of primary memory?

Ans. Primary memory can be:

i. RAM (Random Access Memory)

ii. ROM (Read Only Memory)

10. What are Peripheral Devices?

Ans. An internal or external device that is used to connect directly to a computer but does not contribute to the computer's primary function is called a peripheral device.

11. What is a 'Joystick'?

Ans. The joystick is a device that is used to play games on the computer and consists of a vertical stick that can be moved to control objects on the computer screen.

12. What is a Light pen?

Ans. A light pen is a pointing device that is used to draw directly on the computer screen. It is used to point to an object or option directly on the computer screen.

13. Define Graphic Tablet.

Ans. A graphic tablet is a device that is used to create digital drawings by making hand-drawing images on a flat surface called the tablet and by using a special pen known as a stylus.

14. Define Protocol.

Ans. A protocol is a set of rules to be followed while communicating or transferring data on the internet.

15. What is HTTP?

Ans. HTTP (Hypertext Transfer Protocol) is the protocol that defines the rules to be followed while transferring the information, which may be in the form of text, images, videos, etc. This is the most common protocol used over the world wide web.

16. What do you mean by a blog?

Ans. A blog is a website that is maintained by an individual. Any person who creates and maintains the blog is known as the blogger.

17. What is Twitter?

Ans. Twitter is a social networking microblogging service that allows registered members to broadcast short messages to communicate with their friends or followers. Short messages (tweets) of up to 140 characters may be sent.

18. What is Facebook?

Ans. Facebook, founded by Mark Zuckerberg, is the most popular social networking site.

19. Define YouTube.

Ans. YouTube allows people to watch and share self-created videos.

20. What is WhatsApp?

Ans. WhatsApp is a free messenger app used in smartphones. WhatsApp uses the internet to send text messages, pictures, audio, or video. You can make audio and video calls to any person having WhatsApp in his/her smartphone, in any location of the world.

21. Define operating system.

Ans. An operating system is the first program that gets loaded into computer memory.

22. What is the function of an operating system?

Ans. The operating system acts as an interface between hardware and software.

23. Define desktop.

Ans. A desktop is the first screen that is displayed after switching on Windows.

24. What is a file system?

Ans. A File System defines the ways in which files are named and placed for storage and retrieval.

25. Define a computer virus.

Ans. A computer virus may be defined as a program or a set of programs that disrupt the normal operation of a computer.

26. What is the full form of VIRUS?

Ans. VIRUS stands for Vital Information Resources Under Seize.

27. What do you mean by antivirus software?

Ans. Antivirus software is a computer program designed to identify, prevent, and remove viruses from a computer.

28. Which device controls the basic computer operations?

Ans. Basic computer operations are controlled by operating systems.

29. What is the meaning of 'Tap' and its action?

Ans. Briefly touching the surface with a fingertip is called tap. It activates a control or selects an item.

30. Give two examples of ICT devices.

Ans. ICT devices are tablets, smartphones, and laptops.

31. Give two examples of Mobile Operating systems.

Ans. Android, Symbian, Windows Phone, iOS, etc.

32. Define router.

Ans. A device used to transfer information between computer networks is called a router.

33. What is the main function of the keyboard?

Ans. A keyboard is an input device that is used to type text, numbers, and commands into the computer.

34. Why is the normal 101 keyboard called QWERTY keyboard?

Ans. The first six alphabets of the first row of alphabet keys in a 101 keyboard contain alphabets Q, W, E, R, T, Y., and hence, it is known as the QWERTY keyboard.

35. How many function keys are present on a keyboard?

Ans. 12 Keys from F1 to F12 in the Keyboard are function keys.

36. Why are function keys called so?

Ans. The function keys are used to perform specific functions. Their functions differ from program to program. For example, the function of the F1 key in most programs is to get help on that program.

37. What do you mean by VIRUS in computer science?

Ans. A computer virus is defined as a piece of software code written to enter the computer system and infect files. It can damage or even destroy precious data.

38. What is 'drag and drop'?

Ans. To move an item, click it, and then hold the mouse button down, move the item to a new location and release it. This action is known as drag and drop.

39. What do you mean by files on a computer?

Ans. The Files in computers are used for storing the Data of the users for a long time period, and the files can contain any type of information, which means that they can store the text, or images or Pictures, or any data in any format.

40. Define a folder in computer science.

Ans. A folder is like a container in which similar types of files can be stored. It helps in arranging the files into organised groups, which makes it easy for the user to locate any particular file.

41. What is a Mac Operating System?

Ans. It is a UNIX-based operating system which is developed by the Apple company and is mainly used by Mac users.

42. What do you mean by Linux?

Ans. Linux is a freeware and open-source software that can be installed and used on a variety of computers ranging from mobile phones, tablet computers, video game consoles, mainframes, and supercomputers. Linux is a high-level secured operating system.

43. What is Android?

Ans. Android is a Linux-based operating system that is designed basically for mobile phones, which is also used for devices such as notebooks and tablets. The first version of the Android launched in 2007 was Android OS 2.1.

44. Define Symbian.

Ans. Symbian is an OS developed by Symbian Limited, and it uses GEOS (Graphical Environment Operating System). It is used by most advanced smartphones. It allows the user to install applications on the phone, just like Windows allows installing applications onto a computer.

45. Give four examples of programming languages.

Ans. The programming languages are C++, Java MIDP, Java Personal profile, OPL, Visual Basic, Python, Simkin, and Flash Lite.

46. Which OS was also called a Plug and Play (PnP) operating system?

Ans. Windows 95

47. Expand FAT.

Ans. File Allocation Table.

48. What is Microsoft Edge?

Ans. Microsoft Edge is a new web browser introduced in Windows 10.

49. Name Microsoft's intelligent personal assistant.

Ans. Cortana, which is included in Windows 10 to replace Windows' embedded search feature and support both text and voice input.

50. Can a computer work without software?

Ans. No. No hardware would be able to function without software.

51. What do you mean by backup the data?

Ans. Backing up data is a process to save the information present on your computer on another device, like CD/DVD drives or hard disk.

Figure 3.7 Robo Shalu and its creator Mr Dinesh Patel

3.3.9 Short Answer Type Questions

1. Differentiate between digital technology and analog technology.

Ans. In digital technology, translation of information is done into binary form (zero or one), whereas each bit represents two distinct amplitudes. While in analog technology, data is translated into electric pulses of varying magnitude.

2. How is ICT affecting our life?

Ans. People use technology every moment at home and in the workplace. ICT tools enable people anytime, anywhere, access to information and resources. The different ICT tools that are used include computers at the workplace, smartphones, through which we talk, the internet for getting information, communicating with others through email and social networks like Facebook, watching movies and TV shows like on Netflix, etc. For example, to find a job, one may have to search the internet for job openings, create a resume on a computer, use email to send the resume, send messages through your phone to communicate for a telephonic interview, and get your offer letter through email.

3. How is the information stored?

Ans. The information available today can be recorded or stored in many ways. It may be hand-written on paper, typed using a typewriter or a computer, and so on. When a piece of information is stored and recorded on electronic devices, it is converted into a 'digital' form.' ICT devices are tablets, smartphones, and laptops.

4. What are the basic ICT Skills?

Ans. The basic ICT skills that you require are:

i. knowing how to operate computers; and

ii. knowing the ways to browse the internet for collecting, storing, and disseminating information.

5. Mention two applications of ICT in governance.

Ans. ICT in governance means using the internet, other electronic media by the central and state governments and by local administrative bodies to improve the efficiency, transparency, efficiency of the government.

ICT in governance can help:

i. Delivering government services effectively.

ii. E-governance sites allow people to perform various tasks online, like filling an employment form, applying for a PAN card or a passport, paying bills, property tax, etc., even sitting at home.

6. How is ICT helpful in business?

Ans. ICT in business can be used to perform many tasks like:

i. Maintaining a database of a routine of staff and details of customers.

ii. Keeping records of the stock.

iii. Preparing accounts and balance sheets.

iv. E-commerce websites enable people to buy and sell products online for 24 x 7 hours.

v. An E-banking facility helps in making banking transactions at all times of the day.

7. What are the physical components of a computer?

Ans. A computer consists of the following physical components:

i. Input unit

ii. Processing unit

iii. Storage unit

iv. Software

v. Auxiliary storage

vi. Output unit

8. What are the functions of the Central Processing Unit?

Ans. The functions of CPU are as follows:

i. It controls the sequence of operations within the computer

ii. It commands to other parts of the computer.

iii. It controls the use of main memory for storing data and instructions

9. Write the functions performed by ALU.

Ans. The ALU performs all the following arithmetic operations:

a) + (addition)

b) -(subtraction)

c) *(multiplication)

d) /(Division)

e) ^(Exponent)

10. Which Logical operations are performed by ALU?

Ans. The ALU performs the following logical operations:

< (less than)

< (greater than)

<= (less than or equal to)

>= (greater than or equal to)

≠ (not equal to)

11. Enlist the functions of the Control Unit.

Ans. It controls the flow of data from the input devices to memory and from memory to output devices. It does not process the data.

When the processing begins, the first instruction of the program is selected and fed into the control section of the primary storage area. It is then interpreted there, and then the signals are sent to other components to perform the necessary action.

The next instruction is then selected, interpreted, and executed. This is continued until all the instructions are processed.

12. Enlist the various types of computer software.

Ans. The various categories of software used in computers are as follows:

i. System Software

ii. Operating System

iii. Language Processors

iv. Compiler Assembler Interpreter

v. Utility Software

vi. Application Software

vii. General Purpose

viii. Customized Software

13. What is System Software?

Ans. The system software is defined as a set of one or more programs designed to control the operation of a computer system. Operating systems and language processors are system software.

14. What do you mean by Operating System (OS)? Give two examples.

Ans. The operating system is a master control program that runs the computer. When the computer is switched on, the operating system is the first program loaded into the computer's memory.

Examples of the operating system are Windows, UNIX, MS-DOS, Mac OS, Solaris, etc.

15. Define Language Processors?

Ans. A computer understands instructions in the form of machine code, i.e., 0 and 1. The programs are written in English like a high-level language called source code. Any source code should be converted into machine language to be executed. The translator program that is used to convert source programs written in a high-level language to machine code is called a language processor. The program translated into machine code is called the object program.

16. What are the three types of 'Language Processor'?

Ans. Language processor is of three types as follows:

(a) **Assembler**: It is a program that translates an assembly language program into machine language.

(b) **Compiler**: It is a program that translates a high-level language program into machine language. For example, the C++ compiler.

(c) **Interpreter**: It is a program that translates a high-level language into a machine language program line by line. For example, Visual basic Interpreter.

17. What do you mean by Application Software?

Ans. Application software is a computer program that is designed to perform a certain type of work. This type of software pertains to one specific application. For example, software written to calculate the salary of the school employees cannot be used to prepare school results.

18. Explain two types of Application software.

Ans. Application software can be classified as general-purpose software and Specific purpose application software.

(a) General-purpose application software includes word processing software, like, Microsoft Word., spreadsheet software, like, Microsoft Excel, etc.

(b) Specific purpose application software includes the software that performs a particular task. Examples of specific purpose application software: accounting management software, Reservation system, Payroll system, etc.

19. What is Utility Program?

Ans. A utility program is used to perform maintenance work on an order or the components of the computer.

Examples of Utility program: antivirus software, file management programs, etc.

20. Explain different types of utility programs.

Ans. Utility programs are of the following types:

(a) **Antivirus software**: This program helps in detecting and removing viruses. Examples: Norton antivirus, McAffee virus scan, etc.

(b) **File management tools**: These tools help in storing, searching, and sorting files and folders on the system. For example, Windows Explorer.

(c) **Compression**: This program helps in the compression of large files so that they take less storage space. For example, WinZip.

21. Differentiate between HTTP and HTTPs.

Ans. HTTP (Hypertext Transfer Protocol) is the protocol that defines the rules to be followed while transferring the information, which may be in the form of text, images, videos, etc. HTTPs is the secured version of HTTP. It ensures better protection against data theft.

22. Explain Disk Management Tools.

Ans. Disk Management Tools include:

(i) **Disk Cleaner** for scanning for the files that have not been used for long. These files may be occupying a large amount of space. It prompts the user to delete such files to create more disk space.

(ii) **Disk Defragmenter** for rearranging the files and free space on the computer so that files are stored in contiguous and free space is consolidated in one contiguous block. This speeds up the disk access.

(iii) **Backup** for duplicating the files and data stored on the computer. This program is used to make a backup copy of the data. In case the original data is lost, the backed-up data can be used.

23. Why is RAM called so?

Ans. RAM is used to hold active information of data and instructions. Information in RAM is stored in random order. That's why it is known as Random Access Memory.

24. What will happen sequentially on starting a computer?

Ans. When the computer is turned on, lights on the keyboard may blink for a while, along with a beep sound indicating the starting of Power-on-self text (POST). Here, POST is a sequence of tests that determines if the computer hardware like Keyboard, RAM, disk drives, etc., are working correctly or not. The monitor may display a message when a component is not functioning well.

After this, the computer starts the operating system, and this process of bringing up the operating system is known as booting. The instructions of booting are inbuilt into a chip called BIOS (Basic Input/ Output System).

After the operating system starts, say Windows 7, Windows welcome screen appears. The first screen that appears after Windows 7 is successfully loaded is called desktop.

25. Define and illustrate Internet Browser.

Ans. A web browser is a program that is used to view websites. It acts as an interface between the web server and the world wide web. Some commonly used web browsers are Google Chrome, Firefox, Safari, Microsoft Internet Explorer, Microsoft Edge, Opera, etc.

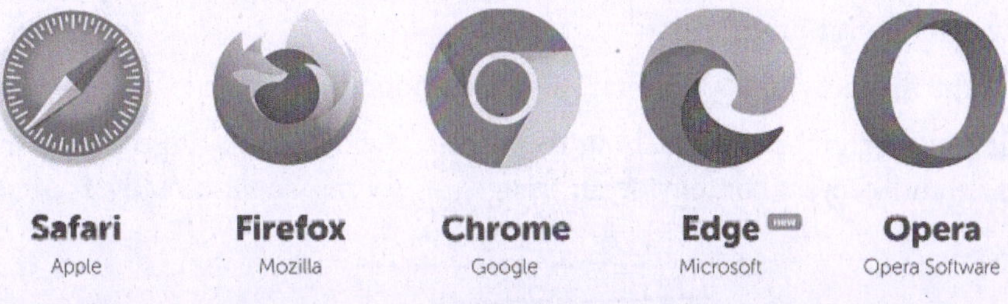

Figure 3.8

26. Mention two functions of a web browser.

Ans. A web browser performs the following tasks:

i. It connects to the web server and sends a request for the information.

ii. It displays information on the computer.

27. What do you mean by 'Digital India'? What is its aim?

Ans. Digital India is a campaign that was launched by the Government of India in 2015 to ensure that the government's services are made available to citizens electronically by improved online infrastructure. It also aims at increasing Internet connectivity and making the country digitally empowered in the field of technology.

28. How has ICT become an integral part of our lives?

Ans. ICT has become an integral part of our work in all sectors of the economy, starting from money transactions via the online banking system to the development of textbooks or research papers in educational institutions. At the workplace, we use different computer software and applications to complete tasks like making documents, calculations, tables, graphs, etc. We can also use applications to do everyday work like purchasing things, booking trains, air or bus tickets, Internet banking, and making payments of bills online, etc. Modern ICT employs various media forms, which include text, graphics, cartoons, animation, audio, and video, etc. It also involves creating, editing, managing images, and documents, collecting and processing data, working with audio and video tools to create media-rich communications, etc. So, employees are expected to possess a sound knowledge of all these to work independently on various software and computers.

29. What are the functions of primary memory?

Ans. Functions of primary memory are:

i. Here data is fed and held until it is ready to be accessed.

ii. It is used to hold the data being processed and the intermediate results of processing.

iii. It holds the result of the processing.

iv. It holds the processing instructions.

30. Enlist four software.

Ans. System Software, Operating System, Language Processors, Compiler Assembler Interpreter, Utility Software, Application Software, General Purpose, Customized Software, etc.

31. What are the five basic operations a computer performs?

Ans. A computer performs five basic operations to carry out any task: Input, Process, Output, Storing, and Controlling.

32. What is the meaning of 'Double-tap' and its action?

Ans. Double-tap means rapidly touching the surface twice with a fingertip. Its action includes zooms in and centers content or an image, or zooms out it already zoomed in or select items.

33. How will you ensure the proper working of the hardware components of a computer?

Ans. Proper working of the hardware components of a computer can be ensured by physically cleaning them, keeping them in a proper manner, and repairing them whenever required.

34. Why will a computer be useless in the absence of an OS?

Ans. An Operating System (OS) performs basic tasks, like recognizing input from the keyboard, sending output to the screen, keeping track of files and directories, controlling the devices (like disk drives and printers), etc. Without a computer Operating System, a computer would be useless.

35. Explain Interactive or Graphical User Interface (GUI) Operating System.

Ans. In GUI operating system, commands can be entered by clicking/double-clicking/right-clicking a mouse. Examples: MS-DOS, MS-Windows, OS/2, Windows/NT, UNIX, Mac-OS, etc.

36. Explain Character User Interface (CUI).

Ans. CUI Operating System requires the user to interact by typing commands. Examples: UNIX, DOS, etc.

37. Mention some steps to ensure safety against computer virus infection.

Ans. Some of the steps to avoid virus infection are as follows:

i. Get good virus scanning software.

ii. Scan frequently.

iii. Update scanning software.

iv. Stay informed of virus alerts.

38. How can you save the computer from Viruses?

Ans. For the Personal Computer, get a good, dependable, highly rated Anti-Virus Software package. Update your software's virus definition frequently. Another method that can be used is to monitor the byte size of your files and programs, especially your .exe and .com files.

3.3.10 Long Answer Type Questions

1. Explain the role of ICT in education.

Ans. ICT for education is related to the development of information and communication technology, specifically for teaching/learning processes. Use of ICT has now become an important part of the teaching-learning process, like in 2020-21, during COVID 19, online classes for all students were conducted by the schools. ICT, in collaboration with the traditional chalkboard method, has improved the learning rate of the students. Students are also using their smartphones or other similar devices during the learning process.

The "flipped classroom" is becoming popular in several countries where students interact with lecturers or teachers online while staying at home and use classroom time for more interactive exercises.

Using ICT tools in education can lead to:

- higher-order thinking skills
- provide creative and individualized learning options for students to express their understandings.
- Students are better prepared to face the ongoing technological changes in society, in the world, and in the workplace.

Some advantages of ICT in education are as follows:

i. Complex topics of many subjects can be easily explained to the learners with the help of ICT-enabled pictures, videos, presentations, etc.

ii. The use of images and videos used during teaching improves the retention memory of the students.

iii. A practical demonstration may be given to the students to clarify the concepts.

iv. It makes the teaching process in the class more interactive and enjoyable.

v. An e-learning program provides the opportunity for students to learn at their own pace, at any convenient time, and from any place in the world.

2. How is ICT used in the healthcare sector?

Ans. ICT plays an important role in the healthcare sector. Some of the uses of ICT in the healthcare sector are described below:

i. ICT-enabled devices like MRI, CT-scan, ultrasound, etc., are used in hospitals, diagnostic centres, etc., are used in diagnosing diseases.

ii. Through the proper communication media, a doctor can easily deliver treatment and care to the patient who is located far away. The doctor can also continuously monitor the patient's history, diagnostic report and track the current health condition. The doctor can also interact with the patient, recommend taking a medical examination, and prescribe medicine.

iii. Life support systems may be provided to the patients.

iv. Searching for information on any disease, medicines, etc., on the internet is easy.

v. By using the ICT tool or a suitable communication system, the government makes efforts to create awareness among the public about communicable diseases, prevention measures, and various current diagnostic, etc.

vi. ICT in healthcare research helps to find possible preventive measures to eradicate and reduce the spread of endemic and pandemic.

vii. Through ICT, the traditional healthcare systems may be modified, and new models can be framed for effective quality healthcare.

viii. Hospitals may use different electronic media to store medical data to help to retrieve the information easily, and the same can be transferred to the patient or the Doctors for consultation.

3. Explain the various types of ICT tools.

Ans. Smartphones and tablets are becoming part and parcel of our lives as most people carry them around and use them in daily activities like sending emails and messages, sharing pictures, etc. The following ICT tools are used nowadays:

i. **Smartphones**: Mobile phones are ICT tools for communicating with persons, but smartphones are more advanced tools. With a simple mobile phone, one can only make phone calls and receive calls, while with a smartphone, one can make calls and do things that you usually do use a computer, such as browsing the web, sending emails, making video calls, playing games, listening to music, watching movies, watching live matches, live TV programmes, etc. Smartphones are also called mobile phones because they can be used anywhere, like at home, in the office, or on the road. They use wireless devices and do not need a telephone line to connect with an internet connection. Various popular operating systems for smartphones are Android OS, Apple iOS, and Windows Mobile.

ii. **Tablets**: The screen of the mobile is too small for some activities, like reading a book for a long time, etc. For such activities, a tablet is used, which is a mini-computer with input, output, and processing functions that are all combined into one 'touchscreen,' where you can do various tasks just by touching its screen. Tablet has more features than a smartphone or computer has, and all the functions can be performed here.

iii. **TV and Radio**: TV and radio have been used as an ICT tool used since a long time. Radio is used to broadcast audio, whereas TV is used to transmit audio-visual programmes. Radio and TV are being used for both entertainment and education. Various items like the news, songs, stories, speeches, cricket commentaries, etc., may be listened to on radio and TV are used for watching movies, news, weather forecasts, songs, cartoons, and educational lectures.

iv. **Applications or apps**: A smartphone performs so many functions smoothly with the help of software applications (Apps). A lot of small pictures (or 'icons') are depicted on the screen of a Smartphone or Tablet. If you touch any of them, they start programs or functions required, like watching movies, playing games, using a camera, etc. Apps are software programs that perform different functions. (Software program is a set of instructions or a set of modules or procedures that allow for a certain type of computer operation.) Some of the apps are already uploaded on the smartphone or tablet. These are called "default" apps. Also, there are a large number of other apps that can be purchased and downloaded or downloaded free of cost from online stores. There are several online stores, like Google Play Store for Android and Apple App Store for Apple.

4. Discuss the main default apps installed on a smartphone.

Ans. Main default Apps installed on smartphones and other mobile phones are given below:

i. **Phone**: This app is used to make telephonic calls and to store the names and phone numbers of people you communicate with.

ii. **Camera:** It connects to the camera on the smartphone and takes photos and videos.

iii. **Calendar:** This app shows a calendar to enter appointments, reminders, etc.

iv. **Mail:** An email app to send and receive emails using your Email account in Gmail, Yahoo, Outlook, etc.

v. **Photos:** This app helps to store all your photos and video and arrange them into various albums.

vi. **Clock:** This app shows the time, and it is used to set the alarms, timers, etc.

vii. **Maps**: This app is used to find directions to where you want to go. It uses GPS (Global Positioning System)

viii. **Messages**: This app is used for sending and receiving SMS.

ix. **Web Browser**: This app allows users to open a browser to search and visit different websites.

x. **Music**: This app is used to play and listen to music.

xi. **Google Play store**: This app is the Google store from where many free apps may be downloaded, like Facebook, WhatsApp, etc.

xii. **Apple Store:** This app is used by Apple devices to download various Apple apps.

5. Differentiate between ROM and RAM.

Ans.

Random Access Memory (RAM)	Read-Only memory (ROM)
(i) RAM is used to hold active information of data and instructions. Information in RAM is stored in random order.	(i) ROM is a part of the computer's main memory. It is used to store the instructions provided by the manufacturer to check basic hardware and to load the operating system from a storage device.
(ii) It is a temporary memory.	(ii) The storage of data and instructions in ROM is permanent until it is written over.
(iii) It is also known as reading/writing memory, as information can be read from RAM and also written onto it.	(iii) The content of the ROM is not lost when the power supply is switched off.
(iv) Information stored in RAM may be erased or written over.	(iv) Information stored in RAM may not be erased or written over.

6. What are the main functions of OS?

Ans. An operating system is basic software that controls the computer. It serves as an interface between the user and the computer.

Some of the functions of the Operating system is:

i. It manages all the devices of a computer and keeps track of the status of the device, whether it is busy or not.

ii. It also checks whether the device is functioning properly or not.

iii. It also controls the software resources of the computer.

iv. It manages the computer memory and keeps track of which memory space is in use by which program and which space is free.

v. It manages the structure of the files and directories on a computer system.

vi. It keeps track of the amount of disk space used by a specific file.

vii. It allows you to create, copy, move, and delete files.

7. Explain the three types of Operating Systems.

Ans. Types of Operating Systems Some commonly used operating systems are as follows:

(i) DOS: DOS (Disk Operating System) is an operating system for a personal computer. Early computers were able to run one program at a time. It had a command-line interface in which a user had to remember the commands to run the program and do other operating system tasks. For example, the DOS command, dir, will display the list of files in the current directory.

(ii) Windows: Windows is an operating system developed by Microsoft. Some popular versions of the Windows operating system are- Windows 98, Windows 2000, Windows XP, Windows 7, Windows 8, and Windows 10.

(iii) Linux: It is an operating system designed for personal computers. It is free and open-source software, which means it can be modified and redistributed.

8. Discuss various types of keys available on a keyboard.

Ans. A keyboard is an input device that is used to type text, numbers, and commands into the computer.

Function keys: Keys labelled from F1 to F12 are function keys and are used to perform specific functions. These functions differ from program to program. For example, the function of the F1 key in most programs is to get help on that program. Some keyboards may have fewer function keys.

Control keys: These are special control keys that perform special functions depending on when and where they are used, like Control (Ctrl), Shift, Spacebar, Alt, Caps Lock, Tab, etc

Enter key: The key is labelled either Enter or Return. By using Enter or the Return key, a new line is started. In some programs, this key is used to send commands and to confirm a task on a computer.

Punctuation keys: These keys include keys for punctuation marks, such as a colon (:), semicolon (;), full stop (.), question mark (?), single quotation marks (' '), double quotation marks (" "), etc.

Navigation keys: Navigation keys include the keys, like the arrow keys, HOME, END, PAGE UP, and PAGE DOWN, etc. These keys are used to move up or down, right or left in a document. The Home and End key move the cursor to the left and right end of a line of text, respectively, while for moving one page up and one page down, the keys the page Up and Page Down are used to respectively.

Command keys: These are the keys like Insert, Delete, and Backspace. When the Insert key is tapped, it overwrites characters to the right of the cursor. The Delete key is used to remove typed text or characters, and the Backspace key is used to keep other objects on the left side of the cursor.

Windows key: Pressing this key opens the Start menu.

9. What are the functions of a mouse? Explain.

Ans. A mouse is a small device that can be used to move, select, and open items on the computer screen. Some functions that can be performed by using a mouse are as follows:

(a) **Rollover/hover**: Some actions can be done by simply rolling over or hovering over an item. When you bring the mouse over a file in File Explorer, it will show the details of that file.

(b) **Point and click**: As the mouse is moved on your desk, a pointer moves correspondingly on the computer screen. The mouse allows you to select an item on the screen. When a particular file is clicked, it gets selected.

(c) **Drag and drop**: For moving an item, click it, and then holding the mouse button down, move the item to a new location of your choice. After moving the item to the new location, release the mouse button. This process is called drag and drop.

(d) **Explorer**: Pick it up from the present location and drop it in a new location when you release the mouse.

(e) **Double-click**: It means two quick clicks on the left mouse button. On double-clicking the file icon, it will open the file.

10. Enumerate the advantages of email.

Ans. Some of the advantages of email are as follows:

i. It is easy to send and receive.

ii. It is the fastest means of communication. A message can reach any part of the world in a fraction of a second.

iii. It is used to send text messages, pictures, sound messages across the globe.

iv. Message can consist of a few lines or more. It is not charged by weight or by length.

v. Nothing is paid extra for sending or receiving the email except the payment for the internet connection.

vi. Email can be sent from any computer or online.

vii. Emails are paperless and eco-friendly.

viii. Bulk messages to a large number of people can be sent at the same time.

11. What do you mean by URL (Uniform Resource Locator)? Explain.

Ans. Each webpage has a unique address that identifies its location on the network. This unique address is called the URL.

The URL has two parts:

Protocol identifier: It identifies the name of the protocol used.

Resource name: It specifies the complete address to the resource on the internet.

For example, http://www.myfreewebsite.com

here, http is the protocol

www.myfreewebsite .com is the resource name

12. Enlist the main applications of the internet.

Ans. Various services provided by the internet are:

i. Email
ii. Chatting
iii. Video conferencing
iv. Social networking
v. E-learning
vi. E-shopping
vii. E-reservation
viii. E-banking, etc.

13. Differentiate between smartphone and tablet.

Ans. The difference between smartphones and tablets is enlisted below:

Smartphone	Tablet
(i) It is a phone with additional features like a camera, Internet surfing, sending and receiving email.	(i) It is considered a useful device like a computer. Most of the tablets do not offer a phone (calling) feature.
(ii) It is mainly considered as a communication device.	(ii) It is considered an entertainment platform.
(iii) The screen display is smaller than a tablet.	(iii) The screen display is larger than a smartphone and smaller than a notebook.
(iv) It is handy and safe to carry anywhere.	(iv) It is not carried everywhere except for meetings or on long trips.
(v) It requires to be charged (depends on usage).	(v) It has a longer battery life than a smartphone.
(vi) Editing, watching movies, reading e-books is difficult.	(vi) Editing, watching movies, reading e-books is easier.

14. Mention the various steps to create a new folder.

Ans. The steps to create a new folder are as follows:

- Double-click the Computer icon.
- Choose/Select the drive in which you want to create a new folder. Say, Local Disk D.
- A window will open up showing files and folders in Local Disc D.
- Click New Folder on the toolbar.

Or

Right-click anywhere in the blank area of the right column, and a shortcut menu appears. Select New Folder from the shortcut menu and click; a new folder is created with the name 'New Folder.'

15. Discuss the main features of OS.

Ans. Some features of an operating system are as follows:

(i) **Single-user/ Single-task Operating System**: This operating system is used by one user to do a task on the computer.

(ii) **Multi programming**: Multiprogramming system allows more than one program to reside in the memory simultaneously. As one program is executed, the CPU executes the other program.

(iii) **Multi-user Operating System**: A multi-user operating system enables multiple users to work on the same computer at different times or simultaneously. Multi-terminal or nodes are attached to a host computer, and more than one user can work on the nodes.

(iv) **Single-user and Multi-task Operating System**: This type of operating system is used in PC, Desktop computers, and laptops, where a single user can operate on several programs at the same time. Examples: Windows, Apple macOS, etc.

(v) **Batch Processing/Spooling:** Batch Operating System places the task in a queue for execution. Tasks are marked according to their priority, and the computer executes them accordingly.

(vi) **Multi-Processing**: A multi-Processing system enables several processes to run concurrently. It means that multi-processing has the ability to execute more than one process at the same time.

(vii) **Multi-threading**: Different parts of a program are called threads. Multi-threading executes different parts of a program simultaneously. It means that multi-threading allows different parts of a software program to run concurrently.

(viii) **Real-Time OS**: A real-time operating system is a computing environment that reacts to input within a specific period of time. A real-time operating system is used to control machinery, scientific instruments, like robots, in complex animations and computer-controlled automated machines. It manages the resources of the computer to execute an operation in the same amount of time every time it is executed.

(ix) **Distributed Operating System:** This operating system runs on a set of computers that are interconnected by a network. It combines all the different computers in the network, forming a single integrated computer and storage location. Some examples: Windows, UNIX, LINUX, etc.

16. Discuss the steps to copy/cut, and paste a file or folder.

Ans. The following steps are used to copy and paste a file or folder:

Step 1: Click the file/folder that you want to copy/cut.

Step 2: On the Home tab, in the Clipboard group, click the Copy button.

Step 3: Click the folder where you want the file/folder to be placed.

Step 4: On the Home tab, in the Clipboard group, click the Paste button.

The file/folder will be placed at the selected place.

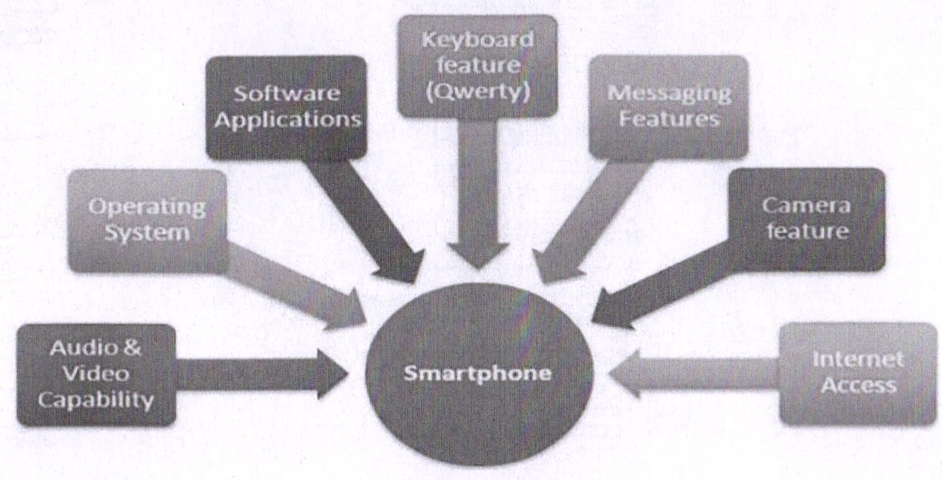

Figure 3.9

3.3.11 HOTS Questions

1. Why is secondary memory called non-volatile memory?

Ans. As the computer's main memory stores the data and information temporarily, the secondary memory is used to store the bulk of information. The information stored in secondary memory is not lost, so it is also non-volatile memory.

Secondary storage devices include a hard disk, CD, DVDs, Pen drive (PD), etc.

2. How is the data recovered from the backup data?

Ans. Data can be recovered from the backup data when the computer stops working completely or computers crash due to human mistakes and / natural disasters, like floods. Hence, it is essential for companies, hospitals, banks, etc., to keep their information safe so that their business can function smoothly and the customers do not face any problems.

3. How can you increase computer performance?

Ans. On using a computer for a long time, a lot of unnecessary files and data, such as temporary files and images, is gathered in the computer. When these files use too much hard-disk space, the performance of the computer degrades. It is important to keep cleaning by removing any extra files. Use some disk cleaner software to clean up the unnecessary files.

4. How will you, as an administrator, avoid the entry of Trojan into the computers?

Ans. The following steps assist the administrator in avoiding a Trojan attack on a system:

i. Install strong antivirus on your system

ii. Take regular backups of your sensitive data.

iii. Deploy hardware-based firewalls on computer systems.

iv. Must have some idea, how the structure of a malicious program looks like.

v. Be very specific while opening a suspicious email.

vi. Avoid third-party downloads.

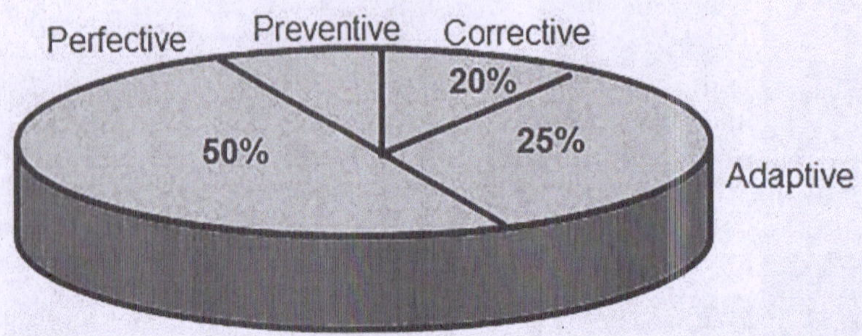

Figure 3.10

3.4 PRACTICE QUESTIONS

1. What do you mean by ICT?
2. What are ICT tools?
3. What is the impact of ICT on education?
4. List four apps found in smartphones.
5. What are the main three parts of a computer?
6. What do you mean by the operating system?
7. Write two functions of the control unit.
8. Mention two antivirus software.
9. Define storage devices?
10. Mention two output devices.
11. What are the different types of printers?
12. What do you mean by byte?
13. What do you mean by command keys?
14. What are the main components of the Taskbar?
15. What is Android?
16. What are the steps to start a computer?
17. Define hardware.
18. What is the full form of CPU?

19. What do you mean by VGA?
20. Define input devices.
21. Write two storage devices.
22. What are the three parts of a computer?
23. List three output devices.
24. What are the main functions of the CPU?
25. What are the differences between RAM and ROM?
26. List the different ports and connections on a computer.
27. Discuss the important features of a mobile device.
28. Mention various parts of a mobile device and list their functions.
29. Describe the functions of at least five types of keys.
30. Describe the functions of a mouse.
31. Explain the applications of the internet.
32. Write the steps to open an internet connection on a computer.

UNIT 4 Entrepreneurial Skills

4.1 UNIT IN BRIEF

- Any economic activity which is related to continuous and regular production and distribution of goods and services for satisfying human needs is called business.
- Business can be done for earning profit or for social service (non-profit). The business caters to the needs of society.
- The gap between demand and availability can be utilised as an opportunity by some people who are ready to take some risk and fill the gap by providing necessary products and services. Such people are termed entrepreneurs.
- The word "entrepreneur" is derived from the French word 'enterprendre' which means 'to undertake.

Fig 4.1

- An entrepreneur is a person who always searches for change, responds to it, and exploits it as an opportunity.
- Innovation is a specific tool of entrepreneurs, how they exploit change as an opportunity for different businesses or services.
- Entrepreneurship is defined as the process of creating business enterprises is called entrepreneurship.
- Entrepreneurship is an act of establishing and managing a new enterprise while undertaking various risks and rewards associated with it.
- One of the main aspects of entrepreneurship is to master the art of planning the business.
- The terms entrepreneur and entrepreneurship are often used interchangeably, but they tend to differ conceptually.

- Innovation is the process of introducing something new in the business. It may be a new product, service, or process.
- An entrepreneur is a person who is self-employed and is willing to take a calculated risk to bring in a new idea to start a business.
- Merchandising/Trading are the businesses that do not produce the goods themselves but purchase the goods for selling them to end-consumers.
- Hybrid business is a mixture of two or more types of businesses. They are engaged in service as well as manufacturing businesses.
- A Joint-Stock company is a form of voluntary association governed under The Companies Act, 2013. As per The Companies Act, 2013, "Company means a company formed and registered under this Act or an existing company.
- A private company is a company whose shares are non-transferable and are not issued to the general public.
- A public company is a company that is not a private company. In public companies, shares are transferable and issued to the general public through invitation.
- Innovative entrepreneurs believe in creating a new product, adding to an existing product, introducing a new process or technique, or creating a new market for his/her product or service.
- Imitative or Adoptive entrepreneurs are the entrepreneurs who adopt the already introduced innovations of innovative entrepreneurs.
- Fabian entrepreneurs are the entrepreneurs who prefer to change things only in circumstances when they are incurring losses.
- Drone entrepreneurs are the entrepreneurs who will not change under any circumstances, even if they are incurring losses.
- An entrepreneur must be a 'Doer' and not merely a 'Dreamer.'
- The basic quality which every entrepreneur must have is the willingness to do hard work.
- Entrepreneurship comes with its rewards. It is associated with the 'Self-Actualisation' need of the 'Need Hierarchy Theory of Motivation' proposed by Abraham Maslow.
- A family where all members are descendants of a common ancestor is called an undivided Hindu family. It includes male members, their wives, and unmarried daughters.
- Business is an economic activity that is related to the continuous and regular production and distribution of goods and services.
- There are three types of business: Product, service, and hybrid.
- A product business is a business where a seller and buyer exchange a thing, which can be seen and touched, is called a product-based business.
- A service business is a business where a seller helps the buyer to finish some work, which cannot be seen or stored. For example, plumbing, teaching, hairdressing, etc., are is called service-based businesses.
- Hybrid businesses are a mix of two or more types of businesses.

- The process of developing a new business plan, launching and running a business using innovation to meet customer needs, and earning a profit is termed entrepreneurship.
- Entrepreneurship development is the process of strengthening entrepreneurs by overviewing their entrepreneurial journey.
- Entrepreneurship development involves training entrepreneurs to improve their skills and knowledge to enable entrepreneurs for business efficiency.
- The process of entrepreneurial development is divided into 3 phases: The stimulatory phase, the Support phase, and the Sustenance phase.

Figure 4.2

4.2 CBSE/NCERT SECTION (SOLVED CBSE/NCERT EXEERCISES)

4.2.1 Multiple Choice Questions

1. Business is a (an) ______________________ activity.

   a) social b) socio-economic

   c) hazardous d) selling

2. What is the aim of entrepreneurship?

   a) Earn a profit b) Solve customers' needs innovatively

   c) Both of the above d) None of the above

ANSWERS
1. (b) 2. (c)

4.2.2 Match the following:

Column A	Column B
1. Business idea	A. Arun goes to the bank to get a loan for the shop
2. Get money	B. Arun and Shyam are thinking about selling tea in front of their school
3. Customer needs	C. Arun and Shyam decide to sell tea along with free biscuits
4. Attract customers	D. Shyam takes his tea samples to customers to understand their taste preferences

ANSWERS
1. B 2. A 3. D 4. C

4.2.3 Statement Based Question

1. Read the following statement and write "Yes" or "No" as to whether the person is an entrepreneur or not.

   Statement Yes/No

   1. Ravi made tea for his friends in the office. Everyone liked the tea very much and told him that he is very good at making tea.
   2. Savita, a housewife, needs extra money for her kids' tuition. She notices that in the afternoon, the children coming out of a nearby college look tired and hungry. She makes refreshing Neembu Pani and samosas and sells them to the students.
   3. Rahul loves dogs. He plays with dogs from his friends' families. One day when they were going out-of-station, they asked Rahul to take care of their dog. Rahul thought that this was a good idea, "taking care of dogs when the owner is traveling ."He started his own Company, which is like a "hotel for dogs ."When the dog-owners travel, they leave their dogs at this hotel and pay the company money for each day they take care of the dog. Is Rahul an entrepreneur?
   4. Monica noticed that her neighbours used to face a problem. They had to leave their young baby behind when they went to work. Monica started going to this house in the evening to take care of the baby for them. Her neighbours were very happy and used to give her chocolates for doing that.

ANSWERS
1. No 2. Yes 3. Yes 4. No

4.2.4 Short Answer Type Questions

1. My customers are not buying my food product because they do not like the flavour of it. What step of the business should I follow next?

Ans. I will improve the taste of food items as per the need of the customers by hiring a good cook.

2. Write the four steps of entrepreneurship development. Give one example.

Ans. The four steps of entrepreneurship development are as follows

i. Idea generation.

ii. Decision making and business planning.

iii. Project creation

iv. Management and control.

Example: One an entrepreneur gets an idea to start a café having fun books and board games near a college. He decides, plans and starts working on the idea to convert into reality. He creates the café with these facilities and manages it.

3. List three businesses seen around you. Share details of what the business does, and how they run it?

Ans. (i) Mr NK Bansal is a person who runs a medical store next to our home. He stocks various types of medicines in his shop and sells them at a discounted rate. His way of dealing with the people is very good.

a) He keeps the stocks up to date.

b) Sometimes, he does the stocks home-delivery.

c) He deals with customers politely.

(ii) Mrs Sunanda Kalita runs a beauty parlour. She employs four girls and is a nice person to her customers.

a) She provides a variety of services to her customers as per their needs and requirements.

b) She deals with her employees and customers very nicely.

c) She started this business in her 17.

(iii) Mr Trilok Chand Suryavanshi is a person who runs a travel agency in our city. He runs the business very decently. He is a calm and peaceful person.

a) He books tickets for all types of transports and levels it by giving discount on every first bookings.

b) He provides vehicles for lease for people at decent price.

c) He is also started a new business of electronic mechanics and is getting a good benefit from it.

4. Give examples of three entrepreneurs you know who live around you. Write how they are helping your city?

Ans. I have three entrepreneurs in my neighbourhood:

(i) Mr Babulal Pandey who manufacture eco-friendly toys in his company.

(ii) Mrs Sudha Raman who runs a beauty parlour and employs four ladies.

(iii) Mrs Geetika Agrawal who runs a NGO working for the welfare of old orphans/ ladies. All these persons are helping the society by providing the products/services at cheaper rates. They are creating employment too.

5. What are the 3 types of business activities? Explain with examples.

Ans. Three types of business activities are as follows:

i. Product/ Manufacturing (Producing some items in large quantities, like toys, earthen pots, artificial jewellery items, etc)

ii. Service (Providing some services, like barber shop/beauty parlour, mason repairing work, etc)

iii. Hybrid (when product and services are provided simultaneously, like sales and service of vehicles, home appliances, etc)

6. What are the key differences between product- and service-based businesses?

Ans. In Product based service items are manufactured for supply to the society while in service-based business, no product is manufactured.

7. If you had a choice to start a business of your own, which business will you start (include in your reply the product or service that you would like to take up)? Why do you want to start this type of business?

Ans. I want to start a service- based business, i.e., Career Counselling Services for school going children, where they will be provided guidance about various courses and help to choose the right career as per their dreams and potential.

8. What is the meaning of manufacturing and trading based business?

Ans. In manufacturing- based business products are manufactured for supply while traders use these products to sell to the customers. Traders do not manufacture any item.

9. Identify the qualities of the following entrepreneurs. Also, write why you think this person has this quality or the qualities.

(a) Anil wanted to do something very different and something no one had thought of before. He decided to start a special travel service for old people/ senior citizens.

(b) Rakesh loves playing outdoors. He used to spend his evenings with his friends, playing games. But he had seen that many of his friends didn't like playing outdoors because they didn't feel safe. He decided to open a playground for children of all ages, with proper security. He found an unused playground, got permission to use it, and asked his friends to help him clean it. He hired a security guard for the playground. He charged a small fee for people who wanted to play. Both parents and children liked his idea and started playing there regularly. His business helped children who would not play outdoor before.

(c) Radhika was a cook in a small restaurant in her area. She made enough money to support her husband and children. She decided to start her own food stall to sell Punjabi food. She would make special parathas. A few days after starting her business, the police came and told her that she was not allowed to run her stall in the area. Radhika did not give up. She started a Tiffin service through which she would deliver fresh food to people.

Ans. (a) Anil is innovative, creative, risk-taker, and emphatic as he thinks about the well-being of old people.

(b) Rakesh is empathetic towards the needs of small children. He is an innovative, leader, creative, and team builder.

(c) Radhika is innovative, creative, hardworking, and a risk-taker as she left her job to convert her dream into reality.

10. List any four characteristics of entrepreneurship.

Ans. Innovative, Leader, Risk-taker, Hardworking

11. List any two characteristics of wage employment.

Ans. Fixed salary, no responsibility.

12. Name any one factor that is common to both entrepreneurship and wage employment on a contract basis.

Ans. A common factor to entrepreneurship and wage employment is Labour market institutions that include wage-setting policies, social insurance provisions, employment security, and the enforcement of restrictive covenants.

12. Answer the following questions in your own words.

(i) Gulab lives in a small village in Rajasthan. She noticed that all the women in her village were good at making paintings and handicraft products. She collected money and started a business. Gulab would help the women to get material from cities and support them in making the latest designs. She would then arrange for these paintings and handicraft products to be sold in big cities. How do you think Gulab is helping her society as an entrepreneur?

Ans. Gulab is helping the ladies to get employment and earn money in the village itself. Moreover, he is exposing the creativity of the ladies to the world. Thus, he is helping society.

13. State whether the person engaged in the activity mentioned below is an entrepreneur or an Employee

(a) Rahul starts a shop to sell Chaat and special Paani Puri. He is an ____________.

(b) Shahid becomes the manager of a dealership selling food products. He is an ____________.

(c) Ritu leaves the company she worked for and starts catering food for marriage programmes. She is an ____________.

Ans. (a) Entrepreneur

(b) Employee

(c) Entrepreneur

14. State the type of business—product, service or hybrid

(a) Arun bakery, which makes and sells bread to people. ____________

(b) Ram's repair shop, which repairs motorcycle. ____________

(c) Hari's hair-salon, where he cuts hair for women and men. ____________

Ans. (a) Hybrid

(b) Service

(c) Service

15. Write P- Product, S- Service and H- Hybrid for the following businesses.

    (a) Ice-cream seller: ___________

    (b) Restaurant/Cafeteria Owner: __________

    (c) Car-driving School owner: ___________

Ans. (a) Service (b) Hybrid (c) service

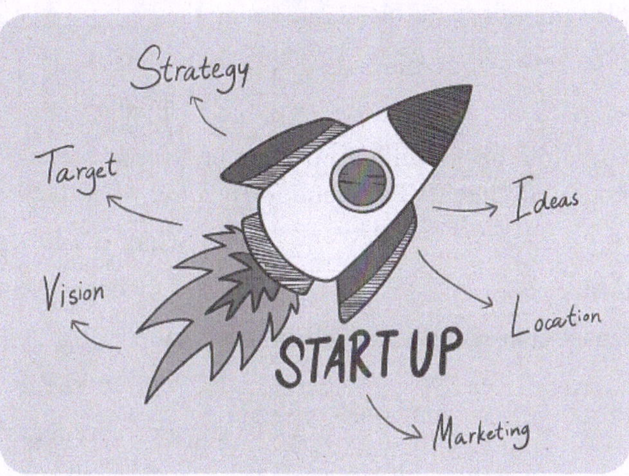

Figure 4.3

4.3 SOLVED EXERCISES

4.3.1 Multiple Choice Questions

Choose the correct option out of the four given options for each question.

1. Which of the following is not a phase of the entrepreneurship process?

   a) Stimulatory phase
   b) Support phase
   c) Elimination phase
   d) Sustenance phase

2. The entrepreneurs who follow the traditional methods of business and do not adapt at all are called:

   a) Fabian entrepreneurs
   b) Innovative entrepreneurs
   c) Drone entrepreneurs
   d) Imitative entrepreneurs

3. ____________ are the entrepreneurs who prefer to change things only in circumstances when they are incurring losses.

   a) Fabian entrepreneurs
   b) Innovative entrepreneurs
   c) Drone entrepreneurs
   d) Imitative entrepreneurs

4. Who defined entrepreneurship as 'the creation of new business in 1985?

   a) Amartya Sen
   b) SP Rana
   c) Peter F. Drucker
   d) Man Mohan Singh

5. Who is an entrepreneur?
   a) A person born with a silver spoon in their mouth
   b) A notorious person
   c) A visionary
   d) A deceptive person
6. Entrepreneurs play an important role in increasing the ____________ of living in a society.
   a) Confidence b) Gender gap
   c) Efforts d) Quality
7. Sneha has employed ten people in her business of Nagpur News Services. Every day, she spends half an hour with them to listen and learn about what they've done that day. She:
   a) Takes risks b) Creates a new product
   c) Manages the business d) Divides income
8. Anyone who manages to establish a new business is called:
   a) Businessman b) Entrepreneur
   c) Visionary d) Entrepreneurship
9. A method for accepting credit card payments is:
   a) SQUARE b) TRIANGLE
   c) CIRCLE d) All of the above
10. Entrepreneurship has a critical role in the ____________ of society.
    a) Evolution b) Functioning
    c) Demolition d) Planning
11. Which of the following is the role of entrepreneurship?
    a) It creates employment opportunities by initiating new ventures.
    b) It increases productivity through technical and other innovative approaches.
    c) It aids the transfer of technology.
    d) All of these.
12. A business set up by the communities facing challenges together in developing the business. For example, shops, call centres, farms, etc., is called:
    a) Industrial unit b) Business
    c) Community business d) Entrepreneur
13. Which of the following abilities allows an entrepreneur to put everything at stake to convert his idea into a reality?
    a) Time management b) Self-confidence
    c) Self-motivation d) Risk-taking ability

14. Which of the following is a microblogging and social networking service?

a) Relax b) Facebook c) Twitter d) Crooks

15. Which of the following options is the correct set of tasks of an entrepreneur?

i. Owning the full income/profit
ii. Creating a New Method, Idea, or Product
iii. Making Effective Decisions
iv. Managing the Business
v. Taking Risk
vi. Distributing the dividend

a) (ii) (iii) (iv) (v) b) (ii) (iii) (iv) (v) (vi)
c) (i) (iii) (iv) (v) (vi) d) All of the above

16. Which of the following abilities refers to the ability of an entrepreneur to bring out the new ways to run a business?

a) Creativity b) Hard work
c) Patience d) Self-motivation

17. Study the following statements and choose the correct set of roles of an entrepreneur.

i. Coordinating role to coordinate the various factors for production.
ii. Risk Assumption role in taking a risk in the new venture.
iii. Capital formation role in mobilizing the idle savings for carrying business
iv. Balancing role to provide development in the big cash of nation-building
v. Employment Generation role in providing employment to the youths
vi. Society's interest protector role to safeguards the interest of society
vii. Catalytic role in increasing the rate of economic development of the region

a) (ii) (iii) (iv) (v) b) (ii) (iii) (iv) (v) (vi)
c) (i) (iii) (iv) (vi) (vii) d) All of the above

18. Anand Mohan runs a Fresh Vegetable shop. A customer comes to his shop and starts shouting at him. He does not get angry, but he listens to what his customer is saying. He is:

a) Confident b) Creative c) Hardworking d) Patient

19. Which Company is headed by Azim H Premji as its chairman?

a) Tata b) OIL c) Wipro d) Infosys

20. Study the following statements to choose the correct set of myths about entrepreneurs.

i. A person who has a big business is an entrepreneur.
ii. Entrepreneurs are not in the industry for the money.
iii. Entrepreneurs take lots of risks.
iv. An entrepreneur cannot borrow from banks.

v. A new business always flourishes.

vi. One must be young and restless to be an entrepreneur.

a) (ii) (iii) (iv)
b) (iii) (iv) (v) (vi)
c) (i) (iii) (iv) (v) (vi)
d) (i) (ii) (iii) (iv) (v) (vi)

21. ____________ are the entrepreneurs who offer a piece of advice and help to customers.
    a) Builders
    b) Advisors
    c) Administrators
    d) Communicators

22. Which of the following businesses involves more than one type of business?
    a) Manufacturing Business
    b) Hybrid Business
    c) Service Business
    d) None of these

23. Suppose Zakir has a pharmaceutical company in Salim Pur. He decides to sell his Company's products in Tunisia. It does not sell, and he has a loss. He apologizes to the people who work for him. He says that he will plan better next time and will bring new products. This incident shows that he:
    a) Does not give up
    b) Takes responsibility for his actions
    c) Thinks before making a decision.
    d) Both a and b

24. Entrepreneurs also invest in community projects, and they provide financial support to:
    a) Industry
    b) Communal disharmony
    c) Charities
    d) Collaboration

25. Arman has a Cold Storage to keep the produce of farmers and employs more than 25 persons. He pays his employees on the 7th of every month. He:
    a) Do nothing special.
    b) Takes risk
    c) Manages the business
    d) Creates a new product

26. Who reaps the most benefits of Entrepreneurship?
    a) Society only
    b) Entrepreneur only
    c) Entrepreneur and his family
    d) Entrepreneur and society

27. Entrepreneurship is not only beneficial for the entrepreneur itself, but it is also important for the ____________ of the economy.
    a) Decline
    b) Flexibility
    c) Growth
    d) None of these

28. Which pair is incorrect?
    a) Tilak Mehta - Papers N Parcels
    b) Advait Thakur- Piramal Enterprises Ltd
    c) Farhad Acidwala - Rockstar Media.
    d) Sunil Mittal - Bharti Enterprises

29. Who believes in creating a new product, adding to an existing product, introducing a new process or technique, or creating a new market for his/her product or service?
    a) Fabian entrepreneurs
    b) Innovative entrepreneurs
    c) Drone entrepreneurs
    d) Imitative entrepreneurs

30. ____________ do not innovate anything themselves, but they imitate successful innovations.
    a) Fabian entrepreneurs
    b) Innovative entrepreneurs
    c) Drone entrepreneurs
    d) Imitative entrepreneurs

Figure 4.4

ANSWERS									
1. (c)	2. (c)	3. (a)	4. (c)	5. (c)	6. (d)	7. (c)	8. (b)	9. (a)	10. (b)
11. (d)	12. (c)	13. (d)	14. (c)	15. (b)	16. (a)	17. (d)	18. (d)	19. (c)	20. (d)
21. (b)	22. (b)	23. (d)	24. (c)	25. (c)	26. (d)	27. (c)	28. (b)	29. (b)	30. (d)

4.3.2 Fill in the blanks

1. An ____________ is a person who is self-employed and is willing to take a calculated risk to bring in a new idea to start a business.
2. ____________ is the entrepreneur who imitates the methods and technologies innovated by others to begin his own business.
3. One of the main aspects of ____________ is to master the art of planning the business.
4. ____________ is the process of introducing something new in the business. It may be a new product, service, or process.
5. Entrepreneurs are often seen as visionaries and ____________ who take well-calculated risks.
6. ____________ is defined as the ability of an entrepreneur to provide things in a Novel or creative manner.

7. The ____________ by new businesses is the primary goal of economic development.
8. ____________ is the entrepreneur who is cautious and sceptic about bringing any change in his enterprise.
9. ____________ is a type of business that deals with intangible products, such as accounting, banking, consulting, cleaning, etc.
10. ____________ is the entrepreneur who makes profits through commissions obtained by customer purchases.
11. Entrepreneurs play a key role in increasing the ____________ of living in a community.
12. A ____________ company is a company that is not a private company. In public companies, shares are transferable and issued to the general public through invitation.
13. There is a ____________ relationship between the entrepreneur and entrepreneurship.
14. Successful entrepreneurs ____________ any distraction that might stop them from achieving their goals.
15. The basic quality which every entrepreneur must have the ____________ to do hard work.

ANSWERS			
1. Entrepreneur	2. Imitative Entrepreneur	3. Entrepreneurship	4. Innovation
5. risk-takers	6. Innovation	7. job creation	8. Fabian Entrepreneur
9. Service business	10. Trader	11. quality	12. public
13. direct	14. eliminate	15. willingness	

4.3.3 True or False

1. Entrepreneurs do research to find out the need of customers and plan to introduce an innovative product to meet the demand.
2. Entrepreneurs create employment.
3. Entrepreneurship may be described as starting a business by using the resources available to a person.
4. Entrepreneurs play no role in increasing the quality of living in a community.
5. An entrepreneur must be a 'Doer' and not merely a 'Dreamer'.
6. New and improved products, services, and technology from entrepreneurs enable to development of new markets and create new wealth.
7. The job creation by new and existing businesses is the primary goal of economic development.
8. Entrepreneurs are not considered visionaries and risk-takers.
9. Entrepreneurship is an act of establishing and managing a new enterprise while undertaking various risks and rewards associated with it.
10. The Indian Government has started offering various incentives and concessions, which comprise capital subsidy, marketing facilities, technical know-how, industrial facilities, etc.
11. Government regulations play a significant role in promoting entrepreneurship.

12. Entrepreneurs do not realize that every event and situation is a business opportunity.
13. Entrepreneurs identify a need in the market to build a product or service for it.
14. Entrepreneurship comes with no rewards.
15. Entrepreneurship is defined as the process of creating business enterprises.

ANSWERS									
1. T	2. T	3. T	4. F	5. T	6. T	7. T	8. F	9. T	10. T
11. T	12. F	13. T	14. F	15. T					

4.3.4 Matching Type Questions

(I) Match the items of column A with those of column B correctly.

Column A(Entrepreneur)	Column B (Associated Company)
(i) Adar Poonawalla	(a) Wipro
(ii) Ritesh Agrawal	(b) Balaji Telefilms
(iii) Azim Premji	(c) Ola Cabs
(iv) Bhavish Aggarwal	(d) OYO Rooms
(v) Ekta Kapoor	(e) Serum Institute of India

(II) Match columns A and B correctly.

Column A	Column B
(i) Shivani opens four more restaurants in her state.	a. Survive
(ii) Out of many competition coaching classes in Shimla, Anita Chauhan started morning batches in her coaching centre to attract more students to her classes.	b. Enter
(iii) Sudeep Sharma has started her boutique on the Internet.	c. Grow

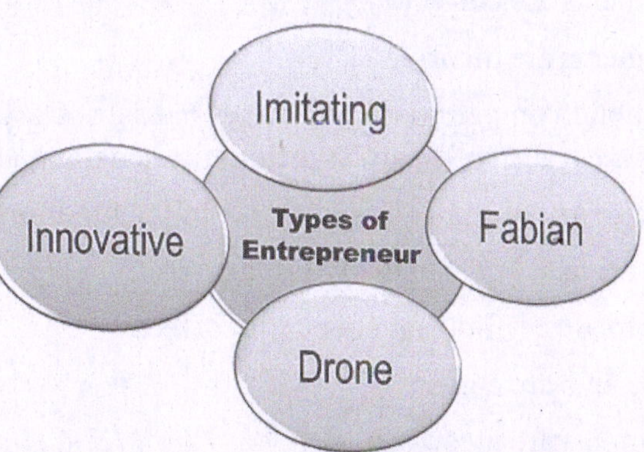

Figure 4.5: Types of Entrepreneurship

ANSWERS					
(I)	(i)-e,	(ii)-d,	(iii)-a,	(iv)-c,	(v)-b
(II)	(i)-c,	(ii)-a,	(iii)-b		

4.3.5 Statements Based Questions

1. Statement 1: Fabian Entrepreneur is an entrepreneur who is cautious and sceptic about bringing any change in his enterprise.

   Statement 2: The basic quality which every entrepreneur must have is the willingness to do hard work.

   a) Statement 1 is correct, but statement 2 is incorrect.

   b) Statement 1 is incorrect, but statement 2 is correct.

   c) Both the statements are correct.

   d) Both the statements are incorrect.

2. Statement 1: Small scale entrepreneurs are called the backbone of our country and many other developing countries.

   Statement 2: The job creation by new and existing businesses is the secondary goal of economic development.

   a) Statement 1 is correct, but statement 2 is incorrect.

   b) Statement 1 is incorrect, but statement 2 is correct.

   c) Both the statements are correct.

   d) Both the statements are incorrect.

3. Statement 1: Innovative entrepreneurs are the entrepreneurs who will not change under any circumstances, even if they are incurring losses.

   Statement 2: A service Entrepreneur is an entrepreneur who is involved in manufacturing and rendering services rather than goods.

   a) Statement 1 is correct, but statement 2 is incorrect.

   b) Statement 1 is incorrect, but statement 2 is correct.

   c) Both the statements are correct.

   d) Both the statements are incorrect.

4. Statement 1: A public company is a company that is not a private company. In public companies, shares are transferable and issued to the general public through invitation.

   Statement 2: Entrepreneurship has a crucial role in the functioning of society.

   a) Statement 1 is correct, but statement 2 is incorrect.

   b) Statement 1 is incorrect, but statement 2 is correct.

   c) Both the statements are correct.

   d) Both the statements are incorrect.

5. Statement 1: The two important personality traits that entrepreneurs possess are creativity and laziness.

   Statement 2: A public company is a company whose shares are non-transferable and are not issued to the general public.

a) Statement 1 is correct, but statement 2 is incorrect.

b) Statement 1 is incorrect, but statement 2 is correct.

c) Both the statements are correct.

d) Both the statements are incorrect.

6. Statement 1: A 'Private Entrepreneur' is an entrepreneur who establishes and operates private enterprises without any government control. He works for personal interest.

   Statement 2: A business venture does not need to have a novel element or process to make it acceptable and thrive in the market.

   a) Statement 1 is correct, but statement 2 is incorrect.

   b) Statement 1 is incorrect, but statement 2 is correct.

   c) Both the statements are correct.

   d) Both the statements are incorrect.

7. Statement 1: Merchandising/Trading are the businesses that do not produce the goods themselves but purchase the goods for selling them to end-consumers.

   Statement 2: Hybrid business is a mixture of two or more types of businesses and they are engaged in service as well as manufacturing businesses.

   a) Statement 1 is correct, but statement 2 is incorrect.

   b) Statement 1 is incorrect, but statement 2 is correct.

   c) Both the statements are correct.

   d) Both the statements are incorrect.

8. Statement 1: Innovation is the process of introducing something new in the business which may be a new product, service, or process.

   Statement 2: A daily wager is a person who is self-employed and is willing to take a calculated risk to bring in a new idea to start a business.

   a) Statement 1 is correct, but statement 2 is incorrect.

   b) Statement 1 is incorrect, but statement 2 is correct.

   c) Both the statements are correct.

   d) Both the statements are incorrect.

9. Statement 1: Any economic activity which is related to continuous and regular production and distribution of goods and services for satisfying human needs is called an entrepreneur.

   Statement 2: One of the main aspects of entrepreneurship is to master the art of planning the business.

   a) Statement 1 is correct, but statement 2 is incorrect.

   b) Statement 1 is incorrect, but statement 2 is correct.

   c) Both the statements are correct.

   d) Both the statements are incorrect.

10. Statement 1: The gap between demand and availability can be utilised as an opportunity by entrepreneurs who are ready to take some risk and fill the gap by providing necessary products and services.

    Statement 2: The word "entrepreneur" is derived from the Arabian verb 'enterprendre' which means 'to undertake.

    a) Statement 1 is correct, but statement 2 is incorrect.
    b) Statement 1 is incorrect, but statement 2 is correct.
    c) Both the statements are correct.
    d) Both the statements are incorrect.

ANSWERS									
1. (c)	2. (a)	3. (b)	4. (c)	5. (d)	6. (a)	7. (c)	8. (a)	9. (b)	10. (a)

4.3.6 Assertion Reason Type Questions

1. Assertion (A): An entrepreneur is a person who always searches for change, responds to it, and exploits it as an opportunity.

   Reason (R): Entrepreneurs are often seen as visionaries and risk-takers who take well-calculated risks.

   a) Both A and R are correct, and R is the correct reason for A.
   b) Both A and R are correct, and R is not the correct reason for A.
   c) A is correct, but R is incorrect.
   d) A is incorrect, but R is correct.

2. Assertion (A): Imitative entrepreneurs are the entrepreneurs who prefer to change things only in circumstances when they are incurring losses.

   Reason (R): Innovation is a specific tool of entrepreneurs, how they exploit change as an opportunity for different businesses or services.

   a) Both A and R are correct, and R is the correct reason for A.
   b) Both A and R are correct, and R is not the correct reason for A.
   c) A is correct, but R is incorrect.
   d) A is incorrect, but R is correct.

3. Assertion (A): Entrepreneurs are called the community life-change agents.

   Reason (R): Entrepreneurs play an important role in improving the quality of living in a community.

   a) Both A and R are correct, and R is the correct reason for A.
   b) Both A and R are correct, and R is not the correct reason for A.
   c) A is correct, but R is incorrect.
   d) A is incorrect, but R is correct.

4. Assertion (A): An entrepreneur is a person who establishes a business or a venture that generates some value for the customer and proves to be profitable for him.

   Reason (R): Entrepreneurship is the act of establishing and managing a new enterprise while undertaking various risks and rewards associated with it.

   a) Both A and R are correct, and R is the correct reason for A.

   b) Both A and R are correct, and R is not the correct reason for A.

   c) A is correct, but R is incorrect.

   d) A is incorrect, but R is correct.

5. Assertion (A): An innovative Entrepreneur is an entrepreneur who imitates the methods and technologies innovated by others to begin his own business.

   Reason (R): A Drone Entrepreneur is an entrepreneur who regularly intends to bring in new products in the market, new technologies, etc.

   a) Both A and R are correct, and R is the correct reason for A.

   b) Both A and R are correct, and R is not the correct reason for A.

   c) A is correct, but R is incorrect.

   d) A is incorrect, but R is correct.

6. Assertion (A): Manufacturing Entrepreneur looks forward to developing alternative projects by giving responsibility to run the business to someone else and moves on to a new idea or a new venture after selling the running business.

   Reason (R): Entrepreneurship can be described as starting a business by using the resources available to a person.

   a) Both A and R are correct, and R is the correct reason for A.

   b) Both A and R are correct, and R is not the correct reason for A.

   c) A is correct, but R is incorrect.

   d) A is incorrect, but R is correct.

7. Assertion (A): Business can be done for earning profit or for social service (non-profit).

   Reason (R): The business caters to the needs of society.

   a) Both A and R are correct, and R is the correct reason for A.

   b) Both A and R are correct, and R is not the correct reason for A.

   c) A is correct, but R is incorrect.

   d) A is incorrect, but R is correct.

8. Assertion (A): New and improved products, services, and technology from entrepreneurs enable to development of new markets and create new wealth.

   Reason (R): Manufacturing Entrepreneur is an entrepreneur who manufactures goods, mobilizes resources and supplies to sell those products.

a) Both A and R are correct, and R is the correct reason for A.

b) Both A and R are correct, and R is not the correct reason for A.

c) A is correct, but R is incorrect.

d) A is incorrect, but R is correct.

9. Assertion (A): A family where all members are descendants of a common ancestor is called an undivided Hindu family.

   Reason (R): Undivided Hindu Family includes male members, their wives, widows, and unmarried daughters.

   a) Both A and R are correct, and R is the correct reason for A.

   b) Both A and R are correct, and R is not the correct reason for A.

   c) A is correct, but R is incorrect.

   d) A is incorrect, but R is correct.

10. Assertion (A): Entrepreneurship is defined as the process of creating business enterprises is called entrepreneurship.

    Reason (R): Fabian entrepreneurs are the entrepreneurs who adopt the already introduced innovations of innovative entrepreneurs.

    a) Both A and R are correct, and R is the correct reason for A.

    b) Both A and R are correct, and R is not the correct reason for A.

    c) A is correct, but R is incorrect.

    d) A is incorrect, but R is correct.

Figure 4.6

ANSWERS									
1. (b)	2. (d)	3. (a)	4. (b)	5. (c)	6. (d)	7. (a)	8. (b)	9. (c)	10. (c)

4.3.7 Competency-Based Questions

1. Suppose Nandita Prasad wants to start a new business, "Nandita Handicrafts ." She has the following steps in her mind:

   i. Improving Product/ service

   ii. Having a business Idea

iii. Understanding customer needs

iv. Arranging resources (money and material)

The correct sequence of steps to start the business is:

a) (i) (ii) (iii) (iv)

b) (iv) (iii) (ii) (i)

c) (ii) (iv) (iii) (i)

d) (i) (iv) (iii) (ii)

2. Consider the following statements:

   i. Entrepreneurs lead to the provision of new and distinguished ideas to society, which may hold some value to them.

   ii. Entrepreneurs are empowered by the sense of owning and controlling a business.

   iii. Entrepreneurs undertake entrepreneurship to fulfill his/her need for self-expression.

   iv. Entrepreneurs earn more income in the form of profit as compared to wage employment.

   These are the advantages of:

   a) Entrepreneurship

   b) Entrepreneurship development

   c) Skills development

   d) Think tank

3. Suppose Diksha Adhikari wants to become a successful entrepreneur. Which of the following set of qualities is a must for her?

   a) Innovation, creativity, hardworking, risk-taker

   b) Innovation, dreamer, authoritative attitude,

   c) Empathy, doer, belief in traditional routes, positive attitude

   d) Creative, Fabian, liar, strict discipline

4. Consider the following features of a process:

   i. It fosters creativity.

   ii. It accelerates economic growth.

   iii. It encourages the welfare of society.

   iv. It provides solutions to the problems of society.

   v. It stimulates innovation and efficiency.

   vi. It creates jobs and employment opportunities.

   This process is termed:

   a) Entrepreneurship　　b) Questioning

   c) Innovation　　d) Data mining

5. The government of India launched a policy whose objective is to meet the challenge of skilling at scale with speed and standard, and it aims to provide an umbrella framework to all skilling activities being carried out within the country, for aligning them to common standards and link the skilling with demand centres. This is called:
   a) Start-up India
   b) Ujjavala Yojana
   c) PMJDY
   d) Pradhan Mantri Yuva Udyamita Vikas Abhiyan

ANSWERS				
1. (c)	2. (b)	3. (a)	4. (a)	5. (d)

4.3.8 VSA

1. How will you define a business?

Ans. Any economic activity which is related to continuous and regular production and distribution of goods and services for satisfying human needs is called business.

2. Why do some people do business?

Ans. Business can be done for earning profit or for social service (non-profit). The business caters to the needs of society.

3. Who are entrepreneurs?

Ans. The gap between demand and availability can be utilised as an opportunity by some people who are ready to take some risk and fill the gap by providing necessary products and services. Such people are termed entrepreneurs.

4. What do you mean by innovation?

Ans. Innovation is a specific tool of entrepreneurs, how they exploit change as an opportunity for different businesses or services.

5. Whether entrepreneur and entrepreneurship are same/

Ans. No, the terms entrepreneur and entrepreneurship are often used interchangeably, but they tend to differ conceptually.

6. Define trading.

Ans. Merchandising/Trading are the businesses that do not produce the goods themselves but purchase the goods for selling them to end-consumers.

7. What is hybrid business/

Ans. Hybrid business is a mixture of two or more types of businesses. They are engaged in service as well as manufacturing businesses.

8. What do you mean by a Joint -Stock company?

Ans. A Joint-Stock company is a form of voluntary association governed under The Companies Act, 2013. As per The Companies Act, 2013, "Company means a company formed and registered under this/her Act or an existing company.

9. What is a private company?

Ans. A private company is a company whose shares are non-transferable and are not issued to the general public.

10. Who are innovative entrepreneurs?

Ans. Innovative entrepreneurs believe in creating a new product, adding to an existing product, introducing a new process or technique, or creating a new market for his/her product or service.

11. Define imitative entrepreneurs.

Ans. Imitative or Adoptive entrepreneurs are the entrepreneurs who adopt the already introduced innovations of innovative entrepreneurs.

12. Who are Fabian entrepreneurs?

Ans. Fabian entrepreneurs are the entrepreneurs who prefer to change things only in circumstances when they are incurring losses.

13. Which entrepreneurs are called Drone entrepreneurs?

Ans. Drone entrepreneurs are the entrepreneurs who will not change under any circumstances, even if they are incurring losses.

14. Define entrepreneurial management.

Ans. Effective management of an enterprise is an essential role of an entrepreneur. Poor management may lead to the failure of the business.

15. Who are innovative entrepreneurs?

Ans. Innovative entrepreneurs are the entrepreneurs who take the route of innovation for their enterprises. They believe in creating a new product, adding to an existing product, introducing a new process or technique, or creating a new market for his/her product or service.

16. What are the characteristics of Imitative or Adoptive entrepreneurs?

Ans. Imitative or Adoptive entrepreneurs are the entrepreneurs who adopt the already introduced innovations of innovative entrepreneurs. They do not innovate anything themselves, but they imitate successful innovations.

17. Who are called Fabián entrepreneurs?

Ans. Fabian entrepreneurs are the entrepreneurs who prefer to change things only in circumstances when they are incurring losses. They do not like facing risks and resist changing anything about their business.

18. Who are drone entrepreneurs?

Ans. Drone entrepreneurs are the entrepreneurs who will not change under any circumstances, even if they are incurring losses.

19. Who became the youngest billionaire at the age of 23 years in 2007?

Ans. Mark Zuckerberg, founder and CEO of Facebook became one of the youngest billionaires in the world in 2007 when he was just 23 years old.

20. Who is not included in the Undivided Hindu Family?

Ans. Widows

21. A person establishes a business or a venture that generates some value for the customer, and it is profitable for him. Who is he/she?

Ans. An entrepreneur.

22. What is entrepreneurship?

Ans. Entrepreneurship may be described as starting a business by using the resources available to a person. Entrepreneurship has a crucial role in the functioning of society.

23. What is the main feature of a business to be successful in the market?

Ans. A business venture must have a novel element or process to make it acceptable and thrive in the market.

24. Who is called the backbone of our country and many other developing countries?

Ans. Small scale entrepreneurs.

25. Who initiated the company" MakeMyTrip"?

Ans. Mr. Deep Kalra

26. Who initiated the idea of 'Nirma' washing powder?

Ans. Mr Karsanbhai Patel

27. Who is known as a manufacturing entrepreneur?

Ans. Manufacturing Entrepreneur is an entrepreneur who manufactures goods, mobilizes resources and supplies to sell those products.

28. Who is a 'private entrepreneur'?

Ans. A 'Private Entrepreneur' is an entrepreneur who establishes and operates private enterprises without any government control. He works for personal interest.

29. Which entrepreneur is called a service entrepreneur?

Ans. A service Entrepreneur is an entrepreneur who is involved in manufacturing and rendering services rather than goods.

30. When was National Skill Development Mission launched?

Ans. The NSD Mission was launched in 2015.

31. When was the 'Make in India' initiative launched by the Govt of India?

Ans. 'Make in India' initiative of the Government of India was launched on 25th September 2014.

32. What is Instagram?

Ans. Instagram is a photo-sharing app (social media) that uses filters to enhance photos.

33. Who is a trading entrepreneur?

Ans. A trading entrepreneur is an entrepreneur who carries out trading activities only.

34. Who is a trader?

Ans. A trader is an entrepreneur who makes profits through commissions obtained by customer purchases.

35. What is the primary goal of economic development?

Ans. The job creation by new and existing businesses is the primary goal of economic development.

36. Why are entrepreneurs considered visionaries and risk-takers?

Ans. Entrepreneurs are considered visionaries and risk-takers because entrepreneurs play an important role in increasing the quality of living in a community by bringing improvised products and services.

37. What are the two important personality traits that entrepreneurs must possess?

Ans. The two important personality traits that entrepreneurs must possess are perception and intuition.

38. Define EDP.

Ans. Entrepreneurship Development Programme (EDP) is an ongoing process of training and motivating entrepreneurs to establish profitable enterprises.

39. What types of incentives are provided by the Indian govt for entrepreneurs?

Ans. The Indian Government has started offering various incentives and concessions, which comprise capital subsidy, marketing facilities, technical know-how, industrial facilities, etc.

Figure 4.7

4.3.9 Short Answer Type Questions

1. Enlist the features of a business.

Ans. Some of the features of a business are enlisted as below:

i. Business is an activity related to some trade.

ii. Business involves the purchase and sale of goods or services.

iii. Business is done to earn profits, and therefore it is referred to as a source of income.

iv. Business is mainly run to maximize profits by creating value for customers through goods or services.

2. What are the main advantages of being an entrepreneur?

Ans. Being an entrepreneur imbibes life skills, increases creativity and problem-solving skills, provides a better understanding of business and market economics, improves communication, teamwork, and networking skills, and hence, enhances employability.

3. Enlist the advantages of Sole proprietorship.

Ans. The advantage of sole proprietorship are as follows:

i. Easy Formulation
ii. Full control
iii. Quick Decisions
iv. Flexible Management
v. Control on Profits

4. What are the disadvantages of Sole proprietorship?

Ans. There are three disadvantages of Sole proprietorship:

i. Unlimited liability
ii. Limited resources
iii. Lack of stability

5. What are the two important elements of entrepreneurship?

Ans. The two elements of entrepreneurship are 'Innovation' and 'Risk-bearing.'

(i) **Innovation:** Innovation is the process of introducing something new in the business. It may be a new product, service, or process. Innovation is considered a necessary condition for being an entrepreneur.

(ii) **Risk-bearing:** Starting something new service or product always involves risks and uncertainties. The reason for this is that the new business may incur profits or losses. It can also be because of the shortage of supplies for production or excessive cost incurred.

6. Mention advantages of partnership.

Ans. The following are the benefits of partnership:

i. Resources
ii. Flexible Management
iii. Decision making.
iv. Risk-sharing
v. Formulation

7. What are the disadvantages of a partnership business?

Ans. The following are the disadvantages of partnership:

i. Dissolution is difficult.

ii. Conflicts may be there between partners.

iii. Implied Authority

iv. Unlimited Liability

v. Minor

8. What are the four primary areas on which an enterprise requires policies?

Ans. Managing an enterprise requires policies on four primary areas.

i. Need for an environment that is suitable for innovation and adaptable to changes.

ii. Systematic measurement of performance of the business and finding ways to improve performance,

iii. Well-built organisational structure with the focus on policies for staffing and compensation and reward structure,

iv. Innovation does not take the focus away from the existing business model. Innovation should be in line with the current business.

9. Explain entrepreneurship development.

Ans. Entrepreneurship development is defined as the process of strengthening entrepreneurs by overviewing their entrepreneurial journey. It involves training the entrepreneurs to improve their skills and knowledge, which in turn will enable the entrepreneurs to run their business effectively and efficiently.

10. Explain the phases of entrepreneurial development.

Ans. The process of entrepreneurial development is divided into the following three phases:

i. Stimulatory phase: This phase involves generating interest and awareness among potential entrepreneurs. It is called the stimulatory phase because it includes activities that stimulate the individual's need for being an entrepreneur.

ii. Support phase: This phase is all about supporting the new enterprises in their establishment. Various activities such as registration of enterprises; development of the product prototype; an arrangement of finance, land, shed, power, and common facility centre; offering management consultancy services and marketing support; guidance for selecting plant and machinery; and getting approvals and licenses comprise this phase.

iii. Sustenance phase: This phase helps the enterprises to grow after they have been established. It helps in the continuous and efficient functioning of enterprises within a society. It includes activities such as modernization, diversification, expansion, getting additional finance, and research and development support to help an enterprise survive, develop and grow.

6. What are the main advantages of HUF?

Ans. The following are the main benefits of HUF:

i. Stability: Business is not dissolved in case of the death of Karta, and the next senior-most coparcener takes the place of Karta.

ii. Existence: No registration is required for a HUF business as it arises by the status of its member.

iii. **Minor**: Even minors can be coparceners as a person acquires the membership in joint Hindu family business by mere birth into the family.

iv. **Limited liability of coparceners**: Coparceners of a joint Hindu family business are only held liable for the debts of business up to the limit of their share in the ancestral property. Their assets are not charged against the liabilities of the business.

7. Mention some advantages of Entrepreneurship Development.

Ans. The following advantages are associated with entrepreneurship:

i. Entrepreneurs lead to the provision of new and distinguished ideas to society, which may hold some value to them.

ii. Entrepreneurs are empowered by the sense of owning and controlling a business.

iii. Entrepreneurs undertake entrepreneurship to fulfill his/her need for self-expression.

iv. Entrepreneurs earn more income in the form of profit as compared to wage employment.

v. Entrepreneurship enables one to be his/her own master and allows one to achieve what is important to him/her.

vi. Entrepreneurs often contribute to society in the form of creating jobs and utilizing idle resources.

vii. Entrepreneurs reduce regional imbalances and promote equal income distribution by improving the overall standard of living.

8. Enlist the disadvantages of HUF.

Ans. The following are the disadvantages of HUF:

i. **Unlimited Liability of Karta**: Karta is personally responsible for the debts of a business in case the assets of the business are insufficient. His/her assets can be used to repay the debts.

ii. **Implied Authority:** In the case of a joint Hindu family business, Karta has the implied authority to bind all members for his/her Act. Thus, they have to face the impact of his/her wrongdoings.

iii. **Female Members**: Female members of the family have restricted rights in the ownership of the business. They are not treated at par with their male counterparts. They can get ownership only under certain circumstances. However, under the Dayabhaga system, they have more rights as compared to the Mitakshara system, where they can get the rights on the death of male coparceners.

9. Give the important advantages of a Cooperative society.

Ans. The following are the important advantages of a cooperative society:

i. **Stability:** A cooperative society has a separate identity from its members and therefore has no impact on its working by entry or exit of any member. It has a perpetual life.

ii. **Limited liability**: The liabilities of the members are limited to the extent of the capital contributed by them. No charge is made against their wealth.

iii. **Open – membership**: Any person can be a member of the society provided s/he shares the common objectives and subscribe to the shares.

iv. **Smooth formulation**: Setting up a cooperative society is easy as any ten individuals can voluntarily form the society and get it registered.

v. **Social service**: Such societies are formed for providing monetary as well as nonmonetary help to their members and community.

10. Enlist three disadvantages of cooperative society business.

Ans. The following are the three disadvantages of co=operative society business:

i. **Inefficient Management:** The management of the business affairs of the society lacks efficiency as the members of the managing committee may not have business experience.

ii. **Absences of Motivation:** Members lack the motive to carry the business efficiently and effectively as there is no direct relationship between efforts and rewards.

iii. **Conflict among members:** There might be a possibility that groups are formed between the members. This leads to a problem when personal interests take over the common interest of society.

11. Enumerate the advantages of a company.

Ans. Running a business through a company has the following advantages:

i. **The pool of resources:** A company can tap on a large number of resources due to its form. It can raise funds either by issuing more shares or by issuing more debentures and hence can invest more in acquiring resources.

ii. **Limited Liability:** The liability of the shareholders is limited to the number of shares subscribed by them or by the amount of guarantee given by them.

iii. **Transferability of shares:** In the case of public companies, members can transfer their shares to others, which provides liquidity to an investment made by members.

iv. **Stability:** A company has a perpetual life, and its existence is not affected by the death or insolvency of any members.

v. **Future growth:** A company has better opportunities for expansion and growth because of a large amount of financial as well as non-financial resources.

vi. **Effective management:** Companies are led by individuals who have immense experience in running a business and are highly qualified.

12. Mention some of the disadvantages of company business.

Ans. Running a business through a company has the following disadvantages:

i. **Complex Formulation:** Setting-up, a company, is not an easy job. It requires time and effort. There are several compliances that have to be completed before a company is incorporated.

ii. **Rigidity:** A company has to function on the exact lines of the objectives decided in its memorandum of association and article of association. Hence, to deviate from the path, it has to take consent from its shareholders in its General Meetings.

iii. **Government interventions:** Since the interest of a large number of people is vested in the Company, their functioning is monitored by the Government.

iv. **Decision-making:** Companies have different levels of management working in a single organisation. This creates a hierarchy of communication, which often delays the decision.

13. Differentiate between an industrialist and an entrepreneur.

Ans. An industrialist is a person who owns and manages a large industrial unit/ company, whereas an entrepreneur is a person who makes a profit by starting a new venture or running businesses involving financial risks. Thus, all industrialists who manufacture goods may be called a businessman. The basic difference between industrialists and entrepreneurs is that an industrialist is a person involved in the ownership or management of an industrial unit, while an entrepreneur is a person who organises and operates a business and assumes much of the associated risk.

14. Write a short note on the Ministry of Skill Development and Entrepreneurship.

Ans. It started as a department of skill development and entrepreneurship but was transformed into a Ministry in 2014. The Ministry of Skill Development and Entrepreneurship (MSDE) is responsible for implementation and coordination of all skill development initiatives and efforts across the country, like removal of disconnect between demand and supply of skilled manpower, the building of a vocational and technical framework for training and skilling, implementation of training programs, sensitization of people on entrepreneurship and large execution of entrepreneurship development programs. National Skill Development Agency (NSDA), National Skill Development Corporation (NSDC), and National Skill Development Fund (NSDF) operate as functional arms of the ministry.

15. What is the objective of National Policy on Skill Development and Entrepreneurship 2015 (Pradhan Mantri Yuva Udyamita Vikas Abhiyan)?

Ans. The objective of this policy is to meet the challenge of skilling at scale with speed and standard, and it aims to provide an umbrella framework to all skilling activities being carried out within the country, for aligning them to common standards and link the skilling with demand centers. The objective of the entrepreneurship framework in the policy is to foster the growth of entrepreneurship across the country.

16. What are the aims of 'Start-Up India'?

Ans. The main aim of Start-up India is to encourage entrepreneurship among the youth of India. The 'Start-up India: Stand up India' promotes bank financing for start-ups and offers incentives to enhance entrepreneurship and job creation. This initiative aims to provide a new dimension to entrepreneurship and help in setting up a network of start-ups in the country.

17. What is Digital India?

Ans. Digital India is an important program of the Government of India with a vision to transform India into a digitally empowered society and sound economy. It is a campaign launched to ensure that the Government's services are made available to all citizens electronically by using improved online infrastructure and by improving the facility of Internet connectivity.

Figure 4.8: Digital India

18. How can society contribute towards the development of entrepreneurship?

Ans. The society also plays the following role in boosting entrepreneurship:

i. Creating needs and demands
ii. Enabling financial support
iii. Providing raw materials
iv. Facilitating networking
v. Creating a need for education
vi. Supporting infrastructural development

4.3.10 Long Answer Type Questions

1. Explain various types of business.

Ans. There are different types of businesses engaged in different sectors of the economy, but broadly they are classified as follows:

(i) Service: These are the businesses that deal with providing services, e.g., banking, transportation, accounting, education, healthcare, insurance, etc.

(ii) Product: These are the businesses that deal in the production of goods. Production of goods requires the conversion of raw material, labour, capital, and other resources into finished goods. These finished goods are then offered to the end-consumers, e.g., Apparel and accessories, automobiles, spare parts, etc.

There are two types of product-based businesses:

(a) Manufacturing businesses: These are the businesses that make one or more products in an industrial unit called a factory. Factories may have many people working together. It may be run on a small scale or on a large scale.

(b) Merchandising/Trading: These are the businesses that do not produce the goods themselves but purchase the goods for selling them to end-consumers. They act as the link between the producers and consumers. These entrepreneurs also transport the product from the factory to warehouses and then finally to shops near the customers. Some examples of such businesses are retail stores, departmental stores, and distributors.

(iii) Hybrid: Hybrid business is a mixture of two or more types of businesses. They are engaged in service as well as manufacturing businesses. They neither offer pure intangible nor pure tangible commodities. For example, in the case of restaurants, they provide services in the form of a dining experience and the food served is the product.

2. Differentiate between product business and service business.

Ans. The main differences between product and service business activities are given below:

Product Business	Service Business
i. The product can be seen and touched.	i. Service cannot be seen or touched.
ii. The customer pays for physical exchange.	ii. The customer here pays for an experience of things.
iii. A product can be prepared and stored in a a shop or a warehouse (usually).	iii. A service cannot be stored. Service is provided when a customer asks for it.
iv. A product can be either prepared at home Or in a factory. It can then be transported to	iv. A service cannot be prepared or transported. It is given to the customer at the time different places where shopkeepers sell it or deliver it.
v. The quality and quantity of the product be the same every time.	v. The quality and quantity of service will different at different times.

3. What are the different forms of business organisations based on the types of ownership? Explain.

Ans. Business organisations are classified under different forms based on their type of ownership, as given below:

(i) Sole proprietorship: A sole proprietorship is defined as a business having only a single owner. It is the most simple business. It does not require any registration and can be opened without any legal formalities.

(ii) Partnership: A partnership firm is a business entity owned and operated by two or more individuals to earn profits. A partnership firm is governed under the Indian Partnership Act, 1932, which states that "Partnership is the relation between persons who have agreed to share the profits of a business carried on by all or any of them acting for all" (Partnership Act). This relationship should be voluntary. Each individual in the firm is called "Partner," and collectively, it is called "Firm."

(iii) Joint Hindu Family Business (HUF): When the members of a joint Hindu family own and run a business entity, it is called Joint Hindu family Business or HUF. It is governed by 'Hindu Law' and is only prevalent in India. It is also known as 'Hindu Undivided Family Business' or HUF – business. There are two forms of Joint Hindu family business – the 'Mitakshara system,' which applies to the whole country except Bengal and Assam, where the 'Dayabhaga System' is prevalent. Under the Mitakshara system, any male member born in the family acquires the right of ownership in the ancestral property, whereas, in the Dayabhaga system, a son can get the rights only after the death of his/her father.

(iv) **Cooperative Society:** According to the Indian Co-operative Societies Act, 1912, "Cooperative society is a society which has the objective of promoting the economic interests of its members following cooperative principles. It is a voluntary organisation of individuals to promote a common interest. The minimum number of persons required to form a cooperative society is 10. Cooperative societies can get themselves registered with the Registrar of Cooperative Societies in the State where their registered office is situated.

However, registration is not mandatory, but a registered society has more benefits than an unregistered society. A cooperative society enjoys the status of a separate legal entity and has perpetual succession and a common seal. A registered cooperative society enjoys the benefits of tax exemption.

(v) **Joint-Stock Company:** A Joint-Stock company is a form of voluntary association governed under The Companies Act, 2013. As per The Companies Act, 2013, "Company means a company formed and registered under this/her Act or an existing company. An existing company means a company formed and registered under any of the previous Companies Acts." Hence, it can be noted that the registration of the Company is mandatory. A company is an organisation of individuals or a group of individuals to undertake some industrial, trading or commercial activity with a motive for earning profits. The Company's capital is fixed under its Memorandum of Association and is divided into several shares. A company has a separate legal entity, perpetual life, and a common seal. The liabilities of the members of the Company can be –

- Limited by shares
- Limited by guarantee or
- Unlimited.

There are two kinds of companies – Private companies and public companies.

(a) A private company is a company whose shares are non-transferable and are not issued to the general public.

(b) A public company is a company that is not a private company. In public companies, shares are transferable and issued to the general public through invitation. The minimum number of members for a private company is two, and the maximum number is 200 persons, whereas in a public company, a minimum number of members are seven people, and there is no limit for maximum members (COMPANIES ACT, 2013).

4. Discuss the types of entrepreneurs.

Ans. The entrepreneurs have been classified into different types based on the qualities and work culture they adopt. Although there are various classifications, the most popular has been given by Clarence Danhof. He provided four types of entrepreneurs:

i. **Innovative entrepreneurs:** These are the entrepreneurs who take the route of innovation for their enterprise. They believe in creating a new product, adding to an existing product, introducing a new process or technique, or creating a new market for his/her product or service. Innovation is the process of commercializing a new invention. Entrepreneurship involves innovation and not invention.

ii. **Imitative or Adoptive entrepreneurs:** These are the entrepreneurs who adopt the already introduced innovations of innovative entrepreneurs. They do not innovate anything themselves, but they imitate successful innovations. Such a type of entrepreneur is found in developing countries where resources are scarce to innovate things on their own.

iii. **Fabian entrepreneurs**: These are the entrepreneurs who prefer to change things only in circumstances when they are incurring losses. They do not like facing risks and resist changing anything about their business. They will only adopt new things when they are sure that by not doing so, they will suffer loss.

iv. **Drone entrepreneurs**: These are the entrepreneurs who will not change under any circumstances, even if they are incurring losses. They follow the traditional methods of business and do not asapt any change at all.

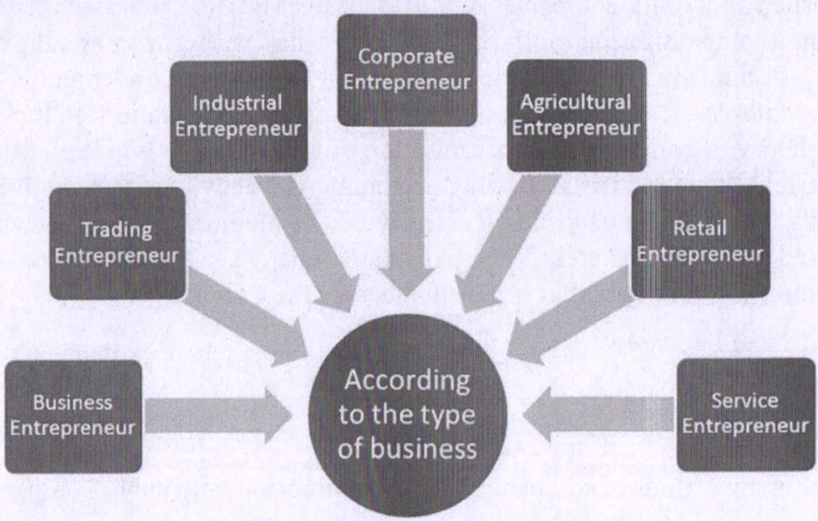

Figure 4.9: Types of entrepreneurs

5. Differentiate between Entrepreneur and Entrepreneurship.

Ans. The difference between entrepreneur and entrepreneurship is given below:

Entrepreneur	**Entrepreneurship**
(i) Person	(i) Process
(ii) Organiser	(ii) Organisation
(iii) Innovator	(iii) Innovation
(iv) Risk- bearer	(iv) Risk-bearing
(v) Motivator	(v) Motivation
(vi) Creator	(vi) Creation
(vii) Visualiser	(vii) Vision
(viii) Leader	(viii) Leadership
(ix) Imitator	(ix) Imitation

6. Explain the objectives of Entrepreneurship Development.

Ans. The objectives of Entrepreneurship development are as follows:

i. Creating a business environment that is suitable for entrepreneurship.

ii. Educating the entrepreneurs about the process of entrepreneurship,

iii. Adjusting the rules and policies for helping new enterprises established in the dynamic economy,

iv. Providing some incentives, tax benefits, and subsidies to new enterprises,

v. Training the entrepreneurs for developing the required skills for running the business,

vi. Increasing the rate of investments in research and development,

vii. Providing financial assistance from institutions,

viii. Aiding in the availability of technology or providing rebates in purchasing raw materials,

ix. Ensuring the infrastructure is adequate for entrepreneurial activities,

x. Developing the motivational needs of entrepreneurs to maintain the quality of entrepreneurial activities.

xi. Helping entrepreneurs in learning the skills required for managing the enterprise,

xii. Helping the entrepreneurs in creating a business plan,

xiii. Providing incubation for new ideas.

7. Enlist and explain the important characteristics of entrepreneurs.

Ans. Every entrepreneur deals in his/her unique way, but the following qualities are found common in all successful:

i. Leadership: Capacity to lead a team

ii. Innovativeness/Initiative: Ability to initiate new plans

iii. Goal-Oriented: Self-motivated to set his goals

iv. Risk Taking: Ability to take risks

v. Highly optimistic: With a positive attitude to see the brighter part.

vi. Motivation: Ability to motivate the team

vii. Creative: Full of new ideas and plans

viii. Self-confident: Having confidence and trust in himself/herself

ix. Decision maker: Ability to make correct decisions

x. Action-Oriented: Ability to take actions after proper planning

xi. Dynamic agent: Capable of changing the scene by proper actions

xii. High achiever: Capable of achieving higher goals

8. Explain the objectives of entrepreneurship development.

Ans. The following are the important objectives of entrepreneurship development:

i. Providing incubation and acceleration to new ideas

ii. Providing financial assistance from banks
iii. Assisting entrepreneurs who are undergoing the process of entrepreneurship.
iv. Developing the motivational needs of entrepreneurs
v. Helping in the availability of technology or raw material
vi. Helping aspiring entrepreneurs start and grow a dynamic business.
vii. Imparting training to entrepreneurs
viii. Supporting entrepreneurs in creating effective business plans
ix. Encouraging research and development across industries
x. Providing incentives, subsidies, and tax relief benefits to new enterprises

9. How are entrepreneurs contributing to the developmental process of society? Explain.

Ans. An entrepreneur performs the following roles to help society:

i. **Improving Quality in Life by Sharing of Wealth:** Wealth may be defined as having enough money to live a comfortable life. Because entrepreneurs grow their business, the people working for them and in related businesses also grow. They have more money to live a quality life.

ii. **Fulfilling Customer Needs**: Demand may be defined as a product or service that people want. Entrepreneurs search and research what people want. Then, they use their creativity to nurture a business idea that will meet that particular demand. Example: During the time of COVID19, many entrepreneurs started the manufacturing of low-cost masks and sanitizers because these items were required for the safety of people.

iii. **Helping society:** Entrepreneurs make profits through activities that benefit society, and hence, they have a positive relationship with society. Many entrepreneurs work towards saving the environment by making bio-degradable products; some start schools and hospitals for the weaker section of society.

iv. **Using Local Resources and Materials**: Entrepreneurs use the material and people available locally to make their manufacturing cost of the products low and to supply the products at reasonable prices to society.

v. **Creating Jobs:** With the growth of a business, entrepreneurs employ more people to help them, and they buy more material from more people. They create jobs and also hire more people to work for their venture. Thus, more people get jobs.

vi. **Lowering Price of Products:** As the entrepreneurs are using the materials and resources available locally for manufacturing their products, the price of the product goes down. Moreover, when a large number of entrepreneurs do the same business, the cost of products goes down. For example, when more mobile phones are getting sold in India, the price of the mobile became lesser.

10. "Entrepreneurship plays a variety of roles in society." Justify the statement.

Ans. Entrepreneurship plays the following roles:

i. It enhances the living standards of people.
ii. It aids the effective utilization of local resources.

iii. It increases productivity through technical and other innovative approaches.

iv. It helps in transforming the economy.

v. It involves a strategic role in commercializing new products and inventions.

vi. It creates employment opportunities by developing new enterprises.

vii. It aids the transfer of technology.

viii. It creates new markets for enabling expansion into global markets.

ix. It drives the industries forward by bringing in innovative products.

11. Describe the tasks of an entrepreneur.

Ans. An entrepreneur has to perform the following tasks:

i. **Creating a New Method, Idea, or Product:** An entrepreneur is always trying new ideas to create things. He/she does this to increase his/her importance and income.

ii. **Making Effective Decisions**: An entrepreneur makes many decisions each day as per his daily planning/weekly planning/monthly planning/ annual planning. This may include what to produce or sell, how much and where to sell, etc.

iii. **Managing the Business**: An entrepreneur makes futuristic plans for his/ her business. Through this process, he/she arranges raw material, hires people for work, and tells everyone what to do. He/she also checks if the plan is being followed.

iv. **Taking Risk:** Risk is defined as the chance of something going wrong. All entrepreneurs take risks against fires, lost items, theft, etc.

v. **Dividing Income**: The Entrepreneur divides business profit money into many groups. He/she spends money to buy raw materials, pays rent of the building, salaries to people, etc.

12. Explain the advantages of entrepreneurship.

Ans. Following are the advantages of entrepreneurship:

i. **Work satisfaction**: One can choose the work he/she like to do, use their strengths and skills, and follow their own style of working and doing things. This can result in more work satisfaction.

ii. **Excitement**: Entrepreneurship may be exciting as many entrepreneurs find their work highly enjoyable. Each day is filled with new hopes and opportunities to challenge one's abilities, skills, and determination.

iii. **Freedom**: It gives freedom to work whenever they want, wherever they want, and however they want, draws many people. Most entrepreneurs don't consider their work as actual work because they are doing something they love.

iv. **Flexibility**: Entrepreneurs may schedule their work hours around other commitments, including spending quality time with their families.

v. **Rational salary**: As an entrepreneur, one's income is directly related to their efforts and the success of the business.

13. What are the main disadvantages/limitations of entrepreneurship?

Ans. Following are the main disadvantages/limitations of entrepreneurship:

i. **No regular salary**: Being an entrepreneur means giving up the security of a regular paycheque. If business slows down, one's personal income can be at risk.

ii. **No Set Work schedule**: The work schedule of an entrepreneur may be unpredictable. A major disadvantage for an entrepreneur is that it requires more work and longer hours than being an employee.

iii. **Administration**: While making all the decisions that can be taken as a benefit, it may also be taken as a burden. Becoming an entrepreneur involves a lot of paperwork that can take up time and energy.

iv. **Loneliness:** He/she will be lonely and scared to be completely responsible for the success or failure of his/her business.

v. **Competition:** Staying competitive in the market is critical as a small business owner. One needs to differentiate their business from others in order to build a solid customer base and be profitable.

4.3.11 HOTS QUESTIONS

1. Why should a cooperative society be registered?

Ans. Registration of a cooperative society is not mandatory, but a registered society has more benefits than an unregistered society. A cooperative society enjoys the status of a separate legal entity and has perpetual succession and a common seal. A registered cooperative society enjoys the benefits of tax exemption. That's why a cooperative society is to be registered.

2. Why are entrepreneurs important in the economic process of the country?

Ans. Entrepreneurs are associated with the following important tasks in the economic development process of the country:

i. Free market evolution is encouraged by entrepreneurs.

ii. Efficiency improvements is initiated by entrepreneurs.

iii. New values are developed and nurtured in the market for professional growth.

iv. Entrepreneurs act as catalyst for bringing prosperity to society.

v. Promoters of research and development for fostering economic development.

3. How can entrepreneurship create an impact on society?

Ans. Entrepreneurship has the following impact on society:

i. It fosters creativity.

ii. It accelerates economic growth.

iii. It encourages the welfare of society.

iv. It provides solutions to the problems of society.

v. It stimulates innovation and efficiency.

vi. It creates jobs and employment opportunities.

4. What steps are considered important for the entrepreneurial process?

Ans. The entrepreneurial process comprises six steps as mentioned below:

i. Deciding to become an entrepreneur

ii. Identifying and evaluating the opportunities

iii. Developing a business plan

iv. Determining the required resources

v. Converting the idea to an enterprise

vi. Managing and growing the enterprise

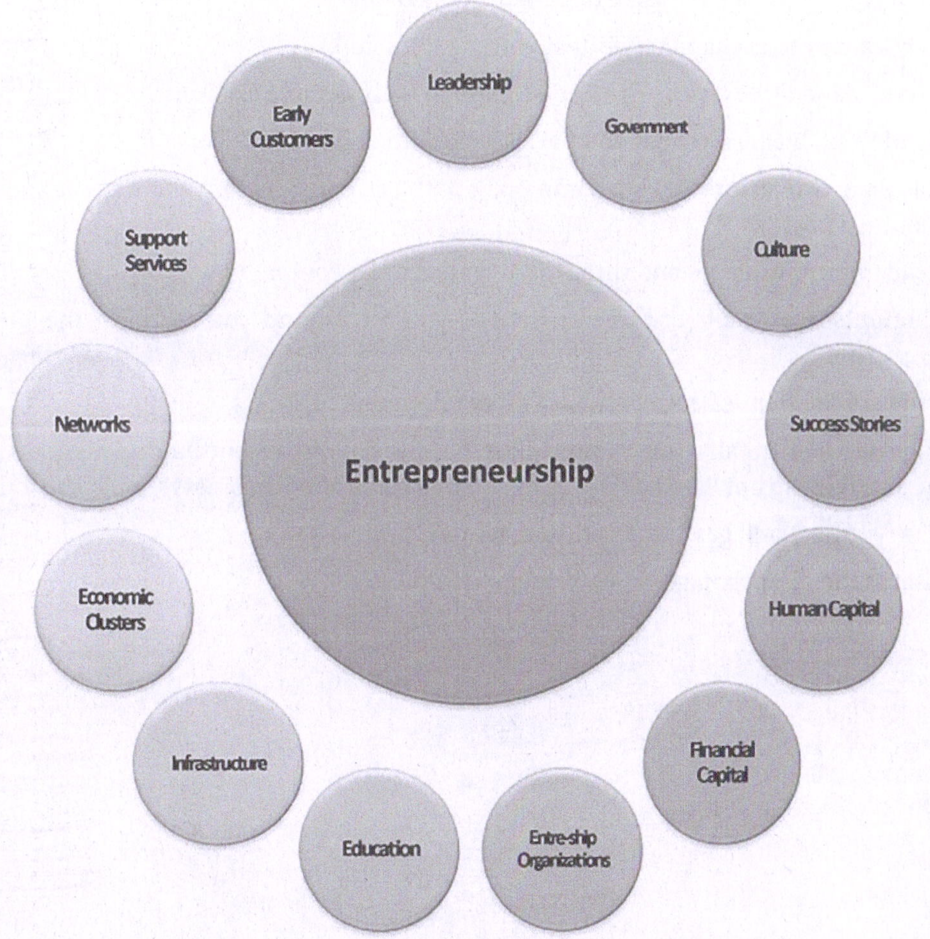

Figure 4.10

4.4 PRACTICE QUESTIONS

1. Define a hybrid business.
2. What do you mean by trading?
3. Differentiate between product business and the service business.
4. Define a joint-stock company.
5. What is solo-proprietorship?
6. What do you mean by rigidity concerning a company?
7. What is a cooperative society?
8. What is HUF?
9. What do you mean by entrepreneurship?
10. List any two characteristics of daily wage employment.
11. Mention any four characteristics of entrepreneurship.
12. What are the three types of business? Explain with suitable examples.
13. Mention six businesses that you have seen around you.
14. Name any two factors that are common to both entrepreneurship and wage employment on a contract basis.
15. Write three advantages and three disadvantages of a company?
16. Mention some details of three businesses you see around you and how they are run by people?
17. What are the steps of entrepreneurship development? Discuss.
18. Suppose Laxmi Sinha runs a hotel, but his customers are not buying his food products because they do not like the flavour of it. What steps of the business should she follow next?
19. Clarify the advantages and disadvantages of HUF.
20. Discuss the disadvantages of entrepreneurship.

Green Skills

5.1 UNIT IN BRIEF

- The environment around us affects our life.
- A resource may be defined as any natural or artificial substance, energy, or organism, which is used by human beings for their welfare.
- Natural resources fall under the four main categories: Inexhaustible, exhaustible, renewable, and non-renewable.
- When harvesting of resources exceeds their reproduction or replenishment, it results in overexploitation.

Figure 5.1

- Deforestation is defined as the clearance of a forest or stands of trees where the land is converted to a non-forest use.
- Sustainable development is defined as 'development that meets the needs and requirements of the present generations without compromising the ability of future generations to meet their own needs.'
- The Sustainable Development Goals (SDGs) are a set of goals for a universal call to take action to end poverty, protect the planet, and ensure that all people enjoy peace and prosperity.
- The Green Economy is defined as the economy that results in improved human wellbeing and social equity while significantly reducing environmental risks and ecological scarcities.
- The skills used for promoting Green Economy are known as green skills.
- Green skills are also termed as skills for sustainability.

- Sustainable development is defined as the economic development that is conducted without the depletion of natural resources.
- Green skills are defined as the technical skills, knowledge, values, and attitudes required in the workforce to develop and support sustainable social, economic, and environmental outcomes in business, industry, and the community.
- Article 48-A of the Indian Constitution empowers the state to take action for protecting and improving the natural environment and safeguarding the forests and wildlife of the country.
- The natural world, like the land, air, and water, in which people, animals, and plants live, is called the environment.
- There are three types of environments- Natural, industrial, and social environment.
- The natural environment encompasses all living and non-living things occurring naturally.
- The interaction of society with the environment sometimes affects the ecological balance in the environment.
- With the increase in population and economic activities, people's interference with nature has started destroying the environment.
- Industrial development and intensive agriculture that provide the goods for our increasingly consumer-oriented society consume large amounts of natural resources, like water, minerals, petroleum products, wood, etc.
- A resource is defined as any natural or artificial substance, energy, or organism that is used by human beings for their welfare.
- The environment, climate change, safe operation, people, ethics and transparency, and innovation and technology are known as the six pillars of the 'Green economy.'
- Ever since the earth was inhabited, all living organisms depended on things that existed freely in nature for their survival.
- The things available freely in nature include water, land, soils, rocks, forests, animals, fossil fuels, and minerals. These resources are called natural resources as they are the basis of life on earth.
- Natural resources may be consumed by organisms directly or indirectly.
- Some of the human activities, which cause damage to the environment, are overexploitation of resources, pollution, deforestation, mining, destruction of natural habitats, construction, etc.
- The resources that have been developed by human beings during the growth of civilisation, are called artificial resources. For example, biogas, thermal electricity, plastics, etc.
- The term 'Green economy' was first used in 1989 by a pioneering committee in a report entitled 'Blueprint for a Green Economy 'for the UK government; the committee consisted of environmental economists.
- A green economy must be not only efficient but also fair. Fairness implies recognizing global and country-level equity dimensions, particularly in assuring a just transition to an economy that is low-carbon, resource-efficient, and socially inclusive.
- Green Economy is the economy in which growth in income and employment should be taken off by public and private investments(PPP model), and it ensures the reduction in carbon emissions

and pollution, enhance energy and resource efficiency and prevent the loss of biodiversity and ecosystem services.

- Sustainable development is defined as the development that satisfies the needs of the present generations without compromising the capacity of future generations, ensuring the balance between economic growth, care for the environment, and social wellbeing.
- Sustainable Development Goals (SDGs) are also termed the Global Goals.
- Sustainable Development Goals are a set of goals for a universal call for action to end poverty, protect the planet, and ensure that all people enjoy peace and prosperity.
- Conservation is defined as the proper management of a natural resource to prevent its exploitation, destruction, or degradation.
- Conservation is the total of activities, which can derive benefits from natural resources but at the same time prevent excessive use, which may lead to destruction or degradation.
- The green economy combines together a vast area of policies and research, and many of the issues are linked together.
- The private sector is a key player in strengthening city governance; the private sector has the innovation potential to develop solutions that fit the new urban challenges.
- The projects which are initiated to manufacture products or to do something to save the environment are called green projects.

Figure 5.2

5.2 CBSE/NCERT SECTION (SOLVED CBSE/NCERT EXERCISES)

5.2.1 Multiple Choice Questions

1. What are some of the environmental changes caused due to modern methods of agriculture?

   a) Chemical pollution due to fertilisers

b) Improvement in the environment

c) Lower air pollution due to crops

d) Decrease in forest areas

2. How can we conserve our health and environment?

a) Grow organic crops
b) Use natural fertilisers
c) Manage wastewater
d) Use more air conditioning

3. Which of the following is an example of renewable resources?

a) Coal
b) Solar Energy
c) CNG
d) Petroleum

4. Which of the following options describe a green economy correctly?

A green economy __________________.

a) uses fewer resources
b) uses more resources
c) wastes fewer items
d) wastes more items

5. Steel factory burns firewood and charcoal for heating and melting the steel? What are the possible effects on the environment?

a) Increase in global temperature
b) Decrease in global temperature
c) Increase in water pollution
d) Decrease in air pollution

ANSWERS
1. (a) 2. (b) 3. (b) 4. (c) 5. (a)

5.2.2 Short Answer Type Questions

1. What are the five sources of energy available to us?

Ans. The following examples are sources of energy:

i. Solar energy
ii. Hydropower
iii. Wind energy
iv. Geothermal energy
v. Nuclear energy
vi. Biofuel energy
vii. Tidal energy

2. What are the sources of pollution?

Ans. The main sources of pollution are human activities, excessive misuse of natural resources, uncontrolled population growth, deforestation, and rapid industrialisation.

3. What are green skills?

Ans. Green skills are defined as the technical skills, knowledge, values, and attitudes required in the workforce to develop and support sustainable social, economic, and environmental outcomes in business, industry, and the community.

4. Give two examples of green skills that you can start learning from now.

Ans. Self-Awareness, Critical thinking, empathy, social responsibility.

5. Write any three actions which you can take to conserve energy.

Ans. i. Switching off the lights and fans when not required.

ii. Using CFL /LED in place of bulbs.

iii. Using pressure cooker in place of simple container for preparing food.

6. Describe any three methods of water conservation.

Ans. The following are the methods for water conservation:

i. Careful use of water in our day-to-day life to avoid wastage is to be promoted.

ii. Sewage and Industrial wastes (effluents) should be treated, and only the treated and clear water should be released into the rivers.

iii. Rainwater harvesting should be encouraged for storing rainwater and recharging groundwater.

7. What is the purpose of soil conservation?

Ans. The purpose of soil conservation is to stop/check soil erosion and improve soil fertility by adopting various methods.

8. State any three ways by which we can save energy.

Ans. i. Cleaning the dust from the tube lights to get more light,

ii. Regular servicing and maintenance of home appliances

iii. Switching off lights and devices when not in use.

9. Classify the following under the three respective categories of natural resources: Air, iron, sand, petroleum, wind, clay, fish, forest, gold, pearls.

i. Inexhaustible

ii. Renewable

iii. Non- renewable

Ans. These are classified as follows:

i. Inexhaustible- Air, wind,

ii. Renewable – Air, wind, sand

iii. Non- renewable- forest, iron, petroleum, fish, pearls, clay,

10. What does conservation of energy mean? (Choose all options that apply)

(a) Saving energy (b) Producing energy

(c) Using energy efficiently (d) Creating energy sources

Ans. (a) and (c)

11. Which of the following are non-renewable resources? (Choose all options that apply)

(a) Coal (b) Diesel (c) Sun (d) Water

Ans. (a) and (b)

Figure 5.3

5.3 SOLVED EXERCISES

5.3.1 Multiple Choice Questions

1. ____________ skills are defined as the technical skills, knowledge, values, and attitudes required in the workforce to develop and support sustainable social, economic, and environmental outcomes in business, industry, and the community.

   a) Soft b) Hard c) Green d) Creative

2. The resources that have been developed by human beings during the growth of civilisation, are called ____________ resources. For example, biogas, thermal electricity, plastics, etc.

   a) Natural b) Artificial

   c) Both a and b d) None of the above

3. Which of the following R's is not part of Three R's principle?

   a) Reuse b) Reproduce c) Reduce d) Recycle

4. What is the combination of sustaining and boosting the economy, environment, and social welfare?

   a) Green Skills b) Green Economy c) Environment d) Resource

5. Which international organisation has launched the Sustainable Development Goals?

   a) UNEP b) AEC c) UNO d) UNICEF

6. Which of the following is an example of an exhaustible resource of energy?

   a) Wind energy b) Solar energy c) Hydro energy d) Coal energy

7. When was the United Nations Commission on Environment and Development (UNCED) created?

   a) 1973 b) 1983 c) 1993 d) 2003

8. Which one of the following is a man-made resource?

   a) Forest b) Pond c) Airways d) Air

9. Which of the following consists of the living organisms that reciprocally take advantages and benefits from each other?

   a) Ecosystem b) Culture
   c) Green skills d) Natural resource

10. WCED stands for:

    a) World Committee on Environment and Development
    b) World Commission on Environment and Development
    c) Weird Commission on Environmental Detoxification
    d) None of the above

11. Which factor is not responsible for causing soil erosion?

    a) Uncontrolled runoff of surface water
    b) Grazing of land
    c) Deforestation
    d) Improper farming techniques

12. The United Nations formed the World Commission on Environment and Development. This commission is also known as:

    a) Huxley Commission b) Brundtland Commission
    c) Geneva Commission d) Tom and Hillary Commission

13. Which is not a benefit from the green economy?

    a) Reduce waste and inefficiency b) Environmentally-friendly
    c) Create a white job d) Generate healthful society

14. Which of the following ministries is not considered the key stakeholders of the Green economy?

    a) Ministry of Environment and Forests
    b) Ministry of Energy and natural resources
    c) Ministry of Home
    d) Ministry of Economic and Natural Resources

15. Which of the following is considered the key stakeholders of the Green economy?

    a) Environmental protection and Natural resources committee,
    b) Economic policy committee,
    c) An international organisation like the International Centre for Environmental Research and Economic vision, the Union for Sustainable Development.
    d) All of the above

16. According to the UNO, which of the following options is not a sustainable development goal?
    a) Clean Water and Sanitation
    b) Population
    c) Gender Equality
    d) No poverty
17. What is described by using the term development?
    a) Political goals
    b) Economic progress
    c) Social justice
    d) Political goals and economic progress
18. What is the process of building sensitivity towards all cultures and celebrating diversity called?
    a) Social inclusion
    b) Cultural diversity
    c) Cultural inclusion
    d) Environmental protection
19. Which of the following form the important components of an ecosystem?
    a) Energy and air
    b) Water and soil
    c) Land, air, and water
    d) both (a) and (b)
20. Sustainable development is a long-term, ____________ approach to development.
    a) Integrated
    b) Inclusive
    c) Exclusive
    d) Submissive
21. Which report was issued in 1987, which highlighted that equity, growth, and environmental maintenance are simultaneously possible?
    a) The Brundtland Report
    b) Future of Earth
    c) Stockholm Report on Environment
    d) None of the above
22. Which country became first to complete the Sustainable Developmental Goals in the world?
    a) Norway
    b) Sweden
    c) USA
    d) Switzerland
23. Which of the following statements are related to sustainable development?
    i. Use of digital media instead of paper
    ii. Deforestation
    iii. Use of energy-saving devices like LED.
    iv. Use of drip irrigation
    v. The practice of crop rotation

    a) (ii) (iii) (iv)
    b) (ii)(iii)(iv)(v)
    c) (iii) (iv) (v)
    d) All of these
24. Which statement is related to the promotion of sustainable development?
    a) Use of hybrid cars instead of conventional cars to reduce air pollution
    b) Use of biofuels (biogas in the kitchen)

c) Treatment of Industrial waste and sewage before releasing in the water bodies

d) All of the above

25. Which of the following is included in the six pillars of 'Green Economy'?

a) Climate change
b) Safe operation
c) Ethics and transparency
d) All the above

26. Which of the following is not included in the components of a 'Green Economy'?

a) Renewable energy
b) Ethics and transparency
c) Green Building
d) Sustainable transport

27. Which of the following is not included in Sustainable development?

a) Reducing excessive use of natural resources,
b) Enhancing natural resource conservation,
c) Scientific management of renewable resources, especially bio-resources
d) None of the above

28. Suppose Harendra has more than 50 acres of agricultural land and is using soil conservation techniques. Soil conservation is useful for:

a) Maintenance of soil fertility
b) Control on grazing
c) Contour ploughing
d) All the above

29. ____________ satisfies the needs of the present generations, and that's too without compromising the capacity of future generations, ensuring the balance between economic growth, care for the environment, and social wellbeing.

a) Sustainable development
b) Green development
c) Affordable development
d) None of the above

30. What was the name of the report released by the World Commission on Environment and Development in1987?

a) Future of Our Planet
b) Futuristic Approach towards Earth
c) Our Common Future
d) Brundtland's Final Report

31. How many are sustainable development goals (SDGs) approved by the United Nations?

a) 16
b) 17
c) 18
d) 19

32. Which one of the following is not an example of an abiotic resource?

a) Plants
b) Forest
c) Water
d) People

33. Deforestation is the clearance or removal of a forest or trees to convert the land for non-forest use, such as:

a) Mining
b) Agriculture
c) Construction of houses or developing industrial units
d) All of these

34. Which of the following is not included in India's Eight-Point Intended Nationally Determined Contribution towards Green Economy?
    a) To put forward and propagate a healthy and sustainable way of living based on traditions and values of conservation and moderation.
    b) To adopt a climate-friendly and cleaner path than the one followed hitherto by others at a corresponding level of economic development.
    c) To reduce the emissions intensity.
    d) None of the above
35. Which of the following is included in India's Eight-Point Intended Nationally Determined Contribution towards Green Economy?
    a) To achieve about 40 percent cumulative electric power installed capacity from non-fossil fuel-based energy resources by 2030
    b) To create an additional forest and tree cover by 2030.
    c) To better adapt to climate change by enhancing investments in development programmes in sectors like agriculture, water resources, the Himalayan region, coastal regions, health, and disaster management.
    d) All of the above
36. Which of the following features is not related to Green Economy?
    a) The transition from fossil fuels to renewable energy is the basis of the green economy.
    b) There are weak links between conserving nature and reducing poverty.
    c) Green energy promotes the steps required to avoid irreversible climate change.
    d) Re-focusing of the development model at the global level with increasing weight of economic sectors based on energy and the environment.
37. ________ Economy must be not only efficient but also fair. Fairness implies recognizing global and country-level equity dimensions, particularly in assuring a just transition to an economy that is low-carbon, resource-efficient, and socially inclusive.
    a) Capitalist b) Green c) Mixed d) Traditional

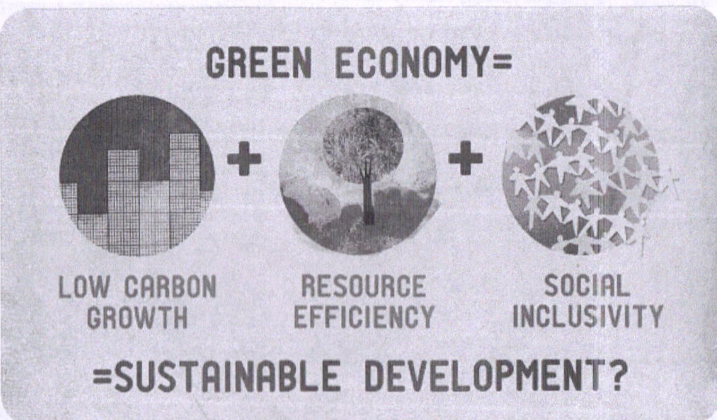

Figure 5.4

ANSWERS									
1. (c)	2. (b)	3. (b)	4. (b)	5. (c)	6. (d)	7. (b)	8. (c)	9. (a)	10. (b)
11. (a)	12. (b)	13. (c)	14. (c)	15. (d)	16. (b)	17. (d)	18. (b)	19. (d)	20. (a)
21. (a)	22. (b)	23. (c)	24. (d)	25. (d)	26. (b)	27. (d)	28. (d)	29. (a)	30. (c)
31. (b)	32. (c)	33. (d)	34. (d)	35. (d)	36. (b)	37. (b)			

5.3.2 Fill in the blanks

1. Article ____________ of the Indian Constitution empowers the state to take action for protecting and improving the natural environment and safeguarding the forests and wildlife of the country.
2. The SDGs have been adopted by 193 member countries of the ____________.
3. Vegetable waste, sewage waste, wood, cattle dung, agriculture waste, etc., are examples of ____________ pollutants.
4. Kitchen dry waste should be utilized to make compost that can be used as an ____________ fertilizer.
5. A ____________ aims to improve human wellbeing and social equity and also supports the environment and ecological system.
6. ____________ are the abilities, knowledge, and attitudes that are needed in the manpower to support economic, social, and environmental outcomes in the business and industry.
7. In 1987, the Brundtland Commission released the report entitled ____________.
8. There are ____________ Sustainable Development Goals (SDGs) were adopted by world leaders in 2015 in the Agenda 2030.
9. ____________ resources include living beings and organic material.
10. ____________ refers to fostering economic growth and development while ensuring that natural assets continue to provide the resources and environmental services.
11. The term 'ecology' was coined by German scientists ____________ in 1866.
12. The undesirable development has resulted in the depletion of the limited ____________ resources globally.
13. The contamination of the environment with harmful (toxic and poisonous) substances due to some natural phenomena and human activities is called environmental ____________.
14. The protection, restoration, preservation, and rational use of all the natural resources in the total environment is collectively known as natural resources ____________.
15. ____________ is defined as the economic development that is conducted without the depletion of natural resources.

ANSWERS			
1. 48-A	2. United Nations Organisation	3. biodegradable	
4. organic	5. green economy	6. Green skills	
7. Our Common Future	8. seventeen	9. Biotic	10. Green development
11. Ernst Haeckel	12. Non-renewable	13. pollution	14. conservation
15. Sustainable development			

5.3.3 True or False

1. The term 'Green economy' was first used in 1989 by a pioneering committee in a report entitled 'Blueprint for a Green Economy 'for the UK government; the committee consisted of environmental economists.
2. Ever since the earth was inhabited, all living organisms depended on things that existed freely in nature for their survival.
3. Careers in Green construction are related to constructing new Green (eco-friendly) buildings.
4. There is no need to conserve resources for future generations by using more environmentally friendly materials.
5. As per the concept of sustainable development, the environment and development are separable issues.
6. Conventionally, the environment was considered as a separate entity, detached from human emotion or action.
7. Green skills are defined as the technical skills, knowledge, values, and attitudes required in the workforce to develop and support sustainable social, economic, and environmental outcomes in business, industry, and the community.
8. The skills used for promoting a green economy are known as red skills.
9. Sustainable development may be defined as economic development that is conducted without the depletion of natural resources.
10. Green Economy is defined as the economy that results in the growth and development of social wellbeing and that also aims at improving the safety of the environment.
11. Sustainable development demotes prosperity and economic opportunity, greater social wellbeing, and protection of the environment.
12. In sustainable development, the objective of social inclusion is attained by creating high-quality development with accessible local services for the community.
13. The key to using resources in sustainable development is the optimum use of resources for the maximum benefit without wastage.
14. Green skills are also termed as skills for sustainability.
15. Sustainable development is defined as the development that satisfies the needs of the present generations without compromising the capacity of future generations, ensuring the balance between economic growth, care for the environment, and social wellbeing.

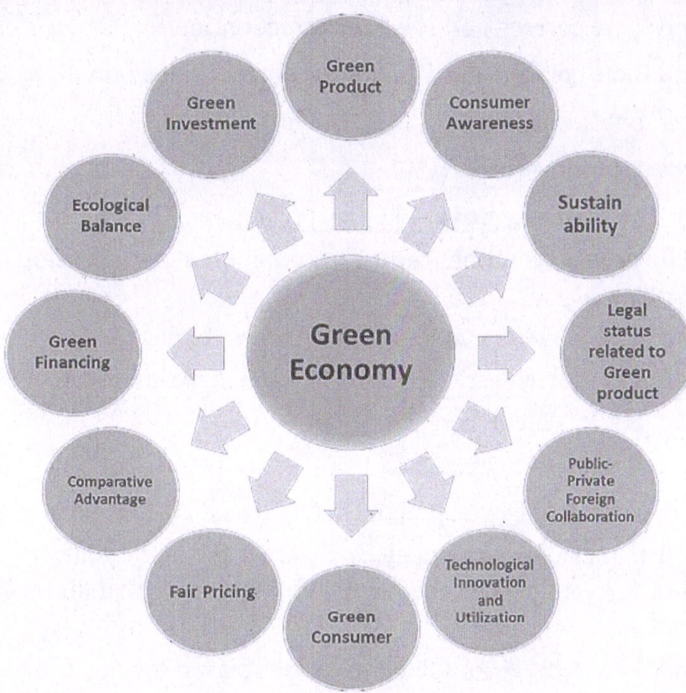

Figure 5.5

ANSWERS						
1. (T)	2. (T)	3. (T)	4. (F)	5. (F, inseparable)	6. (T)	7. (T)
8. (F, green skills)	9. (T)	10. (T)	11. (F, promotes)	12. (T)	13. (T)	14. (T) 15. (T)

5.3.4 Matching type

Match the SDG with the related field correctly.

SDG	Related Field
(i) No Poverty	(a) Actions to reduce inequality within and among countries
(ii) Zero Hunger	(b) Eradicating extreme poverty
(iii) Reduced Inequality	(c) Empowering all women and girls
(iv) Quality Education	(d) Achieving food security, and improved nutrition
(v) Gender Equality	(e) Free, equitable, and quality education

ANSWERS				
(i) -b	(ii) -d	(iii) -a	(iv) -e	(v) -c

5.3.5 Assertion Reason Type Questions

1. Assertion (A): Conservation is defined as the proper management of a natural resource to prevent its exploitation, destruction, or degradation.

   Reason (R): Conservation is the total of activities, which can derive benefits from natural resources but at the same time prevent excessive use, which may lead to destruction or degradation.

a) Both A and R are correct, and R is the correct reason for A.
b) Both A and R are correct, and R is not the correct reason for A.
c) A is correct, but R is incorrect.
d) A is incorrect, but R is correct.

2. Assertion (A): The private sector is a key player in strengthening city governance.
   Reason (R): The private sector has the innovation potential to develop solutions that fit the new urban challenges.
   a) Both A and R are correct, and R is the correct reason for A.
   b) Both A and R are correct, and R is not the correct reason for A.
   c) A is correct, but R is incorrect.
   d) A is incorrect, but R is correct.
3. Assertion (A): Sustainable Development Goals (SDGs) are also termed as the Global Goals.
   Reason (R): Sustainable Development Goals are a set of 20 goals for a universal call for action to end poverty, to protect the planet, and to ensure that all people enjoy peace and prosperity.
   a) Both A and R are correct, and R is the correct reason for A.
   b) Both A and R are correct, and R is not the correct reason for A.
   c) A is correct, but R is incorrect.
   d) A is incorrect, but R is correct.
4. Assertion (A): Green Economy is the economy in which growth in income and employment should be taken off by public and private investments (PPP model).
   Reason (R): Green economy ensures the reduction in carbon emissions and pollution, enhances energy and resource efficiency, and prevents the loss of biodiversity and ecosystem services.
   a) Both A and R are correct, and R is the correct reason for A.
   b) Both A and R are correct, and R is not the correct reason for A.
   c) A is correct, but R is incorrect.
   d) A is incorrect, but R is correct.
5. Assertion (A): Natural resources may be consumed by organisms directly only.
   Reason (R): Some of the human activities, which cause damage to the environment, are overexploitation of resources, pollution, deforestation, mining, destruction of natural habitats, construction, etc.
   a) Both A and R are correct, and R is the correct reason for A.
   b) Both A and R are correct, and R is not the correct reason for A.
   c) A is correct, but R is incorrect.
   d) A is incorrect, but R is correct.
6. Assertion (A): Natural resources are things that include water, land, soils, rocks, forests, animals, fossil fuels, and minerals.
   Reason (R): Natural resources are the basis of life on earth.

a) Both A and R are correct, and R is the correct reason for A.
b) Both A and R are correct, and R is not the correct reason for A.
c) A is correct, but R is incorrect.
d) A is incorrect, but R is correct.

7. Assertion (A): The environment was taken as a separate entity detached from human emotions or actions.

   Reason (R): Green economy is defined as the economy that results in improved human wellbeing and social equity by reducing environmental risks and ecological scarcities.

   a) Both A and R are correct, and R is the correct reason for A.
   b) Both A and R are correct, and R is not the correct reason for A.
   c) A is correct, but R is incorrect.
   d) A is incorrect, but R is correct.

8. Assertion (A): The principles of sustainable development are based on the integration of environmental, social, and economic concerns into all aspects of decision-making.

   Reason (R): The projects which are initiated to manufacture products or to do something by harnessing the environment are called green projects.

   a) Both A and R are correct, and R is the correct reason for A.
   b) Both A and R are correct, and R is not the correct reason for A.
   c) A is correct, but R is incorrect.
   d) A is incorrect, but R is correct.

9. Assertion (A): Green Economy is a boon to mankind.

   Reason (R): The Green Economy is the economy that results in improved human wellbeing and social equity and simultaneously reduces environmental risks and ecological scarcities significantly.

   a) Both A and R are correct, and R is the correct reason for A.
   b) Both A and R are correct, and R is not the correct reason for A.
   c) A is correct, but R is incorrect.
   d) A is incorrect, but R is correct.

10. Assertion (A): The soft economy is also defined as the economy that results in improved human wellbeing and social equity and simultaneously reduces environmental risks and ecological scarcities significantly.

    Statement 2: Economic development refers to giving people what they need without compromising their quality of life, especially in the developing world.

    a) Both A and R are correct, and R is the correct reason for A.
    b) Both A and R are correct, and R is not the correct reason for A.
    c) A is correct, but R is incorrect.
    d) A is incorrect, but R is correct.

ANSWERS									
1. (b)	2. (a)	3. (c)	4. (a)	5. (d)	6. (b)	7. (b)	8. (c)	9. (a)	10. (d)

5.3.6 Statements Based Questions

1. Statement 1: Sustainable development is defined as the economic development that is conducted without the depletion of natural resources.

   Statement 2: Article 48-A of the Indian Constitution empowers the state to take action the protect and improve the natural environment and safeguard the forests and wildlife of the country.

   a) Statement 1 is correct, but statement 2 is incorrect.

   b) Statement 1 is incorrect, but statement 2 is correct.

   c) Both the statements are correct.

   d) Both the statements are incorrect.

2. Statement 1: A resource is defined as any natural or artificial substance, energy, or organism that is used by human beings for their welfare.

   Statement 2: The environment, climate change, safe operation, people, ethics and transparency, and innovation and technology are known as the six pillars of the 'Red economy.'

   a) Statement 1 is correct, but statement 2 is incorrect.

   b) Statement 1 is incorrect, but statement 2 is correct.

   c) Both the statements are correct.

   d) Both the statements are incorrect.

3. Statement 1: The natural world, like the land, air, and water, in which people, animals, and plants live, is called the environment.

   Statement 2: There are three types of environments- Natural, industrial, and social environment.

   a) Statement 1 is correct, but statement 2 is incorrect.

   b) Statement 1 is incorrect, but statement 2 is correct.

   c) Both the statements are correct.

   d) Both the statements are incorrect.

4. Statement 1: Green skills are also known as global skills.

   Statement 2: With the increase in population and economic activities, people's interference with nature has started destroying the environment.

   a) Statement 1 is correct, but statement 2 is incorrect.

   b) Statement 1 is incorrect, but statement 2 is correct.

   c) Both the statements are correct.

   d) Both the statements are incorrect.

5. Statement 1: Industrial development and intensive agriculture that provide the goods for our increasingly consumer-oriented society consume fewer amounts of natural resources, like water, minerals, petroleum products, wood, etc.

Statement 2: Capitalist Economy combines together a vast area of policies and research, and many of the issues are linked together.

a) Statement 1 is correct, but statement 2 is incorrect.

b) Statement 1 is incorrect, but statement 2 is correct.

c) Both the statements are correct.

d) Both the statements are incorrect.

6. Statement 1: The natural environment encompasses all living and non-living things occurring naturally.

   Statement 2: The interaction of society with the environment sometimes affects the ecological balance in the environment.

   a) Statement 1 is correct, but statement 2 is incorrect.

   b) Statement 1 is incorrect, but statement 2 is correct.

   c) Both the statements are correct.

   d) Both the statements are incorrect.

7. Statement 1: The three objectives of sustainable development are economic growth, environmental protection, social inclusion, and cultural diversity.

   Statement 2: The skills used to demote a green economy are called green skills.

   a) Statement 1 is correct, but statement 2 is incorrect.

   b) Statement 1 is incorrect, but statement 2 is correct.

   c) Both the statements are correct.

   d) Both the statements are incorrect.

8. Statement 1: The objectives to achieve effective and sustainable development must be applied simultaneously, interacting with one another in a consistent and committed effort.

   Statement 2: Green skills are also known as skills for sustainability.

   a) Statement 1 is correct, but statement 2 is incorrect.

   b) Statement 1 is incorrect, but statement 2 is correct.

   c) Both the statements are correct.

   d) Both the statements are incorrect.

9. Statement 1: The principles of sustainable development do not require the integration of environmental, social, and economic concerns into all aspects of decision-making.

   Statement 2: Sustainable Development Goals (SDGs) are the collection of 17 global goals set by the United Nations General Assembly in 2015, which are to be achieved by the year 2030.

   a) Statement 1 is correct, but statement 2 is incorrect.

   b) Statement 1 is incorrect, but statement 2 is correct.

   c) Both the statements are correct.

   d) Both the statements are incorrect.

10. Statement 1; Clean drinking and usable water are called effluent.

    Statement 2: SDGs are not required for the welfare of people and the environment at all.

    a) Statement 1 is correct, but statement 2 is incorrect.

    b) Statement 1 is incorrect, but statement 2 is correct.

    c) Both the statements are correct.

    d) Both the statements are incorrect.

ANSWERS									
1. (c)	2. (a)	3. (c)	4. (b)	5. (d)	6. (c)	7. (a)	8. (c)	9. (b)	10. (d)

5.3.7 Competency-Based Questions

1. Suppose Sudipta Dey working with Council for Economic Affairs, was considering the following benefits of a type of economy:

    i. It makes the quality of life better.

    ii. It accelerates the development of new technologies.

    iii. The resource efficiency increases.

    iv. The environmental balance becomes harmonized.

    v. New economic commodities generate in conformity with the environment.

    All these benefits are related to:

    a) Capitalist Economy　　b) Green Economy

    c) Traditional Economy　　d) Mixed Economy

2. Which of the following actions is not required to save 'Marine Life'?

    a) Use natural light as much as possible.

    b) Reduce waste because most of the waste that we produce on land ends up in the oceans.

    c) Never buy bottled water; instead, use boiled and filtered water or stored rainwater.

    d) Stop using plastic bags because the wrong disposal of plastic is a major cause of marine pollution.

3. Suppose Prof DK Batra was explaining the main features of the importance of an economy that was as follows:

    i. It combines together a vast area of policies and research, and many of the issues are linked together:

    ii. There are strong links between conserving nature and reducing poverty.

    iii. Ideas about valuing nature could have a huge impact on how the environment is conserved.

    iv. New economic sectors based on the environment could change our use of nature and natural resources.

He was talking about:

a) Capitalist Economy

b) Socialist Economy

c) Green Economy

d) Mixed Economy

4. Suppose Navin Singhal is residing in a Smart City ZXV 2341 and is thinking to initiate the following actions:

   i. Use energy-efficient lights (LED bulbs) and appliances.

   ii. Use energy-saving and water-saving techniques.

   iii. Use biodegradable items.

   iv. Use natural light as much as possible.

   v. Save energy by switching off electrical appliances, like tube lights and fans, when these items are not used.

   The actions required for 'Sustainable Cities' are:

   a) (ii) (iii)

   b) (ii) (iii) (iv)

   c) (iii) (iv) (v)

   d) (ii) (iii) (iv) (v)

5. Which of the following is included in Sustainable development?

   i. Recycling and reuse of waste products/materials,

   ii. Recycling and reuse of waste products/materials,

   iii. Promoting afforestation/planting more trees,

   iv. Promoting green grassy patches between concrete buildings,

   v. Using more environmentally friendly material promoting products made of biodegradable material,

   vi. Use of environmental-friendly technologies based on the efficient use of resources.

   a) (i) (ii) only b) (iii) (iv) only

   c) (v) (vi) only d) All of the above

6. Consider the following human activities:

   i. Afforestation

   ii. Overexploitation of resources

   iii. Pollution

   iv. Using forest for making furniture and medicines

   v. Mining and destruction of natural habitats

   vi. Construction of buildings and infrastructure

Which of the above activities do cause damage to the environment?

a) (ii) (iii) only
b) (iii) (v) only
c) (ii) (iii) (iv) (v) (vi) only
d) All of these

Figure 5.6

ANSWERS					
1. (b)	2. (a)	3. (c)	4. (d)	5. (d)	6. (c)

5.3.8 VSA

1. Define Green Economy.

Ans. Green Economy is defined as the economy that aims at making issues of reducing environmental risks and ecological scarcities, and also that aims for sustainable development without degrading the environment.

2. Expand UNEP.

Ans. United Nations Environment Programme

3. Expand PAGE.

Ans. Partnership for Action on Green Economy (PAGE)

4. What is sustainable development?

Ans. Sustainable development may be defined as the development that ensures the needs of the present generation without compromising the needs of future generations too.

5. Define the relationship between environment and development.

Ans. Conventionally, the environment was considered a separate entity detached from human emotion or action, while development was a term used to describe both political goals and economic progress.

6. What are the main objectives of sustainable development?

Ans. The objectives of sustainable development are economic growth, environmental protection, social inclusion, and cultural diversity.

7. How do we achieve sustainable development?

Ans. The objectives to achieve effective and sustainable development must be applied simultaneously, interacting with one another in a consistent and committed effort.

8. On which points, the principles of sustainable development are based?

Ans. The principles of sustainable development are based on the integration of environmental, social, and economic concerns into all aspects of decision-making.

9. What are SDGs?

Ans. Sustainable Development Goals (SDGs) are the collection of 17 global goals set by the United Nations General Assembly in 2015, which are to be achieved by the year 2030.

10. When were SDGs implemented?

Ans. SDGs were implemented with effect from 1 Jan. 2016.

11. Define green economy.

Ans. The green economy is also defined as the economy that results in improved human wellbeing and social equity and simultaneously reduces environmental risks and ecological scarcities significantly.

12. What are green skills?

Ans. The skills used to promote a green economy are called green skills.

13. Define green projects.

Ans. The projects which are initiated to manufacture products or to do something to save the environment are called green projects.

14. What is the term used for 'skills for sustainability?

Ans. Green skills are also known as skills for sustainability.

15. Define economic development.

Ans. Economic development refers to giving people what they need without compromising their quality of life and damaging the environment, especially in the developing world.

16. What do you mean by potable water?

Ans. Clean drinking and usable water is called potable water.

17. What do you mean by forest conservation?

Ans. Forest conservation means the retention of existing forests or the creation of new forests at the levels prescribed by the State or local authorities.

18. What is important for the success of the forest conservation programme?

Ans. Participation of the community living in and around the forest is important for the success of the forest conservation programme.

19. Mention three types of environments.

Ans. Three types of environments include Natural, industrial, and social environments.

20. What do you mean by Green Skills?

Ans. Green skills are defined as the technical skills, knowledge, values, and attitudes required in the workforce to develop and support sustainable social, economic, and environmental outcomes in business, industry, and the community.

21. Which Article of the Indian Constitution empowers the state to take action for protecting and improving the natural environment and safeguarding the forests and wildlife of the country?

Ans. Article 48-A

22. Which major factor is responsible for the destruction of the environment?

Ans. With the increase in population and economic activities, people's interference with nature has started destroying the environment.

23. Why are natural resources depleting at a fast rate?

Ans. Industrial development and intensive agriculture that provide the goods for our increasingly consumer-oriented society consume large amounts of natural resources, like water, minerals, petroleum products, wood, etc.

24. Define resource.

Ans. A resource is defined as any natural or artificial substance, energy, or organism that is used by human beings for their welfare.

25. Why are natural resources called so?

Ans. Natural resources are called so because they are the basis of life on earth.

26. Who used the term 'Green Economy' the first time?

Ans. The term 'Green economy' was first used in 1989 by a pioneering committee in a report entitled 'Blueprint for a Green Economy 'for the UK government; the committee consisted of environmental economists.

27. What is the main condition for becoming an economy to Green Economy?

Ans. A green economy must be not only efficient but also fair. Fairness implies recognizing global and country-level equity dimensions, particularly in assuring a just transition to an economy that is low-carbon, resource-efficient, and socially inclusive.

28. What are global goals?

Ans. Sustainable Development Goals (SDGs) are also termed the Global Goals.

29. Why are SDGs known as Global Goals?

Ans. Sustainable Development Goals are a set of goals for a universal call for action to end poverty, protect the planet, and ensure that all people of the world enjoy peace and prosperity. That's why SDGs are called Global Goals.

30. Define conservation.

Ans. Conservation is defined as the proper management of a natural resource to prevent its exploitation, destruction, or degradation.

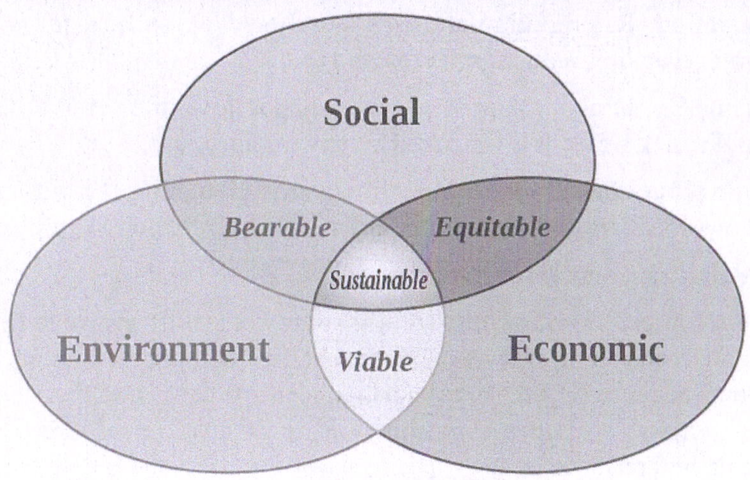

Figure 5.7

5.3.9 Short Answer Type Questions

1. What is the 4Rs concept used in environmental protection?

Ans. The protection of the environment is suggested by applying the concept of 4 Rs (reduce, recover, recycle, and reuse) in businesses. It encourages the use of technologies for keeping their carbon emissions low and defines the ways and means to protect ecosystems, air quality, integrity, and sustainability of our resources.

2. What are the three pillars of sustainable development?

Ans. Three pillars of sustainable development are economic development, social development, and environmental protection.

3. What does a school environment comprise of?

Ans. The physical environment of the school includes the school building and the classrooms, library, laboratories corridors, kitchen, toilets, garden, and also the playground. The sociocultural environment is manifested by the school, with climate teaching, by the teachers, student activities, inclusivity, attitude towards learning, social behaviour, discipline, respect for each other's caste, religion, and creed, the achievement of students, etc.

4. How do humans depend on forests directly?

Ans. Human beings depend directly on forests for food, biomass, health, recreation, and increased living comfort. Indirectly forests help in regulating climate, preventing flood, storm protection, and nutrient cycling.

5. How is soil conservation useful?

Ans. Soil conservation can be useful for the following:

i. **Maintenance of soil fertility**: The fertility of soil can be maintained by adding manure and fertilizers regularly. Moreover, the process of rotation of crops ensures the increased fertility of the soil.

ii. **Control on grazing:** Grazing should be controlled, and it may be allowed only in specified areas.

iii. **Reforestation:** Reforestation/afforestation should be encouraged as the planting of trees and vegetation reduces soil erosion.

iv. **Terracing:** Terracing is the process of dividing a slope into several flat fields to control the rapid run of water. It is practiced mostly in hilly areas.

v. **Contour ploughing**: Contour ploughing is the ploughing at right angles to the slope that allows the furrows to trap water and checks soil erosion by rainwater.

6. Define and illustrate renewable resources.

Ans. Renewable resources are those resources that are constantly available (like water) or can be reasonably replaced or recovered, like vegetative lands. Even though some renewable resources may be replaced, they may take many years to form, and that does not make them renewable. Renewable resources are some of the exhaustible resources that are naturally regenerated after consumption.

For example, Forest trees and plants, hydel power, solar energy, wind power, etc.

7. Discuss the components of a Green Economy.

Ans. A green economy includes the following components:

i. **Renewable Energy**: Renewable energy from renewable resources like wind, water, Sun, Earth, biomass, etc., are available in large quantities and cause less pollution. India is ranked amongst the top 10 countries for the production of renewable energy through solar, wind, and biomass.

ii. **Green Buildings**: Green buildings are buildings that cause minimum damage to the environment during their construction and operation. They use energy, water, and other resources wisely, with minimum waste.

iii. **Sustainable transport**: Sustainable means what is good for the economy as well as the future of the environment. A sustainable transport system will cost less, help more people to move quickly, and cause less or no damage to the environment.

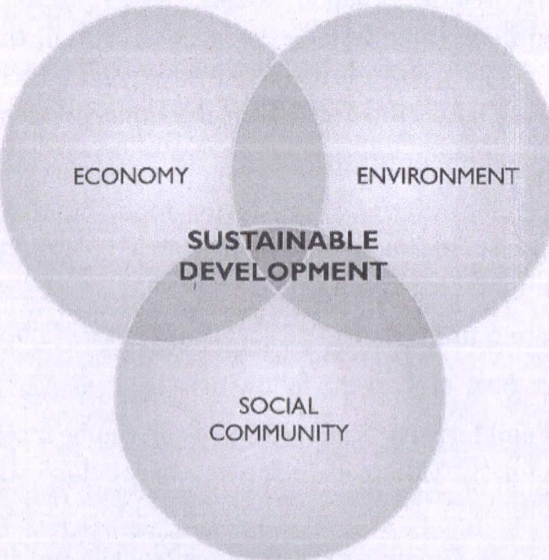

Figure 5.8

8. What do you mean by overexploitation?

Ans. When harvesting of resources exceeds their reproduction or replenishment, then it results in overexploitation. It means that when we exploit the species faster than the natural populations can recover, then it may result in the extinction of the species, thus affecting directly or indirectly the ecological cycle and our environment. For example, the removal of wild medicinal plants, excessive grazing of pastures by animals, destruction of forests and water aquifers.

9. How can we initiate conservation activities?

Ans. As a first step, we can conduct the resource audit to examine the consumption of the resources and accordingly take measures to conserve them. For example, for an energy use audit, we can examine the use of the air conditioning system, ventilation system, light system, and entry of sunlight into the room or the building.

10. What are the two main objectives of the Green economy?

Ans. The main two objectives of 'Green Economy' are:

i. To reduce environmental risks and ecological scarcities that aim for sustainable development without degrading the environment.

ii. To achieve efficiency in energy usage, to development of new environmental dependent business sectors such as food and tourism.

11. What is the role of the Government in the Green Economy?

Ans. The Government has an important role in setting policies that serve, advance, and protect the public's interest in transitioning towards an energy system that is more sustainable from both a supply and environmental standpoint. The Government can play a crucial role in helping to plug gaps by conducting research.

12. What are the major advantages gained by using 'Kulhads' in place of plastic cups on railway stations?

Ans. The major advantages gained by using 'Kulhads' in place of plastic cups on railway stations are as follows:

i. To reduce plastic waste,

ii. To reduce the cutting of trees for making paper cups.

iii. To create jobs for potters,

iv. To enhance contributions to the economy.

13. What actions are required from a responsible consumer?

Ans. A responsible consumer will take the following small acts:

i. Stop leakage in taps and pipes to avoid wasting water.

ii. Taking cloth bags to market for carrying fruits and vegetables.

iii. Reusing paper, glass, plastic, water, etc.

iv. Buying and eating seasonal fruits and vegetables from local farmers.

v. Donating things we do not use, such as clothes, books, furniture, food, etc.

vi. Sorting and treating garbage before properly disposing of it.

14. What is the main purpose of Sustainable Development Goals (SDGs)?

Ans. The 17 Sustainable Development Goals (SDGs) are a universal call of action from the United Nations to protect the planet, end poverty, and ensure that all people enjoy peace and prosperity. The Sustainable Development Goals (SDGs) have pre-decided targets that the countries have to should work towards and achieve by 2030.

15. Explain organic farming.

Ans. Organic farming is farming where farmers do not use chemical pesticides and fertilizers to enhance soil fertility and to increase their crop production. The farmers use organic and natural fertilizers, like cattle dung, to help in growing crops.

16. How is organic farming contributing towards sustainable development?

Ans. The use of organic and natural fertilizers during organic farming helps in better quality chemical-free crops and at the same time maintaining the soil quality for future use. This is an example of sustainable development in which humans are using the earth's resources, and at the same time, they are also preserving them for our future generations.

17. What are the three primary goals of Sustainable Development?

Ans. There are three primary goals of SD:

i. To minimize the depletion of natural resources while creating new developments.

ii. To provide methods to retrofit the existing developments to make them environmentally friendly facilities and projects.

iii. To create and promote a development that can be maintained and sustained without causing any further harm to the environment.

18. Explain recycling with suitable examples.

Ans. Recycling is defined as reusing some components of the waste having some economic value. Some materials, such as aluminum, copper, gold, silver, iron, etc., can be recycled many times. Metal, paper, glass, and plastics are recyclable. Plastic items are recycled to make new plastic products. Wet garbage includes most kitchen wastes, which can be used for preparing vermicompost. Most dry garbage is recyclable. Several innovative technological breakthroughs have recently been made to extract material from industrial waste. Non-toxic solid waste should be properly segregated and disposed of in landfills that are properly sealed to avoid leakage and contamination of surrounding land and groundwater.

19. Why are solar power and wind power called clean fuels?

Ans. When we use solar power, wind power, or hydropower, then the power generation process does not use cause pollution as it does not require the burning of non-renewable fuels, like coal, and hence, these are called clean fuels/energy sources. The use of biogas and hydro energy is also an eco-friendly alternative to natural gas.

20. What steps can be taken to reduce inequalities?

Ans. The following steps may be undertaken to reduce inequalities:

i. Behave in a friendly manner with everyone.

ii. Be helpful to one another.

iii. Include everyone while working or playing.

iv. Help others without any bias, whether they are small or big, girl or boy, belong to any class or caste.

21. Mention the six pillars of the Green Economy.

Ans. Six pillars of 'Green economy' are:

i. The environment,

ii. Climate change,

iii. Safe operation,

iv. People,

v. Ethics and transparency, and

vi. Innovation and technology.

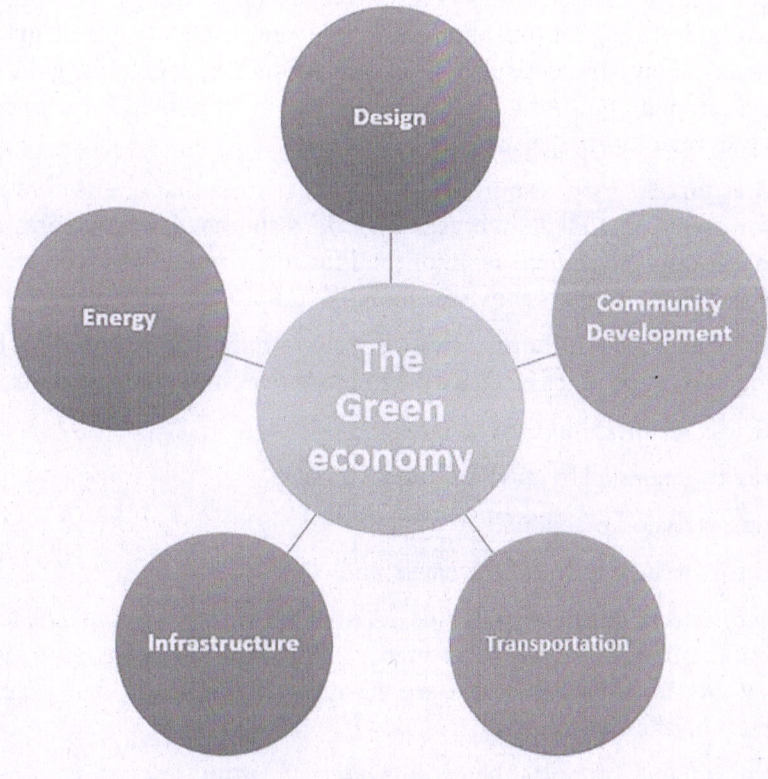

Figure 5.9

5.3.10 Long Answer Type Questions

1. Explain different types of natural resources.

Ans. Natural resources exist in many forms. It may be a solid, liquid, or gas. It may also be organic or inorganic. It may also be metallic or non-metallic.

i. **Land Resources**: Human beings thus, use the land as a resource for production as well as residence and recreation. It is a finite resource that is subject to agricultural and non-agricultural uses, such as infrastructure development.

ii. **Forest Resources**: A forest is a natural, self-sustaining community characterised by a vertical structure created by the presence of trees. Wood is used for making many items, like furniture, tool handles, railway sleepers, matches, ploughs, bridges, boats, etc., and as a source of energy for cooking purposes and for keeping warm. Tannins, gums, drugs, spices, insecticides, waxes, honey, horns, musk, ivory, hides, etc., are all provided by the flora and fauna of forests.

iii. **Water Resources**: Water covers about three-quarters of the earth's surface and is a necessary element for life. Water resources include rivers, lakes, oceans, and underground aquifers, etc. Water is a vital resource in agriculture, industrial, household, and recreational and environmental activities.

iv. **Mineral Resources**: A mineral deposit is defined as a concentration of naturally occurring solid, liquid, or gaseous material in the earth's crust, and such form and amount can be extracted and converted into useful materials or items in a profitable and economical manner. Mineral resources are non-renewable resources and include metals (e.g., iron, copper, and aluminium) and non-metals (e.g., salt, gypsum, clay, sand, phosphates). Some minerals consist of only a single element, like gold, silver, diamond (carbon), sulphur, etc., while some are present in combined form as compounds, like haematite (ore of iron), galena (ore of lead), etc.

v. **Food Resources**: Food resources are those resources that are used as food or provide food for organisms. Plants are used as food resources for herbivores and omnivores. Animals and birds are the source of food for many organisms who are carnivores and omnivores. Agriculture is the main source of crops (food resources) for human beings.

vi. **Energy Resources**: An energy resource is something that can produce heat, power life, move objects, or produce electricity. There are five fundamental sources of energy:

(a) Nuclear fusion in the Sun (solar energy),

(b) Gravity generated by the Earth and Moon,

(c) Nuclear fission reactions,

(d) Energy in the interior of the earth, and

(e) Energy stored in chemical bonds. Most of the energy we consume today is obtained from fossil fuels (stored solar energy). But fossils fuels have the disadvantage that they are non-renewable and are a source for causing other potentially harmful effects on the environment.

2. Explain with suitable examples the various types of natural resources.

Ans. Natural resources fall under the following main categories:

i. **Inexhaustible Resources**: The resources that cannot be exhausted by human consumption are known as inexhaustible resources. These resources include energy sources like solar radiation, wind power, hydel power, and tidal power, etc.

ii. **Exhaustible Resources**: These are the resources that are available in limited quantities and are going to be exhausted as a result of continuous consumption by human beings. For example, the coal and petroleum in the earth's crust are available in limited quantity only, and one day there may be no coal available for our use.

iii. **Renewable Resources**: Renewable resources are those resources that are constantly available (like water) or can be reasonably replaced or recovered, like vegetative lands. Even though some renewable resources may be replaced, they may take many years to form, and that does not make them renewable. Renewable resources are some of the exhaustible resources that are naturally regenerated after consumption. For example, Forest trees and plants that make a forest may be destroyed, but new ones grow in their place. But if the forest is cut down to get land for the construction of buildings, it is lost forever. Renewable energy sources are constantly replaced and are usually less polluting. Examples include hydropower (or hydel power), solar energy, wind power, and geothermal energy (energy from the heat inside the earth).

iv. **Non-renewable Resources**: Non-renewable resources are those resources that cannot easily be replaced once they are consumed. For example, fossil fuels, minerals, etc. Non-renewable resources can be called inorganic resources if they come from non-living things. For example, minerals, wind, land, soil, rocks, etc.

3. Explain the main human activities responsible for the degradation of the environment. Give suitable examples too.

Ans. The various human activities are damaging our earth and environment. Some of them are as follows:

i. **Overexploitation**: When harvesting of resources exceeds their reproduction or replenishment, then it results in overexploitation. It means that when we exploit the species faster than the natural populations can recover, then it may result in the extinction of the species, thus affecting directly or indirectly the ecological cycle and our environment. For example, the removal of wild medicinal plants, excessive grazing of pastures by animals, destruction of forests, and water aquifers, overfishing, and overhunting result in overexploitation of forests and natural habitats.

ii. **Mining**: Mines are dug below the earth's surface to get ores. The ores are then refined to extract valuable elements, such as metals, gems, minerals, etc. Some of the environmental impacts of mining are erosion, the formation of sinkholes, contamination of soil, groundwater, loss of biodiversity, pollution of surface water by chemicals from the mining processes, etc.

iii. **Deforestation**: It is the clearance of a forest or stands of trees where the land is converted to non-forest use, such as agriculture and construction of houses. It results in the loss of habitat for many plants and animals living in the forest. It may also lead to the extinction of plant and animal species.

iv. **Pollution**: This word is derived from the Latin word "pollut," meaning " soiled" or "defile (contaminate) ."Pollution is caused by pollutants, which may be solid, liquid, or gaseous. Pollution is defined as the effect of undesirable changes in our surroundings that have harmful effects on plants, animals, and human beings. Pollutants are produced due to human activity, which has a detrimental effect on our environment. For example, factories consume a lot of water and electricity and release harmful chemicals in the air, land, and water, thus contaminating the atmosphere. Water pollution caused by factories and other industrial units is one of the most serious problems. They also pollute the air through fossil fuel emissions. These emissions include carbon dioxide, methane, and nitrous oxide, which are harmful to living beings.

The other factors responsible for polluting the environment are as follows:

- Exhaust fumes released from vehicle pollutes the air.
- Excessive use of chemicals in agriculture (like insecticides and fertilisers) affects the alkalinity of the soil or the soil pH (pH is a scale on which acidity or alkalinity of a solution is measured. The value of pH less than 7 means the acidic nature of the sample, while the value of pH more than 7 represents alkalinity of the sample). It adversely affects the health of microorganisms and other organisms in the soil.
- Plastic waste like bottles, bags, etc., thrown on land and sea pollutes the water and destroys flora and fauna.
- Dangerous gases (chlorofluorocarbons or CFCs, methane, carbon dioxide, etc.) are released into the air.

4. What is soil conservation? Why is soil conservation useful?

Ans. Soil conservation means checking soil erosion and improving soil fertility by adopting various methods. Soil conservation can be useful for the following:

i. **Maintenance of soil fertility:** The fertility of soil can be maintained by adding manure and fertilizers regularly. Moreover, the process of rotation of crops ensures the increased fertility of the soil.

ii. **Control on grazing:** Grazing should be controlled, and it may be allowed only in specified areas.

iii. **Reforestation:** Reforestation/afforestation should be encouraged as the planting of trees and vegetation reduces soil erosion.

iv. **Terracing**: Terracing is the process of dividing a slope into several flat fields to control the rapid run of water. It is practiced mostly in hilly areas.

v. **Contour ploughing**: Contour ploughing is the ploughing at right angles to the slope that allows the furrows to trap water and checks soil erosion by rainwater.

5. Which methods are adopted for Water conservation? Enlist them.

Ans. Conservation and management of water are essential for the survival of humanity, plants, and animals. This can be done by adopting the following methods:

i. Growing vegetation in the catchment areas holds water in the soil and allows it to percolate into deeper layers and contribute to the formation of groundwater.

ii. Constructing dams and reservoirs is required to regulate the supply of water to the fields, as well as to enable the generation of hydroelectricity.

iii. Sewage should be treated, and only the treated and clear water should be released into the rivers.

iv. Industrial wastes (effluents) should be treated in effluent treatment plants to prevent chemical and thermal pollution of freshwater bodies.

v. Careful use of water in our day-to-day life is to be promoted.

vi. Rainwater harvesting should be encouraged for storing rainwater and recharging groundwater.

vii. Watershed, which is a single unit of land with its water drainage system, includes soil and water management for developing vegetative cover in the area.

Figure 5.10

6. Enlist various methods adopted for energy conservation.

Ans. The following methods may be adapted to conserve energy:

i. Switch off lights, fans, TV, and other electrical items when not in use.

ii. Use tube lights and energy-efficient bulbs that save energy rather than bulbs.

iii. Keep the bulbs and tubes clean.

iv. Remove dust on the tubes and bulbs to improve lighting levels by 10 to 20%.

v. Use a pressure cooker to save the energy required for cooking.

vi. Keep vessels covered with a lid during cooking. It is useful in cooking food faster and saving energy.

vii. Electrical items like air conditioners, geysers, heaters, and dryers use a lot of electrical power. Use them when necessary.

viii. Do not keep the door of a refrigerator open for a long time.

ix. Cool the hot food before putting it in the refrigerator.

x. Use methods of cooking that use less energy, like using a pressure cooker or solar cooker to cook food.

xi. Traveling in a bus or traveling in a group in a carpool is better than going alone in a car.

7. Enlist some Green Projects.

Ans. In our country, many people and organisations are undertaking Green Projects to manufacture products or do something to save the environment. Some of the green projects undertaken by some of the organisations are given below:

i. Solid Waste Management by 'Swachh Cooperative,' Pune (MS).

ii. Modern Chulha of 'Society of Development and Environment Protection,' Solan (HP)

iii. Bio toilet by 'Green Solution Foundation,' Vadodara (Gujarat)

iv. Rooftop farming by The Living Greens, Jaipur (Rajasthan)

v. Rainwater harvesting by D&D Ecotech Services, Mumbai (MS)

vi. Taking leftover food to the poor by Feeding India, New Delhi

vii. Recycling plastic by Banyan Nation, Hyderabad (Telangana)

viii. Recycling waste flowers by HelpUsGreen, Kanpur (UP)

8. What steps are required for effective environmental protection and conservation programme?

Ans. Educating people about the environment through awareness programmes, through the environment, and for the environment will ensure the utilizing their knowledge and skills for saving the environment as responsible world citizens.

i. **Creating awareness about the environment**: Learning about the environment focuses mainly on the acquisition of knowledge and understanding of our surroundings and related issues.

ii. **Learning through the environment**: Learning through the environment refers to the processes of learning while being engaged with the environment inside and outside the classroom. It focuses on the learning process, such as observation, hands-on experience, learning-by-doing, problem-solving through exposure to the environment, and learning. Direct contact with the environment provides the relevant context for acquiring knowledge, skills, aesthetic appreciation, and practical experience to learning. Environmental damage can be minimized by developing the skills and knowledge required for efficient resource utilisation, green processes, and technologies and integrating these into our businesses and daily activities.

iii. **Learning for the environment**: Learning for the environment aims at the development of an informed response and responsibility towards the environment.

iv. **Concept of the three Rs (Reduce, Reuse, Recycle):** There are the three Rs that you can apply for saving the environment – Reduce, Reuse, and Recycle. It is a concept of modern waste management.

(a) **Reduce**: Do not use what you do not need. If we reduce at source, there is a lesser chance of a waste generation, and the pressure on our already stretched natural resources is reduced. Every citizen may work at an individual level also like storing fewer items, reducing the purchasing of unnecessary items while shopping, buying items with minimal packaging, avoiding disposable buying items, avoiding asking for plastic carry bags, etc.

(b) **Reuse**: Reuse the materials for other purposes, such as making pillow covers or rags out of used shirts or ladies' suits.

(c) **Recycling**: Recycling is defined as reusing some components of the waste having some economic value. Recycling has easily visible benefits, like conservation of resources, reduction in energy used during manufacture, reducing pollution levels, etc. Some materials, such as aluminium, copper, gold, silver, iron, etc., can be recycled many times. Metal, paper, glass, and plastics are recyclable. Plastic items are recycled into new plastic products. Wet garbage includes most kitchen wastes, which can be used for preparing vermicompost. Most dry garbage is recyclable. Several technological breakthroughs have recently been made to recover material from industrial waste. Non-toxic solid waste should be properly segregated and disposed of in landfills that are properly sealed to avoid leakage and contamination of surrounding land and groundwater.

9. Discuss the main sectors of the Green Economy.

Ans. The main Sectors of the Green Economy are as follows:

i. **E-waste Management**: E-waste comprises discarded electronic devices. Which can be reused, resale, salvaged or recycled, or disposed of.

ii. **Green Transport:** Green transport refers to making efficient and effective use of resources, modification of transport structures, and making healthier travel choices. Green transport factors in climatic and environmental impact globally. Green transport is also termed as Smart transportation that supports and enhances walkable urbanization. It reduces congestion, reduces our dependency on cars and foreign oil, green transport is safer and less costly, and helps save our planet.

iii. **Renewable energy:** This is the energy that is obtained from renewable resources, which are naturally replenished on a human timescale, sunlight, wind tide, rain waves, geothermal heat.

iv. **Green construction**: Green construction is also referred to as the construction of sustainable buildings, and it includes both the structure and processes that are environmental-friendly, responsible, and resource-efficient through the building lifecycle, i.e., from design, operation, maintenance renovation, and demolition. Thus, green construction is the practice of erecting buildings and using processes that are environmentally responsible and resource-efficient. Green buildings are used to limit their environmental impact by conserving more energy and water, and these are constructed of recycled or renewable materials to have maximum resource efficiency.

v. **Water Management:** Water management is also referred to as optimisation of water usage. It is the management of water resources under a set of policies and regulations. Water, once an abundant natural resource, has become a valuable resource due to droughts and overuse.

10. Explain various methods and strategies of water management.

Ans. The five key water management strategies are widely used for proper water management as given below:

i. **Wastewater systems- recycling and treating**: Sewage systems help to dispose of wastewater cleanly and safely, and it involves recycling water and treating it so that it is safe to be piped back into people's homes for various purposes like for drinking, washing, irrigation, etc.

ii. **Irrigation systems:** Good quality irrigation systems may be used to nourish crops in drought-hit areas without wasting water and by using recycled water. Rainwater harvesting devices are also used to avoid unnecessarily depleting water supplies.

iii. **Conserving water:** Big, medium, and small companies, as well as individuals, can conserve many gallons of water each day simply by not wasting water like running taps without use. Water may also be conserved by generally consuming water as required only.

iv. **Caring for the natural water supplies**: Caring for natural water sources such as lakes, rivers, and canals is urgently required since these are the sources of freshwater ecosystems. Moreover, seas and oceans are home to a wide variety of different marine organisms. Because without the support of these ecosystems, these organisms would most likely become extinct.

v. **Effective implementation of plans/Afforestation**: In many parts of the world, people have to walk many miles to get clean water. So, good water management systems are praiseworthy when they are implemented throughout the world properly so that every world citizen can get a benefit. Good water management means not just a convenient and safe water supply for some people but water for everyone to use.

11. Give some methods for creating sustainable development?

Ans. The various methods for creating sustainable development may include:

i. Recycling and reuse of waste materials;

ii. Reducing excessive use of natural resources and enhancing resource conservation;

iii. Scientific management of renewable resources, especially bio-resources;

iv. Emphasizing afforestation (planting more trees);

v. Developing green grassy patches and planting small trees between concrete buildings;

vi. Using more environmentally friendly material or biodegradable material;

vii. Use of environmentally friendly technologies that are based on efficient use of resources.

12. What steps are required for effective water management?

Ans. The following steps are required for effective water management:

i. All citizens must take measurable steps by promoting awareness to keep water sources clean and to minimize water pollution.

ii. Conservation and management of water are crucial requirements for the survival of humanity, plants, and animals. This can be done by using the following methods:

iii. Industrial wastes (effluents) should be treated in effluent treatment plants to prevent chemical and thermal pollution of freshwater bodies.

iv. Sewage should be treated, and only the treated and clear water should be released into the rivers.

v. Growing vegetation in the catchment areas holds water in the soil and allows it to percolate into deeper layers and contribute to the formation of groundwater.

vi. Constructing dams and reservoirs is required to regulate the supply of water to the fields, as well as to enable the generation of hydroelectricity.

vii. Careful use of water in our day-to-day life is to be promoted.

viii. Rainwater harvesting should be encouraged for storing rainwater and recharging groundwater.

ix. A Watershed is a single unit of land with a water drainage system and includes soil and water management for developing vegetative cover in the area.

13. What methods are adopted for energy conservation?

Ans. The following methods may be adapted to conserve energy:

i. Switch off electrical appliances like lights, fans, TV, etc., when not in use.

ii. Keep the bulbs and tubes clean.

iii. Keep cooking vessels covered with a lid during cooking. It is useful in cooking food faster and saving energy.

iv. Use tube lights and energy-efficient bulbs that save energy rather than bulbs.

v. Use a pressure cooker to save the energy required for cooking.

vi. Use methods of cooking that use less energy, like using a pressure cooker or solar cooker to cook food.

vii. Remove dust from the tubes and bulbs to improve lighting levels by 10 to 20%.

viii. Electrical items like air conditioners, geysers, heaters, and dryers use a lot of electrical power. Use them when necessary.

ix. Do not keep the door of a refrigerator open for a long time.

x. Cool the hot food before putting it in the refrigerator.

xi. Traveling in a public transport vehicle, like roadways bus or traveling in a group using a carpool, etc., is better than using a car.

Figure 5.11

Young Environmentalist: Eiha Dixit

Figure 5.12: Eiha Dixit with The President of India

Creating awareness about conservation of nature through own actions can be learnt from little eiha Dixit. A friend of Prime Minister Sh Narendra Modi (as he introduced on an Instagram post), Eiha Dixit is like an ignited mind working for the welfare of the society. Eiha Dixit from Meerut is infusing the motivation among others for doing plantation. She is herself doing plantation since last 195 weeks (5 saplings per Sunday and hundreds of saplings on special occasions.) through her initiative Green Eiha Smiles Club. The consistency in planting saplings started at a very tender age of 4 years is the key for success in spreading awareness about conservation of environment.

A student of class IV at Saint Francis World School Meerut, she became the iconic image of the country of becoming the youngest awardee of the Prime Minister's **National Child Award (2019)** in Social Services Category. She was awarded by Honourable President of India Sh RN Kovindji. She was also honoured by honourable Prime Minister of India Sh Narendra Modi ji. She also participated in Republic Day parade on 26 Jan 2019.

She was awarded with **"National Balveer Award 2018"** by Union Minister of Social and Justice Empowerment. She got **3rd International Humanitarian & Activist Award 2021**, and **Green Angel Award 2021**. She was selected for her entry in **"India Book of Record (2017)"** for making a record of planting 1008 saplings at the age of 5 years. Again in 2018, she got the entry in **"Asia Book of Record"** for planting 2500 saplings at the age of 6 years. She became **Brand Ambassador of Clean India-Green India in 2020.**

Besides she is honoured and awarded by more than 60 organisations and institutions at International and National level.

5.3.11 HOTS QUESTIONS

1. Why is Green Economy important?

Ans. Green Economy is important because of following reasons:

i. It makes the quality of life better.

ii. The environmental balance becomes harmonized.

iii. The resource efficiency increases.

iv. It accelerates the development of new technologies.

v. New economic commodities generate in conformity with the environment.

2. What norms may be applied to convert cities into smart/sustainable cities?

Ans. For creating Sustainable Cities, apply the following norms:

i. Use energy-efficient lights (LED bulbs) and appliances.

ii. Save energy by switching off electrical appliances, like tube lights and fans, when these items are not used.

iii. Use energy-saving and water-saving techniques.

iv. Use biodegradable items.

v. Use natural light as much as possible.

3. How does sustainable development helpful in enhancing economic, social, and environmental wellbeing?

Ans. The sustainable development of the environment is a way to enhance the long term economic, social, and environmental wellbeing of people and social communities by:

i. Promoting social justice and equality of opportunity, and

ii. Enhancing the natural and cultural environment.

iii. Sustainable development includes:

iv. Reducing excessive use of natural resources,

v. Recycling and reuse of waste products/materials,

vi. Promoting afforestation/planting more trees,

vii. Scientific management of renewable resources, especially bio-resources,

viii. Using more environmentally friendly material promoting products made of biodegradable material,

ix. Using environmental-friendly technologies based on the efficient use of resources.

Figure 5.13

5.4 PRACTICE QUESTIONS

1. Define sustainable development.
2. What are sustainable goals?
3. 'Water management is important.' Justify the statement.
4. Mention the sectors of the green economy.
5. What do you mean by Green Skills?
6. Define environmental pollution.
7. Define green projects.
8. What is the purpose of soil conservation?
9. What do you mean by the Green economy?
10. What are the sources of water pollution?
11. Mention any three methods of water conservation.
12. Mention two green skills you can start learning from school days.
13. Mention a few examples of Green projects.
14. Mention the importance of the Green economy.
15. State any five ways by which we can save energy.
16. Discuss the role of the Government in the Green economy.
17. Explain the policies of the Indian govt for the Green economy.
18. Discuss the methods employed for water management.

Figure 5.14

Introduction to AI

6.1 UNIT IN BRIEF

- AI is now considered as: a form of intelligence, a type of technology, and a field of study.
- A fully automatic washing machine may work on its own, and it requires human intervention to select the parameters of washing.
- AI bias is defined as a phenomenon that occurs when an algorithm produces results that are systematically biased due to erroneous theories in the machine learning process.

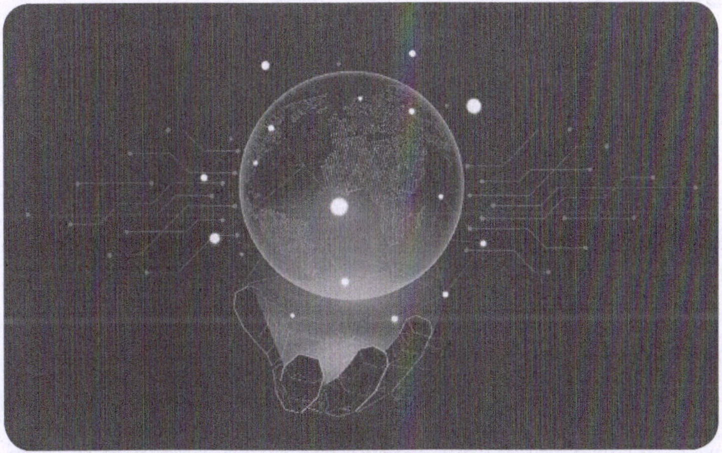

Figure 6.1

- AI theory and development of computer systems (both machines and software) are capable of performing tasks that normally require human intelligence.
- AI can only do what it is programmed for. Unlike a real person, it is not capable of making split-second judgments. A fully automatic washing machine may work on its own, and it requires human intervention to select the parameters of washing. It is not AI.
- Alan Turing in 1950 created the Turing Test to determine the intelligence of a computer.
- An AI-enabled machine should not only recognize but should also do something with its gathered information.
- An AI code of ethics is a policy statement defining the role of artificial intelligence as it is applicable to the continued development of the human race.
- Artificial Intelligence can be sub-divided into three categories: Artificial Intelligence, Machine Learning, and Deep Learning.

- Artificial Intelligence is also defined as the science of making machines do things that would require intelligence if done by man.
- Artificial Intelligence may be defined as a technique that enables computers to mimic human intelligence.
- Artificial Intelligence means a human-made interface with the power to reason and integrate knowledge.
- China has started the functioning of autonomous cars (self-driving cars) in 2021 to become the first country to do so.
- Deep learning is taken as a subset of machine learning wherein artificial neural networks and algorithms are inspired by the human brain and learn from large amounts of data.
- Explanation Based Learning (EBL) was introduced by Gerald Dejong in 1981, allowing a computer to create a set of rules based on training data.
- Geoffrey Hinton coined the term "deep learning" to explain new algorithms that empower computers to distinguish objects and images, and video.
- In 2011, Nevada in the USA became the first jurisdiction in the world where autonomous vehicles can be legally operated on public roads.
- In 2015, Google DeepMind's AlphaGo (version Fan) defeated three-time European Go champion two dan professional Fan Hui by five games to 0.
- In 2018, Nvidia introduced its GPU cloud, which promises to be another interesting alternative to training Deep Learning models.
- Isaac Asimov 1950 published his famous 'Three Laws of Robotics.
- It makes sense to have a large dataset as is required to include variety, subtlety, and nuance to make the model viable for practical use.
- Machines lack the ability to be creative.
- Machines or software can also fail anytime due to some bug or human error.
- Marvin Minsky and Dean Edmunds in 1951 built SNARC (Stochastic Neural Analog Reinforcement Calculator), the first artificial neural network which used 3000 vacuum tubes to simulate a network of 40 neurons.
- Self-learning in neural networks was introduced in 1982, along with a neural network capable of self-learning named Crossbar Adaptive Array (CAA).
- Semantic indexing is a common method of processing meaning from natural language.
- Terry Sejnowski, in 1985 created 'NetTalk,' which learnt to pronounce words.
- The AI devices must be trained with information / large data to produce the best possible accurate results.
- Artificial Intelligence (AI) is the ability of a computer or computer-controlled RobotRobot to perform tasks generally associated with intelligent human beings.
- The goal of AI is to develop machines that behave as though they are intelligent.

✦ The main three domains of AI are Data, Computer Vision (CV), and Natural Language Processing (NLP).

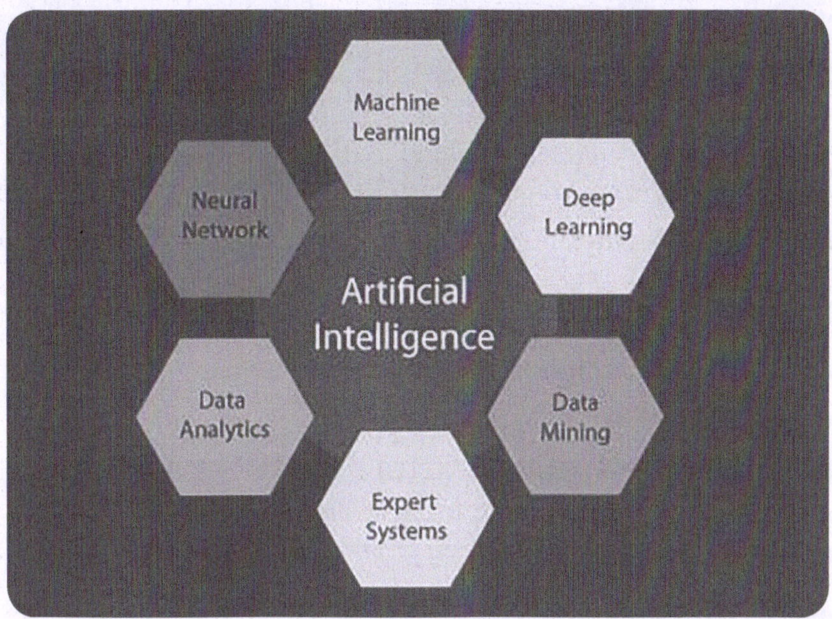

Figure 6.2

6.2 CBSE/NCERT SECTION (SOLVED CBSE/NCERT EXERCISES)

6.2.1 Fill in the Blanks:

1. The basis of decision making depends upon the availability of ____________and how we experience and understand it.

Ans. information or data.

2. A machine can also become intelligent if it is trained with __________ that helps them achieve their tasks.

Ans. Data

6.2.2 True/False:

1. A machine is artificially intelligent when it can accomplish tasks by itself.
2. Is a smart washing machine an example of an Artificially Intelligent device?
3. Platforms like Netflix, Amazon, Spotify, YouTube, etc., show us recommendations on the basis of what we like.

ANSWERS
1. T 2. F 3. T

6.2.3 VSA:

1. What do you understand by linguistic intelligence?

Ans. Linguistic intelligence is an intelligence that helps to understand and interpret natural human language and try to extract meaning out of it.

2. What do you understand by Interpersonal Intelligence?

Ans. Understanding human emotions, feelings and being influenced by them is known as interpersonal intelligence.

3. Define Artificial Intelligence.

Ans. A machine is artificially intelligent if it can accomplish tasks by itself - collect data, understand it, analyse it, learn from it, and improve it.

4. Mention two types of machines that have evolved with time.

Ans. (i) Television (ii) Mobile Phones (iii) Ceiling Fans

5. What do you understand by mathematical and logical reasoning?

Ans. Mathematical and logical reasoning is the ability of a person to regulate, measure, and understand numerical symbols, abstraction, and logic is called

6.2.4 Short Answer Type Questions

1. Mention four examples of artificially intelligent applications in our smartphones.

Ans. (i) Phone Smart Lock (ii) Snapchat filter (iii) Shopping websites (iv) Netflix (v) YouTube (vi) Face Detection

2. How does a machine become Artificially Intelligent?

Ans. A machine may become intelligent by training with data and algorithms. AI machines keep updating their knowledge to optimise their output.

3. Mention four examples of machines that are not AI but confused with AI.

Ans. (i) Automatic gates in shopping malls (ii) Remote control drones (iii) A fully automatic washing machine (iv) Air Conditioner/ Refrigerator (v) Robotic toy cars

4. How does learning and adapting help an AI machine in improvising itself?

Ans. An artificially intelligent machine collects real-time data and tries to figure out new patterns in it. Machines learn in a similar way to human beings, i.e., by supervision or by observation. Also, a machine learns from its mistakes. The more the machine gets trained on data, the more accurate results it gives. For example, Any virtual assistant is initially trained with a few basic instructions. after that the machine captures the data fed by the user, which may be the wake-up time of the user, sleeping time, dinner time, etc. Later on the machine gives reminders of similar things on the basis of data and adapts these new commands.

5. Pick the odd one out and justify your answer:

a. Snap Chat Filter
b. Face Lock in Phone
c. Chatbot
d. Image search Option

Ans. Chatbot, as it is NLP-based, the other three are Computer Vision-based.

6. Explain how AI works in the following areas (any two):
   a. Google Search Engine
   b. Voice Assistants
   c. E-commerce websites

Ans. **a. Google Search Engine**: Using AI, Google Search Engine has been become Intelligent search engine and a new network of systems that produces direct answers. It uses voice and image searches both and has incorporated deep learning to fasten the searches with more accuracy.

b. Voice Assistant: AI used in voice assistants helps to recognise words spoken by the user. NLP has capabilities like "Speech-to-Text" to convert the natural language of the user into text for further processing. When digital assistant answers more queries, it "learns" users through ML algorithms. The more tasks it performs, its ML algorithms help it "learns" from the tasks. It can make preferences of the user. Thus, the digital assistant improves its performance over time.

c. E-commerce website: AI in E-Commerce is using big data and impacting customer choices by recording/analysing the data of previous purchases, searched products, and online browsing habits. It provides product recommendations. E-commerce retailers, including a higher number of returning customers, etc., get benefits.

7. How has AI changed the gaming world?

Ans. AI has changed the world of video gaming by making the game more intelligent. This happens due to providing the users the ability to learn using machine learning algorithms. Online games these days try to understand human patterns to give responses on the basis of it and also give new difficulty levels.

8. Why training with information/Data is important in Artificial Intelligent devices?

Ans. Like human beings, AI devices need the experiences to give better results and improve in every next iteration. The machine must be trained with some real data for giving better results. The more the amount of accurate the data, the better predictions will be made by the machine. So, data is very important in AI devices.

6.2.3 Long Answer Type Questions

1. What is Intelligence? Explain in brief any three types of intelligence that are mainly perceived by human beings?

Ans. Intelligence is defined as the "ability to perceive or infer information, and to retain it as knowledge for its application towards adaptive behaviour within an environment or context."

As per major researches, there are mainly nine types of intelligence;

(i) **Mathematical Logical Intelligence:** Mathematical Logical intelligence is an ability of a person to regulate, measure, and understand numerical symbols, abstraction, and logic.

(ii) Linguistic Intelligence: Language processing skills both in terms of understanding/ implementation in writing or speech is called liguistic intelligence.

(iii) Spatial Visual Intelligence: It is the ability to perceive the visual world and the relationship of one object to another.

(iv) Kinaesthetic Intelligence: It is the ability that is related to how a person uses his limbs in a skilled manner.

(v) Musical Intelligence: This intelligence is about a person's ability to recognise and create sounds, rhythms, and sound patterns.

(vi) Intrapersonal Intelligence: It describes the level of self-awareness someone has, starting from realising weakness, strength, feelings, interests,etc

(vii) Existential Intelligence: It is related to religious and spiritual awareness.

(viii) Naturalist Intelligence: This intelligence is related to the ability to process the information on the environment around us.

(ix) Interpersonal Intelligence: Interpersonal Intelligence is the ability to communicate with others after understanding other people's feelings.

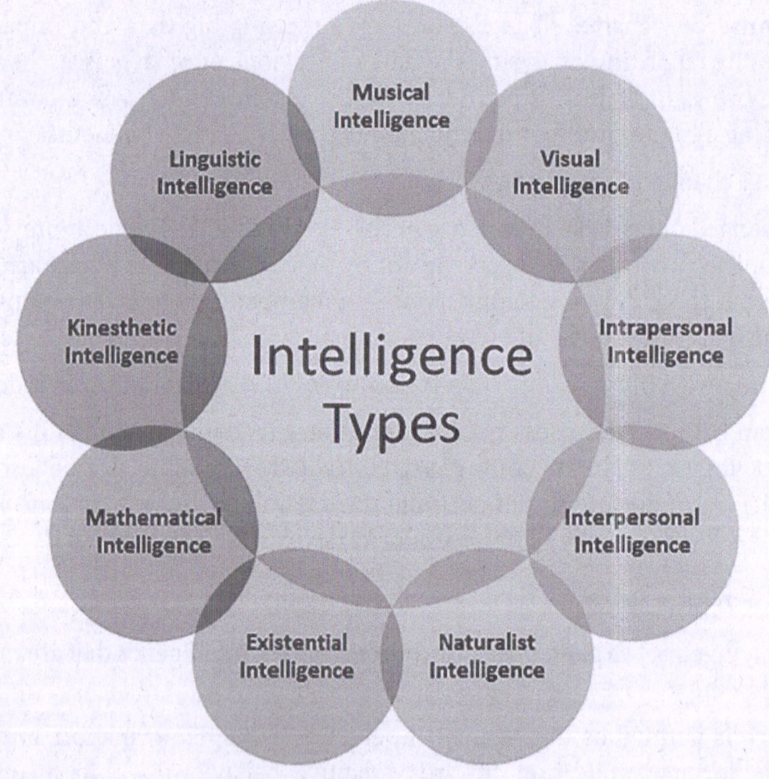

Figure 6.3

2. Differentiate between what is AI and what is not AI with the help of an example?

Ans.

AI Machine	Not AI Machine
(i) AI machines are trained with data and algorithms.	(i) Smart machines which are not AI do not require training data as they work on algorithms only.

(ii) AI machines learn from mistakes and experience and try to improvise on their next iterations.	(ii) Smart machines work on specific/fixed algorithms, and they always work with the same level of efficiency, which is programmed into them.
(iii) AI machines can analyse the situation and can make decisions.	(iii) Machines that are not AI cannot make decisions on their own.
(iv) AI-based drones capture the real-time data during the flight, processes it in real-time, and make an independent human decision based on the processed data.	(iv) An automatic door in an office/ shopping mall is built with only sensor technology. It is not AI.

3. How can AI be integrated with non-AI technologies? Explain with the help of an example.

Ans. Today's world is changing by using IoT (Internet of Things). IoT is helping in collecting a tremendous amount of data from different sources. The use of AI (Artificial Intelligence) and IoT is changing the way industries, business, and economy functions. AI-enabled IoT creates intelligent machines that simulate smart behaviour and supports decision-making with a little human interference. Here, IoT provides data, and artificial intelligence acquires the power to unlock responses, offering both creativity and context to drive smart actions.

Here are some examples:

(a) **Self-driving Cars**: Tesla's self-driving cars are the best example of IoT and AI working simultaneously. With the power of AI, self-driving cars predict the behaviour of pedestrians and cars in various circumstances. For example, these cars can determine road conditions, optimal speed, weather, and getting smarter with each trip.

(b) **Robots in Manufacturing Units**: Manufacturing industries are using new technologies like artificial intelligence, IoT, facial recognition, deep learning, Robots, etc. Robots working in factories are turning smarter with the support of implanted sensors, which facilitate data transmission. The robots are embedded with artificial intelligence algorithms, they can learn from newer data. This approach saves time, cost and makes the manufacturing process better over time.

(c) **Weather Forecasting System**: In a weather forecasting system, IoT temperature sensors and humidity sensors collect data from the physical world and AI figure out patterns from previous data collected to interpret and give actual predictions of upcoming day weather.

(d) **Smart Drones**: Initially, drones were only able to capture photographs; these were not AI drones. As the scientists used to analyse the data collected through drones. Nowadays the drones incorporated with AI helps them to make decisions also on the basis of the picture they capture.

4. Read the given scenario and answer the question that follows:

A farmer keeps rabbits in three large hutches that stand in a row in his backyard. Each of the hutches is painted in different colours – red, yellow, and green. Until recently, the number of rabbits in the green hutch was twice as large as the number of rabbits in the yellow hutch.

Then, one day, the farmer took five rabbits out of the left-side hutch and gave them away to the local school's pet corner. He also took half of the rabbits that remained in the left-side hutch and moved them to the red hutch.

a. What was the colour of the left-side hutch? Justify your answer with an explanation.

Ans. Yellow. Explanation: As we already know that the number of rabbits in the green hutch was twice as large as the number of rabbits in the yellow hutch. This clearly shows that the number of rabbits in the green hutch was an even number. When the farmer removes five rabbits from the left side hutch, then the number of rabbits remained there becomes an even number as proved by the fact that it was divisible by 2. So, before the removal of five rabbits were removed, the left side hutch contained an uneven number of rabbits and hence, the left side hutch cannot be the green one. Moreover, based on the given information, it also cannot be the red hutch. Hence, it is yellow.

5. A scenario is given to you below. Read it and answer the questions that follow:

Late one night, a car ran over a pedestrian in a narrow street and drove away without stopping. A policeman who saw the vehicle leave the scene of the accident reported it moving at a very high speed. The accident itself was witnessed by six bystanders. They provided the following conflicting accounts of what had happened: - It was a blue car driven by a man; - The car was moving at high speed, and its headlights were turned off; - The car did have license plates; it wasn't going very fast; - It was a Toyota, and its headlights were turned off; - The car didn't have license plates; the driver was a woman; - It was a grey Ford. When the car and its driver were finally apprehended, it turned out that only one of the six eyewitnesses gave a fully correct description. Each of the other five provided one true and one false piece of information.

a. What was the car's brand?

Ans. Car's brand was FORD.

b. What was the colour of the car?

Ans. Colour of car: BLUE

c. Was the car going fast or slow?

Ans. FAST

d. Did it have license plates?

Ans. No licence plate

e. Were its headlights turned on?

Ans. Headlights were turned Off.

f. Was the driver a man or a woman?

Ans. Driver was a WOMAN.

Explanation: Out of the statements of 6 bystanders, the third statement becomes false. This is because the policeman who saw the vehicle leave the scene of the accident reported it moving at a very high speed. After eliminating all false statements of bystanders, the above results are extracted.

6. A firefighter has to get to a burning building as quickly as he can. There are three paths that he can take. He can take his fire engine over a large hill (5 miles) at 8 miles per hour. He can take his fire engine through a windy road (7 miles) at 9 miles per hour. Or he can drive his fire engine along a dirt road which is 8 miles at 12 miles per hour. Which way should he choose? (speed=distance/time)

Ans. To reach the destination quickly, the firefighter has to calculate the time required on the basis of given data. Driving his fire engine 5 miles at 8 miles per hour takes 37.5 minutes. Driving his fire engine 7 miles at 9 miles per hour takes about 47 minutes. Driving his fire engine 8 miles at 12 miles per hour takes 40 minutes. Hence, he should choose to drive his fire engine over the hill.

7. *A thief has just found a pair of ancient treasure caves. One of the caves is filled with unbelievable treasure, and the other has a fire-breathing monster that will eat anyone who opens that cave. One cave has a black door decorated with diamonds, and the other cave has a brown door decorated with sapphires. Each of the doors has an engraved description on top. The descriptions say:*

   a. Black Door: Monster is here.

   b. Brown Door: Only One Door speaks the truth.

   Which door should the thief open?

Ans. The treasure is in the Black door. Explanation: Look at the description of the Brown door that can be correct or wrong.

Scenario 1: If the description on the Brown door is true, then the description on the Black door has to be false. It means that the inscription on the Black door is false, and the cave with the black door contains the treasure!

Scenario 2: If the description of the Brown door is false, then either the descriptions are false, or both are true. Both cannot be true at all . It means that both descriptions are false.

8. How do intelligent robots help us in accomplishing dangerous jobs?

Ans. Robots help humans as follows:

(i) Lifting up heavy/big material at the construction site.

(ii) Stirring and mixing metals /liquids at high temperatures.

(iii) Collecting and packing of radioactive waste.

(iv) Working in polluted, and contaminated environment.

9. How AI helps in giving you personalized experience online?

Ans. AI helps in many ways in giving personalised experience online as enlisted below:

i. **AI-based recommendations**: AI uses advanced machine learning algorithms to analyse data , like browser history, page clicks, social interactions (likes/ shares), past purchases, experiences ,the duration for which a page was viewed, location, etc., to find /predict customers' interests and preferences. AI can help in product recommendations based on frequently bought items or related products. It can also help customise web pages and elements to suit a customer's needs. For example, Netflix does intense behaviour analysis based on behaviour and emographic data to finalise the content that will resonate with the customers.

ii. **Chatbots and Automated Messaging**: AI-powered chatbots and messaging agents enhance the customer experiences. across channels. They can answer simple queries, engage customers, efficiently handle multiple interactions,

iii. **Automated Service Interactions**: AI-driven programs can send automated messages to customers regarding a pending service, a part replacement, or a regular order.

iv. **Curating Select Products**: Amazon has come up with the concept of the Amazon 4-star retail store. Products that have received a multitude of 4-star ratings will be offered in this physical store. Amazon will use its product recommendation engine to identify trending products and customers' favourites and bring them to a brick-and-mortar setting.

6.3 SOLVED EXERCISES

6.3.1 Multiple Choice Questions

1. Both Machine learning and ____________ are parts of Data Science.

   a) Data Mining b) Data scrapping c) NLP d) CV

2. Which of the following SDGs is related to ending hunger?

   a) No Poverty b) Reduced inequalities
   c) Zero hunger d) Life under Sea

3. Which subjects are not covered in the field of study of AI?

   a) Human behaviour, biology
   b) Psychology, language, and linguistics
   c) Statistics, computer science
   d) None of the above

4. ____________ is the ability to understand, apply knowledge, and improve skills.

   a) Artificial Intelligence b) CV
   c) Creativity d) Intelligence

5. Which feature is not related to Artificial Intelligence?

   a) Creativity b) Preciseness c) Consistency d) Accuracy

6. Multitasking Which properties are not related to Natural Intelligence?

   a) Non-Precise b) Non-creative
   c) Non-consistent d) Not easy to handle

7. This is the ability of machines to perform cognitive tasks, which a human brain can do, like thinking, perceiving, learning, problem-solving, decision making, etc. It is called:

   a) Supervised Learning b) ANN
   c) Artificial Intelligence d) CNN

8. Rock-Paper-Scissors game is based upon:
   a) Data
   b) NLP
   c) Computer Vision
   d) All of the above
9. Which game is based on computer vision?
   a) Rock-Paper Scissors
   b) Identify the Mystery Animal
   c) Emoji Scavenger Hunt Game
   d) None of these
10. Which is not regarded as a domain of AI?
    a) NLP
    b) CNN
    c) Data
    d) Computer Vision
11. Which of the following is not a sub-category of Machine Learning?
    a) Project-Based Learning
    b) Supervised Learning
    c) Unsupervised Learning
    d) Reinforcement Learning
12. Which Indian Robot was created by Mr Dinesh Patel -a teacher of Kendriya Vidyalaya, IIT Campus Mumbai, and that can speak 9 Indian and 37 foreign languages?
    a) Robot Shalu
    b) Robot Sophia
    c) Robot Manav
    d) Robot George
13. Which of the following products is used in a smart home?
    a) Cameras
    b) Thermostat (controlling the temperature of AC or fridge)
    c) Motion sensors
    d) All the above
14. Which of the following products is not a part of Smart home?
    a) LED lights are controlled by using the smartphone.
    b) Turning lights and appliances at home on or off from the mobile device.
    c) Door locks and garage doors are controlled by using a smartphone.
    d) None of the above
15. Which of the following will possess more cognitive capabilities than gifted human beings?
    a) AGI
    b) ASI
    c) ANN
    d) None of the above
16. Which statements are part of AI Ethics?
    i. Financial investments in AI should be accompanied by funding for research on ensuring its beneficial use.
    ii. If an AI system causes harm, it should be possible to determine why.
    iii. A culture of cooperation, trust, and transparency must be raised among researchers and developers of AI.

iv. Teams developing Al systems should actively cooperate to avoid money saving on safety standards.

v. Al systems should be safe and secure throughout their operational lifetime.

vi. The designers and makers of advanced AI systems are considered as the stakeholders in the moral implications of the use, misuse, and actions of these systems/devices, with a responsibility and opportunity to shape those implications.

vii. Highly autonomous Al systems should be designed so that their goals and behaviours can be assured to align with human values throughout the operation.

a) (ii) (iii) (iii)
b) (iv) (v) (vii)
c) (vi) (ii) (i)
d) All of the above

17. How many UN Sustainable Development Goals (SDGs) are suggested by UNO?

a) 10
b) 13
c) 17
d) 24

18. Which of the following has the potential to resolve the key challenges posed by excessive urban population?

a) Artificial Intelligence (AI)
b) IoT
c) Genome Sequencing
d) Both (a) and (b)

19. Rashmi is an Indian realistic lip-syncing multilingual humanoid robot that can speak four languages (English, Hindi, Bhojpuri, and Marathi). Who was its developer in 2019?

a) Divakar Vaish
b) Dinesh Patel
c) Ranjit Srivastava
d) Rashmi Ahuja

20. How many vacuum tubes were used in creating the first artificial neural network (SNARC) of 40 neurons?

a) 30
b) 300
c) 3000
d) 30000

21. What is the full form of BNN?

a) Biological Neural Network
b) Bio Neural Network
c) Biological Network of Neurons
d) Biology of Neural Networking

22. Which part is not a framework part of Smart city?

a) Smart Governance
b) Smart Environment
c) Smart Economy
d) Smart Transport

23. Which of the following dimension is a core element of sustainable development?

a) Social inclusion
b) Economic growth
c) Environmental protection
d) None of these

24. Which of the following pairs of subject and domain is/are incorrect?

i. Computer Science: Building computers

ii. Mathematics: Algorithms, proof, computability, methods of representation, tractability and decidability

iii. Neuro-Science: How the basic information processing units, i.e., neurons Process Information

iv. Statistics: Grammar, syntax, knowledge representations

v. Linguistics: Learning from data, uncertainty/ certainty of modelling

vi. Economics: Rational economic agents, the usefulness of data & models, decision Theory

vii. Cognitive Sciences: Processes and things in nature, interpretation of different phenomena & their impact

a) (ii) b) (iv) (v)

c) (vi) (vii) d) All of the above

25. Who gave 'Three Laws of Robotics' in 1950?

a) Arthur Samuel b) Isaac Asimov

c) Alan Turing d) William Stanford

26. The full form of NLP in relation to AI :

a) Neural Learning Process b) Neuro-Linguistic Processing

c) Natural Language Processing d) Natural Logic Processing

27. Which of the following is associated with the study of computer algorithms that improve their efficiency automatically through experience?

a) Data science b) Machine Learning (ML)

c) Deep Learning (DL) d) None of the above

28. An Indian Robot, Shalu, can speak 9 Indian and 37 foreign languages and is developed by a teacher of Kendriya Vidyalaya, IIT Campus, Mumbai. Who is he?

Figure 6.4: Robo Rashmi with its creator Ranjit Srivastava

a) SP Saxena b) Ranjit S. c) Diwakar Vaish d) Dinesh Patel

29. Which SDG is not proposed by UNO?

a) No Poverty b) Zero illiteracy

c) Zero hunger d) Low-Quality education

30. ____________ is a common method of processing meaning from natural language.
   a) Sematic Analysis b) Semantic Indexing
   c) Supervised Learning d) Reinforcement Learning
31. Who created NetTalk, which learned to pronounce words?
   a) Terry Sejnowski b) Alan Turing
   c) Asimov d) Gerald Dejong
32. Who created the Turing Test to determine the intelligence of a computer?
   a) Isaac Asimov b) Alan Turing c) James Turing d) Alan Samuel
33. Which of the following systems defeated the World Chess Champion in 1997?
   a) IBM's Deep Blue system b) Google's DeepMind system
   c) IBM's Watson d) AlphaGo
34. Who was the first computer scientist to coin the term "artificial intelligence" in 1955?
   a) Arthur Samuel b) Alan Turing
   c) John McCarthy d) Frank Rosenblatt
35. Who prepared the first computer learning application in1952?
   a) Alan Turing
   b) Asimov
   c) Arthur Samuel
   d) John McCarthy

Figure 6.5

36. When was Deep Learning introduced?
   a) 1986 b) 2003
   c) 2010 d) 2015
37. In 2018, who became the first automaker to launch a self-driving vehicle?
   a) Audi b) Tesla c) Mercedes d) Suzuki
38. What is the art of the study of algorithms that learn from examples and experience known as?
   a) Deep Learning b) Machine Learning
   c) Supervised Learning d) PBL
39. Which of the following companies is considered a giant player in the field of data?
   a) Google b) Facebook c) Amazon d) All the above
40. Which Robot became a Saudi Arabian citizen, the first Robot to become a citizen of any country in the world?
   a) Robot Shalu b) Robot Sophia
   c) Robot Manav d) Robot Rashmi

41. Which Chatbot was created by Microsoft that was forced to close in less than one day?
   a) Tay chatbot
   b) Tina chatbot
   c) Jay chatbot
   d) Toy chatbot
42. What is the name of an assistant that is enabled to communicate with humans through text messages?
   a) Chatterpatter
   b) Chatbot
   c) Airbot
   d) Voicebot
43. Which of the following is NOT a part of Data Science?
   a) Deep Learning
   b) Nano-science
   c) Machine Learning
   d) Artificial Intelligence
44. Which of the following statements is INCORRECT?
   a) Al systems should be designed and operated so that it is compatible with ideals of human dignity, freedoms, rights, and cultural diversity.
   b) The usage of AI to personal data must not unreasonably limit people's real or alleged liberty.
   c) Al technologies should benefit and empower high-powered people.
   d) People should be given the right to access, manage, and control the data they generate, given Al systems' power to analyse and utilize that data.
45. Which of the following robots is India's first 3D printed humanoid RobotRobot that was developed in 2014 by Diwakar Vaish in Noida, UP?
   a) Manavi
   b) Shama
   c) Manav
   d) Rashmi
46. Which of the following statements is correct?
   a) The economic prosperity created by AI can be shared among all countries for the benefit of the world.
   b) The power granted by control of highly advanced AI systems should respect and improve, rather than disrupt, the social and civic processes on which the health of society depends.
   c) The arms race, particularly in lethal autonomous weapons, should be minimized and ultimately avoided by the governments.
   d) All the above
47. Which application is not considered an application of AI?
   a) Remote-controlled Car
   b) Google search
   c) Robot drones
   d) Self-Driving Car
48. Which of the following about the drawbacks of AI is correct?
   a) Unlimited Ability
   b) Can't Handle Emergency Situation
   c) Easy code
   d) Low cost

49. ____________ Intelligence is the ability to understand social situations and the behaviour of other people.

    a) Interpersonal b) Intrapersonal
    c) Musical d) Spatial

50. ____________ is the term that is frequently applied to the project of developing systems endowed with the intellectual processes that are the characteristic of humans, such as the ability to reason, discover meaning, generalize or learn, from past experience.

    a) Neural Network b) Intelligence
    c) Artificial Intelligence d) Creativity

ANSWERS									
1. (a)	2. (b)	3. (d)	4. (d)	5. (a)	6. (b)	7. (c)	8. (a)	9. (c)	10. (b)
11. (a)	12. (a)	13. (d)	14. (d)	15. (b)	16. (d)	17. (c)	18. (d)	19. (c)	20. (c)
21. (a)	22. (d)	23. (c)	24. (b)	25. (b)	26. (c)	27. (b)	28. (d)	29. (b)	30. (b)
31. (a)	32. (b)	33. (a)	34. (c)	35. (c)	36. (a)	37. (b)	38. (a)	39. (d)	40. (b)
41. (a)	42. (b)	43. (b)	44. (c)	45 (c)	46. (d)	47. (a)	48. (b)	49. (a)	50. (c)

6.3.2 Fill in the blanks

1. Computer vision-related projects translate digital ____________ data into descriptions.
2. ____________ is the process of converting sound signals captured by a microphone or mobile/telephone to a set of words (70-100 words/minute with an accuracy of 90%).
3. ____________ works to implement human intelligence in machines and creating systems that understand, learn, think, and behave like humans.
4. ____________ is language processing skills both in terms of understanding or implementation in writing or verbally.
5. ____________ Intelligence is defined as the ability to perceive the visual world and to find the relationship of one object to another.
6. ____________ is responsible for the machine's ability to read and understand human language.
7. ____________ Intelligence is the ability to understand social situations and the behaviour of other people.
8. ____________ refers to the ability of machines to interact with the world (speech, vision, motion, manipulation), ability to model the world and to reason about it, ability to learn, ability to make decisions, and to adapt.
9. ____________ fitted in cameras in the office can recognize shadows or movements, but that doesn't make them an example of artificial intelligence.
10. An automatic washing machine is an example of automation, not ____________.

11. Most ____________ items are ordinary things outfitted with sensors and connected to the Internet.
12. ____________ is the first humanoid given Citizenship by a country-Saudi Arab in Oct. 2017.
13. ____________ is a common method of processing meaning from natural language.
14. Machines also become intelligent once they are ____________ with some information that helps them achieve their tasks.
15. ____________ is a humanoid robot developed in 2015 by "Hanson Robotics," Hong Kong.
16. ____________ like Google assistant, Apple's Siri, Amazon's Alexa, etc., recognize patterns in speech and then understand its meaning and provide a useful response.
17. The main objective of ____________ is to teach machines to collect information from pixels.
18. ____________ is considered the most advanced form of Artificial Intelligence.
19. ____________ inputs machine the ability to read and understand human language.
20. Expert Systems are ____________ used for decision-making.

ANSWERS			
1. visual	2. Speech Recognition	3. Artificial Intelligence	
4. Linguistical Intelligence	5. Spatial/ Visual	6. Natural Language Processing	
7. Interpersonal	8. Intelligence	9. Sensors	10. AI
11. IoT (Internet of Things)	12. Sophia	13. Semantic indexing	14. trained
15. Sophia	16. Smart assistants	17. CV	
18. Deep Learning	19. Natural Language Processing		

6.3.3 True or False

1. Artificial Intelligence means a human-made interface with the power to reason and integrate knowledge.
2. Semantic analysis is a common method of processing meaning from natural language.
3. AI machines also keep updating their knowledge to optimize their output.
4. Alan Turing in 1950 created the Turing Test to determine the intelligence of a computer.
5. Isaac Asimov 1950 published his famous 'Three Laws of Robotics.
6. Marvin Minsky and Dean Edmunds in 1951 built SNARC (Stochastic Neural Analog Reinforcement Calculator), the first artificial neural network which used 3000 vacuum tubes to simulate a network of 40 neurons.
7. It makes sense to have a large dataset as is required to include variety, subtlety, and nuance to make the model viable for practical use.
8. Explanation Based Learning (EBL) was introduced by Gerald Dejong in 2021, allowing a computer to create a set of rules based on training data.

9. AI is not considered a form of intelligence, a type of technology, or a field of study.
10. A fully automatic washing machine may work on its own, and it requires human intervention to select the parameters of washing.
11. Terry Sejnowski, in 1985 created '*NetTalk*,' which learnt to pronounce words.
12. Geoffrey Hinton coined the term "deep learning" to explain new algorithms that empower computers to distinguish objects and images, and video.
13. China has started the functioning of autonomous cars (self-driving cars) in 2021 to become the first country to do so.
14. In 2018, Nvidia introduced its GPU cloud, which promises to be another interesting alternative to training NLP models.
15. The AI devices must be trained with information / large data to produce the best possible accurate results.
16. An AI-enabled machine should not only recognize but should also do something with its gathered information.
17. In 2011, Nevada in the USA became the first jurisdiction in the world where autonomous vehicles can be legally operated on public roads.
18. In 2015, Google DeepMind's AlphaGo (version Fan) defeated three-time European Go champion two dan professional Fan Hui by five games to 0.
19. AI is capable of performing tasks that normally require human intelligence.
20. Artificial Intelligence is not a technique that enables computers to mimic human intelligence.

Figure 6.6

ANSWERS						
1. T	2. F (Semantic indexing)	3. T	4. T	5. T	6. T	7. T
8. F (1981)	9. F	10. T	11. T	12. T	13. T	
14. F (Deep Learning models)		15. T	16. T	17. T	18. T	19. T 20. F

6.3.4 Matching type

(I) Match the bank with the digital assistant used by it correctly.

Column A (Bank)	Column B (Digital Assistant)
(i) Bank of America	(a) iPal
(ii) HSBC Hong Kong	(b) SIA
(iii) SEB Sweden	(c) Ceba
(iv) Commonwealth Bank, Australia	(d) Amy
(v) SBI India	(e) Aida
(vi) ICICI India	(f) Erica

ANSWERS					
(I) (i) f	(ii) d	(iii) e	(iv) c	(v) b	(vi) a

6.3.5 Statements Based Questions

1. Statement 1: In 2018, Tesla became the first automaker to launch a self-driving vehicle.

   Statement 2: A convolutional neural network was designed in 2012 by researchers at the University of Toronto, which achieved an error rate of only 16% in the ImageNet Large Scale Visual Recognition Challenge.

   a) Statement 1 is correct, but statement 2 is incorrect.

   b) Statement 1 is incorrect, but statement 2 is correct.

   c) Both the statements are correct.

   d) Both the statements are incorrect.

2. Statement 1: PathNet, a computer program that plays the board game Go, was developed by Alphabet Inc.'s Google DeepMind in London.

   Statement 2: AlphaGo is a neural network algorithm, and it uses agents embedded in the neural network to discover which parts of the network are to be re-used for new tasks.

   a) Statement 1 is correct, but statement 2 is incorrect.

   b) Statement 1 is incorrect, but statement 2 is correct.

   c) Both the statements are correct.

   d) Both the statements are incorrect.

3. Statement 1: There are three types of Artificial Intelligence (AI): Artificial Narrow Intelligence (ANI) or weak AI, Artificial General Intelligence (AGI) or strong AI, and Artificial Super Intelligence (ASI).

   Statement 2: IBM's Deep Blue system defeated the World Chess Champion in 2017.

   a) Statement 1 is correct, but statement 2 is incorrect.

   b) Statement 1 is incorrect, but statement 2 is correct.

   c) Both the statements are correct.

   d) Both the statements are incorrect.

4. Statement 1: Natural language processing does not use different techniques like parsing techniques, text recognition, and part-of-speech tagging for implementation.

   Statement 2: The range of NLP also includes generating sentences in natural languages by computers just like humans do.

   a) Statement 1 is correct, but statement 2 is incorrect.

   b) Statement 1 is incorrect, but statement 2 is correct.

   c) Both the statements are correct.

   d) Both the statements are incorrect.

5. Statement 1: The main three domains of AI are Data, Computer Vision (CV), and Natural Language Processing (NLP).

   Statement 2: Smart estimation of unknown values by using the given series of past data is termed as Long Term Short Memory (LTSM) that is used in Recurrent Neural Networks (RNN).

   a) Statement 1 is correct, but statement 2 is incorrect.

   b) Statement 1 is incorrect, but statement 2 is correct.

   c) Both the statements are correct.

   d) Both the statements are incorrect.

6. Statement 1: A Neural Network is comprised of interconnections between the set of computing nodes at consecutive layers.

   Statement 2: John McCarthy 1955 coined the term "artificial intelligence."

   a) Statement 1 is correct, but statement 2 is incorrect.

   b) Statement 1 is incorrect, but statement 2 is correct.

   c) Both the statements are correct.

   d) Both the statements are incorrect.

7. Statement 1: Robot Sophia is a social humanoid robot developed by Hanson Robotics, Hong Kong. Sophia was first appeared on Feb.14, 2016.

   Statement 2: In Oct. 2017, Sophia became a Saudi Arabian citizen, the first RobotRobot to become a citizen of any country in the world.

   a) Statement 1 is correct, but statement 2 is incorrect.

   b) Statement 1 is incorrect, but statement 2 is correct.

   c) Both the statements are correct.

   d) Both the statements are incorrect.

8. Statement 1: AI can be defined as a form of intelligence, a type of technology, and a field of study, which is used for making intelligent machines, including robots.

   Statement 2: Computer vision is defined as a field of artificial intelligence that trains computers to interpret and understand the visual world.

a) Statement 1 is correct, but statement 2 is incorrect.

b) Statement 1 is incorrect, but statement 2 is correct.

c) Both the statements are correct.

d) Both the statements are incorrect.

9. Statement 1: Machine learning is not related to getting computers to act without being explicitly programmed and Arthur Samuel prepared the first computer learning application in 1952.

   Statement 2: Oxford University students in 1979 invented the self-navigating Stanford Cart.

   a) Statement 1 is correct, but statement 2 is incorrect.

   b) Statement 1 is incorrect, but statement 2 is correct.

   c) Both the statements are correct.

   d) Both the statements are incorrect.

10. Statement 1: Intelligence has not played a significant role in our evolution and establishing human civilisation.

   Statement 2: Artificial Intelligence is sub-divided into three categories: AI, ML, and DL.

   a) Statement 1 is correct, but statement 2 is incorrect.

   b) Statement 1 is incorrect, but statement 2 is correct.

   c) Both the statements are correct.

   d) Both the statements are incorrect.

ANSWERS									
1. (c)	2. (d)	3. (a)	4. (b)	5. (c)	6. (c)	7. (c)	8. (c)	9. (d)	10. (b)

6.3.6 Assertion Reason Type Questions

1. Assertion (A): Artificial Intelligence covers a wide range of domains and applications.

   Reason(R): The core idea of AI is making machines and algorithms, which are capable of performing computational tasks that would otherwise require human-like brain functions.

   a) Both A and R are correct, and R is the correct reason for A.

   b) Both A and R are correct, and R is not the correct reason for A.

   c) A is correct, but R is incorrect.

   d) A is incorrect, but R is correct.

2. Assertion (A): A biased person favours one side or issue over another.

   Reason(R): Biased means having a preference for one thing over another, and the bias can also be present in Artificial Intelligence.

   a) Both A and R are correct, and R is the correct reason for A.

   b) Both A and R are correct, and R is not the correct reason for A.

c) A is correct, but R is incorrect.

d) A is incorrect, but R is correct.

3. Assertion (A): Artificial Intelligence (AI) is defined as the ability of a digital computer and/ computer-controlled RobotRobot to perform tasks that are generally associated with intelligent humans.

   Reason(R): The intended purpose of AI is to make an intelligent machine that initially thinks as good as a human being.

   a) Both A and R are correct, and R is the correct reason for A.

   b) Both A and R are correct, and R is not the correct reason for A.

   c) A is correct, but R is incorrect.

   d) A is incorrect, but R is correct.

4. Assertion (A): Bias in AI systems may occur in the data or in the algorithmic model used.

   Reason(R): It is not easy to develop and train AI systems with unbiased data and to develop algorithms that can be easily explained and understood.

   a) Both A and R are correct, and R is the correct reason for A.

   b) Both A and R are correct, and R is not the correct reason for A.

   c) A is correct, but R is incorrect.

   d) A is incorrect, but R is correct.

5. Assertion (A): AI is the term that is frequently applied to the project of developing systems embedded with the intellectual processes that are characteristic of humans, like the ability to reason, discover meaning, generalise or learn, from past experience.

   Reason(R): The human-machine interface is also known as the man-machine interface (MMI), computer-human interface, or human-computer interface.

   a) Both A and R are correct, and R is the correct reason for A.

   b) Both A and R are correct, and R is not the correct reason for A.

   c) A is correct, but R is incorrect.

   d) A is incorrect, but R is correct.

6. Assertion (A): At the very core, CV means enabling computers to derive meaning from spoken or written text in natural language input.

   Reason(R): AI is a field of study covering human behaviour, biology, psychology, language, and linguistics.

   a) Both A and R are correct, and R is the correct reason for A.

   b) Both A and R are correct, and R is not the correct reason for A.

   c) A is correct, but R is incorrect.

   d) A is incorrect, but R is correct.

7. Assertion (A): A Neural Network is comprised of interconnections between the set of computing nodes at consecutive layers.

   Reason(R): Frank Rosenblatt designed the first artificial neural network in 1957.

   a) Both A and R are correct, and R is the correct reason for A.

   b) Both A and R are correct, and R is not the correct reason for A.

   c) A is correct, but R is incorrect.

   d) A is incorrect, but R is correct.

8. Assertion (A): The Most commonly used Artificial Neural Network is BNN.

   Reason(R): A Chabot is a computer program designed to simulate conversation with human users, especially over the Internet.

   a) Both A and R are correct, and R is the correct reason for A.

   b) Both A and R are correct, and R is not the correct reason for A.

   c) A is correct, but R is incorrect.

   d) A is incorrect, but R is correct.

9. Assertion (A): One of the key features that distinguish humans from other living things in the world is intelligence.

   Reason(R): Intelligence is the ability to understand, apply knowledge, and improve skills.

   a) Both A and R are correct, and R is the correct reason for A.

   b) Both A and R are correct, and R is not the correct reason for A.

   c) A is correct, but R is incorrect.

   d) A is incorrect, but R is correct.

10. Assertion (A): The goal of AI is to develop machines that behave as though they were intelligent.

    Reason(R): In 1985, John McCarthy, one of the pioneers of AI, was the first to define the goal of artificial intelligence.

    a) Both A and R are correct, and R is the correct reason for A.

    b) Both A and R are correct, and R is not the correct reason for A.

    c) A is correct, but R is incorrect.

    d) A is incorrect, but R is correct.

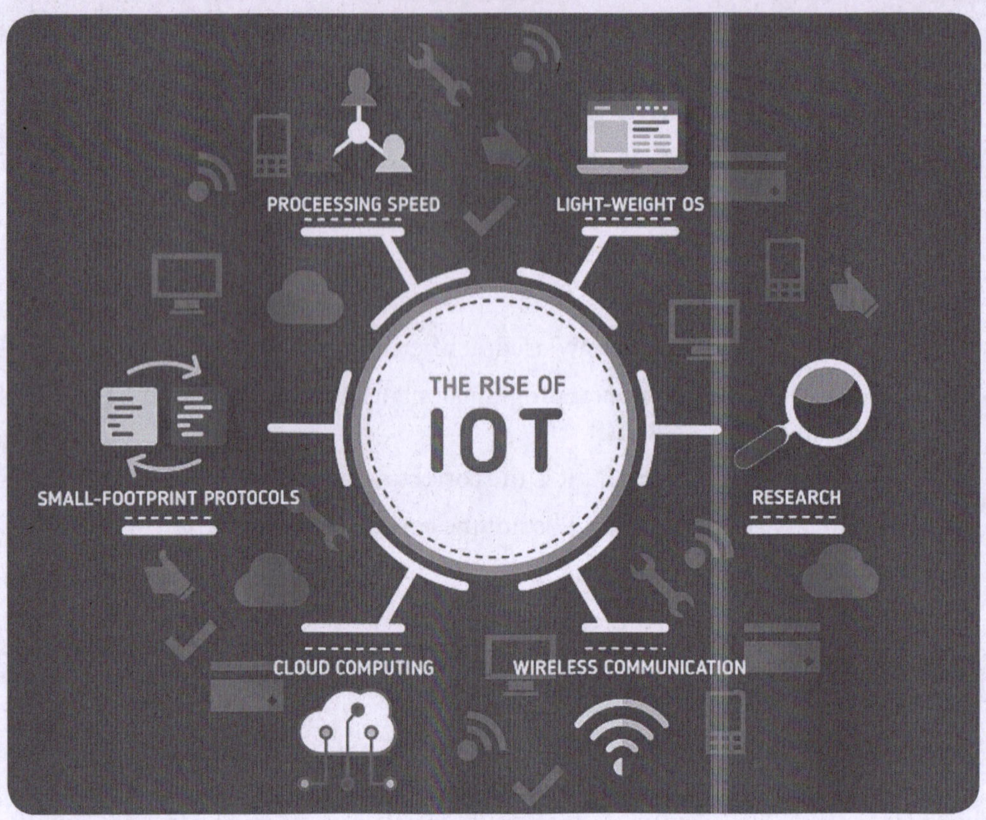

Figure 6.7

ANSWERS									
1. (a)	2. (a)	3. (b)	4. (a)	5. (b)	6. (d)	7. (b)	8. (d)	9. (a)	10. (c)

6.3.7 Competency-Based Questions

1. Suppose Kundan was suffering from a genetic disorder. He wants personalized medical care to treat the disease or disorder that is caused due to gene mutations, and that is achieved by understanding the genetic blueprint of the patient. Doctor asked him for the analysis to identify the order of nucleotides. This process is called:

   a) Genome sequencing   b) DNA analysis

   c) DNA blueprint   d) None of the above

2. Suppose Atharv has purchased a house in *Galaxy Wonderland Apartments* in a city called ***PSK204***. The house has the following features:

   i. Cameras will track the home's exterior even in the dark black outside.

   ii. A thermostat (controlling the temperature of AC or fridge) can be controlled from the bed, the airport, anywhere by his smartphone.

   iii. LED lights in the home can be switched on or off by using a smartphone.

   iv. Motion sensors are used to send an alert when there's motion around the house and to differentiate between pets and burglars.

v. Turning lights and appliances at home on or off from the mobile device.

vi. Door locks and garage doors can be opened automatically by using a smartphone.

vii. Setting Auto alerts from the security system to go to your smartphone.

The city under reference is called:

a) Electronic City b) Noble City

c) Smart City d) Future City

3. Suppose Sugandha is using an AI technique that finds wide applications in email classifying into "Social," "Personal," and "Promotional" categories, image recognition, face recognition, and text recognition systems. The fundamental of this technique/device is to create parameters that draw the line between doing different objects classifying them into two classes. She is using:

   a) Vector Analysis b) Data Analysis

   c) Support Map d) Vector Machines

4. Which type of problem is solved by using Vector machines?

   a) Classification problems b) Regression problems

   c) Typical problems d) None of the above

ANSWERS
1. (a) 2. (c) 3. (d) 4. (a)

6.3.8 VSA

1. Define artificial intelligence.

Ans. An ability of a computer or computer-controlled Robot to perform tasks generally associated with intelligent human beings is called AI.

2. What is the main cause of AI Bias?

Ans. Bias in AI systems occurs due to the data used or fault in the algorithmic model.

3. Define AI Bias.

Ans. AI bias is also known as Machine learning bias or Algorithm bias. It is a phenomenon that occurs when an algorithm produces incorrect results due to erroneous theories in the machine learning process.

4. What is Natural Language Toolkit?

Ans. NLTK is one of the platforms for building Python programs that can work with human language data.

5. Which Chatbot has been produced by Amazon?

Ans. Alexa

6. What are the three sub categories of Artificial Intelligence?

Ans. Artificial Intelligence can be sub-divided into three categories: Artificial Intelligence, Machine Learning, and Deep Learning.

7. What are the three domains of AI?

Ans. The main three domains of AI are Data, Computer Vision (CV), and Natural Language Processing (NLP).

8. Who was the first person to define the goal of artificial intelligence?

Ans. John McCarthy (1955)

9. What is the primary goal of AI?

Ans. 'The goal of AI is to develop machines that behave as though they were intelligent.'

10. Define Intelligence?

Ans. Intelligence is the ability to understand, apply knowledge, and improve skills that have played a significant role in our evolution and in establishing human civilization.

11. Who gave the following definition of AI?

"*The science of making machines for doing things that would require intelligence if done by man is termed as Artificial Intelligence.*"

Ans. Alan Turing

12. Who created NetTalk, which learned to pronounce words in 1985?

Ans. Terry Sejnowski

13. Which system in 1997 defeated World Chess Champion?

Ans. IBM's Deep Blue system

14. Who first used the term "artificial intelligence" in 1955?

Ans. John McCarthy

15. Who, in1952, prepared the first computer learning application?

Ans. Arthur Samuel

16. What is Deep Learning?

Ans. In deep learning, the machine uses different layers to learn from the data.

17. Define Machine Learning.

Ans. Machine Learning is the art of the study of algorithms that learn from examples and experience.

18. Which automobile company became the first one to launch a self-driving vehicle in 2018?

Ans. Tesla

19. What is the full form of SDGs?

Ans. Sustainable Development Goals

20. What is the full form of NLP?

Ans. Natural Language Processing

21. What is the foundational element that makes AI so powerful?

Ans. Data

22. What is the full form of AGI?

Ans. Artificial General Intelligence

23. Which RobotRobot is a social humanoid robot developed by Hanson Robotics, Hong Kong, in 2016?

Ans. Robo Sophia

24. What is genome sequencing?

Ans. Genome sequencing is the analysis to identify the order of nucleotides.

25. Define Collaborative filtering.

Ans. Collaborative filtering focuses on identifying similar users and recommending items preferred by related users.

26. What are Content-based recommendations?

Ans. It understands users' interests based on the ratings/feedback provided for a few items and suggests similar items to them.

27. What do you mean by IoT?

Ans. The network of interconnected things or devices having sensors, software, network connectivity, and necessary electronics; that are used to collect and exchange data, making them responsive, is called the Internet of Things (IoT).

28. Define Artificial General Intelligence (AGI).

Ans. AGI is the intelligence that can be as intelligent as human beings and perform intellectual tasks as humans can do.

29. What is PathNet?

Ans. PathNet is defined as a neural network algorithm that uses agents embedded in the neural network to discover what parts of the network are to be re-used for new tasks.

30. What is Artificial Super Intelligence?

Ans. Artificial Superintelligence has the ability to surpass or outperform the most intelligent human beings in every intellectual factor and by an extreme margin.

31. What is a smart city?

Ans. A Smart city is a city or urban area that uses different types of electronic gadgets, sensors, and the Internet of Things (IoT) for collecting data and then using the insights gained from the collected data to manage assets, resources, and services efficiently.

32. What are the other terms used for HMI?

Ans. Man-machine interface (MMI), computer-human interface, or human-computer interface.

33. What is a chatbot?

Ans. A Chabot is a computer program designed to simulate conversation with human users, especially over the Internet.

34. Give two examples of Chatbot.

Ans. Alexa, Slush, Vainu, Dominos, etc.

35. What is the full form of PCA?

Ans. Principal Component Analysis

36. Define feature extraction.

Ans. Feature extraction is the process of identifying a minimal set of informative features or attributes from the provided dataset.

37. What is CAA?

Ans. Crossbar Adaptive Array is a neural network capable of self-learning.

38. Define a neural network.

Ans. A Neural Network is comprised of interconnections between the set of computing nodes at consecutive layers.

39. What do you mean by CNN?

Ans. Convolutional Neural Networks (CNN) rolls the received input with the learned spatial filters/patterns to identify features at the convolution layer, and these signals are feed-forwarded to the next layers for performing recognition tasks.

40. What is the full form of RNN?

Ans. Recurrent Neural Networks.

41. How does deep learning perform?

Ans. The deep learning framework performs automatic feature extraction along with classification learning in a better way.

42. What is ANN?

Ans. An artificial neural network comprises a collection of simulated neurons.

43. Define node.

Ans. Each neuron in ANN is called a node that is connected to other nodes via links that correspond to biological axon-synapse-dendrite connections.

44. What is the use of Vector machines?

Ans. Vector machines or support vectors are capable of solving classification problems.

45. What are SDGs?

Ans. The Sustainable Development Goals (SDGs) or the Global Goals were adopted by all United Nations Member States as a universal call to take action to end poverty, protect the planet, and ensure peace and prosperity by 2030.

46. What is Park Adelaide?

Ans. This is a mobile app installed by 'The city of Adelaide' as a smart parking system in February 2018 that provides the user with accurate and real-time parking information.

47. Which Chatbot was created by Microsoft that was forced to close in less than one day, on March 23, 2016?

Ans. Tay chatbot

48. Define data mining.

Ans. Data mining is all about extracting meaningful knowledge from data.

49. What is HMI?

Ans. Human-machine interaction (HMI) is the communication and interaction between a human and a machine via a user interface.

50. How many SDGs were adopted by the UNO?

Ans. 17 SDGs.

51. What do you mean by Roboethics?

Ans. The term "robot ethics" or "robotics" refers to the morality of how humans design, construct, use, and treat robots, and it considers both how artificially intelligent devices may be used to harm or benefit humans and how they may be used to benefit humans.

52. Define computer vision (CV).

Ans. Computer Vision is defined as the ability of a machine to extract information from an image that is necessary to solve a task.

53. What is the purpose of Machine Learning?

Ans. Its main purpose is to enable machines to learn by themselves using the provided data for making accurate Predictions/ Decisions.

54. A Robot can speak 9 Indian and 37 Foreign languages. It was developed by a teacher of Kendriya Vidyalaya, IIT Campus, Mumbai- Mr. Dinesh Patel. What is its name?

Ans. Robot Shalu.

55. Name two common machine learning applications.

Ans. Targeted marketing, recommendation engine, Customer churn prevention, Sentiment analysis, Risk Management, Anti-money laundering, Fraud detection (any two).

56. Define NLP.

Ans. Natural Language Processing inputs machines the ability to read and understand human language.

57. What is the goal of CV?

Ans. The goal of Computer vision is not only to see but also to process and provide useful results based on the observations.

58. Give two examples in which CV is used.

Ans. Self-driven car, facial recognition device, face filter techniques, medical imaging, etc

59. What do you mean by Espionage?

Ans. Espionage (spying) involves the disclosure or theft of many types of information, especially secrets, political, military, business, or industrial information.

60. What is Identity theft?

Ans. Identity theft is the use of an individual's personally identifying information by someone else (often a stranger) without that individual's permission or knowledge.

61. What do you mean by Data Retrieval?

Ans. This is the process of identifying and extracting data from a database as per the query provided by the users.

62. What is Copyright infringement?

Ans. Copyright infringement is the use or reproduction of copyright-protected material without the permission of the copyright holder.

63. What are the sources to collect data?

Ans. Data is collected from various sources, like Surveys, Sensors, Observations, Web scrapping (Internet), Interviews, Documents and records, Oral histories, etc.

64. Which form of AI is the most advanced form of Artificial Intelligence?

Ans. Deep Learning (DL)

65. Define data privacy?

Ans. Data privacy is defined as a branch of data security concerned with the proper handling of data -consent, notice, and regulatory obligations.

66. What are the different forms in which data is collected?

Ans. Numeric, text, audio, video, or image

67. An AI domain is used by search engines like Google, Yahoo, Bing, Ask, and AOL. Name it.

Ans. Data science

68. What is web scraping?

Ans. Web Scraping is the collection of Web data from websites on the Internet using a web browser.

69. What is the main function of sensors?

Ans. Sensors or Transducers convert real-world phenomena like temperature, force, and movement to voltage or current signals that can be used as inputs.

70. What is a spreadsheet?

Ans. A spreadsheet is defined as a computer program used for accounting and recording data using rows and columns to enter information.

71. What is the full form of SQL?

Ans. Structured Query Language.

72. What is a chatbot?

Ans. Any computer program designed to simulate human conversation through voice commands or text chats, or both is called a chatbot.

73. What is a corpus?

Ans. A structured but large set of texts that can be read by machines and have been produced in a natural communicative setting is called a corpus.

74. What is the full form of NLTK?

Ans. Natural Language Toolkit

75. What is the most common source of data collection by many companies?

Ans. Smartphones

76. Expand IoT.

Ans. Internet of Things

77. What do you mean by AI Ethics?

Ans. The ethics of AI lies in the ethical quality of its Prediction, the ethical quality of the end outcomes drawn out of that, and the ethical quality of the impact it has on human beings.

78. What is dealt in Deep Learning?

Ans. Deep Learning deals with a large amount of data which enables software to train itself to perform tasks dealing.

79. What do you mean by genome sequencing?

Ans. The personalized medical care to treat diseases or disorders that are caused due to gene mutations is achieved by understanding the genetic blueprint of the patient. Genome sequencing is the analysis to identify the order of nucleotides.

Figure 6.8: Robo Sophia

6.3.9 Short Answer Type Questions

1. Define the Internet of Things (IoT).

Ans. Internet of Things (IoT) is the network of interconnected things or devices having sensors, software, network connectivity, and necessary electronics that are used to collect and exchange data, making them responsive.

2. Explain the concept of 'Smart City.

Ans. A Smart city is a city or urban area that uses different types of electronic gadgets, the Internet of Things (IoT), and sensors to collect data and then use the insights gained from the collected data to manage assets, resources, and services efficiently.

Artificial Intelligence (AI), along with IoT, has the potential to resolve the key challenges posed by the excessive urban population because it can help in many areas like traffic management, healthcare, energy distribution, energy and water crisis, etc. IoT data and AI technology can be used to improve the lives of the citizens and businesses that inhabit a smart city. Consider some of the most popular cases that have already been implemented in smart cities across the world.

3. Explain Machine Learning (ML).

Ans. Machine learning is related to getting computers to act without being explicitly programmed. Machine learning is the type of artificial intelligence where we create an algorithm that can learn from data rather we write rules to generate intelligence. In conventional programming, logic is written and is given input, and the program produces the output. In Machine learning, the system is given a set of inputs and outputs that is associated, and once that is done, we can use the system to produce output from another set of inputs.

4. How will you differentiate between ML and Data Mining?

Ans. The process of ML is similar to Data Mining, with the key difference that data mining is all about extracting knowledge from data, while machine learning is related to learning to work on future data from the actual data available. Both Machine learning and Data Mining are parts of Data Science.

5. How will you correlate AI with machines' abilities?

Ans. Artificial Intelligence has always been a thing of curiosity among people. Artificial Intelligence (AI) now is known as the ability of machines to perform cognitive tasks, which a human brain can do, like thinking, perceiving, learning, problem-solving, decision making, etc. The development of AI is inspired by the ways people use their brains to perceive, learn, reason out and decide the action.

6. Differentiate between artificial Intelligence and Natural Intelligence.

Ans. The main difference between artificial Intelligence and Natural Intelligence is given below:

Artificial Intelligence	Natural Intelligence
(i) Non-creative	(i) Creative
(ii) Precise	(ii) Non-Precise
(iii) Consistency	(iii) Non-consistent
(iv) Multitasking	(iv) Not easy to handle

7. How is artificial intelligence related to the traits of the human mind?

Ans. Artificial Intelligence is defined as the ability to design smart machines or to develop self-learning software applications that work like the traits of the human mind, such as reasoning, problem-solving, planning, decision making, etc.

8. Define AI, ML, and DL.

Ans. **Artificial Intelligence:** Most smartphones and other internet devices use artificial intelligence.

Machine Learning: Machine Learning is the art of the study of algorithms that learn from examples and experience.

Deep Learning: In deep learning, the machine uses different layers to learn from the data.

9. What kind of bias may be present in data used in AI systems?

Ans. Bias in AI systems occurs due to the data used or fault in the algorithmic model. Since humans and AI work together to make decisions, data researchers are trying to find new ways to ensure that human bias does not affect the data or algorithms used to inform those decisions. AI systems are good till the data we put into them is unbiased. Some data may contain biases, like implicit racial, gender, ideological biases, etc.

10. What is the harm of using biased data in AI systems?

Ans. Many AI systems are continued to be trained using biased data, making this an alarming problem. It is believed that bias can be tamed. The AI systems tackling bias well will be the most successful ones. Avoiding bias remains a crucial principle for both humans and machines to prevent racial discrimination.

11. How is AI used in Intelligent Disaster Response systems?

Ans. Modern disaster rescue systems normally use AI-powered drones, robots, sensors to quickly collect specific information during crisis time about the exact location of trapped victims, the extent of damage, and topographical details of the landscape. AI systems assist rescue workers to identify the nearest and safest assemble points also for evacuating people from disaster-hit areas. These modules are used in mock disaster drills for identifying potentially vulnerable locations, planning precautionary actions, and monitoring the allocation of resources.

12. How is Data important in AI?

Ans. While the AI scenarios highlight the technology's incredible computational power, the practical, effective applications begin with data. Indeed, data is the foundational element that makes AI so powerful.

Google, Facebook, Amazon, etc., are considered leaders in AI because they have tons of data to crunch and for research. Other companies may not have massive amounts of data to use and apply it to.

13. What is the use of CV in AI systems?

Ans. By using digital images from cameras and videos and deep learning models, machines can identify and classify objects correctly and then respond to what they "see." In order to do so, the field includes activities, like processing and understanding images/ visual data. The need for incorporating vision capabilities in the existing applications being developed and deployed in the industry has increased at a noticeable pace. Applications like surveillance systems, object detection and recognition, activity recognition, image interpretation are in high demand.

14. Explain the types of AI.

Ans. There are three types of AI, as discussed below:

i. Artificial Narrow Intelligence (ANI) or Weak Artificial Intelligence

Narrow artificial intelligence (narrow AI) is a specific type of artificial intelligence in which a technology outperforms humans in some very narrowly defined task. Narrow enable a high-functioning system that replicates – and perhaps surpasses -- human intelligence for a dedicated purpose. At present, many systems can be classified as narrow

AI. Most of the AI systems as of today are known as systems based on Weak Artificial Intelligence. These systems were designed to solve a specific problem. AlphaGo was able to beat human champions on the board game, but it was considered to be a narrow AI (Weak AI).

ii. Artificial General Intelligence (AGI)

AGI is the intelligence that can be as intelligent as human beings and perform intellectual tasks as humans can do. Artificial General Intelligence (AGI) is the hypothetical intelligence of a machine having that is capable of understanding or learning any intellectual task that human beings can do. It is regarded as a primary goal of some artificial intelligence research and a common topic in science fiction and future studies.

iii. Artificial Super Intelligence

Artificial Superintelligence is considered as the last step in AI, having the ability to surpass or outperform the most intelligent human beings in every intellectual factor and by an extreme margin. Its learning and knowledge will be infinite and will also have the ability to create better machines than human beings.

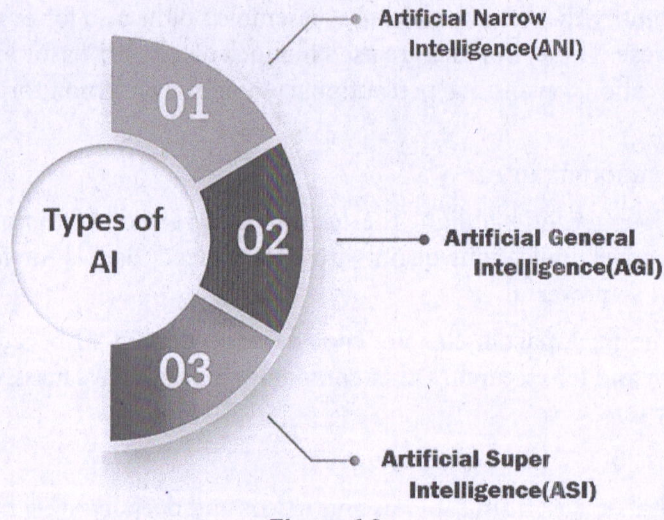

Figure 6.9

15. What is the biggest challenge of creating AGI? Explain.

Ans. The biggest challenge to solve when we are creating such intelligence is that one should be capable of figuring out how the human brain works exactly. That can make creating General artificial intelligence much tougher than one could ever imagine. The human brain is considered a state-of-the-art machine, which is a product of millions of years of evolution. It may simulate the future from the current state and give us consciousness, and may enable rational thinking. So, even if we could know how a single neuron works, it would not be very easy to know how this 20 W machine is able to load correct information at the correct time.

16. Explain the purpose of AI.

Ans. The intended purpose of AI is to make an intelligent machine that initially thinks as good as a human being, but eventually much better, even to the degree of far superior. The advantages and benefits offered by AI upgraded modules are based on two important factors:

(i) **Minimal Human Intervention:** AI-powered systems are regarded as the best-fit solutions in the environment, where human life is at risk. For example, space exploration, defense operations like bomb defusing, workplaces characterized by intense heat, Mineral mining, etc.

(ii) **Faster and Accurate:** The performance of well-trained AI-enabled applications reduces the chance for human errors to creep to a great extent. These AI versions are faster at tasks, especially in scientific research and in some time-consuming tasks. The routine, trivial, and repetitive type tasks can be automated with proper AI drove the technology to improve operational efficiencies.

17. Explain Human-Machine Interaction (HMI).

Ans. Human-machine interaction (HMI) is the communication and interaction between a human and a machine via a user interface. HMI is considered an interface that allows humans to interact with the machine. Examples of HMI physical aspects could be a machine with a touch display, a push button, a mobile device, a computer with a keypad, etc. The interface consists of hardware and software that allows user inputs to be translated as signals for machines that provide the required result to the user. Human-machine interface technology is being used in various industries, like electronics, entertainment, military, medical, etc. Human-machine interfaces help in integrating humans into complex technological systems.

The human voice is used to control smart thermostats or commands the intelligent speaker to play a song in the devices used at home. A few taps on the smartphone's touch screen are enough to view photos from Switzerland or Canada and enlarge individual pictures. Chatbots/AI Assistants conduct automatic dialogs with customers in messengers. Engineers in the industry use Virtual Reality (VR) glasses to enable them to walk through planned factory buildings. For all that to be possible, we need human-machine interaction (HMI).

18. How does human-machine interaction work?

Ans. **The devices are either controlled directly:** Users touch the smartphone's screen or issue a verbal command.

Or **the systems automatically identify what people want:** Chatbots, for instance, reply automatically to requests from customers and keep on learning, is also an example of HMI.

19. How is Chatbot helpful for entrepreneurs?

Ans. A Chatbot is an assistant that is enabled to communicate with humans through text messages. It may be a virtual companion that integrates into websites, applications, or instant messengers and thus, helps entrepreneurs to have more close relations with the customers.

20. There will be a growing demand for AI in the future. Are you agree with the statement? Justify your answer.

Ans. Yes, the demand for AI and related fields is going to rise in the future. In a survey, it is estimated that ML and Al alone have at least 1.4 million open jobs. There is no confusion that training in Data Science or Machine Learning and Al is the best way to give new jobs.

As per the AI talent report, the number of AI-related jobs has increased by 119 percent. Many industries like manufacturing, transportation, healthcare, finance, agriculture, retail, and customer service will receive growing business value from AI.

AI working/teaching companies have witnessed a strong demand for its Al and ML course for their unique value proposition. Its futuristic curriculum provides hands-on experience on various industry-relevant programming and tools and covers advanced concepts, like Robotic Process Automation, Developing Intelligent Bots, etc.

The availability of tremendous data has given birth to Data Science, which has further divided into Machine Learning, Artificial Intelligence, Deep Learning, etc. It is estimated that an increase of 364,000 to 2,720,000 openings will be generated in AI-related fields in the near future.

The demand for data scientists will rise tremendously. Many companies are offering programs that are designed to an upscale working knowledge of Statistics, Data Science with R, Python or SAS, understanding the concepts of Data Mining, Application of ML, Deep Learning and AI, Software Programming Languages, Database Management, and lastly Data Visualisation can help to succeed in this new field.

21. Explain Neural Networks.

Ans. Self-learning in neural networks was introduced in 1982, along with a neural network capable of self-learning named Crossbar Adaptive Array (CAA). It was a system with only one input, situation, and only one output, action (or behaviour). It had neither external advice input nor external reinforcement input from the environment.

A Neural Network is comprised of interconnections between the set of computing nodes at consecutive layers. The optimal weights of connections are calculated in the learning phase. Each node in NN calculates the weighted sum of values that are propagated to its input. The decision for computed values to feed-forward to the next layer is controlled by some activation functions. The Most commonly used Artificial Neural Networks are CNN.

22. What do you mean by LTSM, and where is it used?

Ans. Smart estimation of unknown values by using the given series of past data is termed as Long-Term Short Memory (LTSM) that is used in Recurrent Neural Networks (RNN).

23. Explain CNN.

Ans. Convolutional Neural Networks (CNN) rolls the received input with the learnt spatial filters/patterns to identify features at the convolution layer, and these signals are feed-forwarded to the next layers for performing recognition tasks. These convolutions to translational variations fuel recognition of labelling of features effectively, which is used in image recognition applications.

24. How do you assess the impact of Artificial Intelligence on Sustainable Development Goals (SDGs) to develop responsible citizenship?

Ans. Artificial Intelligence is frequently used in the headlines these days, sometimes portrayed in negative terms as the technology that will take over jobs or even human lives. But it could also become a valuable tool in the worldwide efforts to achieve the world's Sustainable Development Goals. The emergence of AI and its wider impact on many sectors across society now requires an assessment for understanding its effect on sustainable development.

AI capabilities are used by humans in various ways to match societal goals. An AI application combined with satellite imagery with object detection software is used to enable rescue workers to identify safe escape routes for disaster victims. Al-powered object detection is also at the core of a new application to bring relief to more than 250 million visually impaired people across the world.

25. How is AI Ethics playing its role in the modern world?

Ans. The ethics of artificial intelligence pertains to the ethics of technology specific to robots and other artificially intelligent entities. It may be divided into a concern with the moral behaviour of human beings as they design, construct, use and treat artificially intelligent devices. Machine ethics is related to the moral behaviour of artificial moral agents (AMAs). It also addresses the issues of singularity and superintelligence.

The term "robot ethics" or "roboethics" refers to the morality of how humans design, construct, use, and treat robots, and it considers both how artificially intelligent devices may be used to harm or benefit humans and how they may be used to benefit humans.

Artificial Intelligence (Al) is an effective science that employs strong enough approaches, methods, and techniques to solve unsolvable real-world based problems. Because of its unstoppable rise towards the future, there are also some discussions about its ethics and safety. Shaping an Al-friendly environment for people and a people-friendly environment for Al can be a possible answer for finding a shared context of values for both humans and robots.

26. Explain the principles of AI Ethics.

Ans. There are four principles of AI Ethics that help people trust the AI:

Principle 1: Ethical Purpose -- How to make sure your AI›s actions have a net good to society.

Principle 2: Fairness -- Ensuring your AI›s actions avoid entrenching historical disadvantage and avoid discriminating on sensitive features.

Principle 3: Disclosure -- Disclosing sufficient information to an AI›s stakeholders so that they can make informed decisions.

Principle 4: Governance -- Where there is a risk, apply high standards of governance over the design, training, deployment, and operation of AIs.

Figure 6.10

27. What is AI Bias, and how may biases be introduced in AI systems?

Ans. AI bias (Machine learning bias/ Algorithm bias) is a phenomenon that occurs when an algorithm produces incorrect results due to erroneous theories in the machine learning process.

Biases may find their way into the AI systems designed by humans and are used to make decisions by many users. Sometimes, bad data used to train AI may contain implicit racial and gender biases. Bias in AI systems can lose trust between humans and machines. For example, Microsoft's experimental AI chatbot, Tay, released racist commentary after learning through interaction with its Twitter followers.

28. How is AI influencing the world?

Ans. AI has changed the gaming world in terms of feel and emotions. Some video games react to player skill level. Depending on how well one does, adaptive AI changes the game's difficulty level up and down to give the user a greater challenge when user needs it or to prevent him/her from game-quitting in frustration. AI can also adapt to the playing style of user by making the game more exciting.

6.3.10 Long Answer Type Questions

1. Discuss the definitions of AI as stated by some world bodies, like World Economic Forum.

Ans. According to **World Economic Forum,**

Artificial intelligence (AI) is the software engine that is responsible for the Fourth Industrial Revolution, and its impact can be seen everywhere, be it homes, businesses, or political processes. In the form of robots, it will soon be driving cars, stocking warehouses, and caring for the young and elderly.

As per **European Artificial Intelligence (AI) leadership**: The path for an integrated vision, AI is not taken as a well-defined technology, and no universally agreed definition exists; rather, it is used as a cover term used for techniques related to data analysis and pattern recognition. AI has existed since the 1950s. Moreover, AI is still at a relatively early stage of development in many organisations and industries. In many industries and sectors, the range of potential applications, and the quality of most existing applications, have sufficient margins left for further development and improvement.

NITI Aayog (India) defines AI as follows:

'AI is defined as the ability of machines to perform cognitive tasks like thinking, perceiving, learning, decision making, and problem-solving. Initially taken as a technology that could mimic human Intelligence, AI has been developed in many ways that exceed its original conception. Due to advanced methods used in data collection, processing, and computation power, intelligent systems are being deployed for taking over a variety of tasks, fostering connectivity, and enhancing productivity.'

Alan Turing defined AI as follows:

"The science of making machines for doing things that would require intelligence if done by man is termed as Artificial Intelligence."

2. How will you prove that AI is a multidisciplinary study?

Ans. AI operates in close association with other fields of study or practice. Many times, it has been found that it drives its knowledge as well as has its applications across other domains of knowledge. The following table explains how the school domains of study (both formal and informal) interact with the concepts of Artificial Intelligence. AI Cross Breeds with Other Subjects.

Subject	Domain
Computer Science	Building computers
Mathematics	Algorithms, computability, proof, methods of representation, tractability, and decidability
Neuro-Science	How the basic information processing units, i.e., neurons Process Information
Linguistics	Grammar, syntax, knowledge representations
Statistics	Learning from data, uncertainty/ certainty of modelling
Economics	Rational economic agents, the usefulness of data & models, decision Theory
Cognitive Sciences	Processes and things in nature, interpretation of different Phenomena & their impact

3. Discuss three main applications of AI.

Ans. The main three applications of AI are discussed below:

i. **Recommendation Systems:** The best recommendation systems are those systems that identify or predict users' preferences to items based on items' profiles and inferences about users' behaviour. The willingness of users towards various items may be represented as user-item pairs in the utility matrix. There are two ways of discovering users' responses to items:

(i) Content-based recommendations understand users' interest based on the ratings/ feedback provided for a few items and suggest similar items to them.

(ii) Collaborative filtering focuses is identifying similar users and recommending items preferred by related other users.

ii. **Ethical Gene Editing:** The personalized medical care to treat diseases or disorders that are caused due to gene mutations is achieved by understanding the genetic blueprint of the patient. Genome sequencing is the analysis to identify the order of nucleotides. After having the insights from Genome sequencing, susceptible mutations would be identified to prescribe a sufferer-specific line of treatment.

iii. **Intelligent Disaster Response system:** Modern disaster rescue systems normally use AI-powered drones, robots, sensors to quickly collect specific information during crisis times about the exact location of trapped victims, the extent of damage, and topographical details of the landscape. AI systems assist rescue workers to identify the nearest and safest assemble points also for evacuating people from disaster-hit areas.

These modules are used in mock disaster drills for identifying potentially vulnerable locations, planning precautionary actions, and monitoring allocation of resources.

4. Discuss some examples of Smart Home Products and applications.

Ans. The following are the examples of smart home products and their functions:

i. Cameras will track your home's exterior even in the dark black outside.

ii. A thermostat (controlling the temperature of AC or fridge) can be controlled from your bed, the airport, anywhere by your smartphone.

iii. LED lights in the home can be switched on or off by using a smartphone.

iv. Motion sensors are used to send an alert when there's motion around your house and to differentiate between pets and burglars.

v. Turning lights and appliances at home on or off from the mobile device.

vi. Door locks and garage doors can be opened automatically by using a smartphone.

vii. Setting Auto alerts from the security system to go to your smartphone.

5. Discuss the main features of a smart city.

Ans. The main features of a smart city will be as follows:

(i) Smart Traffic Management

AI and IoT are used to implement smart traffic solutions to ensure that inhabitants of a smart city get from one place to another in the city as safely and efficiently as possible.

For example, one of the most congested cities in the world, Los Angeles, has implemented a smart traffic solution for controlling the flow of traffic. The city has installed road-surface sensors and closed-circuit TV cameras that send real-time updates about the actual traffic flow to a central traffic management system. The data so collected from the sensors and cameras are analysed by computers using AI, and it notifies the users about the congestion and traffic signal malfunctions.

(ii) Smart Parking

Anyone living in a city must have faced the struggle of finding a parking spot. Smart parking can ease the struggle for parking. With road surface sensors fitted in the ground on parking spots, smart parking solutions can determine the availability of parking spots on a real-time parking map. The smart parking system aims to improve traffic flow, reduce traffic congestion, and decrease carbon emissions.

The city of Adelaide installed a smart parking system in February 2018 by launching a mobile app: Park Adelaide. This app provides the user with accurate and real-time parking information. The app can provide users with the ability to locate, pay for, and even extend the parking session remotely.

(iii) Smart Waste Management

Essential city services include waste collection, proper management, and disposal. The explosion of the urban population necessitated the adoption of smart methods for waste management by adopting AI for smart recycling and waste management. For example, Barcelona's waste management system has sensors and devices fitted on waste bins to send notifications to the civil authorities to dispatch the waste collection trucks on filling of these bins. Separate bins for paper, glass, plastic, and waste food items are used in every locality.

(iv) Smart Lighting

Consumption of energy by street lights in cities and towns can be reduced with the use of smart lighting systems. The lamp posts are fitted with additional sensors for serving as Wi-Fi network hotspots. The lamps can also adjust the brightness.

(v) Smart Governance

The main aim of smart cities is to make a comfortable and convenient life for their inhabitants. Therefore, smart city governance is required. Smart governance ensures the use of Information and Communication Technology (ICT) intelligently in order to improve decision-making through better collaboration among different participants, including government and citizens. Smart governance will use data, evidence, and other resources to improve decision-making and compliance with the needs of the citizens.

(vi) Smart homes in smart cities

The scope for smart home technology is quite wide and will certainly have a beneficial effect on the lives of residents. Cities could become a safer, cleaner environment for all if new and future buildings use technology in the design and initial build stages.

Figure 6.11

6. What are the major challenges of AI?

Ans. The use of Artificial Intelligence has the following challenges:

i. Need for Massive Data Corpus

Before the deployment as a real-world solution, intelligent systems learn an optimized model with the help of a large amount of data during training and validation. The availability of large data volumes and the ability to handle them are two major limitations for the conventional systems and software applications while evolving AI-enabled editions. The sophisticated modelling techniques can estimate the model parameters with high precision using limited data samples, and its need is imminent.

ii. **Multimodal Interactions**

The efficiency and precision of perception-based recognition applications encompass computer-vision methods. It can be improved by leveraging the ability to interpret and process multiple modes of data simultaneously. This enables the recognition paradigm to ideally emulate human intelligence that works in conjunction with various senses like touch, vision, hearing, etc.

iii. **Beyond Human Control**

The exceptional capability of AI technology is used to understand and learn vast libraries of information at a faster pace. There are few threatening instances when an AI framework gained an emotional quotient and surpassed the extremities of human logical thinking. In such cases, the unusual behaviour of AI systems would lead to irreparable catastrophe.

iv. **AI can fail too**

Machines or software can fail anytime due to some bug or human error. For example, Facebook created a bot (an automated software program that is designed to create and control a fake Facebook account) that is completely automated software that generates a profile by scraping images and information from other sources. It faced failure when it reached a failure rate of 70%.

Microsoft was forced to close its Tay chatbot in less than one day, which was originally released on March 23, 2016. The chatbot began to post bad, inflammatory, and offensive tweets through its Twitter account.

v. **AI does not understand causal reasoning**

AI can only do for what it is programmed, and it normally does this extremely well, but unlike a real person, it cannot make on-the-spot quick judgments. For example, good marketing personnel will change or cancel any scheduled messaging when a tragic event occurs, but an AI device cannot take such a decision. This is because humans are capable of exhibiting empathy and compassion to the victims and their families whereas a machine, however, does not have the ability to show emotion, so it could get a company in trouble in times of crisis if it's not carefully managed or controlled.

vi. **Lack of Creativity**

Machines can not think and lack creativity, whereas human beings are quite creative. Humans can think and feel, which guides their decision-making skills, but machines cannot think. In terms of originality and creative thinking, a machine cannot be compared with the human brain.

vii. **High Maintenance cost**

High maintenance cost is another key consideration with procuring AI technologies. Businesses that lack in-house skills or are unfamiliar with Al often have to outsource the services, which is where challenges of cost and maintenance come in. Smart technologies may be expensive due to their complex nature, costs for repair, and ongoing support. The computational cost for training data models etc., can also be an additional expense.

7. Discuss the main components and characteristics of AI systems.

Ans. The components or frameworks that majorly contribute to the implementation of various intelligent systems are given as follows:

i. Feature Engineering

Feature extraction is the process of identifying a minimal set of informative features or attributes from the provided dataset. The performance of machine learning processes may be improved by choosing a meaningful set of features carefully.

The efficient feature extraction process ensures:

a) Reduction of the degree of disorders during the process of classifying datasets based on selected features and maximising the information gain.

b) Zero correlation among the features, achieving independence, and minimality of feature-set by using techniques like Principal Component Analysis (PCA), Gram-Schmidt orthogonalization process, etc.

ii. Neural Networks

Self-learning in neural networks was introduced in 1982, along with a neural network capable of self-learning named Crossbar Adaptive Array (CAA). It was a system with only one input, situation, and only one output, action (or behaviour). It had neither external advice input nor external reinforcement input from the environment.

A Neural Network is comprised of interconnections between the set of computing nodes at consecutive layers. The optimal weights of connections are calculated in the learning phase. Each node in NN calculates the weighted sum of values that are propagated to its input. The decision for computed values to feed-forward to the next layer is controlled by some activation functions.

iii. Deep Learning

In Deep learning architecture, more hidden layers between the input and output layers are present as compared to the layers present in artificial neural networks. Thus, the deep learning framework performs automatic feature extraction along with classification learning in a better way. These models use supervised learning to train with well-labeled datasets. Inspite of the presence of a large number of hidden layers and kit complex nature, the learning time of the model may be reduced with the usage of high-performance parallel-computing GPUs.

8. Discuss any four techniques used in AI.

Ans. Many AI techniques have emerged in the past decade for implementing and building AI systems. Some of them are as follows:

i. Natural Language Processing (NLP)

Natural language processing is the study of the interaction between a computer and a human language. AI refers to speech recognition and speech synthesis in human language.

This field of study is already in the application phase, and many companies are using it in many devices like voice assistants. For example, voice devices like Apple's Siri, Google

Assistant, Microsoft's Cortana, and Amazon's Alexa are based on natural language processing.

ii. **Artificial Neural Networks (ANN)**

An artificial neural network comprises a collection of simulated neurons. Each neuron is called a node that is connected to other nodes via links that correspond to biological axon-synapse-dendrite connections.

Neural networks are available in living beings. Humans and animals use a complex network of billions of neurons (which makes neural systems) to make decisions in day-to-day life and learn new things to do. Building artificial neural networks is taken as an attempt to create neural networks modelled on the human brain.

ANN can identify patterns in inputs as it processes a lot of data and learns from it, and uses different learning methods, like supervised learning, unsupervised learning, and reinforced learning. Neural networks are useful in pattern recognition, machine learning, and deep learning.

iii. **Vector machines**

Vector machines are capable of solving classification problems. For example, an email system like Gmail uses a vector machine for classifying emails as 'Social,' 'Promotion,' or 'Personal' in nature and placing them in the respective categories.

The fundamental of vector machines or support vectors is to create parameters that draw the line between doing different objects, classifying them into two classes. This AI technique finds wide applications in image recognition, face recognition, and text recognition systems.

iv. **Heuristics**

This technique is probably the most basic in AI and comes from our understanding of human behaviour in learning processes. As humans, make mistakes and learn, and keep doing things until you chance upon the answer or the right solution. Similarly, heuristics work on the principle of trial-and-error.

Heuristics are good techniques for solving problems where it is difficult to find a solution definitely. For example, telling the shortest route on a map. The best option to solve such a problem is to identify all possible routes and then, to identify the shortest one or the one which has the least traffic.

9. What do you mean by Sustainable Development Goals (SDGs)? Give a brief historical explanation.

Ans. All UN Member States in 2015 adopted **'The 2030 Agenda for Sustainable Development**. This document provided a shared blueprint for peace and prosperity for people and the planet. The Sustainable Development Goals (SDGs) or the Global Goals were adopted by all United Nations Member States like a universal call to take action to end poverty, protect the planet and ensure peace and prosperity by 2030. All the 17 Sustainable Development Goals (SDGs) were taken as an urgent call for action by all countries in a global partnership.

The building of SDGs took decades of time by countries and the UN, including the UN Department of Economic and Social Affairs. Some milestones are as follows:

- In Rio de Janeiro, during the Earth Summit (June 1992), 178 countries adopted Agenda 21 that is a comprehensive plan of action to build a global partnership for sustainable development and to improve human lives by protecting the environment.
- Again, the Member States unanimously adopted the Millennium Declaration at the Millennium Summit in September 2000 at UN Headquarters in New York.
- The Plan of Implementation (POI) was adopted at the World Summit on Sustainable Development in 2002. It was reaffirmed the global community's commitments to eradicate poverty and improve the environment, as it was built on Agenda 21. It gave more emphasis on multilateral partnerships.
- In the UN Conference on Sustainable Development in Rio de Janeiro (June 2012), a document entitled "***The Future We Want***" was adopted to launch a process to develop a set of SDGs.
- In 2013, the UN General Assembly set up a 30-member Open Working Group to develop a proposal on the SDGs.

All the 17 SDGs and their description are enlisted in the table. AI plays an important role in achieving the desired goals.

10. Explain the goals and objectives of SDGs and the use of AI to achieve them.

Ans. The goals and objectives of 17 SDGs and the use of AI to achieve them are enlisted below:

SDG -1 No Poverty: Eradicate extreme poverty for all people everywhere by 2030. AI in improving farming, technologies used in the distribution of farm products to the poorer and war-torn areas.

SDG -2 Zero Hunger: End hunger, achieve food security, and improved nutrition by 2030: enhanced communication interfaces and use of automated transport and logistics systems.

SDG -3 Good Health and Well-being: Ensure healthy lives and promote well-being for all at all ages by 2030.Use of AI in providing healthier, more productive, and accessible work environments for all employees.

SDG -4 Quality Education: Ensure that all girls and boys complete free, equitable, and quality primary and secondary education by 2030. Use of intelligent AI-powered systems to improve the efficiency of educational institutes, lowering their operational costs, robots in assisting the teaching process.

SDG -5 Gender Equality: To achieve gender equality and empower all women and girls. Use of AI and automated machines to understand and confront gender bias at all workplaces.

SDG -6 Clean Water and Sanitation: Ensure availability and sustainable management of water and sanitation for all by 2030. The use of AI, computer vision, and deep learning automatically detect contaminants in water and bring changes in the sanitation industry.

Goal -7 Affordable and Clean Energy: Ensure access to affordable, reliable, sustainable, and modern energy for all by 2030. Use of AI-powered predictive analysis to find out the energy consumption patterns, improved safety, efficiency, and reliability

Goal -8 Decent Work and Economic Growth: Promote sustained, inclusive, and sustainable economic growth. Use of AI in monotonous and dangerous work such as mining, dangerous industrial repetitive work for enhancing decent work culture.

Goal -9 Industry, Innovation, and Infrastructure: Build resilient infrastructure, promote inclusive and sustainable industrialization, and foster innovation by 2030.AI supports the people in various industries during data processing and industry workflows to explore complex reasoning and data analysis.

Goal -10 Reduced Inequality: Reduce inequality within and among countries by 2030.AI applications reduce inequalities like applications developed by Microsoft and Google help visually handicapped in automatic image recognition

Goal -11 Sustainable Cities and Communities: Make cities and human settlements inclusive, safe, resilient, and sustainable: digitalisation and AI algorithms aimed at improving fraud detection technology.

Goal -12 Responsible Consumption and Production: Ensure sustainable consumption and production patterns. Responsible AI to bring fairness and equality of gender, race, or similar attributes.

Goal -13 Climate Action: Take urgent action to combat climate change and its impacts. AI helps farmers to increase crop yields by providing inputs about climate change, and it is used to know the behaviour pattern of poachers to save wildlife.

Goal -14 Life Below Water: Conserve and sustainably use the oceans, seas, and marine resources for sustainable development. AI-empowered new advances in satellite observation, open data, and machine learning are helping in the sustainability of life underwater.

Goal -15 Life on Land: Protect, restore, and promote sustainable use of terrestrial ecosystems, combat desertification, and halt biodiversity loss. AI is providing automated data collection and decision-making to optimise farming processes, save ecosystems, protect endangered areas, etc.

Goal -16 Peace and Justice: Strong Institutions promote peaceful and inclusive societies for sustainable development; provide access to justice for all. Use of AI in fighting against cybercrimes and use of robots for peace, justice, and strong institutions

Goal -17 Partnerships to achieve the goal: Strengthen the means of implementation and revitalize the global partnership for sustainable development. Use of AI initiatives like data analysis and image recognition to develop policies leadership skills, partnering abilities, etc.

11. Explain the main points of the AI code of ethics or AI Principles.

Ans. Although AI developers are still in the early stages of Al adoption, it is important for enterprises to make ethical and responsible approaches when creating Al systems. To that end, a non-profit institute was founded by MIT cosmologist Max Tegmark, Skype co-founder Jaan Tallinn and Deep Mind research scientist Viktoriya Krakovnahas - worked with Al researchers and developers to establish a set of guiding principles which are now referred to as AI Principles.

The AI code of ethics states that:

i. A culture of trust, cooperation, and transparency should be raised among researchers and developers of AI.

ii. Highly autonomous Al systems should be designed so that their goals and behaviours can be assured to align with human values throughout their operation.

iii. Financial investments in AI should be accompanied by funding for research on ensuring its beneficial use.

iv. If an Al system causes harm, it should be possible to determine why.

v. Teams developing Al systems should actively cooperate to avoid money saving on safety standards.

vi. Al systems should be safe and secure throughout their operational lifetime.

vii. The designers and builders of advanced AI systems are considered as the stakeholders. They will plan implementation the use, misuse, and actions, with a responsibility and opportunity to shape those implications.

viii. Al systems should be designed and operated so that it is compatible with ideals of human dignity, freedoms, rights, and cultural diversity.

ix. People should be given the right to access, manage, and control the data they generate, given Al systems' power to analyse and utilize that data.

x. The usage of AI to personal data must not unreasonably limit people's real or alleged liberty.

6.3.11 HOTS QUESTIONS

1. How will you explain the relationship of AI code with its purpose?

Ans. An Al code of ethics or an AI value platform is a policy statement that defines the role of artificial intelligence for its application to the continued development of the human race. The purpose of the Al code of ethics is to provide AI developers with guidance when faced with an ethical decision about the use of artificial intelligence devices.

2. AI is a threat to mankind. How will you justify this statement?

Ans. Yes, Artificial Intelligence may be a threat to human dignity. We require authentic feelings or empathy from people in some positions, and if machines replace them, humans will find themselves alienated, devalued, and frustrated. AI technology must not be used to replace people in positions that require care and respect. For example, the following positions should not be replaced by AI devices:

i. A customer service representative (AI technology is already used today for telephone-based interactive voice response systems)

ii. A therapist

iii. A nursemaid for the elderly

iv. A soldier

v. A judge

vi. Police officer

3. Why is it essential to use unbiased data in AI systems?

Ans. Identifying and removing bias in AI systems is essential for building trust between humans and AI machines. Since AI systems find, understand, and point out human inconsistencies in decision making, these machines can reveal ways and methods in which humans are partial and cognitively biased, leading to adopting more impartial. During the process of recognizing the bias and teaching machines about common values, an improvement in AI is required. We might just improve ourselves.

4. How is AI providing solutions to the biggest challenges faced by humans? Illustrate with examples.

Ans. The AI provides the solution to some of the most pressing problems faced by society. But it also presented some challenges, like mysterial "black box" algorithms, unethical use of data, and potential job profile change. When is rapid advances in machine learning (ML) increase the scope and scale of AI's deployment across all aspects of daily life, then the technology itself may learn and change on its own. Multi-stakeholder collaboration is required to optimise accountability, transparency, privacy, and impartiality to create trust.

5. How can we reduce bias in AI systems?

Ans. The efforts to reduce bias may include using contractual approaches to ethics and describing principles that people should use in decision-making, and determining how human minds apply these principles. The goal is to make machines that apply some human values and principles in decision-making. They have developed an independent bias rating system to determine the fairness of an AI system.

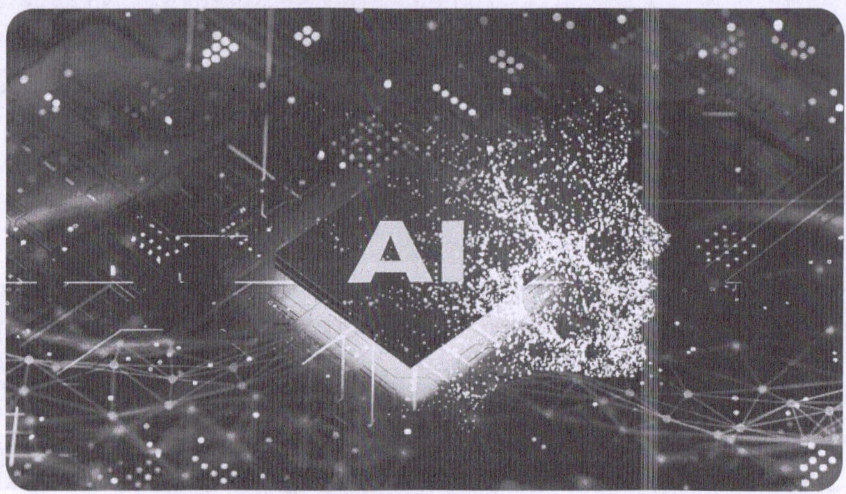

Figure 6.12

6.4 PRACTICE QUESTIONS

1. Why is artificial intelligence important?
2. Define sustainable development.
3. What are SDGs?
4. What do you mean by Machine Learning? Illustrate with a suitable example.
5. What do you mean by Smart City?
6. Mention one application of Deep Learning.
7. What is NLP?

8. Explain the three domains of AI.
9. Write two uses of Smart Governance.
10. Define and illustrate Supervised Learning.
11. Explain Reinforcement Learning.
12. Mention two uses of Machine Learning.
13. Why are smart cities required?
14. Why is AI ethics important?
15. Differentiate between Machine Learning and Deep Learning.
16. Explain the various fields where AI is helpful in sustainable development.
17. What are the framework parts of a Smart City? Explain.
18. Explain various applications of AI for the purpose of supporting sustainable development.
19. Define the main aim of AI.
20. What is Computer Vision?
21. What is importance of a chatbot?
22. What is the purpose of AI?
23. Write three challenges of AI.
24. What do you mean by HMI?
25. Write the names/titles of any 8 SDGs.
26. Discuss the applications of Machine Learning.
27. How may artificial intelligence become a threat to human intelligence?

UNIT 7 Project Cycle

7.1 UNIT IN BRIEF

- AI Modelling refers to developing algorithms or AI models which can be trained to get intelligent output, i.e., writing codes to make a machine artificially intelligent.
- AI models can be classified either on Rule-based or Learning-based approaches.
- AI Project Cycle provides an appropriate framework that can lead us towards the goal.
- All elements in the AI system are interconnected, and one has to understand the elements and relationships between the elements to understand the system. The concept of a loop defines a chain of events in the system and relationships between them.
- Anyone can use decision trees to clarify and find an answer to a complex AI problem. Every branch of the decision tree represents a possible decision, outcome, or reaction, while the farthest branches on the decision tree represent the end results.
- Artificial intelligence (AI) is the ability of a machine to think, learn, and perform tasks usually requiring human intelligence, like speech recognition, visual perception, and decision-making skills.
- Artificial intelligence and machine learning are affecting the processes of researching, purchasing, and implementing IT tools in various industries.

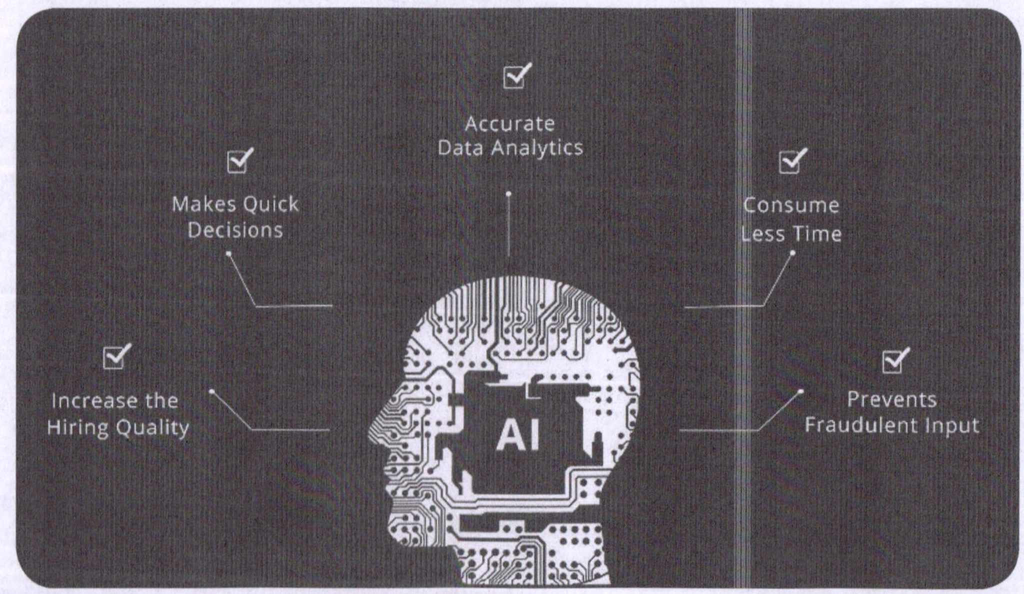

Figure 7.1

- Artificial Intelligence is an umbrella term for ML and DL.
- Copying someone's data from the website/internet without permission is termed a cybercrime.
- Data Acquisition is a process to collect data for the problem scoped, which has to be correct, authentic, and reliable. It is the second component of the AI Project Cycle after the problem scoping.
- Data acquisition is the second stage in the AI project cycle.
- Data acquisition is used to collect data that has to be authentic and reliable.
- Data Analysis consists of Data Requirement Gathering, Data Cleaning, Data Analysis, Data Collection, Data Interpretation, and Data Visualisation
- Data analysis means a process of cleaning, transforming, and modelling data to discover useful information for business decision-making.
- Data features can be collected from various sources like newspapers, cameras, observations, surveys, questionnaires, and so on.
- Data is defined as the raw fact, which is organised together to form information that needs to be processed further for analysis and data visualisation.
- Data may be a piece of information or facts and statistics collected together for reference or analysis purposes.
- Data modelling is the fourth stage in the AI project cycle.
- Datawrapper is a popular choice among media organisations that frequently use it to create charts and present statistics for media coverage.
- Decision tree learning is one of the most successful techniques for supervised classification learning.
- Decision tree learning is the technique used for supervised classification learning.
- Demand for data scientists is increasing continuously. The problems of collecting and normalizing clean and meaningful data for machine learning are to be tackled at a faster rate.
- Evaluation is a testing technique where the model is installed in the real world, and it is tested in as many ways as possible.
- Fusion chart is a widely-used and JavaScript-based charting and visualisation package. It can produce more than 90 different types of charts and integrates with a large number of platforms and frameworks.
- A high chart is often chosen for a fast and flexible solution, with a minimum need for specialist data and visualisation training before it can be put to work.
- In classification, data is categorised under different labels based on some parameters mentioned in the input.
- LOOPY is an interactive tool that can be worked without any knowledge of coding.
- Open-sourced websites are the government portals to provide the information to be used and referred to in data analytics. These websites/portals are authentic, accurate, and reliable. Some of the open-sourced websites are https://www.india.gov.in/data-portal-india , https://data.gov.in/ , https://dbie.rbi.org.in/DBIE/dbie.rbi?site=home , http://mospi.nic.in/data

- Plotly enables more complex and sophisticated visualisations due to the use of its integration with analytics-oriented programming languages, like Python, R, Matlab, etc. It is built using JavaScript.
- Preparing customer data for meaningful ML projects is a difficult task due to the variety of data sources that exist in the organisations.
- Problem scoping is a skill where the learners need to focus on the relevant details related to the problem.
- Regression is defined as the process of finding a model/ function for distinguishing the data into continuous real values in place classes.
- Sensors are often called Transducers.
- Sensors used in AI-enabled machines convert real-world phenomena like temperature, force, movement to voltage or current, etc., into signals.
- Simulation is defined as the method of designing a model in a real-world where you conduct experiments by changing the values of individual elements and seeing the effect in the other elements.
- Simulation refers to the method of designing a model of a real system.
- Sisense provides a full-stack analytics platform, but its visualisation capabilities provide a simple-to-use drag and drop interface which creates charts and more complex graphics with a minimum of hassle.
- Stakeholders are all those humans who are affected the most by the model used in the AI project.
- Testing data is used to assess the AI machine for its efficiency and performance too.
- Text Analytics is the process of extracting useful and structured knowledge from unstructured documents to find useful associations and insights.
- Text, Statistical, Diagnostic, Predictive, and Prescriptive Analysis are the types of Data Analysis.
- The analogy of an Artificial Neural Network may be made with Parallel Processing.
- The Artificial Intelligent project cycle describes all steps required to convert a real-life problem or a challenge into a computer-based Al model.
- The components of the AI Project Cycle Problem are scoping, Data acquisition, Data exploration, Modelling, and Evaluation.
- The data is labelled when entered into the model in a rule-based approach.
- The decision tree is the most potent and accessible tool for classification and prediction. "A Decision tree is a flowchart like a tree structure, in which each internal node represents a test on an attribute, each branch exhibits an outcome of the test, and each leaf node (terminal node) holds a class label."
- The field of Machine Learning (ML) is used by many people and organisations, and till today various businesses are still finding new ways to apply ML methods to their vast, complex, and expanding data sets.
- The larger Neural Network tends to perform better with large data.

- The learning-based Approach performs algorithms on a sample Data set which is called training data.
- The training data needs to be reliable, authentic, and accurate for the AI machine to work efficiently.
- Training data is used to give the AI machine a set of inputs on which the machine will be assessed later on.
- Types of Data Analysis: Text, Statistical, Diagnostic, Predictive, Prescriptive Analysis
- While taking up any AI project in an enterprise, a scientific method is used that is known as the AI Project cycle.
- A loop in the system defines a chain of events that signifies the cause and effects among system elements.
- A classification problem arises when the output variable is a category.
- A decision tree is a tree-like graph having three parts. Nodes represent the place where an attribute is picked and asked a question, edges represent the answers to the question, and the leaves represent the actual output. These are used in non-linear decision-making.
- A technique in which a computer program extracts data from human-readable output coming from another program is termed data scraping.

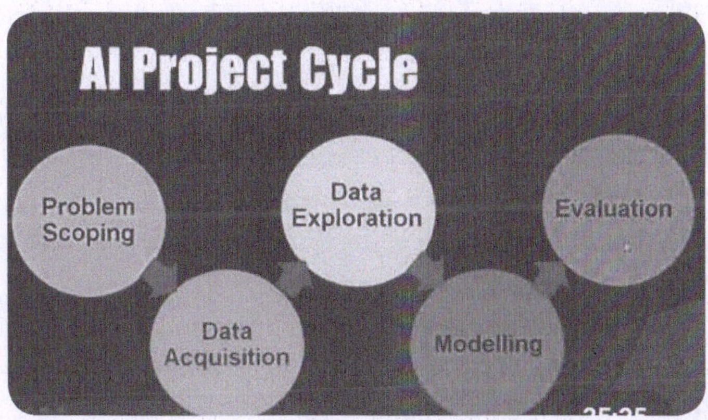

Figure 7.2

7.2 SOLVED CBSE/NCERT EXERCISES

7.2.1 VSA Questions

1. Name all the stages of an AI Project cycle.

Ans. Problem Scoping, Data Acquisition, Data Exploration, Modelling, Evaluation

2. What are sustainable development goals?

Ans. The Sustainable Development Goals (SDGs) or Global Goals are a collection of 17 interlinked goals that are designed to be a "blueprint for achieving a better and more sustainable future for all" so that future generation may live in peace and prosperity.

3. Name the 4Ws of problem canvases under the problem scoping stage of the AI Project Cycle.

Ans. The 4 Ws of problem canvas include: Who, What, Where, Why.

4. What is the objective of the evaluation stage?

Ans. This stage is to evaluate whether the ML algorithm is able to predict with high accuracy or not before deployment.

5. Which of the following is not an authentic source for data acquisition?

   a. Sensors b. Surveys c. Web Scraping d. System Hacking

Ans. System Hacking

6. Which type of graphical representation suits best for a continuous type of data like the monthly exam scores of a student?

Ans. Linear graph

7.2.2 Short Answer Type Questions

1. What is a problem statement template, and what is its significance?

Ans. The problem statement template gives a clear idea about the basic framework required to achieve the goal. It is the 4Ws canvas that segregates; what is the problem, where does it arise, who is affected, why is it a problem? It takes us straight to the goal.

2. Explain any two SDGs in detail.

Ans. (a) **No Poverty:** The Goal 1 strives to end poverty in all its forms everywhere globally by 2030. The goal has a total of seven targets to be achieved.

(b) **Quality Education:** This is Goal 4, which aspires to ensure inclusive and equitable quality education and promote lifelong learning opportunities for all. It has ten targets to achieve.

3. Mention the precautions to be taken while acquiring data for developing an AI Project. It should be from an authentic source and accurate. Look for redundant and irrelevant data parameters that do not take part in prediction.

4. What do you mean by Data Features?

Ans. Data features are columns in a dataset which we would like to give to our machine learning model as input for training.

5. Explain the Data Exploration stage.

Ans. In this stage of the project cycle, interpretation of some useful information out of the data is done. For this purpose, we explore the data and put it uniformly for a better understanding. This stage deals with validating / verification of the collected data and analyzing that:

   i. The data is acs per the specifications decided.

   ii. The data is free from errors.

   iii. The data is meeting our needs.

7.2.3 Long Answer Type Questions

1. Explain the AI Project Cycle in detail.

Ans. The steps involved in the AI project cycle are as given:

The first step is to Scope the Problem by which you set the goal for your AI project by stating the problem which you wish to solve with it. Under problem scoping, we look at various parameters which affect the problem we wish to solve so that the picture becomes clearer.

The next step is to acquire data that will become the base of our project as it will help us in understanding the parameters that are related to problem scoping.

Next, we go for data acquisition by collecting data from various reliable and authentic sources. Since the data we collect would be in large quantities, we can try to give it a visual image of different types of representations like graphs, databases, flow charts, maps, etc. This makes it easier for us to interpret the patterns in which our acquired data follows.

After exploring the patterns, we can decide upon the type of model we would build to achieve the goal. For this, we can research online and select various models which give a suitable output.

We can test the selected models and figure out which is the most efficient one.

The most efficient model is now the base of your AI project, and you can develop your algorithm around it.

Once the modelling is complete, you now need to test your model on some newly fetched data. The results will help you in evaluating your model and hence improving it. Finally, after evaluation, the project cycle is now complete and what you get is your AI project.

2. Draw the 4Ws problem canvas and explain each one of them briefly.

Ans. The 4Ws problem canvas is the basic template. While scoping a problem and using this canvas, the picture becomes clearer.

a) **Who**: The "Who" block helps us in analyzing the people getting affected directly or indirectly due to it? Under this, we find out who the 'stakeholders' to this problem are and what we know about them. Stakeholders are the people who face the problem and would be benefitted from the solution.

b) **What**: Under the "What" block, we need to look into what we have on hand. At this stage, we need to determine the nature of the problem. What is the problem, and how do we know that it is a problem?

c) **Where**: In this block, we had to focus on the context/situation/location of the problem. It will help us look into the situation in which the problem arises, the context of it, and the locations where it is prominent.

d) **Why**: In the "Why" canvas, we think about the benefits which the stakeholders would get from the solution and how it would benefit them as well as the society.

3. What is the need for an AI Project Cycle? Explain.

Ans. The project cycle is the process of planning, organising, coordinating, and finally developing a project effectively throughout its phases, from planning through execution, then completion and review to achieve pre-defined objectives. If we have to develop an AI project, the AI Project Cycle provides us with an appropriate framework that can lead us towards the goal. The major role of the AI Project Cycle is to distribute the development of AI projects in different stages so that the development becomes easier, clearly understandable, and the steps/stages should become more specific to get the best output. It mainly has five ordered stages which distribute the entire development in specific and clear steps: The steps are Problem Scoping, Data Acquisition, Data Exploration, Modelling, and Evaluation.

4. Five sustainable Development Goals are mentioned below. Write two problems under each goal that you think should be addressed for achieving the goal.

   a. Quality Education

   b. Reduced Inequalities

   c. Life on Land

   d. No Poverty

   e. Clean Water and Sanitation

Ans. a. **Quality Education:**

i. Providing education remotely by leveraging hi-tech, low-tech, and no-tech approaches;

ii. Ensuring coordinated responses and avoid overlapping efforts;

iii. Ensuring the return of students to school when they reopen to avoid an upsurge in dropout rates.

b. **Reduced inequalities:**

i. Reduction of relative economic inequalities inequality in some countries having poorest and most vulnerable communities.

ii. Improving the situations in countries with weaker health systems.

c. **Life on Land:**

i. Prevention of Deforestation caused by humans and restoration of land

ii. Preventions and cures of diseases that are transmissible between animals and humans

d. **No Poverty:**

i. Creation of Strong social protection systems to prevent people from falling into poverty

ii. Reduction of social exclusion and high vulnerability of certain populations to disasters and diseases.

iii. Responsible distribution of resources.

e. **Clean Water and Sanitation:**

i. To increase access to clean drinking water and sanitation, mostly in rural areas

ii. Managing our water sustainably to manage our production of food and energy.

5. Do ethics in AI hamper the data acquisition stage? Justify your answer.

Ans. Data acquisition is the most important stage because the entire project development is based on the acquired data. There are several ethical issues that must always be considered when planning any type of data collection. We have to understand that the data which is collected is ethical only if the provider agrees to provide it. For example, in the case of smartphone users, data is collected by clicking on allow when it asks for permission and by agreeing to all the terms and conditions. when one does not want to share his/her data with any user, then this ethical issue hampers the acquisition process and lowers the amount of data required for the development. So, regardless of the type of data collection, it is necessary to gain the approval of the community from which the data will collect otherwise.

7.3 SOLVED EXERCISES

7.3.1 Multiple Choice Questions

1. What is the foundational element that makes AI so powerful?

   a) Neural Networks b) Fusion chart c) Data d) Facts

2. ____________ is a skill where the learners need to focus on the relevant details related to the problem.

   a) Data Scrapping b) Problem scoping c) Data Mining d) Evaluation

3. Which of the following is NOT a data type?

   a) Categorical data b) Time series data
   c) Numerical data d) Classical data

4. How many basic types of data are known from a machine learning perspective?

   a) 3 b) 4 c) 5 d) 6

5. A company has the following data. Identify the time series data out of it.

   i. Server metrics,
   ii. Application performance monitoring,
   iii. Network data, Sensor data,
   iv. Economic indicators
   v. Clicks on social sites

   a) (ii) (iii) b) (v)
   c) (v) d) (ii) (iii) (iv) (v)

6. Which of the following is NOT time-series data?

   a) Weather records b) Economic indicators
   c) Patient health evolution metrics d) None of the above

7. Which of the following type of problems are solved by using a decision tree?

   a) Classification problems b) Regression problems
   c) Both (a) and (b) d) None of the above

8. Which of the following is NOT related to data visualisation?
   a) Histogram b) Sketchy graphs
   c) Vector mechanics d) System Mapping
9. Which one of the following is used as a Data Visualisation tool?
   a) Fusion chart b) Pie chart
   c) Bar diagram d) All of the above
10. Which of the following components of the AI project cycle does select the best model by checking their advantages, disadvantages, and efficiency?
    a) Data Visualisation b) None of the above
    c) Data Mining d) Data Modelling
11. In which step of the AI Project cycle is data collected?
    a) Data Acquisition b) Data Modelling
    c) Data Evaluation d) Project Scoping
12. Which is NOT a part of problem scoping?
    a) Measurable objectives b) Project's purpose, vision, and mission
    c) Concerned stakeholders d) None of the above
13. The AI model is evaluated for its efficiency on the basis of the results while comparing with the results we already have. Name the process.
    a) Problem scoping b) Evaluation
    c) Data Visualisation d) Data Mining
14. Which quality is NOT necessary for the training data used for the AI machine?
    a) Authentic b) Discrete c) Reliable d) Accurate
15. Which Approach is used in AI models?
    a) Rule-based Approach b) Project-based Approach
    c) Learning-based Approach d) both (a) and (c)
16. For which purpose the visualisation technique used is?
    a) For using order, layout, and hierarchy to prioritize
    b) For handling and understanding big data
    c) For enabling to make comparisons easily
    d) All of the above
17. Which tool has a tree-like structure of decisions and their possible outcomes?
    a) Decision tree b) Neural network
    c) Fusion Chart d) Bar Graph
18. What is Data?
    a) A piece of information b) A raw fact

c) A fact and/ visual
d) Any meaningful information

19. Which tool is used to convert the information more meaningful for making decisions?
    a) Python
    b) Excel
    c) QlikView
    d) All of the above
20. What does a branch of the decision tree represent?
    a) A possible decision, outcome, or reaction
    b) End results
    c) Input
    d) Classification of attributes
21. For what purpose is training Data used in the AI machine?
    a) Testing the model
    b) Making predictions
    c) Giving input to the machine
    d) Processing
22. Which quality of the training data is necessary for using it for AI machines?
    a) Authentic
    b) Accurate
    c) Reliable
    d) All of the above
23. Which of the following is NOT a component of the decision tree?
    a) Flowers
    b) Leaf
    c) Nodes
    d) Branches
24. ____________ is the process of extracting useful and structured knowledge from unstructured documents to find useful associations and insights.
    a) Plotly
    b) Text Analytics
    c) Data Analysis
    d) Datawrapper
25. Which of the following Approach is used in a Decision Tree?
    a) Top-down
    b) Bottom-up
    c) Both (a) and (b)
    d) None of the above
26. Which of the following data visualisation tools does use integration with analytics-oriented programming languages, like Python, R, Matlab, etc.?
    a) Datawrapper
    b) Fusion charts
    c) QlikView
    d) Plotly
27. Which stage is the first stage of the AI project cycle?
    a) Problem Scoping
    b) Data mining
    c) Data Acquisition
    d) Evaluation
28. Which of the following is NOT an open-sourced data website?
    a) https://www.india.gov.in/data-portal-india
    b) https://data.gov.in/
    c) https://dbie.rbi.org.in/DBIE/dbie.rbi?site=home
    d) None of the above
29. Which of the following is included in sustainable development.
    a) Recycling and reuse of waste products/materials,

b) Scientific management of renewable resources, especially bio-resources,

c) Promoting afforestation

d) All of the above

30. Which of the following sources is not used for data acquisition?

a) API b) Survey c) DPI d) System map

31. ____________ is a simple graphical representation for classifying examples.

a) Decision Tree b) Fusion chart c) Sisense d) Datawrapper

32. Which of the following features is NOT associated with ANN?

a) Neural networks are able to automatically extract features without input from the coder/programmer.

b) The neural network system is modeled on the human brain.

c) Every artificial neural network (ANN) is controlled by the human brain.

d) Every neural network node is essentially a machine learning algorithm.

33. Which word is not a part of the 4Ws Problem Canvas?

a) Who b) Why c) Where d) What

34. Which of the following data visualisation tool is mostly used by media organisations to create charts and statistics for media coverage?

a) High charts b) Plotly c) Datawrapper d) QlikView

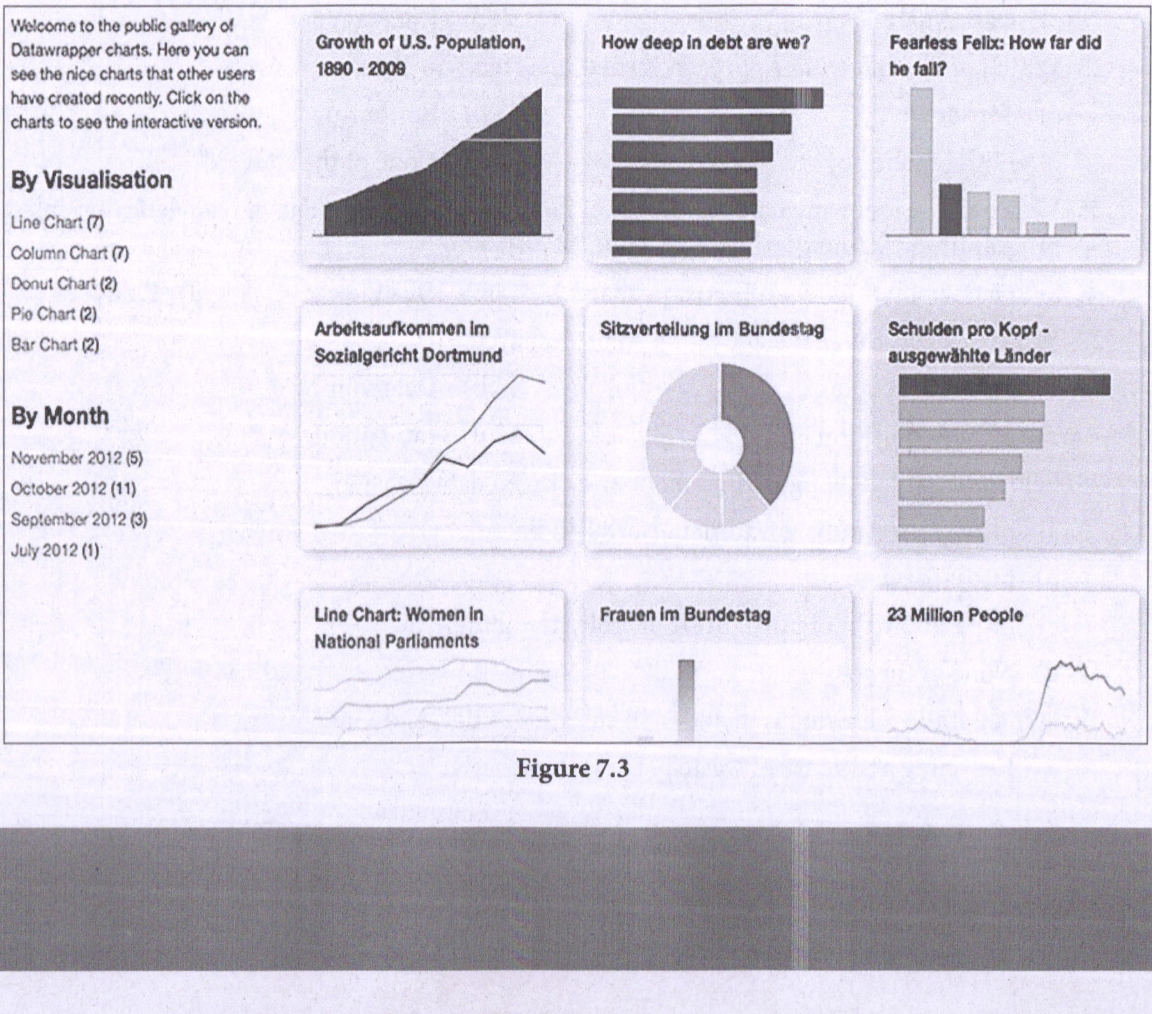

Figure 7.3

35. For which purpose is the visualisation technique used?
    a) Handling and understanding big data
    b) Enabling to make comparisons easily
    c) Using order, layout, and hierarchy to prioritise
    d) All of the above
36. A process of cleaning, transforming, and modeling data to discover useful information for making business decisions is known as:
    a) Data scraping
    b) Data mining
    c) Data analysis
    d) Data acquisition
37. Which of the following is a part of the project charter?
    a) Project's purpose, vision, and mission
    b) Measurable objectives and success criteria
    c) Elaborated project description, conditions, and risks
    d) All the above
38. ____________ refers to the unsupervised learning algorithm that can cluster the unknown data according to the patterns or trends identified out of it.
    a) Sisense
    b) Clustering
    c) Regression
    d) Data analysis
39. Which statement is correct?
    a) The training data needs to be reliable, authentic, and accurate for the AI machine to work efficiently.
    b) Testing data is used to assess the AI machine for its efficiency and performance too.
    c) Data features can be collected from various sources like newspapers, cameras, observations, surveys, questionnaires, etc.
    d) All of the above
40. Which of the following is not categorical data?
    a) Gender of students
    b) Record of the temperature of patients in a hospital
    c) List of hometowns of employees
    d) Player's position in a cricket team
41. Which technique is used in which a computer program extracts data from a human-readable output from another program?
    a) Data scraping
    b) Data acquisition
    c) Data modeling
    d) Vector mechanics
42. Which of the following statements is INCORRECT?
    a) The numerical data is the data where data points are exact numbers.

b) A technique in which a computer program extracts data from a human-readable output from another program is termed data modeling.

c) The time-series data is a sequence of numbers collected at regular intervals over some time.

d) Data is the foundational element that makes AI so powerful.

43. Which of the following statements is NOT correct?

a) The initiation phase aims to define the project.

b) The Project Charter documents the primary requirements for the project.

c) The structured data is not easy to use.

d) The Text data type stores any kind of text data that can contain both single-byte and multibyte characters.

44. Which of the following is NOT a type of data analysis?

a) Predictive Analysis
b) Prescriptive Analysis
c) Statical Analysis
d) Diagnostic Analysis

45. Which of the following statements is INCORRECT?

a) Open-sourced websites are the government portals from where the information can be purchased.

b) Tableau is called 'the grandmaster of data visualisation software.'

c) Fusion charts are a widely-used and JavaScript-based charting and visualisation package.

d) Data visualisation is the graphic representation of data.

46. Which of the following is a type of statistical analysis?

a) Narrative analysis
b) Descriptive Analysis
c) Inferential Analysis
d) Both (b) and (c)

47. For which purpose is the diagnostic analysis performed?

a) To get refined data
b) To identify the behavioural patterns.
c) To predict some decision.
d) None of the above

48. Which of the following phases are included in the data analysis process?

i. Data Requirement Gathering
ii. Data Collection
iii. Data Cleaning
iv. Data Analysis
v. Data Interpretation
vi. Data Visualisation

a) (i)(ii)(iii)
b) (ii)(iii)(v) (vi)
c) (vi)(v)(iv) (iii)
d) (i)(ii)(iii) (iv) (v) (vi)

49. In data visualisation, data is presented as:
    a) Pictorial/Graphs/ charts
    b) Texts
    c) Maps
    d) None of the above
50. Which step of the AI Project is associated with data collected from different sources?
    a) Project Scoping
    b) Data Modelling
    c) Data Exploration
    d) Data Evaluation
51. Which of the following is NOT the SDGs as adopted by UNO?
    a) Zero Hunger
    b) Quality Education
    c) Gender Discrimination
    d) No Poverty
52. Which of the following statements are related to Data visualisation?
    i. It clarifies which factors influence customer behaviour.
    ii. It identifies areas that need attention or improvement.
    iii. It predicts sales volumes.
    iv. It helps human beings understand which products to place where.
    v. It helps to manipulate data.
    a) (i) (ii) (iii)
    b) (iii) (v)
    c) (ii) (iii) (iv)
    d) (i) (ii) (iii) (v)
53. Which of the following tools is regarded as 'the grandmaster of data visualisation software?
    a) Tableau
    b) QlikView
    c) Fusion charts
    d) High charts
54. Which of the following is an advantage of the decision tree?
    a) Easy to use and interpret.
    b) Easy to prepare and simple to explain.
    c) Can handle both categorical and numerical data.
    d) All of the above
55. Which language/script is used in creating Fusion charts?
    a) C++
    b) Java
    c) Python
    d) All of the above
56. Which of the following is NOT a data visualisation tool?
    a) Datawrapper
    b) High charts
    c) Low charts
    d) QlikView
57. What is represented by a node in a decision tree?
    a) A place where an attribute is picked and asked a question
    b) The answers to the question

c) The actual output

d) None of the above

58. What is the number of types of decision trees based on the target variables?

a) 2 b) 3 c) 4 d) 6

59. Which of the following sources is an authentic one for data acquisition?

a) APIs b) Sensors

c) Web Scraping d) All of the above

60. Which of the following is a disadvantage of decision trees?

a) They can handle only one type of data.

b) They are resistant to outliers.

c) Adding new features is easy.

d) They provide strategic answers to uncertain situations.

61. ____________ provides a full-stack analytics platform, but its visualisation capabilities provide a simple-to-use drag and drop interface which creates charts and more complex graphics with a minimum of hassle.

a) Plotly b) SiSense

c) Datawrapper d) Fusion chart

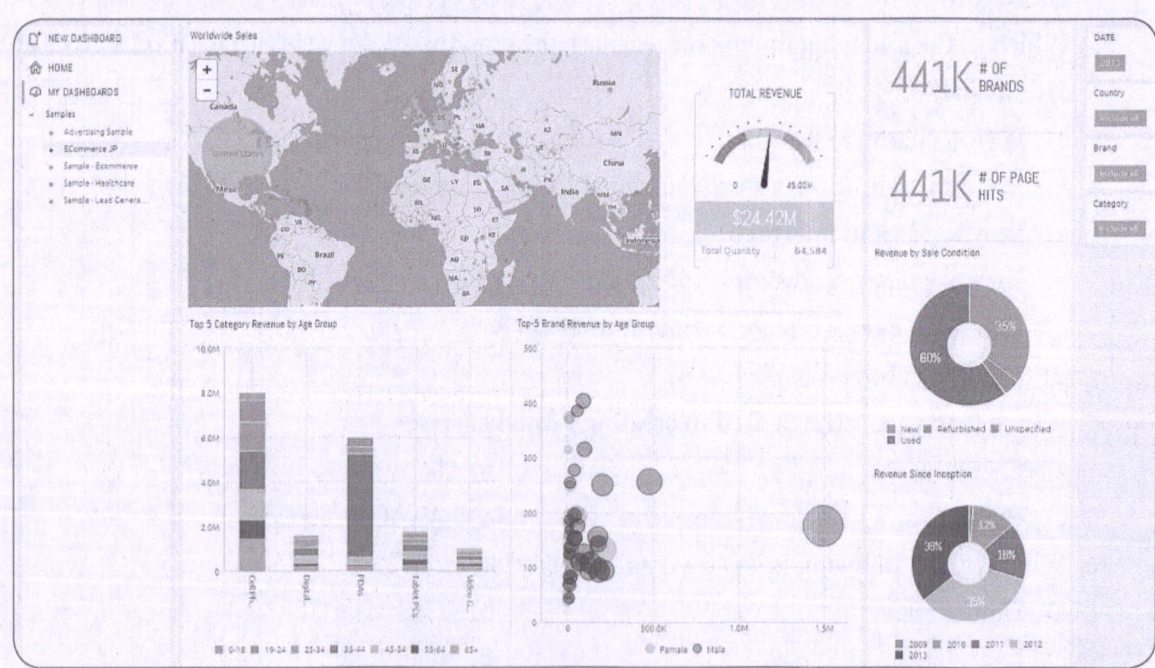

Figure 7.4

ANSWERS									
1. (c)	2. (b)	3. (d)	4. (c)	5. (d)	6. (d)	7. (c)	8. (c)	9. (d)	10. (a)
11. (a)	12. (d)	13. (b)	14. (b)	15. (d)	16. (d)	17. (b)	18. (a)	19. (d)	20. (c)
21. (c)	22. (d)	23. (a)	24. (b)	25. (a)	26. (d)	27. (a)	28. (d)	29. (d)	30. (c)
31. (a)	32. (c)	33. (c)	34. (c)	35. (d)	36. (c)	37. (d)	38. (b)	39. (d)	40. (b)
41. (a)	42. (b)	43. (c)	44. (c)	45. (a)	46. (d)	47. (b)	48. (d)	49. (a)	50. (c)
51. (b)	52. (c)	53. (a)	54. (d)	55. (b)	56. (c)	57. (a)	58. (a)	59. (d)	60. (a)
61. (b)									

7.3.2 Matching Type Questions

I. Match the items of column A and Column B.

Column A	**Column B**
(i) Data Acquisition	(a) An interactive tool
(ii) Raw facts	(b) Factors associated with problem
(iii) Data Features	(c) Designing a model of a real system
(iv) Testing data	(d) Collection of Data
(v) LOOPY	(e) Accurate, reliable, and correct
(vi) Simulation	(f) Data

II. Match the items of column A and Column B

Column A	**Column B**
(i) Data visualisation tools	(a) Machine learns through experience
(ii) Modelling	(b) Project Cycle components
(iii) Deep Learning	(c) reliable, authentic, and accurate
(iv) Graphical tools	(d) most abundant approach
(v) Training data	(e) Pictorial Representation
(vi) Data acquisition, Modelling	(f) It helps in comprehending trends.

ANSWERS						
(I)	(i)- d,	(ii)-f,	(iii)-b,	(iv)-e,	(v)-a,	(vi)-c
(II)	(i)-f,	(ii)-d,	(iii)-a,	(iv)-e,	(v)-c,	(vi)-b

7.3.3 Fill in the blanks

1. Artificial Intelligence is used as an umbrella term for Machine Learning and ____________.
2. ____________ is a tree-like graph having three parts. Nodes represent the place where an attribute is picked and asked a question, edges represent the answers to the question, and the leaves represent the actual output. These are used in non-linear decision-making.

3. ____________ is a widely-used and JavaScript-based charting and visualisation package. It can produce more than 90 different types of charts and integrates with a large number of platforms and frameworks.

4. Data Acquisition is the ____________ stage in the AI project cycle.

5. ____________ enables more complex and sophisticated visualisations due to the use of its integration with analytics-oriented programming languages, like Python, R, Matlab, etc.

6. ____________ provides a full-stack analytics platform, but its visualisation capabilities provide a simple-to-use drag and drop interface which creates charts and more complex graphics with a minimum of hassle.

7. Copying someone's data from the website/internet without permission is termed as a ____________.

8. ____________ is a popular choice among media organisations that frequently use it to create charts and present statistics for media coverage.

9. ____________ is labelled when entered into the model in a rule-based approach.

10. Data acquisition is used to collect data that has to be authentic and ____________.

11. The learning-based Approach performs algorithms on a sample Data set which is called ____________ Data.

12. ____________ is an interactive tool that can be worked without any knowledge of coding.

13. Data modelling is the ____________ stage in the AI project cycle.

14. ____________ is a skill where the learners need to focus on the relevant details related to the problem.

15. ____________ refers to the method of designing a model of a real system.

16. AI ____________ provides an appropriate framework that can lead us towards the goal.

17. ____________ helps the machine to make decisions and learn from large Data sets.

18. ____________ is defined as the process of finding a model/ function for distinguishing the data into continuous real values in place classes.

19. Sensors are often called ____________.

20. ____________ is a simple graphical representation for classifying examples.

ANSWERS				
1. Deep Learning	2. Decision tree	3. Fusion chart	4. second	5. Plotly
6. Sisense	7. cybercrime	8. Datawrapper	9. Data	10. reliable
11. Training	12. LOOPY	13. fourth	14. Problem scoping	
15. Simulation	16. Project Cycle	17. Deep Learning	18. Regression	19. Transducers
20. Decision Tree				

7.3.4 True or False

State the following statements either as True (T) or false (F).

1. Sensors used in AI-enabled machines convert real-world phenomena like temperature, force, movement to voltage or current, etc., into signals.
2. Decision tree learning is the technique used for supervised classification learning.
3. A regression problem arises when the output variable is a category.
4. Data modelling is the third stage in the AI project cycle.
5. The data is labelled when entered into the model in a learning-based approach.
6. Data analysis means a process of cleaning, transforming, and modelling data to discover useful information for business decision-making.
7. Regression is defined as the process of finding a model/ function for distinguishing the data into continuous real values in place classes.
8. Text, Statistical, Diagnostic, Predictive, and Prescriptive Analysis are the types of Data Analysis.
9. The analogy of an Artificial Neural Network may be made with Parallel Processing.
10. Data Analytics is the process of extracting useful and structured knowledge from unstructured documents to find useful associations and insights.
11. A loop in the system defines a chain of events that signifies the cause and effects among system elements.
12. Data acquisition is the fourth stage in the AI project cycle.
13. AI models can be classified either on a Rule-based Approach or a Learning-based Approach.
14. Clustering refers to the unsupervised learning algorithm that can cluster the unknown data according to the patterns or trends identified out of it.
15. Data may be a piece of information or facts and statistics collected together for reference or analysis purposes.
16. The learning-based Approach performs algorithms on a sample Data set which is called training data.
17. The smaller Neural Network tends to perform better with large data.
18. In classification, data is categorised under different labels based on some parameters mentioned in the output.
19. Evaluation is a testing technique where the model is installed in the real world, and it is tested in as many ways as possible.
20. Machine Learning helps the machine to make decisions and learn from large Data sets.

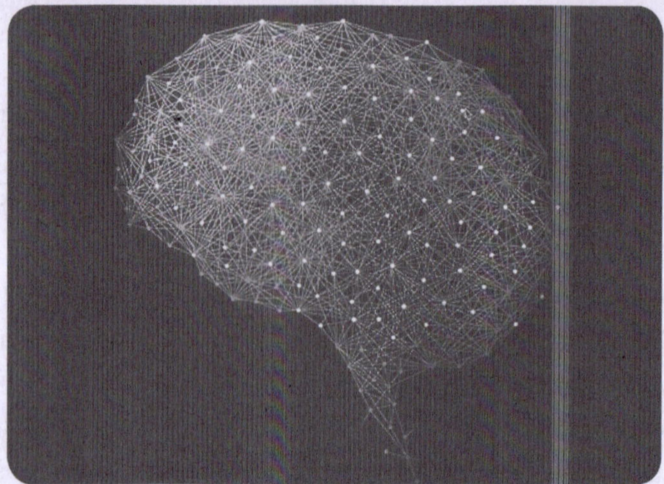

Figure 7.5

ANSWERS						
1. T	2. T	3. F (classification)		4. F (fourth stage)	5. F (Rule-based)	6. T
7. T	8. T	9. T	10. F (Text Analytics)	11. T	12. F (second)	
13. T	14. T	15. T	16. T	17. F (larger)	18. F (input, not output)	
19. T	20. F (Deep Learning)					

7.3.5 Statements Based Questions

1. Statement 1: Data may be a piece of information or facts and statistics collected together for reference or analysis purposes.

   Statement 2: Artificial intelligence (AI) is the ability of a machine to think, learn, and perform tasks usually requiring human intelligence, like visual perception, speech recognition, and decision-making skills.

   a) Statement 1 is correct, but statement 2 is incorrect.

   b) Statement 1 is incorrect, but statement 2 is correct.

   c) Both the statements are correct.

   d) Both the statements are incorrect.

2. Statement 1: Clustering is the process of extracting useful and structured knowledge from unstructured documents to find useful associations and insights.

   Statement 2: Text Analytics refers to the unsupervised learning algorithm that can make clusters of the unknown data as per the patterns or trends identified out of it.

   a) Statement 1 is correct, but statement 2 is incorrect.

   b) Statement 1 is incorrect, but statement 2 is correct.

   c) Both the statements are correct.

   d) Both the statements are incorrect.

3. Statement 1: While taking up any AI project in an enterprise, a scientific method is used that is known as the AI Project cycle.

   Statement 2: The field of Deep Learning is used by many people and organisations in finding new ways to apply ML methods to their vast, complex, and expanding data sets.

   a) Statement 1 is correct, but statement 2 is incorrect.

   b) Statement 1 is incorrect, but statement 2 is correct.

   c) Both the statements are correct.

   d) Both the statements are incorrect.

4. Statement 1: The Artificial Intelligent project cycle describes all steps required to convert a real-life problem or a challenge into a computer-based Al model.

   Statement 2: AI Modelling refers to developing algorithms or AI models which can be trained to get intelligent output, i.e., writing codes to make a machine artificially intelligent.

   a) Statement 1 is correct, but statement 2 is incorrect.

   b) Statement 1 is incorrect, but statement 2 is correct.

   c) Both the statements are correct.

   d) Both the statements are incorrect.

5. Statement 1: The training data need not to be reliable, authentic, and accurate for the AI machine to work efficiently.

   Statement 2: A technique in which a computer program extracts data from human-readable output coming from another program, is termed data modelling.

   a) Statement 1 is correct, but statement 2 is incorrect.

   b) Statement 1 is incorrect, but statement 2 is correct.

   c) Both the statements are correct.

   d) Both the statements are incorrect.

6. Statement 1: Problem scoping is a skill where the learners need to focus on the relevant details related to the problem.

   Statement 2: The Training data must be relevant and authentic for the better efficiency of an AI project.

   a) Statement 1 is correct, but statement 2 is incorrect.

   b) Statement 1 is incorrect, but statement 2 is correct.

   c) Both the statements are correct.

   d) Both the statements are incorrect.

7. Statement 1: Data Analytics is the process of extracting useful and structured knowledge from unstructured documents to find useful associations and insights.

   Statement 2: AI models can be classified either on Rule-based or learning-based approaches.

   a) Statement 1 is correct, but statement 2 is incorrect.

   b) Statement 1 is incorrect, but statement 2 is correct.

c) Both the statements are correct.

d) Both the statements are incorrect.

8. Statement 1: Data exploration is used to collect data that has to be authentic and reliable.

   Statement 2: LOOPY is an interactive tool that can be worked without any knowledge of coding.

   a) Statement 1 is correct, but statement 2 is incorrect.

   b) Statement 1 is incorrect, but statement 2 is correct.

   c) Both the statements are correct.

   d) Both the statements are incorrect.

9. Statement 1: LOOPY is an interactive tool that can be used to play with simulations in real-time with using coding.

   Statement 2: Artificial intelligence and machine learning are affecting the processes of researching, purchasing, and implementing IT tools in various industries.

   a) Statement 1 is correct, but statement 2 is incorrect.

   b) Statement 1 is incorrect, but statement 2 is correct.

   c) Both the statements are correct.

   d) Both the statements are incorrect.

10. Statement 1: AI Project cycle does not provide any appropriate framework that can lead us towards the goal.

    Statement 2: Stakeholders are all those areas that are affected the most by the AI model/ AI project.

    a) Statement 1 is correct, but statement 2 is incorrect.

    b) Statement 1 is incorrect, but statement 2 is correct.

    c) Both the statements are correct.

    d) Both the statements are incorrect.

Figure 7.6

ANSWERS									
1. (c)	2. (d)	3. (a)	4. (c)	5. (d)	6. (c)	7. (b)	8. (c)	9. (b)	10. (d)

7.3.6 Assertion Reason Based Questions

1. Assertion (A): Demand for data scientists is increasing continuously.

   Reason (R): The problems of collecting and normalising clean and meaningful data for machine learning are to be tackled at a faster rate.

   a) Both A and R are correct, and R is the correct reason for A.

   b) Both A and R are correct, and R is not the correct reason for A.

   c) A is correct, but R is incorrect.

   d) A is incorrect, but R is correct.

2. Assertion (A): A regression problem arises when the output variable is a category.

   Reason (R): Datawrapper is a popular choice among media organisations that frequently use it to create charts and present statistics for media coverage.

   a) Both A and R are correct, and R is the correct reason for A.

   b) Both A and R are correct, and R is not the correct reason for A.

   c) A is correct, but R is incorrect.

   d) A is incorrect, but R is correct.

3. Assertion (A): High chart is often chosen for a fast and flexible solution.

   Reason (R): With a minimum need for specialist data and visualisation training, the high chart can be put to work.

   a) Both A and R are correct, and R is the correct reason for A.

   b) Both A and R are correct, and R is not the correct reason for A.

   c) A is correct, but R is incorrect.

   d) A is incorrect, but R is correct.

4. Assertion (A): AI Project cycle provides an appropriate framework that can lead us towards the goal.

   Reason (R): Decision tree learning is the technique used for unsupervised classification learning.

   a) Both A and R are correct, and R is the correct reason for A.

   b) Both A and R are correct, and R is not the correct reason for A.

   c) A is correct, but R is incorrect.

   d) A is incorrect, but R is correct.

5. Assertion (A): Fusion chart is a widely-used and JavaScript-based charting and visualisation package.

   Reason (R): Fusion charts can produce 90 different types of charts and integrate with a large number of platforms and frameworks.

a) Both A and R are correct, and R is the correct reason for A.

b) Both A and R are correct, and R is not the correct reason for A.

c) A is correct, but R is incorrect.

d) A is incorrect, but R is correct.

6. Assertion (A): Classification is defined as the process of finding a model/ function for distinguishing the data into continuous real values in place of classes.

   Reason (R): In classification, data is categorized under different labels based on some parameters mentioned in the input.

   a) Both A and R are correct, and R is the correct reason for A.

   b) Both A and R are correct, and R is not the correct reason for A.

   c) A is correct, but R is incorrect.

   d) A is incorrect, but R is correct.

7. Assertion (A): Anyone can use decision trees to clarify and find an answer to a complex AI problem.

   Reason (R): Every branch of the decision tree represents a possible decision, outcome, or reaction, while the farthest branches on the decision tree represent the end results.

   a) Both A and R are correct, and R is the correct reason for A.

   b) Both A and R are correct, and R is not the correct reason for A.

   c) A is correct, but R is incorrect.

   d) A is incorrect, but R is correct.

8. Assertion (A): The decision tree is the most potent and accessible tool for classification and prediction.

   Reason (R): A decision tree is a flowchart like a tree structure, where each internal node represents a test on an attribute, each branch denotes an outcome of the test, and each leaf node (terminal node) holds a class label.

   a) Both A and R are correct, and R is the correct reason for A.

   b) Both A and R are correct, and R is not the correct reason for A.

   c) A is correct, but R is incorrect.

   d) A is incorrect, but R is correct.

9. Assertion (A): Plotly enables more complex and sophisticated visualisations due to the use of its integration with analytics-oriented programming languages, like Python, R, Matlab, etc. It is built using JavaScript.

   Reason (R): Transponders used in AI-enabled machines convert real-world phenomena like temperature, force, movement to voltage or current, etc., into signals.

   a) Both A and R are correct, and R is the correct reason for A.

   b) Both A and R are correct, and R is not the correct reason for A.

c) A is correct, but R is incorrect.

d) A is incorrect, but R is correct.

10. Assertion (A): Preparing customer data for meaningful ML projects is a difficult task.

Reason (R): There is a variety of data sources and data silos that exist in organisations.

a) Both A and R are correct, and R is the correct reason for A.

b) Both A and R are correct, and R is not the correct reason for A.

c) A is correct, but R is incorrect.

d) A is incorrect, but R is correct.

ANSWERS									
1. (a)	2. (d)	3. (a)	4. (c)	5. (a)	6. (d)	7. (a)	8. (b)	9. (c)	10. (a)

7.3.7 Competency- Based Questions

1. Suppose Sagar prepared a document having the following details:

   i. Project's purpose, vision, and mission

   ii. Measurable objectives and success criteria

   iii. Elaborated project description, conditions, and risks

   iv. Name and authority of the project sponsor

   v. Concerned stakeholders

   What is this document called?

   a) Project cycle
   b) Project charter
   c) Stakeholders' charter
   d) Project file

2. Suppose Neelima is preparing a Decision Tree, where she will show each:

   a) Internal node as a test on an attribute

   b) Branch as an outcome of the test

   c) Leaf node as a class label

   d) All of the above

3. Suppose Matin is using a visualisation package having the following properties:

   i. It is a widely-used visualisation package.

   ii. It has JavaScript-based charting.

   iii. It can produce more than 90 different types of charts.

   iv. It can be integrated with a large number of platforms and frameworks.

   What is used by him?

   a) Plotly
   b) Sisense
   c) Fusion chart
   d) Datawrapper

4. Suppose James is using a visualisation tool that enables more complex and sophisticated visualisations due to the use of its integration with analytics-oriented programming languages, like Python, R, Matlab, etc., and it is built using JavaScript. He is using:

   a) Plotly   b) Sisense   c) Datawrapper   d) Fusion chart

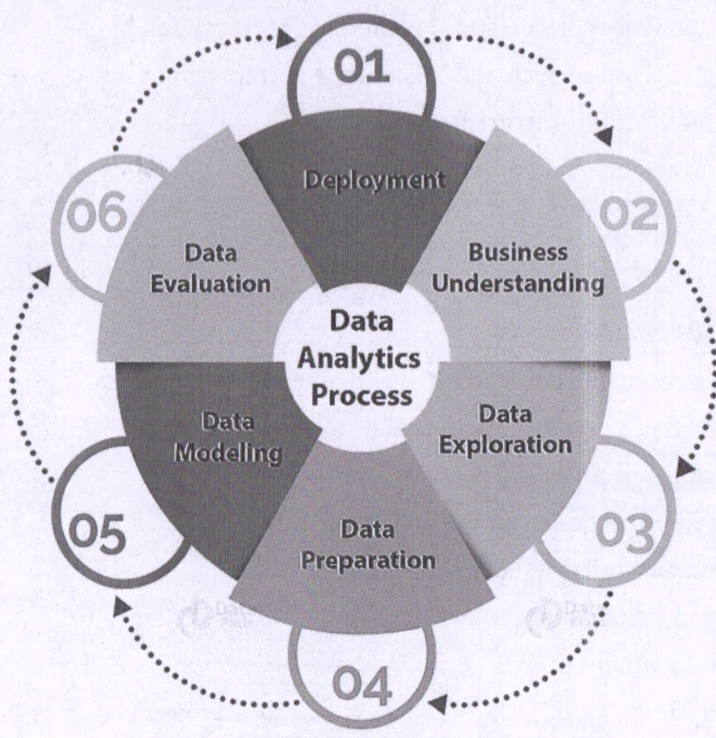

Figure 7.7

ANSWERS
1. (b)   2. (d)   3. (c)   4. (a)

7.3.8 VSA

1. Define data.

Ans. Data is defined as the raw fact, which is organised together to form information that needs to be processed further for analysis and data visualisation.

2. How many stages are there in an AI-project cycle?

Ans. Five stages

3. What is the name of the initial phase of the project cycle?

Ans. Problem scoping

4. Name the second stage of the project cycle.

Ans. Data collection / Data acquisition

5. What is the last stage of the project cycle?

Ans. Evaluation

6. Name the third stage of the project cycle.

Ans. Data exploration

7. What is feature engineering?

Ans. The process of repeating rapidly and testing new data points that can be derived from the data source is called feature engineering.

8. Define the main purpose of Data Analysis.

Ans. The main purpose of Data Analysis (DA) is to extract useful information from huge data and to make decisions.

9. Define data scraping.

Ans. A technique/method in which a computer program extracts data from a human-readable output from another program is called data scraping.

10. What is text data?

Ans. The Text data type stores any kind of text data that can contain both single-byte and multibyte characters that the locale supports.

11. What are open-sourced websites?

Ans. Open-sourced websites are the government portals from where the information can be used and referred to.

12. Define numerical data.

Ans. The data where data points are exact numbers is called numerical data.

13. What is categorical data?

Ans. Categorical data represents characteristics, such as gender, a cricket player's position, team, hometown, etc.

14. Define LOOPY.

Ans. LOOPY is defined as an interactive tool that can be used to play with simulations in real-time without using any coding.

15. What is SiSense?

Ans. SiSense provides a full-stack analytics platform where its visualisation capabilities provide a simple-to-use drag and drop interface which creates charts and more complex graphics with a minimum of hassle.

16. What is data analysis?

Ans. The process of cleaning, transforming, and modeling data to discover useful information for making business decisions is defined as data analysis.

17. Which tool is regarded as 'the grandmaster of data visualisation software?

Ans. Tableau

18. What do you mean by time-series data?

Ans. The time-series data is a sequence of numbers collected at regular intervals over some time.

19. Define descriptive analysis.

Ans. Descriptive analysis is an analysis of complete data or a sample of summarised numerical data to show the mean and deviation for continuous data.

20. What do you mean by text analysis?

Ans. Text Analysis or Data Mining is a method to discover a pattern in large data sets by using databases or data mining tools to extract and examine data.

21. What is a decision tree?

Ans. A Decision tree is a flowchart similar to a tree structure, in which each internal node denotes a test on an attribute, whereas each branch represents an outcome of the test, and each leaf node (terminal node) represents a class label.

22. What is statistical analysis?

Ans. Statistical analysis is the process of collecting, exploring and presenting large amounts of data to discover underlying patterns and trends.

23. Define data visualisation.

Ans. Data visualisation is defined as the graphic representation of data that involves producing images for communicating relationships among the represented data to viewers/users.

24. What do you mean by 'Fusion chart'?

Ans. Fusion chart is a widely-used and JavaScript-based charting and data visualisation package.

25. What does a decision tree display?

Ans. Decision trees display a sequence of steps and give people an effective and easy way to visualise the potential options of a decision and its range of possible outcomes.

26. What do you mean by Datawrapper?

Ans. Datawrapper is a tool for data visualisation and has a simple and clear interface that makes it very easy to upload data and create straightforward charts and also maps.

27. Define categorical variable decision tree.

Ans. A categorical variable decision tree includes categorical target variables that are divided into categories.

28. Name all the components of the Al project Cycle.

Ans. Five components of the AI Project Cycle are Problem scoping, Data acquisition, Data exploration, Modelling, and Evaluation.

29. What do you mean by a problem statement?

Ans. The problem statement gives a clear idea about the basic framework required to achieve the goal.

30. What is the full form of API?

Ans. Application Programming Interface

31. What are the main qualities of training data?

Ans. The training data needs to be reliable, authentic, and accurate for the AI machine to work efficiently.

32. For which purpose is testing data used?

Ans. Testing data is used to assess the AI machine for its efficiency and performance too.

33. What are the main qualities of an open-sourced data website (Govt portal)?

Ans. Open-sourced websites or government portals are authentic, accurate, and reliable.

34. What do you mean by loop?

Ans. The concept of a 'Loop' is used to define a chain of events in the system and relationships between them.

35. What is Data Acquisition?

Ans. Data Acquisition is a process to collect data for the problem scoped, which has to be correct, authentic, and reliable.

36. Define testing dataset.

Ans. A testing dataset is a dataset provided to the model ML algorithm after training the algorithm.

37. What do you mean by evaluation in an AI-based project?

Ans. Evaluation is a testing technique where the model is installed in the real world, and it is tested in as many ways as possible.

38. What is the objective of the evaluation stage?

Ans. The evaluation stage is to evaluate whether the ML algorithm is able to predict with high accuracy or not before deployment.

39. What is a decision tree?

Ans. A decision tree is a simple graphical representation for classifying examples.

40. Which stage is data modelling in the AI Project cycle?

Ans. Fourth stage

41. What do you mean by data exploration?

Ans. Data exploration is a method to collect data that has to be authentic and reliable.

42. What are thc types of data analysis?

Ans. Text, Statistical, Diagnostic, Predictive, and Prescriptive Analysis

43. What are the other names given for web scraping?

Ans. Web data extraction, web harvesting, and Screen Scraping.

44. Define web scraping.

Ans. Web scraping is defined as a technique used for extracting huge amounts of data from websites on the Internet by using a web browser.

45. What is an API?

Ans. Application programming interfaces (API) are the pieces of code that helps to connect one application to another to collect data from it.

46. When is a system map used in the project cycle?

Ans. System Map is used to find relationships between different elements of the problem that is scoped.

47. What do you mean by data modelling?

Ans. Data Modelling is defined as a process in which Al-Enabled algorithms are being designed as per the requirements of the system, and later, the model is implemented.

48. What do you mean by data visualisation in an AI project?

Ans. Data visualisation is defined as a form of visual art that grabs users' interest and keeps their eyes on the message.

49. Define Plotly.

Ans. Plotly enables more complex and sophisticated visualisations due to the use of its integration with analytics-oriented programming languages, like Python, R, Matlab, etc. It is built using JavaScript.

50. Define Datawrapper.

Ans. Datawrapper is a popular choice among media organisations that frequently use it to create charts and present statistics for media coverage.

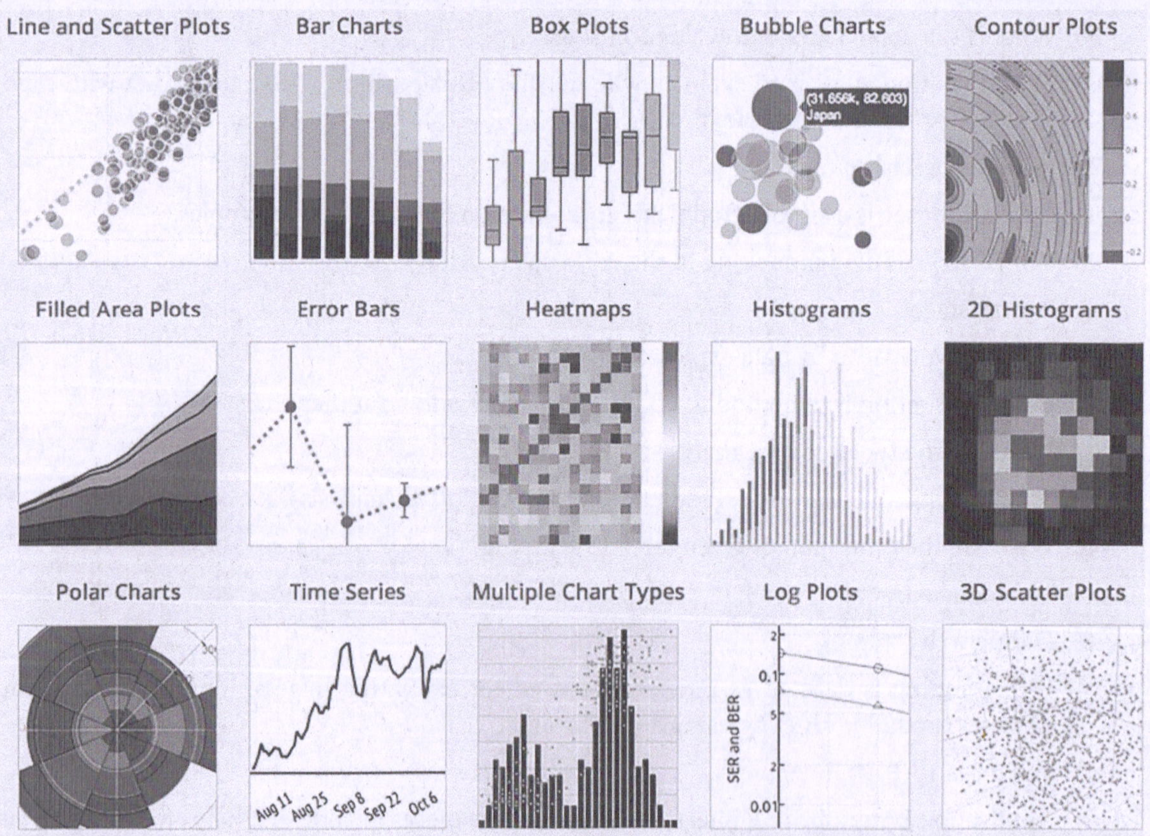

Figure 7.8

7.3.9 Short Answer Type Questions

1. Explain the process of Data Exploration.

Ans. Cleaning and normalising dirty data is the next step in the ML process, where analysts and data scientists normally spend most of their time on analysis projects. This purpose often requires data scientists to make decisions based on data they may not understand, like what to do with missing data, incomplete data, etc. The available data may not be easily correlated to the customer. A data scientist will prepare and collect all of the data from those sources into a format that ML models can interpret. This process can end up being a lengthy one and may require a lot of work before any ML can even occur.

2. What is the purpose of Data Modelling?

Ans. The data modelling is used for prediction. Some part of modelling data for a prediction about customers is to be combined disparate data sets with painting a proper picture of a single customer and includes blending and collecting silos of data, like web, mobile app, offline data, etc.

3. What information is provided in the project charter?

Ans. The Project Charter documents the primary requirements for the project and includes information, like:

i. Project's purpose, vision, and mission

ii. Measurable objectives and success criteria

iii. Elaborated project description, conditions, and risks

iv. Name and authority of the project sponsor

v. Concerned stakeholders

4. What types of questions are to be answered to assess the requirement of data for an AI Project?

Ans. Data requirements of an AI project can be assessed by asking the following questions:

i. How many and types of sources of data do you have?

ii. How is the quality of this data?

iii. Do all of the sources need to be available in a single location?

iv. How large are your datasets?

v. How much transformation will the data need?

vi. Which methods will be used to import the data into the visualisation tool?

vii. Are there any built-in connectors available?

viii. Will it be imported raw or need to be cleaned first?

ix. Where will the data exist?

5. Why is it said that all AI models could not be deployed to production?

Ans. All work culminates in the final step of deploying a model to production, where the ability of model to predict outcomes in the real world is tested. By this point, models should meet some threshold of accuracy necessary to deploy them to production. For this reason, it's important to interpret model performance with stakeholders to agree on what level of risk is acceptable for inaccuracy. Some customer behaviours may not be sufficiently predictable, and thus a model may never achieve accuracy to justify deploying to production.

6. Why is Data called a foundational element?

Ans. While the AI scenarios highlight the technology's incredible computational power, the practical, useful applications begin with data. That's why data is the foundational element that makes AI so powerful. Google, Facebook, and Amazon are regarded as leaders in AI because they have lots of data to crunch. Other companies do not have access to such type huge data sets for the same type of AI technology.

7. For which purpose was SDGs framed?

Ans. The Sustainable Development Goals (SDGs), also known as the Global Goals, were adopted by all United Nations Member States in 2015 as a universal call to action to end poverty, protect the planet and ensure that all people enjoy peace and prosperity.

8. Explain the term 'Predictive Analysis.'

Ans. The predictive analysis shows "what is likely to happen" by using previous data. The simplest example is if last year someone bought two dresses based on the savings and if this year the salary is increasing double, then four dresses can be purchased. Hence, this analysis makes predictions/forecasts about future outcomes based on current or past data. Its accuracy depends on how much detailed information is available.

9. What do you mean by Text Analysis? Explain.

Ans. Text Analysis or Data Mining is a method to discover a pattern in large data sets by using databases or data mining tools. It is used to transform raw data into business information. Business Intelligence tools are used to make strategic business decisions as they offer a way to extract and examine data and derive patterns and, finally, for the interpretation of the data.

10. What do you mean by open-sourced websites? Give some examples.

Ans. Open-sourced websites are the government portals from where the information can be used and referred to. Some of the open-sourced portals of the Indian Govt are as follows:

i. https://www.india.gov.in/data-portal-india

ii. https://data.gov.in/

iii. https://dbie.rbi.org.in/DBIE/dbie.rbi?site=home

iv. http://mospi.nic.in/data

v. http://www.surveyofindia.gov.in/

vi. https://data.uidai.gov.in/

vii. https://www.icegate.gov.in/jsp/DailyReport.jsp

11. Define data analysis. What is the purpose of data analysis?

Ans. Data analysis is defined as a process of cleaning, transforming, and modelling data to discover useful information for making business decisions. The main purpose of Data Analysis is to extract useful information from huge data and to make decisions.

Data analysis tools are used to make the process and manipulate data, analyse the relationships and correlations between data sets easier. It helps to identify patterns and trends for interpretation.

12. Why is data analysis required?

Ans. Data analysis is required for the reasons like to grow your business or to grow in life. When your business is not growing, then you have to look back and acknowledge the mistakes made and then make a plan again without repeating the mistakes made earlier. When your business is growing, then for looking forward to the further growth of a business, data analysis is required.

13. What do you mean by statistical analysis? Explain its types.

Ans. Statistical analysis shows "What happens?" by using past data in the form of dashboards. This analysis includes gathering/collection, analysis, interpretation, presentation, and modelling of data. There are two types of Statistical Analysis; Descriptive Analysis and Inferential Analysis.

(a) **Descriptive Analysis:** It analyses complete data or a sample of summarised numerical data to show mean and deviation for continuous data, whereas percentage and frequency for categorical data.

(b) **Inferential Analysis:** It analyses samples from complete data to find different conclusions from the same data by selecting different samples.

14. Define Data Analysis Process. What are the phases of data analysis?

Ans. The Data Analysis Process is gathering information by using proper application or tool, that allows you to explore the data and find a pattern in it. Based on that, you can make decisions, or you can get ultimate conclusions.

Data Analysis consists of the following phases:

i. Data Requirement Gathering

ii. Data Collection

iii. Data Clcaning

iv. Data Analysis

v. Data Interpretation

vi. Data Visualisation

15. Define data visualisation. How is it achieved?

Ans. Data visualisation is defined as the graphic representation of data that involves producing images for communicating relationships among the represented data to viewers/users. This communication is achieved by using a systematic mapping between graphic marks and data values in the creation of the visualisation.

16. What is the purpose of data visualisation?

Ans. Data visualisation is the presentation of data in a pictorial or graphical format. It enables decision-makers to view analytics presented in a visual format to understand the difficult concepts or to identify new patterns. By using interactive visualisation, one can take the concept a step further to drill down into charts and graphs for more detail.

17. Why is data visualisation essential?

Ans. The human brain processes information by using visuals like charts or graphs to visualise large amounts of complex data. The human brain is more comfortable with visuals than textual data, like spreadsheets, reports, etc. Data visualisation is a quick and easy way to convey concepts universally.

Data visualisation can:

i. Clarify which factors influence customer behaviour.

ii. Identify areas that need attention or improvement.

iii. Predict sales volumes.

iv. Help humans understand which products to place where Large Data and the ever-growing access is the driving force behind AI and the wave of technological change sweeping across all industries.

Some of the data in the world are useless since it may become a liability when it is not understandable. Data visualisation is about how to present the data, to the users/right people, at the right time to enable them to gain insights most effectively.

18. What are the different types of Decision Trees? Explain.

Ans. There are two types of decision trees based on the target variable; categorical variable decision trees and continuous variable decision trees.

(i) Categorical variable decision tree: A categorical variable decision tree has categorical target variables divided into different categories. For example, the categories can be 'yes' or 'no'. Here, the categories mean that every stage of the decision process falls into one of the categories, and there are no in-betweens.

(ii) Continuous variable decision tree: A continuous variable decision tree is a decision tree having continuous target variable. For example, the income of an individual whose income is not known, may be predicted based on available information, like his/her occupation, age, and other continuous variables.

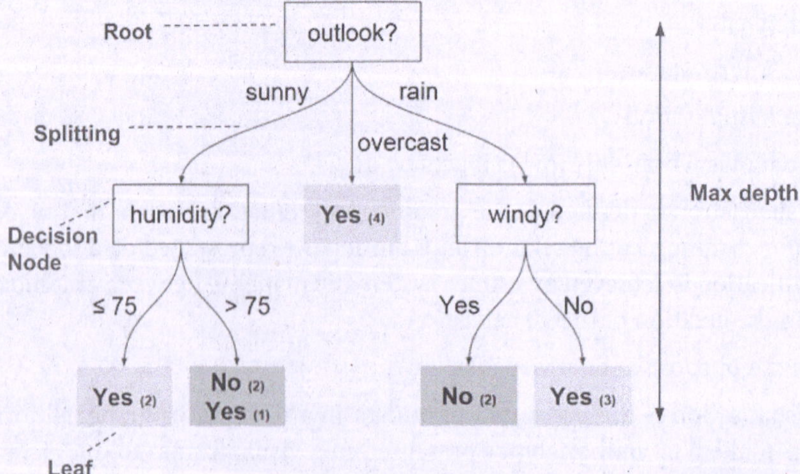

Figure 7.9

19. What are the advantages of a Decision Tree?

Ans. Following are the advantages of decision tree:

i. Easy to use and interpret.

ii. Easy to prepare.

iii. Simple to understand and explain.

iv. Can handle both categorical and numerical data.

v. Resistant to outliers, hence require little data cleaning/pre-processing.

vi. New features can be easily added.

vii. It can be used to build larger classifiers by using ensemble methods.

viii. It provides strategic answers to uncertain situations.

20. Enlist the disadvantages of Decision Tree.

Ans. Following are the disadvantages of decision tree:

i. It is prone to overfitting.

ii. It is less effective in predicting the outcome of a continuous variable.

iii. It requires some kind of measurement to know the efficiency.

iv. It needs careful attention with parameter tuning.

v. It can create biased learnt trees if some classes dominate.

21. Explain 'Fusion Chart.'

Ans. Fusion chart is a widely-used and JavaScript-based charting and visualisation package. It can produce 90 different types of charts and integrates with a large number of platforms and frameworks. It is quite flexible. One feature that has helped make Fusion Charts very popular is that users can pick from a range of "live" example templates, merely plugging in their data sources as needed.

22. Define Decision Tree. Where are Decision trees used?

Ans. A decision tree is a tree-like graph having three parts. Nodes represent the place where an attribute is picked and asked a question, edges represent the answers to the question, and the leaves represent the actual output. These are used in non-linear decision-making.

23. Differentiate between Fusion Chart and High Chart.

Ans. Fusion chart is a widely-used and JavaScript-based charting and visualisation package. It can produce more than 90 different types of charts and integrates with a large number of platforms and frameworks. A high chart is often chosen for a fast and flexible solution, with a minimum need for specialist data and visualisation training before it can be put to work.

24. Why is there an increase in the demand for data scientists?

Ans. Demand for data scientists is increasing continuously. The problems of collecting and normalizing clean and meaningful data for machine learning are to be tackled at a faster rate.

25. What is the main advantage of using a Decision Tree?

Ans. Anyone can use decision trees to clarify and find an answer to a complex AI problem. Every branch of the decision tree represents a possible decision, outcome, or reaction, while the farthest branches on the decision tree represent the end results.

7.3.10 Long Answer Type Questions

1. Explain different data types.

Ans. Data obtained from various sources may be grouped as follows:

a) **Known Data:** This type of data is precious. If the properties of the production plant or my warehouses are not known to a manager, then he is unable to plan anything seriously. Not all data is "as valuable," this is a notion of "good data." The unstructured data is not easy to use. So, good data should be procured. Not all data is available as open-source, and hence, capturing and reselling useful data is a great business.

b) **Unknown Data:** The structure we can find in known data is, in fact, additional data. This is data we did not know initially and that we can extract from the known data. We can classify, we can structure, we can forecast.

From a machine learning perspective, most data can be categorised into four basic types as follows:

i. **Numerical Data:** The data where data points are exact numbers is called numerical data. Numerical data can be characterised as continuous data or discrete data. For example, the number of students taking class IX in a school would be a discrete data set, where only discrete whole number values like 20, 25, or 39 will exist. A class cannot have 22.65 students enrolled. Continuous data are defined as numbers that can fall anywhere within a range. For example, a student could have an average score in the subject of 75.32, which falls between 0 and 100.

ii. **Categorical Data**: Categorical data represents characteristics, such as gender, a cricket player's position, team, hometown, etc. Categorical data can take numerical values. For example, we may use 1 for the colour red and 2 for blue. But these numbers don't have a mathematical meaning. It means that we can't add them together or take the average. This process would also be something like if a person is a man or woman, school is in the urban or rural background, or property is residential or commercial.

iii. **Time Series Data:** The time-series data is a sequence of numbers collected at regular intervals over some time. For example, weather records, economic indicators, patient health evolution metrics, etc., other examples of time series data may be server metrics, application performance monitoring, network data, sensor data, events, clicks, etc. It is essential in some fields like finance.

iv. **Text Data:** Text data is just words. The Text data type stores any kind of text data that can contain both single-byte and multibyte characters that the locale supports. The term simple large object refers to an instance of a TEXT or BYTE data type. A lot of the time, the first thing that you do with text is you turn it into numbers using some interesting functions like the bag of words formulation.

2. Discuss the types of tools for Data Analysis.

Ans. Using data analysis tools makes it easier for users to process and manipulate data, analyse the relationships and correlations between data sets. These are also used to identify patterns and trends for interpretation.

There are various types of data analysis techniques based on business and technology. The major types of data analysis are as follows:

(i) Data Mining / Text Analysis

Text Analysis or Data Mining is a method to discover a pattern in large data sets by using databases or data mining tools. It is used to transform raw data into business information. Business Intelligence tools are used to make strategic business decisions as they offer a way to extract and examine data and derive patterns and, finally, for the interpretation of the data.

(ii) Statistical Analysis

Statistical analysis shows "What happens?" by using past data in the form of dashboards. This analysis includes gathering/collection, analysis, interpretation, presentation, and modelling of data. There are two types of Statistical Analysis: Descriptive Analysis and Inferential Analysis.

(a) **Descriptive Analysis:** It analyses complete data or a sample of summarised numerical data to show mean and deviation for continuous data, percentage and frequency for categorical data.

(b) **Inferential Analysis:** It analyses samples from complete data to find different conclusions from the same data by selecting different samples.

(iii) Diagnostic Analysis

The diagnostic analysis shows "Why did it happen?" by finding the cause from the insight found in Statistical Analysis. This analysis is useful in identifying behaviour patterns of data. If a new problem arrives in the business process, then this analysis is used to find similar patterns of that problem to get solutions.

(iv) Predictive Analysis

The predictive analysis shows "what is likely to happen" by using previous data. The simplest example is if last year someone bought two dresses based on the savings and if this year the salary is increasing double, then four dresses can be purchased.

So, this analysis makes predictions/forecasts about future outcomes based on current or past data. Its accuracy depends on how much detailed information is available.

(v) Prescriptive Analysis

The prescriptive analysis combines the experience from all previous analyses to find out the correct action to be taken in a current problem or decision. Most of the data-driven companies are utilising Prescriptive Analysis because the predictive and descriptive analysis is not enough to improve data performance.

3. Explain the different phases of data analysis.

Ans. The following phases of data analysis are used:

i. **Requirement of Data Collection**

If the purpose or aim of doing the analysis is clear, then a collection of data becomes easier. A project manager has to understand the need for a type of data analysis. In this phase, the type of analysis and mode of its measurement is decided that is based on the investigating and understanding the purpose of analysis.

ii. **Data Collection**

After understanding the requirement of gathering, a clear idea is obtained about what things are to be measured and what the findings should be like. Now, data based on requirements is collected or procured for processing or organising for analysis. The collected data from various sources should be recorded in a log with all details, like collection date, source of the data, etc.

iii. **Data Cleaning**

Since all the data collected may not be useful or relevant as per the aim of analysis, so, it should be cleaned first. The collected data may contain duplicate records, white spaces, or errors. This data should be cleaned to make it error-free. This phase should be done before analysis because, based on data cleaning, the output of the analysis will be closer to the expected outcome.

iv. **Data Analysis**

When the data is collected, cleaned, and processed, then it is ready for data analysis. During this phase, one can use data analysis tools and software, which will help to understand, interpret and derive conclusions based on the requirements.

v. **Data Visualisation**

Data visualisation is very common in day-to-day life as it often appears in the form of charts and graphs. In other words, data is presented graphically so that it will be easier for humans to understand and process it. Data visualisation is often used to find out unknown facts and ongoing trends. By observing relationships and comparing datasets, one can choose a way to find out meaningful information.

vi. **Data Interpretation**

After analysing the data, it is finally time to interpret the results. One may choose the way to communicate the data analysis, either in words or in visual (table or chart). Use the results of the data analysis process for deciding the best course of action.

4. Discuss various tools for data visualisations.

Ans. The following tools are employed for data visualisations:

(i) **Tableau:** Tableau is often regarded as the grandmaster of data visualisation software, and for a good reason. Tableau is quite suitable for handling the huge and very fast-changing datasets that are used in Big Data operations, including artificial intelligence and machine learning applications. Extensive research and testing have been done for enabling Tableau to create graphics and visualisations more efficiently and to make them easy for humans to understand.

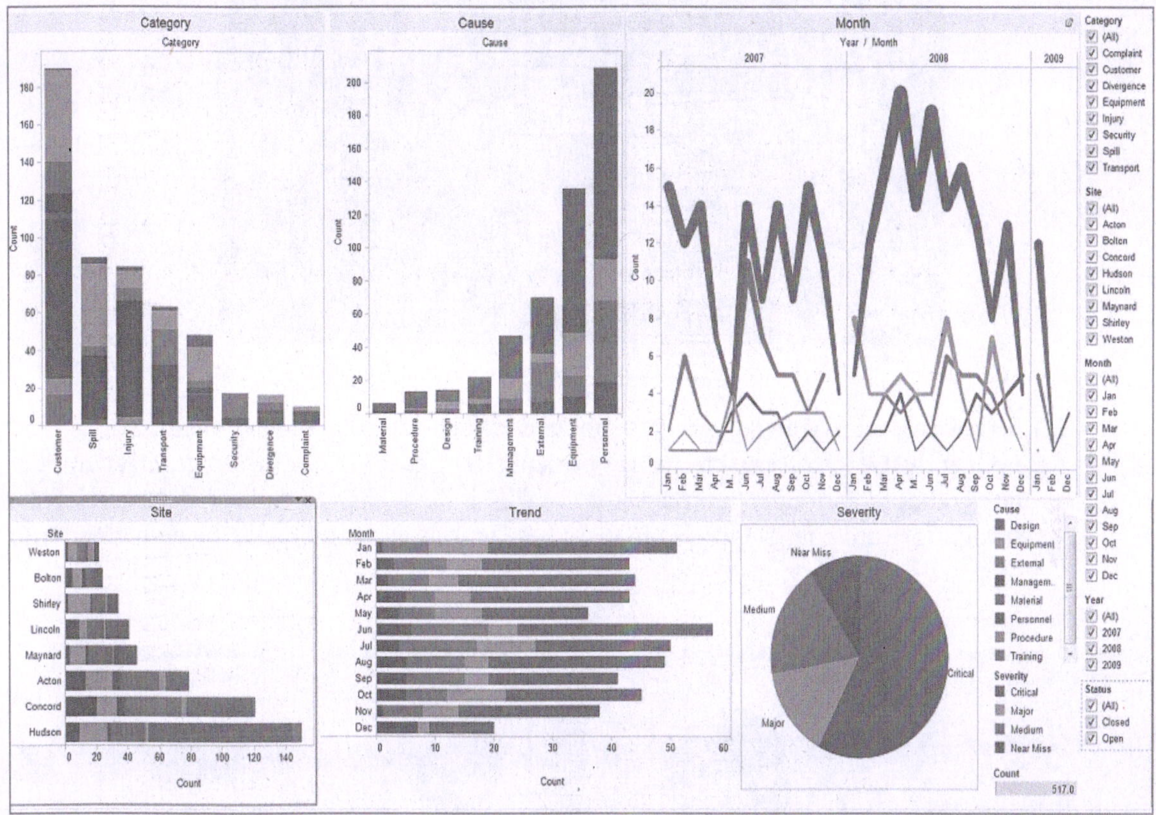

Figure 7.10

(ii) QlikView: In addition to its data visualisation capabilities, QlikView offers powerful business intelligence, analytics, and enterprise reporting capabilities and has a clean and clutter-free user interface. QlikView tool is the major player in this category and Tableau's biggest competitor. It is used by more than 40,000 customers in more than 100 countries.

Figure 7.11

(iii) Fusion Charts: Fusion chart is a widely-used and JavaScript-based charting and visualisation package. It can produce 90 different types of charts and integrates with a large number of platforms and frameworks. It is quite flexible. One feature that has helped make Fusion Charts very popular is that users can pick from a range of "live" example templates, merely plugging in their data sources as needed.

(iv) High Charts: Like Fusion Charts, high charts require a license for their commercial use. According to the website of the company, it is used by 72 out of the world's 100 largest companies. It is often chosen for a fast and flexible solution, with a minimum need for specialist data and visualisation training before it can be put to work. Its main feature is that anyone can view and run its interactive visualisations, which is not always true with newer platforms.

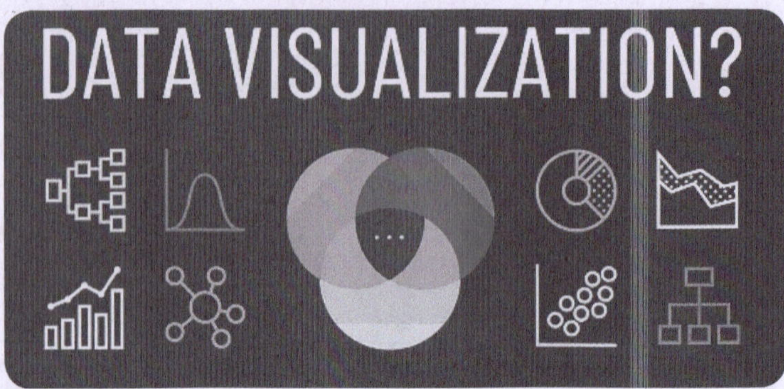

Figure 7.12

(v) **Datawrapper:** Datawrapper is a popular choice among media organisations that frequently use it to create charts and present statistics for media coverage. Datawrapper has a simple and clear interface that makes it very easy to upload data and create straightforward charts and also maps. These graphs etc. can quickly be embedded into reports.

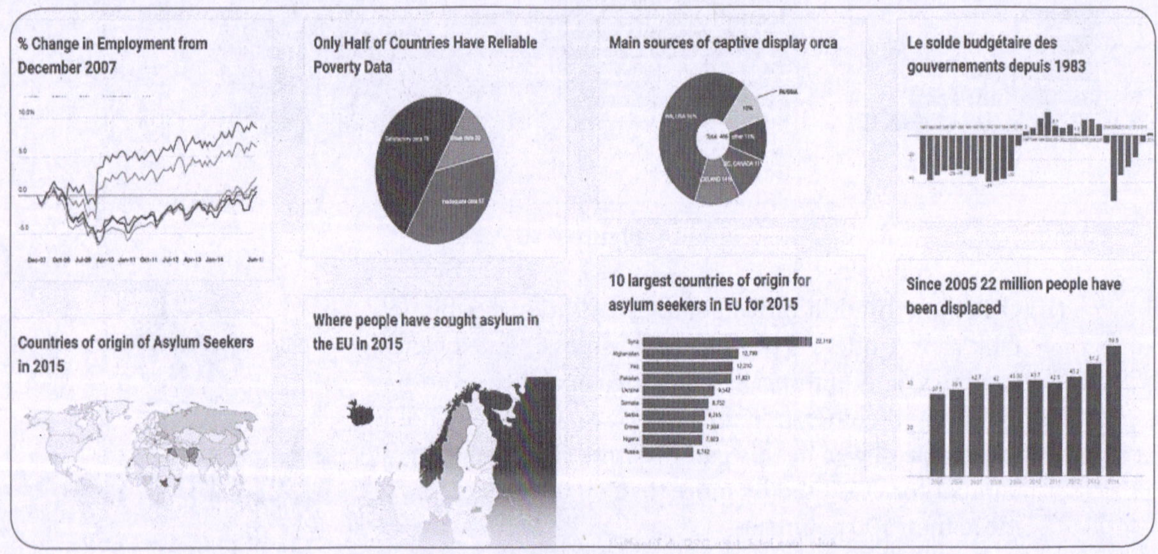

Figure 7.13

(vi) **Plotly:** Plotly enables more complex and sophisticated visualisations due to the use of its integration with analytics-oriented programming languages, like Python, R, Matlab, etc. It is built using JavaScript.

(vii) **SiSense:** SiSense provides a full-stack analytics platform, but its visualisation capabilities provide a simple-to-use drag and drop interface which creates charts and more complex graphics with a minimum of hassle. Multiple sources of data are gathered into one easily accessed repository, where it can be queried through dashboards instantaneously. Dashboards can then be shared among organisations ensuring easy access to even non-technically-minded staff to understand the visuals easily.

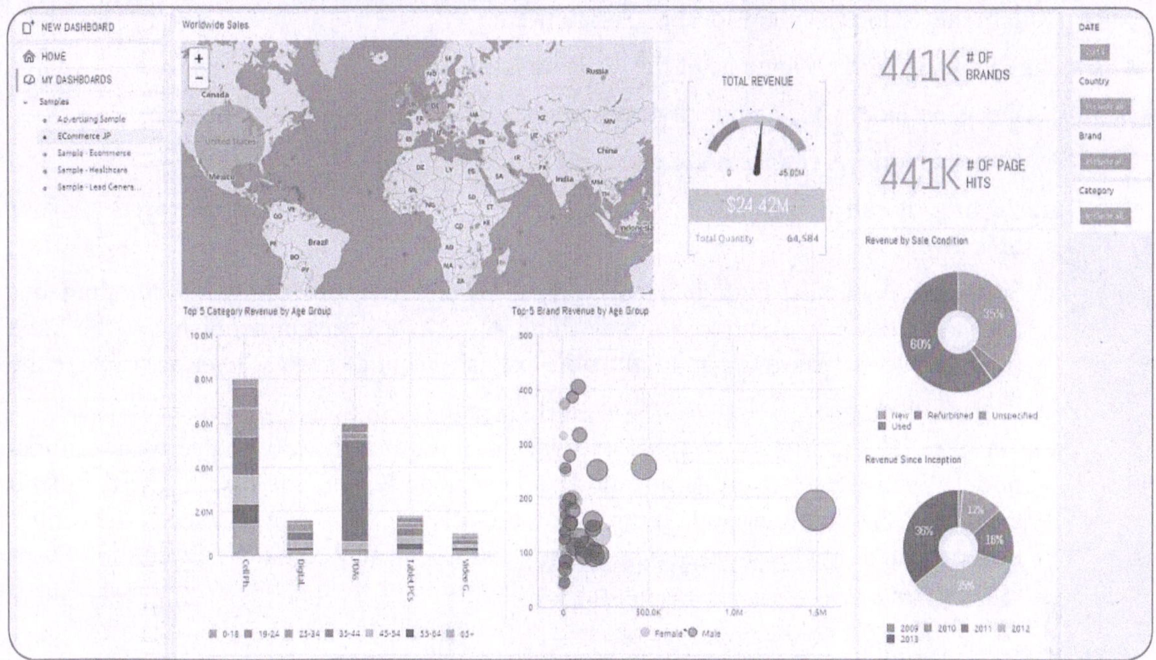

Figure 7.14

5. Explain the Basics of a Decision Tree.

Ans. A decision tree is a tree-like graph having three parts. Nodes represent the place where an attribute is picked and asked a question, edges represent the answers to the question, and the leaves represent the actual output. These are used in non-linear decision-making.

Decision trees are used to classify the examples by sorting them down the tree from the root to some leaf node, whereas the leaf node provides the classification to the example selected. Each node in the decision tree acts as a test case for some attribute. Moreover, each edge descending from that node corresponds to one of the possible answers to the test case. This process is recurrence/recursive in nature and is repeated for every subtree rooted at the new nodes.

Decision trees display a sequence of steps and give people an effective and easy way to visualise the potential options of a decision and its range of possible outcomes. It also helps people identify every potential option and weigh each course of action against the risks and rewards for each option.

An organisation may use decision trees as a kind of decision support system when the structured model allows the user to see how and why one choice may lead to the next, with the use of the branches indicating exclusive options. The decision tree allows users to take any problem with multiple possible solutions and to display those solutions in a simple and easy-to-understand format.

In the decision tree, every end result has an assigned risk and reward weight/number. If a person uses a decision tree to make a decision, he/she look at each final outcome to assess the benefits and drawbacks. The decision tree itself can span as long or as short as needed in order to come to a proper conclusion.

6. Explain the various elements of the 'Decision Tree.'

Ans. The following are the elements of the decision tree:

i. **Decision Node**: It is a node that represents a decision that needs to be made.

ii. **Chance Node**: A chance node represents uncertainty.

iii. **Payoff**: It can be profit, cost, distance, time, or any other measure based on your objective.

iv. **Software:** A parallel node is a node where its children are considered simultaneous decision trees. For example, we may think about two decision problems at the same time. Or we may have two mutually non-exclusive chance events. Then we can use the parallel node.

v. **Terminal Node**: An action node or an Event node may be terminated by a terminal node. When we select an Action node or Event node, we will see the flyover menu exhibiting the Terminal node button. But, a Decision Node or a Chance Node cannot be terminated by a terminal node because these nodes may contain only Action / Event as children.

7.3.11 HOTS Questions

1. Preparing customer data is considered a difficult task? Why?

Ans. Preparing customer data for meaningful ML projects is a difficult task due to the variety of data sources that exist in the organisations. For making an accurate model, it is critical to select data that you hope the model will predict based on other input data.

2. Why is it necessary to train the model before deployment in the real world?

Ans. The training of an AI model is necessary to validate its functioning. When has an organisation deployed the collection and enrichment of meaningful input data, then data scientists take a representative sample of the population (i.e., all types of customers, anonymous visitors, or known prospects) and prepare a portion for training models? The remaining portion is used to validate the models after training is complete.

3. What is feature engineering? Where is it used?

Ans. The process of repeating rapidly and testing new data points that can be derived from the data source is called feature engineering. It is used in the evaluation phase of the project cycle.

4. Why is it difficult to prepare customer data for an ML project?

Ans. Preparing customer data for meaningful ML projects is a difficult task due to the variety of data sources and data silos that exist in the organisations.

5. Why is a Decision tree considered the most potent tool for classification and prediction?

Ans. The decision tree is the most potent and accessible tool for classification and prediction. A Decision tree is a flowchart like a tree structure, in which each internal node represents denotes a test on an attribute, each branch an outcome of the test, and each leaf node (terminal node) holds a class label.

7.4 PRACTICE QUESTIONS

1. Define Data Exploration.
2. What are the different steps of Data Analysis?
3. What do you mean by Data Mining?
4. What are the different Data Analysis techniques?
5. Define Decision Tree.
6. What do you mean by problem scoping to set goals for an AI project?
7. Define Problem Scoping.
8. Explain clustering.
9. Discuss regression with the help of an example.
10. What is the purpose of Data Visualisation?
11. Discuss the ethical issues involved in the AI problem.
12. Mention two types of Data Modelling.
13. What are the different types of Decision Trees?
14. Explain classification in the AI project.
15. Discuss all steps of an AI Project Cycle framework.
16. Why is data required? From where is relevant data is obtained?
17. Explain the use of various types of graphs.
18. Mention various functions of AI Project Management.
19. Write one purpose of Histogram.
20. What is Histogram, and where is it used?
21. Mention two advantages of using visualisation techniques.
22. List any three visualisation techniques with their purpose.
23. How will you differentiate between chart and graph?

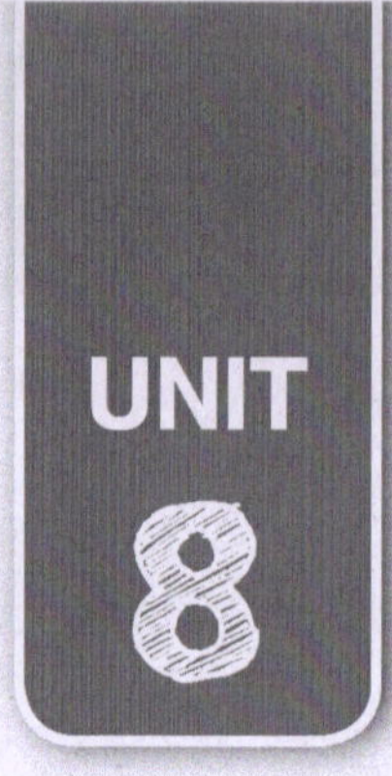

Neural Network

8.1 UNIT IN BRIEF

- A neural network is a computational data model that is capable to capture and represent complex input/output relationships.
- A neural network is either a Biological Neural Network (BNN)that is made up of real biological neurons, or an artificial neural network, for solving artificial intelligence (AI) problems.

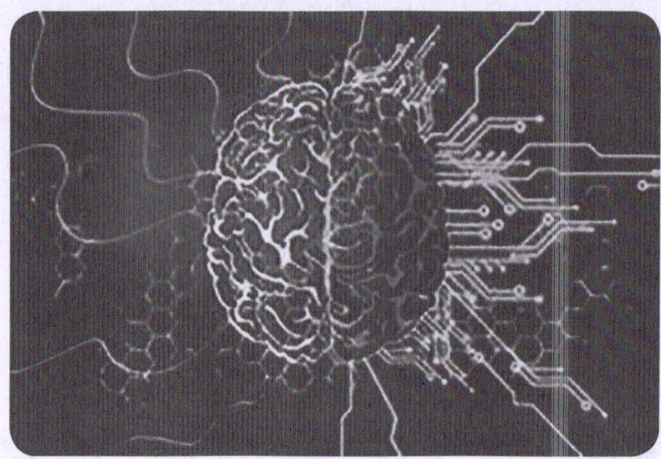

Figure 8.1

- AutoDraw (https://www.autodraw.com/) is a tool by Google Creative Lab.
- AutoDraw is a collaboration between machine learning and the artist community. It can guess hundreds of drawings, and more drawings will be added over time.
- A Feedforward Artificial Neural Network consists of many layers of processing units and each layer is feeding input to the next layer in a feed through manner.
- AutoDraw is a fast drawing tool that acts like a magic wand for everyone to create anything visual and quick.
- Basic Three-Layer Neural Network consists of an input layer, hidden layer, and output layer.
- Classification and clustering work on discrete datasets.
- Classification is defined as a systematic grouping of observations into different categories. Applications of classification are speech recognition, biometric identification, handwriting recognition, and so on.
- Classification is defined as a systematic grouping of observations into different categories.

- Classification is evaluated by measuring accuracy.
- Classification predicts unordered data.
- Clustering is dividing the data points into a number of groups so that data points in the same groups are more similar to other data points in the other group and dissimilar to the data points in other groups.
- Deep learning learns by itself. It means that it learns by using a neural network that acts like a human brain and then analyses the data as humans do.
- Deep learning systems and, thus, the neural networks that enable them are used strategically in many industries and businesses.
- Examples of deep learning are chatbots, automatic translation of the text, adding colours to mono colour images, autonomous vehicles, computer vision, text generation (use of punctuation and grammar), and so on.
- In classification, data is categorised under different labels as per the parameters given in input, and then the labells are predicted for the data.
- In Supervised Learning, all data is labelled, and the algorithms learn to predict the output from the input data.
- In Unsupervised Learning, all data is unlabelled, and the algorithms learn to inherent structure from the input data.
- Machine learning is a component of Artificial Intelligence that learns from the previous dataset.
- Regression can also identify the distribution movement depending on the historical data.
- Regression works with continuous data.
- Reinforcement Learning is a Machine Learning method, and it helps to discover which action yields the highest reward over a longer period.
- Reinforcement learning is used in gaming.
- The Reinforcement Learning method works on interacting with the environment, whereas the supervised learning method works on given sample data.
- RL method is not used when enough data to solve the problem is provided.
- Self-learning resulting from experience may occur within networks, which can derive conclusions from a complex and seemingly unrelated set of information.
- Supervised learning models can make predictions based on labelled datasets.
- The artificial networks may be used for predictive modelling, adaptive control, and applications where they can be trained via a dataset.
- The biggest challenge of the RL method is that parameters may affect the speed of learning.
- The biggest characteristic of RL is that there is no supervisor, only a real number or reward signal.
- The classification algorithms involve decision trees, logistic Regression, etc.
- The function of an axon in a neuron is to transmit information to different neurons, muscles, and glands, while the function of a dendrite in a neuron is to send messages to the neuron

cell body for the cell to function. The cell body is also called soma, which connects to the dendrites so as to bring information to the neuron and the axon, which sends information to other neurons.

- The Neural Network is defined as a combination of algorithms to understand the relationship between various sets of data to process and then takes out some meaningful information from it.
- The objective of unsupervised learning is to model the underlying distribution in the data to learn more about the data.
- There are two types of reinforcement learning- Positive and Negative Reinforcement.
- Unsupervised learning occurs where only input data (X) is available, but no corresponding output variable is available.

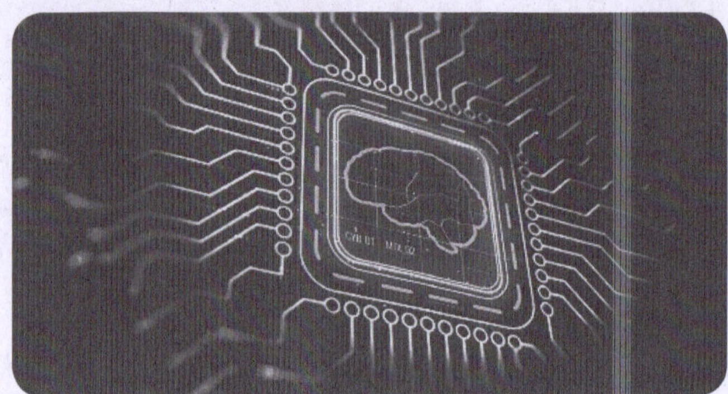

Figure 8.2

8.2 SOLVED CBSE/NCERT EXERCISE

8.2.1 VSA Questions

1. What is the Testing dataset?

Ans. The dataset provided to the model ML. algorithm after training the algorithm

2. Mention the types of learning approaches for AI modelling.

Ans. Supervised, unsupervised, and Reinforcement

8.2.2 Fill in the blanks:

1. The analogy of an Artificial Neural Network can be made with ____________.

Ans. Parallel Processing

2. Neural Network is a mesh of multiple ____________________.

Ans. Hidden Layers / Layers

8.2.3 Short Answer Type Questions

1. What are the two different approaches for AI modelling? Define them.

Ans. There are two approaches for AI Modelling; Rule-based and Learning-based.

Rule-based approach produces pre-defined outputs based on some rules programmed by developers. Learning approach has its own rules that are based on the output and data used to train the models.

2. Draw the graphical representation of the Classification AI model. Explain in brief.

Ans. The classification Model works on the labelled data. For example, we have three coins of the different denominations, which are labelled according to their weights, then the model would look for the labelled features for predicting the output. This model works on a discrete dataset. It means that the data need not be continuous.

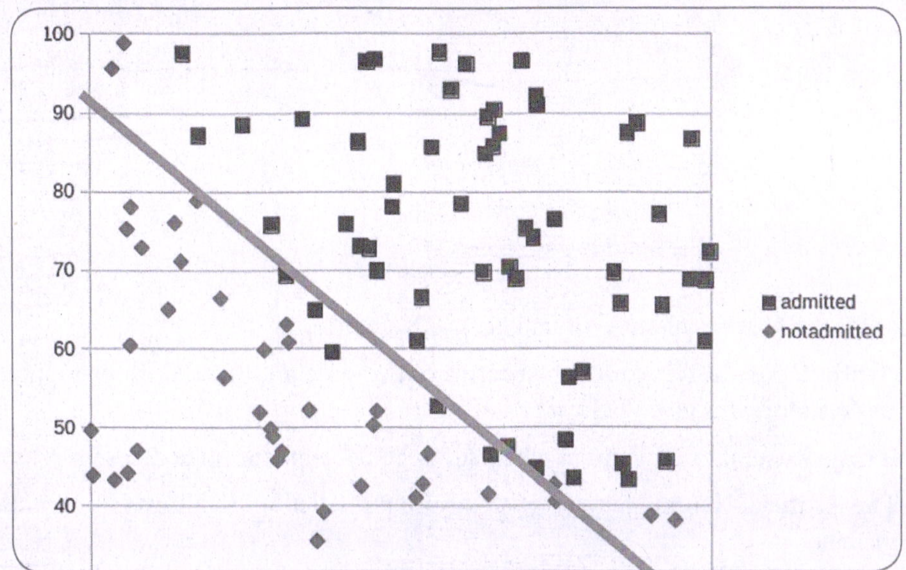

Figure 8.3: Classification

3. Draw the graphical representation of the Regression AI model. Explain in brief.

Ans. This model works on continuous data to predict the output based on patterns. For example, if we wish to predict our next salary, then we would put in the data of our previous salary, any increments, etc., and would train the model. Here, the data which has been fed to the machine is continuous.

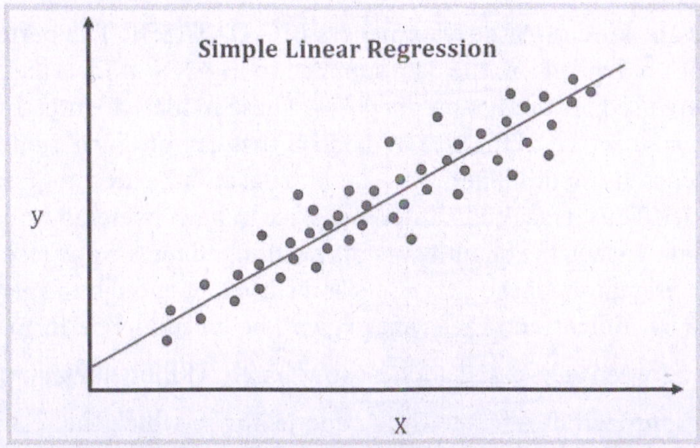

Figure 8.4: Regression

4. Draw the graphical representation of the Clustering AI model. Explain in brief.

Ans. Clustering refers to the unsupervised learning algorithm. It can cluster the unknown data according to the patterns or trends identified out of it. The patterns observed might be the ones that are known to the developer.

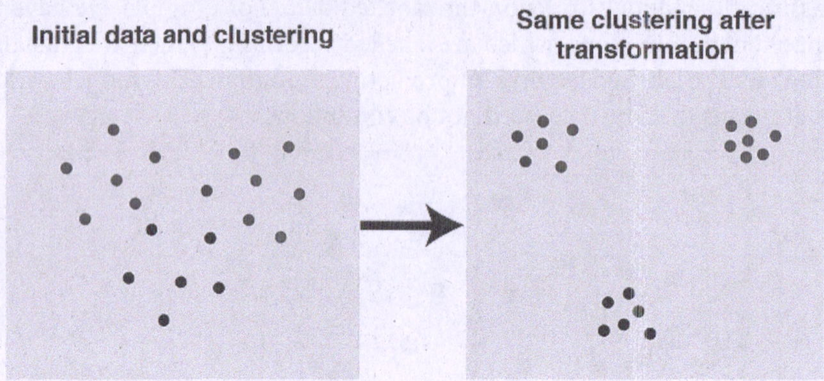

Figure 8.5

5. What are the features of an Artificial Neural Network?

Ans. An Artificial Neural Network, irrespective of the style and logic of implementation, has a few basic features, as given below:

i. It is very useful to implement when solving problems for huge datasets.

ii. The Artificial Neural Network systems are modelled on the human brain and nervous system.

iii. They are able to automatically extract features without feeding the input by developer/programmer.

iv. Every node of a layer in a Neural Network is compulsorily a machine learning algorithm.

8.2.4 Long Answer Type Questions

1. Explain the relation between data size and model performance of an Artificial Neural Network.

Ans. The basis for any kind of AI development is BIG DATASET. The performance of any AI-based application depends on the data supplied to it. ANN models are known as Learning models and are used for prediction purposes. These models are mostly developed without paying much cognizance to the size of datasets that can produce models of high accuracy and better generalisation. Generally, a large dataset is needed to construct a predictive learning model. Thus, what constitutes a dataset to be considered as being big or small is somehow vague. In fact, the quantity of data partitioned for the purpose of training must be of a good representation of the entire sets and sufficient enough to span through the input space. It must be authentic and relevant to give a better model performance.

2. Differentiate between rule-based and learning-based AI modelling approaches.

Ans. **Rule-Based Approach:** It refers to the AI modelling in which the relationship/patterns in data are defined by the developer. The machine follows the rules or instructions mentioned by the developer and performs its task accordingly. For example, suppose you have a dataset comprising 100 images of apples and 100 images of bananas. To train your machine, you feed this data into the machine and label each image as either apple or banana. Now, if you test the machine with the image of an apple, it will compare the image with the trained data, and according to the labels of trained images, it will identify the test image as an apple. This is known as the Rule-based approach. The rules given to the machine in this example are the labels given to the machine for each image in the training dataset.

Learning-Based Approach: In this approach, the machine learns by itself. It refers to AI modelling in which the relationship/ patterns in data are not defined by the programmer. In this approach, random data is fed to the machine to find out patterns and trends by the machine. Generally, this approach is used when the data is unlabelled. For example, suppose we have a dataset of 2000 images of random stray cats of one area. We would put this into a learning approach-based AI machine, and the machine would come up with different patterns it has observed in the features of these 2000 images.

3. What is an Artificial Neural Network? Explain the layers in an artificial neural network.

Ans. **Artificial Neural Network**: A Neural Network was modelled to mimic the functionality of a human brain. The human brain is a neural network made up of a number of neurons. Whereas an Artificial Neural Network (ANN) is made up of a number of perceptrons. A neural network consists of three important layers:

Input Layer: As the name suggests, this layer accepts all the inputs provided by the programmer.

Hidden Layer: Between the input and the output layer is a set of layers known as Hidden layers. In this layer, computations are performed, which result in the output. There can be any number of hidden layers.

Output Layer: The inputs go through a series of transformations via the hidden layer, which finally results in the output that is delivered via this layer.

4. Explain the following: (a) Supervised learning (b) Unsupervised Learning

Ans. **(a) Supervised learning**: Supervised learning is an approach for creating artificial intelligence (AI), in which the program is given labelled input data and the expected output/results.

(b) Unsupervised Learning: An unsupervised learning model works on the unlabelled/ random dataset. The unsupervised learning models are used to identify patterns, relationships, and trends out of the data that is fed into it. It helps the user in understanding the data is about and what are the major features identified by the machine in it.

5. Differentiate between classification and regression algorithms with the help of suitable examples.

Ans. Classification is a process of finding a function that helps in dividing the dataset into classes based on various parameters. In classification, a computer program is trained on the training dataset and based on that training, it categorises the data into various classes. The task of the classification algorithm is to find the mapping function to map the input(x) to the discrete output(y). For example, email Spam Detection. The model is trained on the basis of millions of emails on different parameters. Whenever it receives a new email, it identifies whether the email is spam or not. If the email is spam, then it is moved to the Spam folder.

Regression is the process of finding the correlations between dependent and independent variables. It helps in predicting the continuous variables such as prediction of Market Trends, prediction of House prices, etc. The task of the Regression algorithm is to find the mapping function to map the input variable(x) to the continuous output variable(y). Example: Suppose we want to do weather forecasting, so for this, we will use the Regression algorithm. In weather prediction, the model is trained on the past data, and once the training is completed, it can easily predict the weather for future days.

8.3 SOLVED EXERCISES

8.3.1 Multiple Choice Questions

1. ____________ systems and thus, the neural networks that enable them are used strategically in many industries and businesses.

   a) Machine Learning b) Deep Learning
   c) NLP d) CV

2. Which of the following is NOT a part of a neuron in BNN?

   a) Axon b) Dendrite c) Loaf d) Cell body

3. Which body part is used to send signals away from neurons in the human nervous system?

   a) Nucleus b) Axons c) Dendrites d) Cell body

4. Consider the following features:

   i. These have the ability to learn by themselves and produce the output that is not limited to the input provided to them.
   ii. The input is stored in its own networks instead of a database; hence the loss of data does not affect its working.
   iii. These networks can learn from examples and apply them when a similar event arises, making them able to work through real-time events.
   iv. Even if a neuron is not responding or a piece of information is missing, the network can detect the fault and still produce the output.
   v. They can perform multiple tasks in parallel without affecting the system performance.

   These features are of:

   a) ANN b) BNN
   c) CNN d) None of the above

5. ____________ learning is used in gaming.

   a) Reinforcement b) Supervised
   c) Unsupervised d) Project-based

6. Which type of AI Learning is associated with the following features?
   i. It helps in finding which situation needs action.
   ii. It helps in discovering the action that yields the highest reward over a longer period.
   iii. It provides the learning agent with a reward function.
   iv. It allows to figure out the best method for obtaining large rewards.
   a) Supervised Learning b) Unsupervised Learning
   c) Semi-supervised Learning d) Reinforcement Learning
7. ANN stands for:
   a) Artificial Neural Node b) Artificial Neural Network
   c) Artificial Neural Network d) Artificial Neutral Node
8. Which one of the following examples is not related to SL?
   a) Classifying the patients whether a patient is suffering from a particular disease or not.
   b) Predicting weather
   c) Classifying the received emails whether an email is spam or not.
   d) Predicting house/property price or stock market price
9. What is the meaning of SL in AI?
   a) Slow Learner b) Slow Learning
   c) Supervised Learning d) Slightly Learnt
10. Which of the following terms is NOT related to Neural networks?
   a) ANN b) BNN c) PNG d) CNN
11. Which of the following examples is NOT that of Supervised Learning?
   a) Linear Regression for regression problems.
   b) Random forest for classification and regression problems.
   c) Support vector machines for classification problems
   d) None of the above
12. Which sub-category is related to supervised learning?
   a) Clustering b) Classification
   c) Regression d) Both (b) and (c)
13. Artificial neuron is also known as:
   a) Cluster b) Perceptron
   c) Regression d) ANN
14. Which one of the following layers in ANN is used to take the input from the user?
   a) Input Layer b) Hidden Layer
   c) Output Layer d) None of the above

15. Which of the following is not a type of reinforcement learning?
    a) Positive Reinforcement
    b) Negative Reinforcement
    c) Neutral Reinforcement
    d) None of the above
16. A ____________ Artificial Neural Network consists of many layers of processing units and each layer is feeding input to the next layer in a feed through manner.
    a) Feedforward
    b) Feedbackward
    c) Neutral
    d) Central
17. ____________ is the task of dividing the data points into a number of groups such that data points in the same groups are more similar to other data points in the same group and dissimilar to the data points in other groups.
    a) Regression
    b) Clustering
    c) Classification
    d) Any of the above
18. Which one of the following statements is INCORRECT?
    a) Machine learning is a component of AI.
    b) Classification and clustering work on discrete data.
    c) Classification is defined as a systematic grouping of observations into different categories.
    d) In supervised learning, the algorithm learns from a dataset that is not labelled.
19. Which of the following statements is NOT correct?
    a) Reinforcement Learning (RL) is used in gaming.
    b) Testing data is used to check the efficiency of the model.
    c) QuickDraw is a game by Microsoft where neural net tries to guess what you are redrawing.
    d) SketchCode app is used to convert the handmade drawing into HTML code.
20. Which app is used to convert the handmade drawing into HTML code?
    a) SketchCode
    b) QuickDraw
    c) LearnDraw
    d) Vinci code
21. Which of the following is an application of Artificial Neural Network (ANN)?
    i. Optimisation of logistics for transportation networks,
    ii. Medical and disease diagnosis,
    iii. Character and voice recognition (natural language processing),
    iv. Targeted marketing,
    v. Robotic control systems.
    vi. For financial predictions for stock prices, currency, futures options, bankruptcy, bond ratings, etc.
    vii. Drones

a) (ii) (iii) (iv)
b) (iv) (v) (vii)
c) (vii) (vi) (v) (iv) (iii)
d) (i) (ii) (iii) (iv) (v) (vi)

22. Which of the following is NOT an application of ANN?
    a) Ecosystem evaluation, medical imaging
    b) Forecasting of Electrical load and energy demand, identification of compounds
    c) Outdoor games for children, wood cutting industries
    d) Process and quality control in industries, facial recognition
23. Which one of the following is the function of the Hidden Layer?
    a) Receive data from the Input Layer
    b) Process the data
    c) Give the data to the Output Layer
    d) All of the above
24. Who has developed the AutoDraw tool?
    a) Microsoft AI Learning
    b) Intel AI Models
    c) Google Creative Lab
    d) SatyaNadela Labs
25. How many types of ANN are there?
    a) 2
    b) 3
    c) 4
    d) 5
26. Which of the following is NOT a type of ANN?
    a) FeedForward ANN
    b) Feedback ANN
    c) Neutral ANN
    d) None of the above
27. ____________ learning occurs where only input data (X) is available, but no corresponding output variable is available.
    a) Reinforcement
    b) Supervised
    c) Unsupervised
    d) Project-based
28. What is the usual acceptable range of output in ANN?
    a) Between 0 and 1.
    b) Between −1 and 1.
    c) Between −1 and 0.
    d) Between −1 and 2.

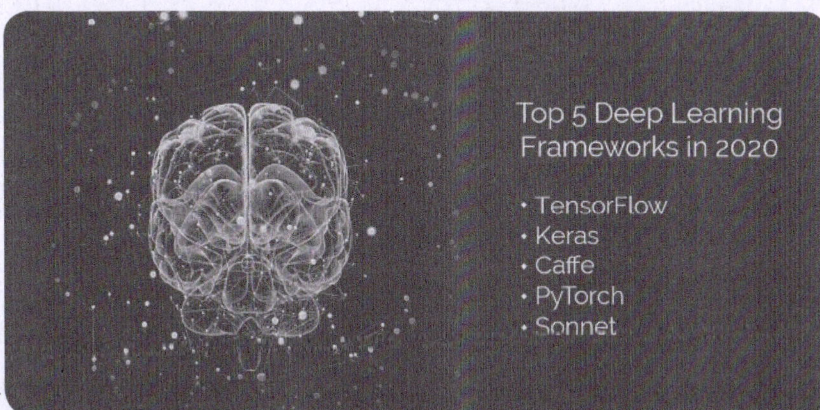

Figure 8.6

ANSWERS									
1. (b)	2. (c)	3. (b)	4. (a)	5. (a)	6. (d)	7. (c)	8. (b)	9. (c)	10. (c)
11. (d)	12. (d)	13. (b)	14. (a)	15. (c)	16. (a)	17. (b)	18. (d)	19. (c)	20. (a)
21. (d)	22. (c)	23. (a)	24. (c)	25. (a)	26. (c)	27. (c)	28. (b)		

8.3.2 Matching Type Question

Match the items of column A and Column B

Column A	Column B
(i) Input Layer	(a) Axon
(ii) Hidden layer	(b) fast drawing tool
(iii) Output Layer	(c) labelled dataset
(iv) Interconnections	(d) responsible for processing
(v) Supervised learning	(e) Synapse
(vi) AutoDraw	(f) Dendrites

ANSWERS
(i) f, (ii) d, (iii) a, (iv) e, (v) c, (vi) b

8.3.3 Fill in the Blanks

1. Classification and ____________ work on discrete data.
2. The two important areas where ANNs have a huge potential for applications are Speech and ____________.
3. ____________ learning is required when there is no labelled data set available with known answers.
4. ____________ is the process of finding /discovering a model (function) which helps in separating the data into multiple categorical classes.
5. In ____________ learning, the algorithm learns from a dataset that is labelled.
6. The ____________ analysis is the statistical model which is used to predict the numeric data instead of labels.
7. ____________ networks are helpful in solving complex problems in real-life situations.
8. ____________ is used to check the efficiency of the model.
9. SketchCode app is used to convert the ____________ drawing into the HTML code.
10. Supervised learning is learning in which we teach or train the machine using ____________ data.
11. Gram Panchayat is the first stage in Panchayati Raj, which acts as an ____________ layer.
12. ____________ (the rice application) uses a method called Neural Sketch learning.
13. ____________ is a game by Google where neural net tries to guess what you are redrawing.

14. Regression is the process of finding a model for identifying the data into continuous real values instead of using ____________ values.
15. ____________ are capable of learning that takes place by altering weight values.

ANSWERS			
1. clustering	2. Image Processing	3. Unsupervised	4. Classification
5. supervised	6. Regression	7. Neural	8. Testing data
9. handmade	10. labelled	11. input	12. Bayou
13. Quick Draw	14. discrete	15. ANNs	

8.3.4 True/False

1. Machine learning is a component of AI.
2. Regression is defined as a systematic grouping of observations into different categories.
3. Deep learning systems and, thus, the neural networks that enable them are used strategically in many industries and businesses.
4. Reinforcement learning is used in gaming.
5. A Feedforward Artificial Neural Network consists of many layers of processing units and each layer is feeding input to the next layer in a feed through manner.
6. Clustering is the task of dividing the data points into a number of groups such that data points in the same groups are more similar to other data points in the same group and dissimilar to the data points in other groups.
7. Supervised learning occurs where only input data (X) is available, but no corresponding output variable is available.
8. Classification can also identify the distribution movement depending on the historical data.
9. A neural network is a computational data model that is capable of capturing and representing complex input/output relationships.
10. The objective of unsupervised learning is to model the underlying distribution in the data to learn more about the data.
11. A neural network is either a biological neural network (BNN) that is made up of real biological neurons, or an artificial neural network used for solving artificial intelligence (AI) problems.
12. The artificial networks may be used for predictive modelling, adaptive control, and applications where they can be trained via a dataset.
13. Self-learning resulting from experience can occur within networks, which can derive conclusions from a complex and seemingly unrelated set of information.
14. In classification, data is categorized under different labels according to some parameters given in input, and then the labels are predicted for the data.
15. The clustering process models a function through which the data is predicted in discrete class labels.

ANSWERS						
1. T	2. F (Classification)	3. T	4. T	5. T	6. T	
7. F (Unsupervised)	8. F (Regression)	9. T	10. T	11. T	12. T	13. T
14. T	15. F (Classification process)					

8.3.5 Statements Based Questions

1. Statement 1: Regression can be evaluated using root mean square error.

   Statement 2: Classification is evaluated by measuring accuracy.

   a) Statement 1 is correct, but statement 2 is incorrect.

   b) Statement 1 is incorrect, but statement 2 is correct.

   c) Both the statements are correct.

   d) Both the statements are incorrect.

2. Statement 1: Clustering is the task of dividing the data points into a number of groups such that data points in the same groups are more similar to other data points in the same group and dissimilar to the data points in other groups.

   Statement 2: Regression trees (e.g., Random Forest) and linear Regression are examples of clustering algorithms.

   a) Statement 1 is correct, but statement 2 is incorrect.

   b) Statement 1 is incorrect, but statement 2 is correct.

   c) Both the statements are correct.

   d) Both the statements are incorrect.

3. Statement 1: Unsupervised learning is a learning in which we teach or train the machine using data that is well labelled, which means some data is already tagged with the correct answer.

   Statement 2: Supervised learning is required when there is no example data set available with known answers.

   a) Statement 1 is correct, but statement 2 is incorrect.

   b) Statement 1 is incorrect, but statement 2 is correct.

   c) Both the statements are correct.

   d) Both the statements are incorrect.

4. Statement 1: SketchCode is a game by Google where neural net tries to guess what the users are redrawing.

   Statement 2: QuickDraw is an app that is used to convert handmade drawings into HTML code.

   a) Statement 1 is correct, but statement 2 is incorrect.

   b) Statement 1 is incorrect, but statement 2 is correct.

   c) Both the statements are correct.

   d) Both the statements are incorrect.

5. Statement 1: A neural network is a computational data model that is capable to capture and represent complex input/output relationships.

   Statement 2: Classification is basically a collection of objects on the basis of similarity and dissimilarity between them.

   a) Statement 1 is correct, but statement 2 is incorrect.
   b) Statement 1 is incorrect, but statement 2 is correct.
   c) Both the statements are correct.
   d) Both the statements are incorrect.

6. Statement 1: The cell body is also called soma.

   Statement 2: Soma connects to the dendrites so as to bring information to the neuron and the axon.

   a) Statement 1 is correct, but statement 2 is incorrect.
   b) Statement 1 is incorrect, but statement 2 is correct.
   c) Both the statements are correct.
   d) Both the statements are incorrect.

7. Statement 1: Regression predicts unordered data while Regression predicts ordered data.

   Statement 2: Classification can also identify the distribution movement depending on the historical data.

   a) Statement 1 is correct, but statement 2 is incorrect.
   b) Statement 1 is incorrect, but statement 2 is correct.
   c) Both the statements are correct.
   d) Both the statements are incorrect.

8. Statement 1: Testing data is used to check the efficiency of the model.

   Statement 2: Unsupervised Learning is defined as a Machine Learning method that helps to discover which action gives the highest reward over a longer period.

   a) Statement 1 is correct, but statement 2 is incorrect.
   b) Statement 1 is incorrect, but statement 2 is correct.
   c) Both the statements are correct.
   d) Both the statements are incorrect.

9. Statement 1: A Feedbackward Artificial Neural Network consisting of several layers of processing units wherein each layer is providing feeding input to the next layer in a feedthrough manner.

   Statement 2: Unsupervised learning models can make predictions based on labelled datasets.

   a) Statement 1 is correct, but statement 2 is incorrect.
   b) Statement 1 is incorrect, but statement 2 is correct.
   c) Both the statements are correct.
   d) Both the statements are incorrect.

10. Statement 1: ANNs are composed of multiple nodes, which are not similar in action to biological neurons.

    Statement 2: The Reinforcement Learning method works on interacting with the environment, whereas the supervised learning method works on given sample data or examples.

    a) Statement 1 is correct, but statement 2 is incorrect.

    b) Statement 1 is incorrect, but statement 2 is correct.

    c) Both the statements are correct.

    d) Both the statements are incorrect.

ANSWERS									
1. (c)	2. (a)	3. (d)	4. (d)	5. (a)	6. (c)	7. (d)	8. (a)	9. (d)	10. (b)

8.3.6 Assertion Reason Type Questions

1. Assertion (A): Deep learning systems and, thus, the neural networks that enable them are used strategically in many industries and businesses.

   Reason (R): The two important areas where ANNs have a huge potential for applications are Speech and Image Processing.

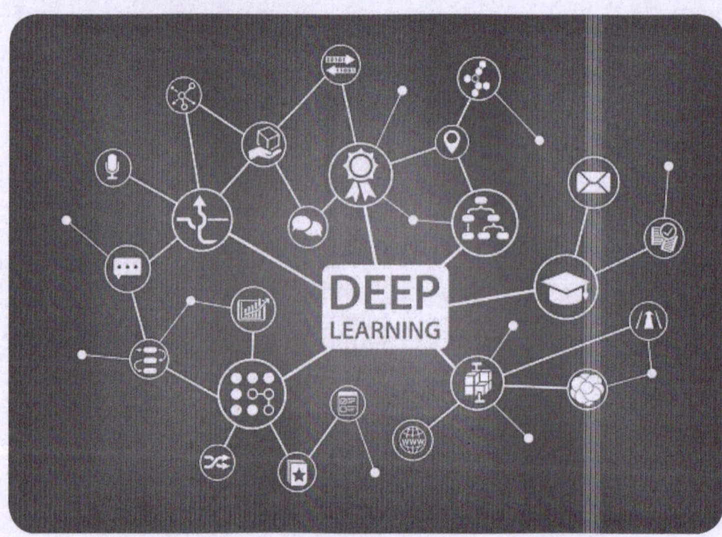

Figure 8.7

   a) Both A and R are correct, and R is the correct reason for A.

   b) Both A and R are correct, and R is not the correct reason for A.

   c) A is correct, but R is incorrect.

   d) A is incorrect, but R is correct.

2. Assertion (A): Clustering is the task of dividing the data points into a number of groups such that data points in the same groups are more similar to other data points in the same group and dissimilar to the data points in other groups.

Reason (R): Clustering is basically a collection of objects on the basis of similarity and dissimilarity between them.

a) Both A and R are correct, and R is the correct reason for A.

b) Both A and R are correct, and R is not the correct reason for A.

c) A is correct, but R is incorrect.

d) A is incorrect, but R is correct.

3. Assertion (A): A Feedforward Artificial Neural Network consists of many layers of processing units and each layer is feeding input to the next layer in a feed through manner.

   Reason (R): Classification is the process of finding or discovering a model (function) which helps in separating the data into multiple categorical classes.

   a) Both A and R are correct, and R is the correct reason for A.

   b) Both A and R are correct, and R is not the correct reason for A.

   c) A is correct, but R is incorrect.

   d) A is incorrect, but R is correct.

4. Assertion (A): Self-learning resulting from experience can occur within networks, which can derive conclusions from a complex and seemingly unrelated set of information.

   Reason (R): Neural networks are not helpful in solving complex problems in real-life situations.

   a) Both A and R are correct and R is the correct reason for A.

   b) Both A and R are correct, and R is not the correct reason for A.

   c) A is correct, but R is incorrect.

   d) A is incorrect, but R is correct.

5. Assertion (A): The Classification process models a function through which the data is predicted in discrete class labels.

   Reason (R): Regression is the process of creating a model which predicts continuous quantity.

   a) Both A and R are correct and R is the correct reason for A.

   b) Both A and R are correct and R is not the correct reason for A.

   c) A is correct, but R is incorrect.

   d) A is incorrect, but R is correct.

6. Assertion (A): Regression analysis is the statistical model which is used to predict numeric data instead of labels.

   Reason (R): Regression is the process of finding a model for distinguishing the data into continuous real values instead of using discrete values.

   a) Both A and R are correct, and R is the correct reason for A.

   b) Both A and R are correct and R is not the correct reason for A.

c) A is correct, but R is incorrect.

d) A is incorrect, but R is correct.

7. Assertion (A): ANNs are capable of learning, which takes place by altering weight values.

   Reason (R): Each link in ANN is associated with weight.

   a) Both A and R are correct and R is the correct reason for A.

   b) Both A and R are correct and R is not the correct reason for A.

   c) A is correct, but R is incorrect.

   d) A is incorrect, but R is correct.

8. Assertion (A): In classification, data is categorised under different labels as per the parameters given in input, and then the labels are predicted for the data.

   Reason (R): The classification algorithms involve decision trees, logistic Regression, etc.

   a) Both A and R are correct and R is the correct reason for A.

   b) Both A and R are correct and R is not the correct reason for A.

   c) A is correct, but R is incorrect.

   d) A is incorrect, but R is correct.

9. Assertion (A): A neural network is either a biological neural network (BNN), made up of real biological neurons, or an artificial neural network, for solving artificial intelligence (AI) problems.

   Reason (R): These artificial networks may be used for predictive modelling, adaptive control, and applications where they can be trained via a dataset.

   a) Both A and R are correct and R is the correct reason for A.

   b) Both A and R are correct and R is not the correct reason for A.

   c) A is correct, but R is incorrect.

   d) A is incorrect, but R is correct.

10. Assertion (A): The objective of supervised learning is to model the underlying distribution in the data to learn more about the data.

    Reason (R): Unsupervised learning occurs where only input data (X) is available, but no corresponding output variable is available.

    a) Both A and R are correct and R is the correct reason for A.

    b) Both A and R are correct and R is not the correct reason for A.

    c) A is correct, but R is incorrect.

    d) A is incorrect, but R is correct.

ANSWERS									
1. (b)	2. (a)	3. (b)	4. (c)	5. (b)	6. (b)	7. (a)	8. (b)	9. (b)	10. (d)

8.3.7 Competency Based Questions

1. Suppose 'Jhoom AI Creations & Solutions' is using the following applications:
   i. computer vision, & speech recognition,
   ii. machine translation, & social network filtering,
   iii. playing board, & video games,
   iv. medical diagnosis.

   Artificial neural networks (ANNs) have been used in:

   a) (i) only b) (i) (ii) only
   c) (iii) (iv) only d) (i) (ii) (iii) (iv) only

2. Suppose Leena wants to employ NN to analyse data, image processing, natural language processing, and some other kinds of cognitive tasks. Which of the following will be employed by her?

   a) ANN b) BNN
   c) CNN d) None of the above

3. Consider the following applications:
   i. Robotics for industrial automation.
   ii. Business strategy planning
   iii. Machine learning and data processing
   iv. In creating training systems that provide custom instruction and materials according to the requirement of learners.
   v. Aircraft control and robot motion control

   These are associated with:

   a) Unsupervised Learning b) Supervised Learning
   c) Reinforcement Learning d) None of the above

4. Suppose Pranav Kalita is using a process that models a function through which the data is predicted in discrete class labels. The algorithms involve decision trees, logistic Regression, etc., and predict unordered data. It is evaluated by measuring accuracy.

   He is using:

   a) Classification b) Regression c) Clustering d) CNN

5. Consider the following features/properties:
   i. It is the process of creating a model which predicts continuous quantity.
   ii. Regression tree (e.g., Random Forest) and linear Regression are examples of this algorithm.
   iii. It predicts ordered data.
   iv. It can be evaluated using root mean square error.

These are associated with:

a) Classification b) Regression

c) Clustering d) BNN

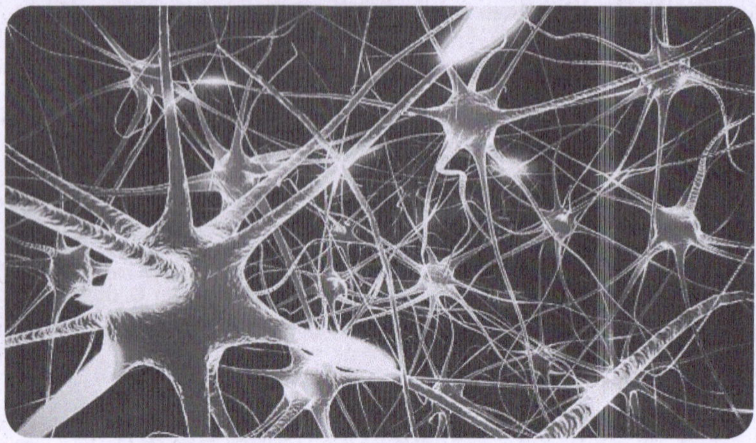

Figure 8.8

ANSWERS				
1. (d)	2. (c)	3. (c)	4. (a)	5. (b)

8.3.8 VSA

1. Define a neural network.

Ans. A neural network is a computational data model that is capable of capturing and representing complex input/output relationships.

2. Mention two uses of ANN.

Ans. Computer vision, speech recognition, machine translation, social network filtering, playing board and video games, and medical diagnosis (any two).

3. What is a Feedforward ANN?

Ans. A Feedforward Artificial Neural Network consists of several layers of processing units wherein each layer provides feeding input to the next layer in a feed through manner.

4. What are the three basic layers of ANN?

Ans. Three layers are An input layer, hidden layer, and output layer.

5. What is the full form of BNN?

Ans. Biological Neural Network

6. Define machine learning.

Ans. Machine learning is a component of Artificial Intelligence that learns from the previous dataset.

7. What is Supervised Learning (SL)?

Ans. In Supervised Learning, all data is labelled, and the algorithms learn to predict the output from the input data.

8. What is done by supervised learning models?

Ans. Supervised learning models can make predictions based on labelled datasets.

9. What are the two important features of 'Unsupervised Learning?

Ans. In Unsupervised Learning, all data is unlabelled, and the algorithms learn to inherent structure from the input data.

10. Define Reinforcement Learning.

Ans. Reinforcement Learning (RL) is defined as a Machine Learning method that helps to discover which action gives the highest reward over a longer period.

11. What is classification in ML?

Ans. Classification is defined as a systematic grouping of observations into different categories.

12. Mention two applications of classification.

Ans. Applications of classification include speech recognition, biometric identification, handwriting recognition, etc.

13. Which type of dataset is used in classification and clustering?

Ans. Classification and clustering work on discrete datasets.

14. With which type of data Regression works?

Ans. Regression works with continuous data.

15. What is the main characteristic of RL?

Ans. The biggest characteristic of RL is that there is no supervisor, only a real number or reward signal.

16. What is the main difference between RL and SL?

Ans. The Reinforcement Learning method works on interacting with the environment, whereas the supervised learning method works on given sample data or examples.

17. What is the main challenge of the RL method?

Ans. The biggest challenge of the RL method is that parameters may affect the speed of learning.

18. Which type of learning is used in gaming by the computer?

Ans. Reinforcement Learning.

19. What are the features of a NN?

Ans. The variables or attributes in the data set are termed as features in a NN.

20. What is the activation value?

Ans. The nodes take input data to perform simple operations on the data, and the result of these operations is passed to other neurons. The output at each node is called activation or node value.

21. What is the main similarity between nodes of ANN and neurons in BNN?

Ans. ANNs are composed of multiple nodes, which are similar in action to biological neurons.

22. For which purpose is testing data used?

Ans. Testing data is used to check the efficiency of the model.

23. What do you mean by QuickDraw?

Ans. QuickDraw is a game by Google where neural net tries to guess what the users are redrawing.

24. What is SketchCode?

Ans. SketchCode is an app that is used to convert handmade drawings into HTML code.

25. How does Deep Learning (DL) occur?

Ans. Deep learning learns by using a neural network that acts like a human brain and then analyses the data as humans do.

26. Give two examples of Deep Learning.

Ans. Chatbots, automatic translation of the text, adding colours to mono colour images, autonomous vehicles, computer vision, text generation (use of punctuation and grammar), etc.

27. What is the function of an axon in a neuron?

Ans. The function of an axon in a neuron is to transmit information to different neurons, muscles, and glands.

28. Who invented the first neurocomputer?

Ans. Dr. Robert Hecht-Nielsen.

29. What does positive and negative weight value exhibit in ANN?

Ans. A positive weight exhibits an excitatory connection, and negative values mean inhibitory connections.

30. What is the usual acceptable range of output in ANN?

Ans. Between –1 and 1.

31. What is the function of a dendrite in a neuron of a human neuron cell?

Ans. The function of a dendrite in a neuron is to send messages to the neuron cell body for the cell to function.

32. What is the other name for the cell body of a neuron?

Ans. The cell body is also called soma.

33. What is the main function of 'Soma'?

Ans. Soma connects to the dendrites so as to bring information to the neuron and the axon.

34. What do you mean by AutoDraw?

Ans. AutoDraw is a fast drawing tool that acts like a magic wand for everyone to create anything visual and quick.

35. Who has developed the Auto Draw tool?

Ans. AutoDraw is a tool developed by Google Creative Lab.

36. What is 'Topology'?

Ans. The organisation or arrangement of the processing elements in ANN, their interconnections, inputs, and outputs are simply known as Topology.

37. Define classification in SL.

Ans. Classification is defined as the process of learning a model that identifies different predetermined classes of data and is a two-step process comprised of a learning step and a classification step.

38. What do you mean by Regression?

Ans. A regression problem is one in which the output variable is a real value, like dollars, weight, etc.

39. Define CNN.

Ans. A Convolutional Neural Network (CNN) is a specific type of artificial neural network that uses perceptrons, a machine learning unit algorithm, for supervised learning to analyse data.

40. What do you mean by perceptrons?

Ans. In Machine Learning (ML), the Perceptron is an algorithm for supervised learning of binary classifiers.

41. Give one example of the unsupervised learning algorithm.

Ans. k-means for clustering problems, or Apriori algorithm for association rule learning problems.

42. What are the types of unsupervised learning?

Ans. Clustering and Association.

43. When is unsupervised learning required?

Ans. Unsupervised learning is required when there is no example data set available with known answers.

44. What is Bayou?

Ans. Bayou is a software-coding application that uses Neural Sketch learning. It is helpful for human programmers to write many codes/programs in response to keywords.

45. How will you define classification with reference to AI?

Ans. Classification is defined as a systematic grouping of observations into different categories.

46. What is the main use of Neural Networks in deep learning?

Ans. Deep learning systems and, thus, the neural networks that enable them are used strategically in many industries and businesses.

47. Give one application of RL.

Ans. Reinforcement Learning is used in gaming.

48. Define feedforward ANN.

Ans. A Feedforward Artificial Neural Network consists of many layers of processing units and each layer is feeding input to the next layer in a feed through manner.

49. What do you mean by clustering?

Ans. Clustering is the task of dividing the data points into a number of groups such that data points in the same groups are more similar to other data points in the same group and dissimilar to the data points in other groups.

50. Define NN.

Ans. A neural network is a computational data model that is capable of capturing and representing complex input/output relationships.

51. What is the objective of unsupervised learning?

Ans. The objective of unsupervised learning is to model the underlying distribution in the data to learn more about the data.

52. What are the two types of NN?

Ans. A neural network is either a biological neural network (BNN) that is made up of real biological neurons, or an artificial neural network used for solving artificial intelligence (AI) problems.

53. For which purpose is ANN used?

Ans. The artificial neural networks can be used for predictive modelling, adaptive control, and applications where they can be trained via a dataset.

54. When does an ANN become useful?

Ans. An Artificial Neural Network will become useful when all the processing elements are organised in an appropriate manner so that they can complete the task of pattern recognition.

55. Expand CNN.

Ans. Convolutional Neural Network.

56. What do you mean by CNN?

Ans. A Convolutional Neural Network (CNN) is a specific type of artificial neural network that uses perceptrons, a machine learning unit algorithm for supervised learning.

57. For which purpose is CNN used?

Ans. CNN is used to analyse data. CNN's apply to image processing, natural language processing, and other kinds of cognitive tasks.

58. Why are Neural Networks called parallel computing devices?

Ans. Neural networks are parallel computing devices, which are basically an attempt to make a computer like the model of the brain.

59. Write two examples of unsupervised learning.

Ans. Examples of unsupervised learning algorithms are; k-means for clustering problems, Apriori algorithm for association rule learning problems.

60. What do you mean by parallel processing capability with reference to ANN?

Ans. ANN has numerical strength that can perform more than one job at the same time. This is called Parallel processing capability.

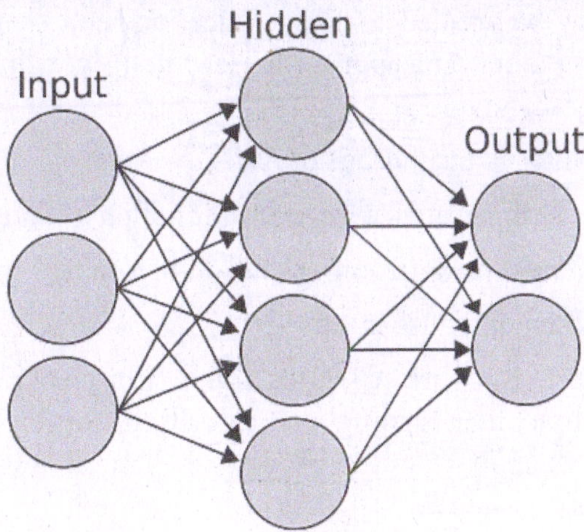

Figure 8.9

8.3.9 Short Answer Type Questions

1. Which types of tasks are performed by using ANN?

Ans. Artificial neural networks (ANNs) have been used for a variety of tasks, including computer vision, speech recognition, machine translation, social network filtering, playing board and video games, and medical diagnosis.

2. What is the similarity between Neural Networks and the human brain?

Ans. Neural networks look like e human brain in two ways:

i. A neural network acquires knowledge through learning.

ii. A neural network's knowledge is stored in synaptic weights (inter-neuron connection strengths).

3. How is ANN related to BNN?

Ans. A neural network is either a biological neural network (BNN), made up of real biological neurons, or an artificial neural network used for solving artificial intelligence (AI) problems. The connections of the biological neuron are modelled as weights. A positive weight exhibits an excitatory connection, and negative values mean inhibitory connections. All inputs are modified by weight and summed, and this activity is termed a linear combination. An activation function has controlled the amplitude of the output. For example, an acceptable range of output is usually between 0 and 1, or it could be −1 and 1.

4. Explain Topology.

Ans. An Artificial Neural Network will become useful when all the processing elements are organised in an appropriate manner so that they can complete the task of pattern recognition. This organisation or arrangement of the processing elements, their interconnections, inputs, and outputs are simply known as Topology.

5. What are the main advantages of ANN?

Ans. The main advantage of ANN is parallel processing which makes it more useful than linear programs. Because of their parallel processing structure, any failure in one particular neural element will not affect the rest of the process.

Neural networks may be applied to any application, and they can be used to solve any complex problem. By embedding appropriate learning algorithms, an ANN can be made to learn without reprogramming.

6. Mention two disadvantages/limitations of ANN.

Ans. (i) All parallel processing requires a huge amount of processing power and time.

(ii) There is a requirement for a "training" period before real-world implementation.

7. What is CNN? For which purpose is it used?

Ans. A Convolutional Neural Network (CNN) is a specific type of artificial neural network that uses perceptrons, a machine learning unit algorithm, for supervised learning. It is used to analyse data. CNN's apply to image processing, natural language processing, and other kinds of cognitive tasks.

8. Compare the functioning of ANN and BNN.

Ans. The comparison between ANN and BNN is summarised as follows:

Artificial Neural Network	Biological Neural Network	Function
Input layer	Dendrites	Takes inputs for the system
Node	Cell-body	Responsible for the processing of information
Interconnections	Synapse	These are the connections between the input and the output
Outer layer	Axon	The result is sent out by this part.

9. What are the main features of NN?

Ans. The variables or attributes in the data set are termed as features in a NN. In a neural network, the features would be the input layer, the hidden layer, nodes. The output is whatever variable (or variables) we are trying to predict.

Neural networks are considered as parallel computing devices, which is an attempt to make a computer like the model of the brain. The main aim is to develop a system to perform various computational tasks faster than any traditional system. These tasks include pattern recognition and classification, optimisation, approximation, and data clustering.

There are three types of layers in Neural networks enlisted as follows:

i. **Input Layer**: Vector data, each input collects one feature/dimension of the data and passes it on to the (first) hidden layer.

ii. **Hidden Layer**: Each hidden unit computes a weighted sum of all the units from the input layer (or any previous layer) and passes it through a nonlinear activation function.

iii. **Output Layer**: Each output unit computes a weighted sum of all the hidden units and passes it through a (possibly nonlinear) threshold function.

10. Define Unsupervised Learning. Give some examples.

Ans. Unsupervised learning occurs where only input data (X) is available, but no corresponding output variable is available. The objective of unsupervised learning is to model the underlying distribution in the data to learn more about the data. It is called unsupervised learning because there are no correct answers, and there is no teacher. Algorithms are left on their own to device and discover an interesting structure in the data.

Examples of unsupervised learning algorithms are;

i. k-means for clustering problems,

ii. Apriori algorithm for association rule learning problems.

11. Identify the areas where Unsupervised Learning is required?

Ans. Unsupervised learning is required when there is no example data set available with known answers. For example, searching for a hidden pattern. In the case of clustering, the process of dividing a set of elements into groups according to some unknown pattern is carried out that is based on the existing data sets present.

12. Mention some applications of Reinforcement Learning.

Ans. Some applications of Reinforcement Learning are given below:

i. Robotics for industrial automation.

ii. Business strategy planning

iii. Machine learning and data processing

iv. In creating training systems that provide custom instruction and materials according to the requirement of learners.

v. Aircraft control and robot motion control

13. What are the advantages of using Reinforcement Learning?

Ans. The following prime reasons for using Reinforcement Learning should be considered:

i. It helps in finding which situation needs action.

ii. It helps in discovering the action that yields the highest reward over a longer period.

iii. Reinforcement Learning provides the learning agent with a reward function.

iv. It allows to figure out the best method for obtaining large rewards.

14. Enlist the limitations of Using Reinforcement Learning.

Ans. In the following conditions, the use of reinforcement learning model is not suggested:

i. When enough data to solve the problem is available for a supervised learning method

ii. When the action space is large because Reinforcement Learning is computing-heavy and time-consuming.

15. What are the key differences between Classification and Regression?

Ans. The main differences between Classification and Regression are as follows:

i. The Classification process models a function through which the data is predicted in discrete class labels. On the other hand, Regression is the process of creating a model which predicts continuous quantity.

ii. The Classification algorithms involve decision trees, logistic Regression, etc. In contrast, regression trees (e.g., Random Forest) and linear Regression are examples of regression algorithms.

iii. Classification predicts unordered data while Regression predicts ordered data.

iv. Regression is evaluated by using root mean square error while classification is evaluated by measuring accuracy.

16. Explain Supervised Learning (SL)?

Ans. Supervised learning is a learning in which we teach / train the machine using labelled data. It means some data is already tagged with the correct answers. Then, the machine is fed with a new set of examples (data) so that the supervised learning algorithm analyses the training data (set of training examples) and produces correct outcome from labelled data.

17. What do you mean by labelled data used in Supervised Learning?

Ans. In a supervised learning model, the labelled dataset is fed to the machine . It means some data is already tagged with the correct answers.

18. Explain 'Unsupervised Learning.'

Ans. Unsupervised learning is the training of a machine using information that is neither classified nor labelled and allowing the algorithm to act on that information without any guidance/supervision. Here, the task of the machine is to group unsorted information according to similarities, patterns, and differences without any prior training of data.

19. Explain Clustering.

Ans. Clustering is the dividing the data points into a number of groups such that data points in the same groups are more similar to other data points in the same group and dissimilar to the data points in other groups. It is basically a collection of objects on the basis of similarity and dissimilarity between them.

20. Differentiate between Classification and Regression.

Ans. Classification is the process of finding a model (function) which helps in separating the data into various categorical classes. In classification, the group membership of the problem is identified, which means the data is categorized under different labels according to some parameters, and then the labels are predicted for the data.

Regression is the process of finding a model /function for distinguishing the data into continuous real values instead of using classes. Mathematically, with a regression problem, one is trying to find the function approximation with the minimum error deviation. In Regression, the data numeric dependency is predicted to distinguish it. The Regression analysis is the statistical model which is used to predict the numeric data instead of labels. It can also identify the distribution movement depending on the available data or historical data.

21. Enlist the main features of ANN.

Ans. The main features of ANN are as follows:

i. It has the ability to learn events and make decisions by commenting on similar events.

ii. It can work with incomplete knowledge and may produce output even with incomplete information.

iii. It has Parallel processing capability, i.e., ANN has numerical strength that can perform more than one job at the same time.

iv. It has fault tolerance which means that corruption of one or more cells of ANN does not prevent it from generating output.

8.3.10 Long Answer Type Questions

1. Explain the functioning of ANN.

Ans. The functioning of an ANN occurs as follows:

Step 1. When is the input node given an image, then it activates a unique set of neurons in the first layer by starting a chain reaction that will have a unique path to the output node?

Step 2. The activated neurons send signals to each connected neuron in the next layer, which directly affects neurons activated in the next layer.

Step 3. Each neuron in the next layer is governed by a rule on what combinations of received signals would activate the neuron (rules are trained when we give the ANN program training data, i.e., images of handwritten digits and the correct answer).

Step 4. When the model has more than two layers, steps 2-3 are repeated for all the remaining layers till it reaches the output node.

Step 5. The output node detects the correct digit based on signals received from neurons in the layer directly preceding it (layer 2). Every combination of activated neurons in layer 2 leads to one solution, and each solution can be represented by different combinations of activated neurons.

2. Explain the importance of Neural Networks in solving real-life situations and problems.

Ans. Neural networks are helpful in solving complex problems in real-life situations. NNs can learn and identify the relationships between inputs and outputs that are nonlinear and complex. They make generalisations and inferences, reveal hidden relationships, patterns, and predictions, and prepare modelling of highly volatile data. These may be used to predict rare events, like fraud detection. Thus, neural networks can improve decision processes in many areas, like credit card fraud detection, medicare, fraud detection, etc.

NNs are also used in:

i. Optimisation of logistics for transportation networks,

ii. Medical and disease diagnosis.

iii. Character and voice recognition (natural language processing),

iv. Targeted marketing,

v. Robotic control systems.

vi. Financial predictions for stock prices, currency, futures options, bankruptcy, bond ratings, etc.

vii. Ecosystem evaluation,

viii. Forecasting of Electrical load and energy demand,

ix. Process and quality control in industries,

x. Identification of Chemical compounds,

xi. In Computer vision to interpret raw photos and videos (for example, in medical imaging, robotics, facial recognition, etc.).

3. Explain the usage of Neural Networks in industries.

Ans. Deep learning systems and, thus, the neural networks that enable them are used strategically in many industries and businesses. For example,

(i) **Life Sciences:** Health and life sciences organisations generally use neural networks to enable predictive diagnostics, biomedical imaging, and health monitoring.

(ii) **Manufacturing:** Companies in the field of energy and manufacturing products use neural networks to optimize supply chains, automatise defect detection, forecast, etc.

(iii) **Banking:** Banks use neural networks for various purposes, like detecting frauds, conducting credit analysis, automating financial adviser services, etc.

(iv) **Public Sector:** Public sector organisations use neural networks in various tasks like to support smart cities, security intelligence, facial recognition, etc.

(v) **Communications & Retail:** The communications and retail industries use neural networks to power conversational chatbots, enhance and deepen customer intelligence, and perform network analysis.

(vi) **Hotel Industry:** To maximize the value of your data for advanced analytics to take marketing management to drive profitable revenue growth and for data management software.

(vii) **In Higher education:** To gain analytical skills, build courses, create degree programs, grant certificates, and conduct academic research, etc.

4. Explain the types of Artificial Neural Networks.

Ans. There are two Artificial Neural Network topologies- FeedForward ANN and Feedback ANN.

i. **FeedForward ANNs:** A Feedforward Artificial Neural Network consists of many layers of processing units and each layer is feeding input to the next layer in a feed through manner. In this ANN, the information flow is unidirectional. A unit sends information to another unit from which it does not receive any information. There are no feedback loops. They are used in pattern generation/recognition/classification. They have fixed inputs and outputs.

ii. **FeedBack ANN:** A feedback ANN is an ANN consists of the feedback element. In the basic structure, a feedback ANN consists of a set of processing units and outputs produced are fed back as inputs to all other units of the same layer. Here, feedback loops are allowed. They are used in content-addressable memories.

5. Enlist the two important areas of applications of ANN.

Ans. The two important areas where ANNs have a huge potential for applications are Speech and Image Processing.

(i) **Applications in Speech**

- Phonetic Typewriter

- ▲ Vowel Classification
- ▲ Recognition of vowel-consonant segments
- ▲ Recognition of stop consonant-vowel utterances in Indian languages
- ▲ NetTalk

Figure 8.10

(ii) Applications in Image Processing

- ▲ Recognition of Symbols (used in Olympics)
- ▲ Recognition of handwriting
- ▲ Segmentation of image
- ▲ Classification and segmentation of texture.

6. Explain Supervised Learning with suitable examples.

Ans. In Supervised Learning, the machine learns by using labelled data. The majority of practical machine learning (ML) uses supervised learning. In other words, supervised learning is where an algorithm is used to learn the mapping function from the input to the output provided input variables (X), and an output variable (Y) is available.

Since the process of an algorithm learning from the training dataset can be thought of as a teacher supervising the learning process and hence, it is called supervised learning. Learning stops when the algorithm achieves a particular level of performance.

Some examples of supervised machine learning algorithms are:

i. Linear Regression for regression problems.

ii. Random forest for classification and regression problems.

iii. Support vector machines for classification problems.

iv. Some real-life examples of SL may be as follows:

v. Suppose Monika gets a bunch of photos with information about what is on them, and then she trains a model to recognize new photos based on the input provided.

vi. Suppose Shailesh has a bunch of molecules and information about which of these are drugs, and he trains a model to answer whether a new molecule is also a drug.

vii. Classifying the patients whether a patient is suffering from a disease or not.

viii. Classifying the received emails whether an email is spam or not.

ix. Predicting house/property price

x. Predicting stock market price

7. Explain the types of Supervised Learning.

Ans. Supervised learning problems is grouped as Regression and Classification problems.

(i) **Classification:** Classification is defined as the process of learning a model that identifies different predetermined classes of data and is a two-step process comprised of a learning step and a classification step. In the learning step, a classification model is constructed, while in the classification step, the constructed model is used to identify the class for given data.

For example, in a bank loan application, the customer may be classified as safe or risky according to his/her age/salary. A classification problem is one when the output variable is a category, such as "red" or "blue" or "disease" and "no disease."

(ii) **Regression:** A regression problem is one in which the output variable is a real value, like dollars, weight, etc. Some common problems built on top of Regression include time series prediction.

8. Explain various types of Unsupervised Learning with suitable examples.

Unsupervised learning problems are further grouped into clustering and association.

i. **Clustering:** A clustering problem is one where discovering the inherent groupings in the data occurs, like grouping customers by their purchasing behaviour.

ii. **Association:** An association ruled learning problem is one where the rules that describe large portions of your data are discovered, like people that buy X item in the market also tend to buy Y item.

Some real-life examples of Unsupervised Learning:

Suppose Satya Prabha has a bunch of photos of 6 people but without information about who is on which photo, and he wants to divide this dataset into six piles, each with the photos of one individual.

Suppose Manisha Jain has molecules, part of them are drugs, and part of them are not, but she does not know which are which, and she want the algorithm to discover the drugs.

9. Differentiate between Supervised and Unsupervised Learning.

Ans. The difference between Supervised and Unsupervised Learning is given below:

Parameter	Supervised learning	Unsupervised learning
Data	Deals with labelled data	Deals unlabelled data
(i) Computational complexity	High	Low
(ii) Analysation	Offline	Real-time
(iii) Accuracy	Produces accurate results	Generates moderate results

(iv) Sub-domains	Classification & Regression	Clustering and Association
(v) Approach	Map labelled input to the discover outputs	Understands patterns and known output
(vi) Training	External supervision	No supervision

10. Explain the types of Reinforcement Learning.

Ans. Two kinds of reinforcement learning methods are discussed as follows:

(i) **Positive Reinforcement:** It is an event that occurs because of specific behaviour and increases the strength and the frequency of the behaviour that positively affects the action taken by the agent. The positive Reinforcement helps in maximising the performance and sustaining change for an extended period. Too much Reinforcement may lead to over-optimisation of the state affecting the results.

(ii) **Negative Reinforcement:** Negative Reinforcement is the strengthening of behaviour that occurs because of a negative condition that should have been avoided. It helps in defining the minimum stand of performance. The main drawback of this method is that it provides enough to meet up the minimum behaviour.

11. Explain Reinforcement Learning and mention its characteristics.

Ans. This strategy is built on observations. The ANNs make a decision by observing their environment. When the observation is negative, then the network adjusts its weights to be able to make a different required decision the next time.

Some important characteristics of reinforcement learning are enlisted below:

i. There is no supervisor, but a real number or reward signal is present.

ii. Time plays an important role in Reinforcement problems.

iii. Sequential decision-making.

iv. Feedback is always delayed, not instantaneous.

v. The agent's actions determine the subsequent data it receives.

12. Differentiate between Reinforcement Learning (RL) and Supervised Learning (SL).

Ans. The difference between supervised learning and reinforcement learning is summarised below;

Reinforcement Learning	Supervised learning
(i) Reinforcement learning helps to	(i) In Supervised Learning, a decision is based take the decisions sequentially on the input given at the beginning.
(ii) Works on interacting with the Environment.	(ii) Works on examples or given sample data.
(iii) Learning decision is dependent. So, labels to all the dependent decisions are Given.	(iii) Supervised learning the decisions which are independent of each other, so labels are given for every decision.

(iv) Supports and works better in AI, where human interaction is prevalent.	(iv) It is mostly operated with an interactive Software systems or applications.
Example: Chess game	Example: Object recognition

8.3.11 HOTS

1. Explain activation or node value?

Ans. ANNs are composed of multiple nodes, which are similar in action to biological neurons. All the neurons are interconnected, and they interact with each other. The nodes take input data to perform simple operations on the data, and the result of these operations is passed to other neurons. The output at each node is called activation or node value.

2. What are the major challenges of Reinforcement Learning?

Ans. The major challenges while doing Reinforcement Learning are as follows:

i. Selection of feature or reward design is not easy.

ii. Parameters selected may affect the speed of learning.

iii. A realistic environment may have partial observability.

iv. Too much Reinforcement may lead to an overload of states, which can diminish the results.

v. Realistic environments can be non-stationary.

3. Why is 'Unsupervised Learning' called so?

Ans. Unsupervised learning occurs where only input data (X) is available, but no corresponding output variable (Y) is available. The objective of unsupervised learning is to model the underlying distribution in the data to learn more about the data. It is called unsupervised learning because there are no correct answers, and there is no teacher. Algorithms are left on their own to a device and discover an interesting structure in the data.

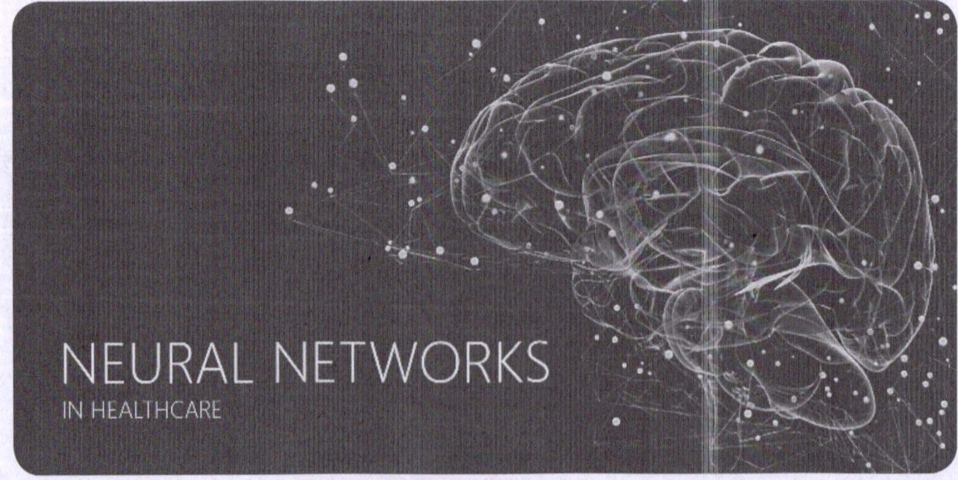

Figure 8.11

8.4 PRACTICE QUESTIONS

1. Define a neural network in AI.
2. What do you mean by Neural Network (NN)?
3. What is Regression?
4. In BNN, mention the functions of Dendrites, Axon, and Soma.
5. Define Deep Learning.
6. Discuss the need for neural networks in Artificial Intelligence.
7. Name three basic layers of NN.
8. Compare BNN with ANN.
9. Write two applications of NN.
10. Mention two types of NN.
11. Define Feedback NN
12. Enlist the three applications of classifications.
13. Mention any two examples of deep learning.
14. Name any two datasets required for Artificial Intelligence modelling.
15. What are the main features of Supervised and Unsupervised learning?
16. Write one important feature of AutoDraw and Sketch2Code.
17. Write the three easy steps to work with the Sketch2Code application.
18. What is Clustering?
19. What do you mean by RL?
20. What are the two types of Reinforcement Learning?
21. Write two advantages of RL.
22. What is classification in ANN?
23. Mention the elements of Reinforcement Learning.
24. Define clustering and association with reference to Unsupervised Learning.
25. Give two examples where Supervised Learning is used?
26. Differentiate between Supervised Learning and Reinforcement Learning.
27. What are the elements of Reinforcement Learning?
28. Write the full form of ANN, BNN, SL, and RL.
29. Differentiate between supervised Learning and Unsupervised Learning.
30. Give two real-life examples of SL.
31. Discuss the important features of the Neural Network.
32. Explain the importance of neural networks in our world.

33. Mention and explain three layers of ANN.
34. Discuss the advantages and limitations of reinforcement Learning.
35. Enlist the advantages and disadvantages of ANNs.

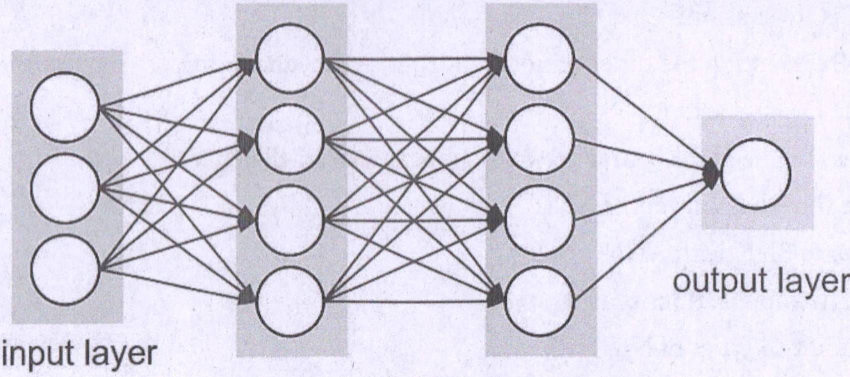

Figure 8.12

UNIT 9 Python Basic

9.1 UNIT IN BRIEF

- A diagrammatic/graphical representation of a sequence of steps to solve a problem is known as a flowchart.
- A List can be traversed forward or backward.

Figure 9.1

- A List within a List is called a nested list.
- A person who writes computer programs using a programming language is called a programmer.
- A program is defined as a series of instructions given in the programming language to make a computer perform an action.
- An operator is a symbol that helps the user to command the computer to do a certain mathematical or logical manipulation.
- Arithmetic operators are special symbols that represent arithmetical computations in a program like Addition (+), subtraction (-), multiplication (*), and division (/).
- Assignment operators are the operators that are used for assigning a value of the right operand to the left operand.
- Class names start with an uppercase letter.
- Different types of elements can be stored in a list.
- Elements in a List are kept in the square [ ] brackets.
- Escape Characters are special characters represented by a backslash followed by the character(s), and they are used for special purposes.
- IDLE is a part of the Python Integrated Development Environment and helps us in writing, editing, running, and debugging python programs.

- If a loop has one control condition and executes as long as the condition is true, then the condition of the loop is evaluated /tested before the body of the loop is executed. Hence, this loop is called an entry-controlled loop.
- If the user knows the number of iterations before entering the loop, then 'For' loops are typically used. It is also known as a definite loop.
- In computer programming, a variable is a quantity whose value can change as many times as required during the execution of the program.
- 'In' operator is used to check whether an element exists in the specified List or not, and hence, the 'in' operator is called the membership operator. The Not in operator is used in a reverse manner to check whether the element is not present in the List.
- Input () function takes the input from the user initially and then, it evaluates the expression, which means Python automatically identifies whether the user entered a string or a number or a List.
- It is easy to convert the flowchart into any programming language code.
- Iteration is the process where a set of instructions or statements is executed repeatedly for a specified number of times until and unless a condition is fulfilled. The iteration is also known as looping.
- List and string indexing are the same and start with 0 index locations.
- List is a sequence in Python which is mutable, i.e., the element in the List may be changed/ modified at any point in time.
- Logical operators in Python are used for conditional statements that are true or false.
- Loops are also known as iteration or iterative statements.
- Membership operators are 'in' and 'not in'.
- Python can be downloaded free of cost from the website www.python.org.
- Python can be used on a variety of hardware platforms and has the same interface on all platforms.
- Python is a case-sensitive language.
- Python is a popular object-oriented programming language that offers a lot of flexibility.
- Python is an Interpreted and Interactive language.
- Python provides various types of conditional statements, including If, If-else and If-elif-else.
- Relational operators are the operators that compare the values on either side of the operand and determine the relation between them.
- The remove function is used to delete an element from the given List.
- Slicing [:] is used to extract a part out of the specified List.
- Starting an identifier with a single leading underscore indicates that the identifier is private.
- Starting an identifier with two leading underscores indicates a strongly private identifier.
- The data type of a variable decides what type of data a variable can store. The three main data types in Python are int, float, and string.

- The elements in a List can be changed. It shows that a list is Mutable.
- The input() function allows a program to take inputs from the user.
- The print() function displays the output on the computer's screen.
- The print() function prints the given object to the standard output device.
- The python files always have an extension of .py.
- The Sort() function arranges the List in ascending order by default, and it arranges the List in the original List itself (in place).
- The Sorted() function arranges the List in order by creating another list.
- There are two ways to traverse elements in the List: forward from beginning to end or backward from end to the beginning.
- Traversing a list can be done using the for loop with len() and range() and while loop.
- We can download Python from the web page https://www.python.org/downloads/.

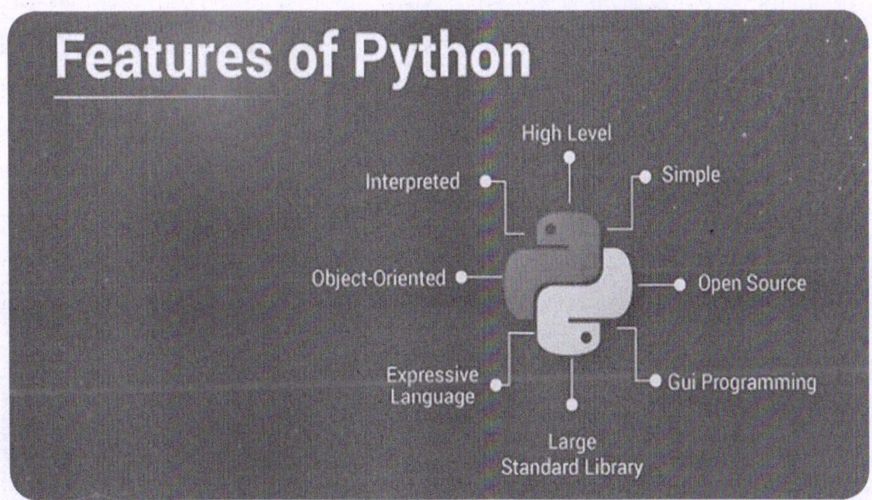

Figure 9.2

9.2 SOLVED EXERCISES

9.2.1 Multiple Choice Questions

Tick (√) the correct option for each question.

1. The appropriate reason to make Python the most suitable coding language for AI Projects is:

   a) Flexibility, Readability, Good visualisation options

   b) A low entry barrier, Platform dependence

   c) A great library ecosystem, No Community support

   d) None of the above

2. Which programming language is exhibited by the following logo?

a) Java b) Prolog c) Python d) Pascal

3. Which geometrical shape is used to show page connector in a flow chart?

a) Triangle b) Square c) Rectangle d) Circle

4. Which of the following statements is correct?

a) Python is machine-dependent when dealing with identifiers.

b) Python is case-sensitive when dealing with identifiers.

c) Python is not case-sensitive when dealing with identifiers.

d) None of these

5. Which geometrical symbol is used to indicate the flow of logic by connecting symbols in a flow chart?

a) Single arrow b) Double arrow c) Diamond d) Triangle

6. The function range(6) will return a sequence:

a) 1, 2, 3, 4,5,6 b) 0, 1, 2, 3,4,5 c) 1, 2, 3,4,5 d) 0, 1, 2, 3,4

7. Which symbol is used while ending all control flow statements in Python?

a) Full Stop (.) b) Colon (:)

c) Semicolon (;) d) Hash sign (#)

8. What is the number of type conversions used in Python?

a) 2 b) 3 c) 4 d) 5

9. What is the output of max(mylist), if mylist%=[7487, 7413, 5393, 3567, 7436]?

a) 5 b) 7436 c) 7487 d) 5393

10. Consider the following reasons for the selection of Python for AI Projects and choose the correct set.

i. A great library ecosystem

ii. Flexibility

iii. A low entry barrier

iv. Platform independence

v. Readability

vi. Good visualisation options

vii. Community support

a) (i) (ii) (iii) (iv) b) (ii) (iii) (vi) (vii)

c) (iii) (iv) (v) (vi) d) All the above

11. Which application does not use Python?

a) Database Access b) Network Programming

c) 2D Graphics d) Desktop Applications

12. Which platform can be used to run Python?

    a) Windows b) macOS, c) Linux d) All of these

13. All other identifiers except ____________ start with a lowercase letter.

    a) Class names
    b) Private identifier
    c) Complex number
    d) None of the above

14. A complex number consisting of an ordered pair of real floating-point numbers is denoted by x +yi, where x and y are the real numbers. What is 'i' in it?

    a) Identifier
    b) Imaginary unit
    c) Both a and b
    d) None of the above

15. Which of the following statements about Python is correct?

    a) It is a high-level and interpreted programming language.
    b) It is a highly useful language focused on rapid application development (RAD), and don't repeat yourself (DRY).
    c) It works perfectly to connect existing components together.
    d) All the above

16. From which weblink can Python be downloaded for free?

    a) www.python.com
    b) www.python.org
    c) www.python.in
    d) None of the above

17. Consider the following reasons for the selection of Python for AI Projects and choose the correct set.

    i. A great library ecosystem
    ii. Flexibility
    iii. A low entry barrier
    iv. Platform independence
    v. Readability
    vi. Good visualisation options
    vii. Community support

    a) (ii) (iii) (iv)
    b) (iii) (vi) (vii)
    c) (iv) (v) (vi)
    d) All the above

18. Which Statement about the flow chart is NOT TRUE?

    a) The flow chart makes program or system maintenance easier.
    b) The flow chart shows the logic of a program in a simple way.
    c) The flow chart is an easy and efficient tool to analyse a problem.
    d) It is difficult to convert the flow chart into any programming language code.

19. What is a graphical representation of a sequence of steps to solve a problem known as?

a) Vector analysis b) Venn diagram c) Flow chart d) Pie chart

20. Which geometrical shape is used in a flowchart to represent the operations having two/ three alternatives, true and false, etc.?

a) Square b) Diamond c) Triangle d) Rectangle

21. Due to which property is Python one of the fastest-growing programming languages?

a) Ease of Learning b) Scalability
c) Adaptability d) All the above

22. What is the other name for 'Iterative statements' in Python?

a) Loops b) Lists c) Operators d) Strings

23. Which of the following applications does use Python?

a) Database Access b) Web and Internet Development
c) Desktop GUI Applications d) All of the above

24. Which of the following is not a Python keyword?

a) except b) Outcome c) as d) Def

25. In which sorts of projects is Python used?

a) Web App, and Mobile App b) IoT, and Data Science
c) AI d) All the above

26. Which Statement is INCORRECT regarding the rules for a variable name?

a) Spaces are allowed in a statement.
b) A statement may begin with a lowercase alphabet.
c) Special characters like @, *, % are allowed in a statement.
d) Letters, numbers, and underscore (_) characters are allowed in a statement.

27. Which of the following statements will check if 'x' is less than or equal to 'y'?

a) if x is less than equal to y: b) if x <= y:
c) if x >= y: d) if x < == y:

28. Which of the following pairs is not a Python keyword?

a) and, pass b) Out, Accept c) as With d) Del, if

29. What is represented by a parallelogram in a flowchart?

a) Beginning and end of flow chart b) Arithmetic operation
c) Input and output operation d) All the above

30. Which of the following type of projects is using Python?

a) Data Science, b) Web App, IoT
c) Mobile App, AI d) All of the above

31. Which one of the following is used to create Strings by enclosing characters inside it?

   a) Single quotes (' ')
   b) Double Quotes (" ")
   c) Triple quotes (""" """)
   d) Any of them

32. The file extension for a Python program is

   a) .python
   b) .py
   c) .pyt
   d) .pt

33. What is the reason for gaining maximum popularity by Python as a programming language?

   a) Easy in writing and Less execution of codes
   b) Availability of prebuilt libraries
   c) Flexibility in providing an API from an existing language
   d) All the above

34. Which geometrical shape is used to represent the start and the end in a flowchart?

   a) Triangle
   b) Oval
   c) Diamond
   d) Square

35. Which function is used to convert a string of digits into an integer?

   a) int()
   b) conv()
   c) string()
   d) str()

36. All control flow statements in Python start with:

   a) Colon (:)
   b) Semicolon (;)
   c) Hash sign (#)
   d) Full Stop (.)

37. Which geometric shape is used for arithmetic operations and data manipulations in a flow chart?

   a) Rectangle
   b) Triangle
   c) Diamond
   d) Square

38. Which of the following is used to add a new element to the end of the List?

   a) add()
   b) push()
   c) append()
   d) insert()

39. Which of the following is used to add an element '15' at index 5 in my List?

   a) mylist.insert(15, 5)
   b) mylist.insert(5, 15)
   c) mylist.add(4,15)
   d) mylist.append(15,5)

40. Which Statement is CORRECT for a variable name?

   a) Spaces are not allowed.
   b) Letters, numbers, and () underscore characters are allowed.
   c) Special characters like @, *, % are allowed.
   d) All the above

41. Which of the following statements does check if a is greater than or equal to b?

   a) if a is less than equal to b:
   b) if a < == b:
   c) if a >= b:
   d) if a < = b:

42. Which command is used to create a list having four elements (1,3,6,9)?

   a) Mylist = list(1,3,6,9)
   b) Mylist = [1,3,6,9]
   c) Mylist = list([1,3,6,9)
   d) All of the above

43. What is the number of white spaces used for indentation?

a) 3 b) 4 c) 5 d) 6

44. What is the output of sum(mylist), if mylist= [2,3,5,9]?

a) Displays an error b) 4 c) 19 d) 21

45. What is the output of min(mylist), if mylist%=[303, 4313, 363, 3313, 404]?

a) 3313 b) 4313 c) 303 d) 404

46. The process where a set of instructions are repeated in a sequence a number of times until and unless a condition is met known as:

a) Iteration
b) Sequential
c) Looping
d) Idealization

47. Which of the following statements is TRUE for the flowchart?

a) A flowchart shows the logic of a program in a simple way.
b) A flowchart is an easy and efficient tool to analyse a problem.
c) Flow chart makes program or system maintenance easier.
d) All the above

48. Which of the following programming languages is considered the most popular programming language?

a) Haskell b) Python c) C++ d) Ruby

49. Consider the following statements about the flowchart and choose the correct set.

i. It exhibits the individual steps and their interconnections.
ii. It represents a workflow or process in a diagrammatic representation.
iii. It exhibits the Sequence of instructions/happenings in a single program.
iv. It shows the logic of an algorithm from start to end.
v. It consists of standardised and acceptable symbols.
vi. It has a clear start point and End/Finish point.
vii. It exhibits the control from one activity to the next one.

a) (ii) (iii) (iv)
b) (iv) (v) (vi)
c) (iii) (v) (vii)
d) All the above

50. Which platform can be used to run Python?

a) Windows
b) macOS,
c) Linux
d) All of these

51. From which weblink can Python be downloaded for free?

a) www.python.com
b) www.python.org
c) www.python.in
d) None of the above

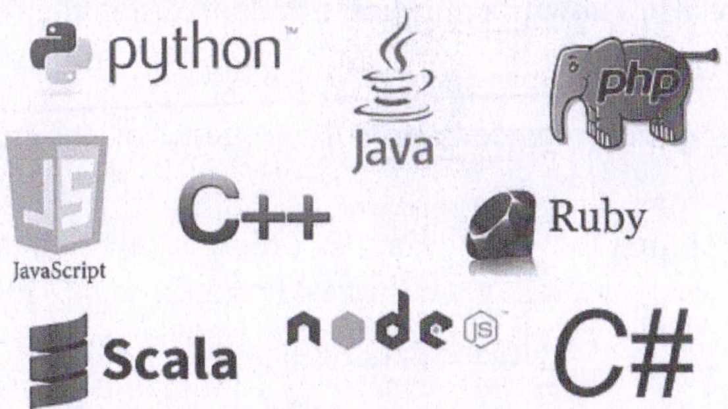

Figure 9.3

ANSWERS									
1. (a)	2. (c)	3. (d)	4. (b)	5. (a)	6. (b)	7. (b)	8. (a)	9. (c)	10. (d)
11. (c)	12. (d)	13. (a)	14. (b)	15. (d)	16. (b)	17. (d)	18. (a)	19. (c)	20. (b)
21. (d)	22. (a)	23. (d)	24. (b)	25. (d)	26. (a)	27. (b)	28. (b)	29. (c)	30. (d)
31. (d)	32. (b)	33. (a)	34. (b)	35. (a)	36. (c)	37. a)	38. (c)	39. (b)	40. (d)
41. (c)	42. (d)	43. (b)	44. (c)	45. (c)	46. (a)	47. (d)	48. (b)	49. (d)	50. (d)
51. (b)									

9.2.2 Fill in the blanks

1. The ____________ is an easy and efficient tool to analyse a problem.
2. ____________ contains items that are separated by commas and enclosed within square brackets ([]).
3. When an ____________ starts with two leading underscores, it indicates that the identifier is a strong private identifier.
4. The plus (+) sign is defined as the string concatenation operator, and the asterisk (*) is the ____________ operator.
5. A List can be ____________ forward or backward.
6. Elements in a List are kept in ____________ brackets.
7. Python has two types of type conversion: Implicit Type Conversion and ____________ Type Conversion.
8. Starting an identifier with two leading ____________ indicates a strongly private identifier.
9. ____________ in Python are identified as a contiguous set of characters represented in the quotation marks.
10. The values stored in a List may be accessed using the slice operator ([ ] and [:]) with indexes starting at ____________ at the beginning of the List and working their way to end -1.
11. Python language supports the operators: Arithmetic Operators, Comparison (Relational) Operators, ____________ Operators, Logical Operators, Bitwise Operators, Membership Operators, Identity Operators.
12. It is easy to convert the flowchart into any ____________ code.

13. ____________ are also known as iteration or iterative statements.
14. Class names start with an ____________ case letter.
15. A diagrammatic/graphical representation of a sequence of steps to solve a problem is known as ____________.
16. A complex number may be defined as an ordered pair of real floating-point numbers denoted by x +yi, whereas x and y are the real numbers and 'i' is the ____________ unit.
17. Python has ____________ standard data types.
18. The ____________ in computer science is a plain language description of all the steps of an algorithm.
19. Python does not allow punctuation/____________ such as @, $, and % within identifiers.
20. Starting an identifier with a single leading ____________ indicates that the identifier is private.

ANSWERS				
1. flowchart	2. List	3. identifier	4. repetition	5. traversed
6. square	7. Explicit	8. underscores	9. Strings	10. 0(zero)
11. Assignment	12. programming language		13. Loops	14. Upper
15. flowchart	16. imaginary	17. five	18. pseudocode	
19. special characters		20. underscore		

9.2.3 True or False

1. In a List, the elements and size can be changed.
2. Flow chart makes program or system maintenance easier.
3. Class names start with lowercase letters.
4. A List contains items that are separated by commas and enclosed within square brackets ([]).
5. Python does allow punctuation/special characters such as @, $, and % within identifiers.
6. The flow chart shows the logic of a program in a simple way.
7. Lists are an important data type of Python.
8. Python has three types of type conversion.
9. A diagrammatic/graphical representation of a sequence of steps to solve a problem is known as a flowchart.
10. Starting an identifier with a single leading underscore indicates that the identifier is private.
11. When the identifier also ends with two trailing underscores, then the identifier is a language-defined special name.
12. It is difficult to convert the flowchart into any programming language code.
13. The elements in a List can be changed. It shows that a list is Immutable.
14. Different types of elements can be stored in a List.

15. List indexing starts from 1.
16. Membership operators are 'in' and 'not in.'
17. A List within a list is called 'Nested List.'
18. The remove function is used to delete an element from the given List.
19. Slicing is used to extract a part out of the specified List.
20. List indexing is the same as string.

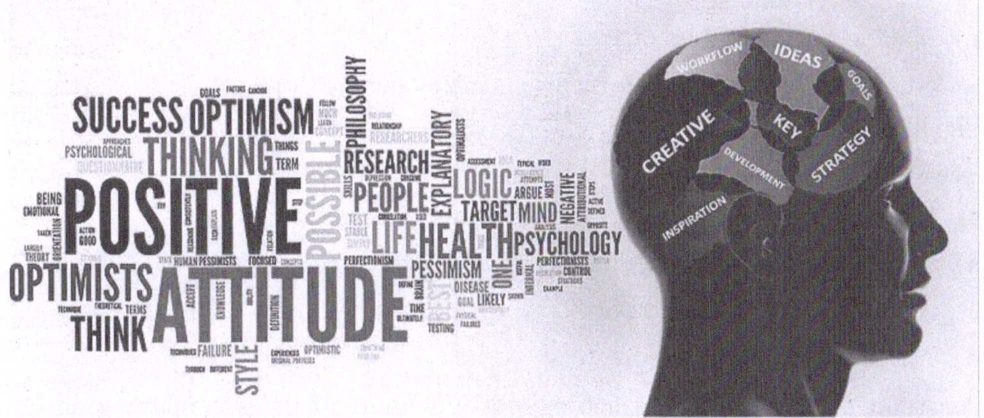

Figure 9.4

ANSWERS						
1. T	2. T	3. F (uppercase)	4. T	5. F (does not allow)	6. T	7. T
8. F (two types)	9. T	10. T	11. T	12. F (easy)	13. F (mutable)	14. T
15. F (zero)	16. T	17. T	18. ??	19. T	20. T	

9.2.4 Matching type Questions:

Match the items of column A and column B correctly.

Column A	Column B
a. len()	i. To create an empty list
b. append()	ii. To return the number of times an element is found in the list
c. list()	iii. Delete the given element from the list
d. insert()	iv. mylist.append(20)
e. count()	v. To calculate the number of elements in list
f. index()	vi. To return the index location of the element in the list
g. remove()	vii. To add an element at the desired index

ANSWERS						
a. (v)	b. (iv)	c. (i)	d. (vii)	e. (ii)	f. (vi)	g. (iii)

9.2.5 Assertion Reason Type Questions

1. Assertion (A): Python is an object-oriented program.

   Reason (R): Python supports Object-Oriented style or technique programming that encapsulates code within objects.

   a) Both A and R are correct, and R is the correct reason for A.

   b) Both A and R are correct, and R is not the correct reason for A.

   c) A is correct, but R is incorrect.

   d) A is incorrect, but R is correct.

2. Assertion (A): In Lists, their elements and size can be changed while the tuples cannot be updated.

   Reason (R): The elements in a List are separated by a semi-colon.

   a) Both A and R are correct, and R is the correct reason for A.

   b) Both A and R are correct, and R is not the correct reason for A.

   c) A is correct, but R is incorrect.

   d) A is incorrect, but R is correct.

3. Assertion (A): A package is a program of Python modules containing an additional application environment.

   Reason (R): Lists are enclosed in a square bracket.

   a) Both A and R are correct, and R is the correct reason for A.

   b) Both A and R are correct, and R is not the correct reason for A.

   c) A is correct, but R is incorrect.

   d) A is incorrect, but R is correct.

4. Assertion (A): Python is platform-independent.

   Reason (R): Python can be used across different platforms and technologies with basic coding.

   a) Both A and R are correct, and R is the correct reason for A.

   b) Both A and R are correct, and R is not the correct reason for A.

   c) A is correct, but R is incorrect.

   d) A is incorrect, but R is correct.

5. Assertion (A): A flowchart is a programming tool that uses different symbols to design a solution to a problem.

   Reason (R): A program is a collection of instructions used to perform a specific task when executed by a computer.

   a) Both A and R are correct, and R is the correct reason for A.

   b) Both A and R are correct, and R is not the correct reason for A.

   c) A is correct, but R is incorrect.

   d) A is incorrect, but R is correct.

6. Assertion (A): Python is a popular object-oriented programming language that offers a lot of flexibility.

   Reason (R): Python is an Interpreted and Interactive language.

   Both A and R are correct, and R is the correct reason for A.

   a) Both A and R are correct, and R is not the correct reason for A.

   b) A is correct, but R is incorrect.

   c) A is incorrect, but R is correct.

7. Assertion (A): Python- an interpreted and object-oriented programming language, has gained popularity due to its clear syntax and readability.

   Reason (R): Guido van Rossum has developed Python.

   a) Both A and R are correct, and R is the correct reason for A.

   b) Both A and R are correct, and R is not the correct reason for A.

   c) A is correct, but R is incorrect.

   d) A is incorrect, but R is correct.

8. Assertion (A): Python is an OOP language.

   Reason (R): Python allows us to create classes, objects, and modular procedures with reusable code.

   a) Both A and R are correct and R is the correct reason for A.

   b) Both A and R are correct and R is not the correct reason for A.

   c) A is correct, but R is incorrect.

   d) A is incorrect, but R is correct.

9. Assertion (A): A List contains items that are separated by commas and enclosed within square brackets ([ ]).

   Reason (R): A package is a directory of Python modules containing an additional application environment.

   a) Both A and R are correct, and R is the correct reason for A.

   b) Both A and R are correct, and R is not the correct reason for A.

   c) A is correct, but R is incorrect.

   d) A is incorrect, but R is correct.

10. Assertion (A): Python's readability makes it a great programming language - it allows the user to think like a programmer.

    Reason (R): Time is not wasted in understanding the mysterious syntax that other programming languages may require.

    a) Both A and R are correct, and R is the correct reason for A.

    b) Both A and R are correct, and R is not the correct reason for A.

    c) A is correct, but R is incorrect.

    d) A is incorrect, but R is correct.

ANSWERS									
1. (a)	2. (c)	3. (d)	4. (a)	5. (b)	6. (b)	7. (b)	8. (a)	9. (b)	10. (a)

9.2.6 Statements Based Questions

1. Statement 1: An algorithm means a procedure or a technique or a sequence of steps to solve a specific problem.

   Statement 2: Strings in Python are identified as a contiguous set of characters represented in the quotation marks.

   a) Statement 1 is correct, but statement 2 is incorrect.

   b) Statement 1 is incorrect, but statement 2 is correct.

   c) Both the statements are correct.

   d) Both the statements are incorrect.

2. Statement 1: The Loop or Repetition allows the Statement (s) to be executed repeatedly based on certain loop conditions.

   Statement 2: A 'for' Statement allows you to repeatedly execute a block of statements till the condition is true.

   a) Statement 1 is correct, but statement 2 is incorrect.

   b) Statement 1 is incorrect, but statement 2 is correct.

   c) Both the statements are correct.

   d) Both the statements are incorrect.

3. Statement 1: A notebook integrates code and its output into a single document that combines narrative text, visualisations, mathematical equations, and other rich media.

   Statement 2: All other identifiers except class names start with a lowercase letter.

   a) Statement 1 is correct, but statement 2 is incorrect.

   b) Statement 1 is incorrect, but statement 2 is correct.

   c) Both the statements are correct.

   d) Both the statements are incorrect.

4. Statement 1: Matplotlib is a package that is used to plot 3D figures.

   Statement 2: NLTK is an open-source Python module that has been developed for NLP.

   a) Statement 1 is correct, but statement 2 is incorrect.

   b) Statement 1 is incorrect, but statement 2 is correct.

   c) Both the statements are correct.

   d) Both the statements are incorrect.

5. Statement 1: Python does not allow punctuation/special characters such as @, $, and % within identifiers.

   Statement 2: A variable whose value cannot be changed even later on is called a 'Constant.'

a) Statement 1 is correct, but statement 2 is incorrect.
b) Statement 1 is incorrect, but statement 2 is correct.
c) Both the statements are correct.
d) Both the statements are incorrect.

6. Statement 1: The plus (+) sign is defined as the string repetition operator, and the asterisk (*) is the concatenation operator.

   Statement 2: A flowchart is considered as a blueprint of a design used for solving any specific problem.

   a) Statement 1 is correct, but statement 2 is incorrect.
   b) Statement 1 is incorrect, but statement 2 is correct.
   c) Both the statements are correct.
   d) Both the statements are incorrect.

7. Statement 1: A List contains items which are separated by commas and enclosed within square brackets ([]).

   Statement 2: Logical operators are used for comparing values, and it either returns True or False as per the condition.

   a) Statement 1 is correct, but statement 2 is incorrect.
   b) Statement 1 is incorrect, but statement 2 is correct.
   c) Both the statements are correct.
   d) Both the statements are incorrect.

8. Statement 1: Strings in Python are identified as a contiguous set of characters represented in the quotation marks.

   Statement 2: Logical operators are three: and, or, not.

   a) Statement 1 is correct, but statement 2 is incorrect.
   b) Statement 1 is incorrect, but statement 2 is correct.
   c) Both the statements are correct.
   d) Both the statements are incorrect.

9. Statement 1: PYTHON is extensively used to create web software, Internet-based applications, mobile apps, and games.

   Statement 2: PYTHON does not support an Object-oriented programming paradigm.

   a) Statement 1 is correct, but statement 2 is incorrect.
   b) Statement 1 is incorrect, but statement 2 is correct.
   c) Both the statements are correct.
   d) Both the statements are incorrect.

10. Statement 1: Python programming language is the most popular among programming languages for AI applications.

Statement 2: In programming, Sequence means to place statements one after the other, and the execution takes place starting from top to bottom.

a) Statement 1 is correct, but statement 2 is incorrect.

b) Statement 1 is incorrect, but statement 2 is correct.

c) Both the statements are correct.

d) Both the statements are incorrect.

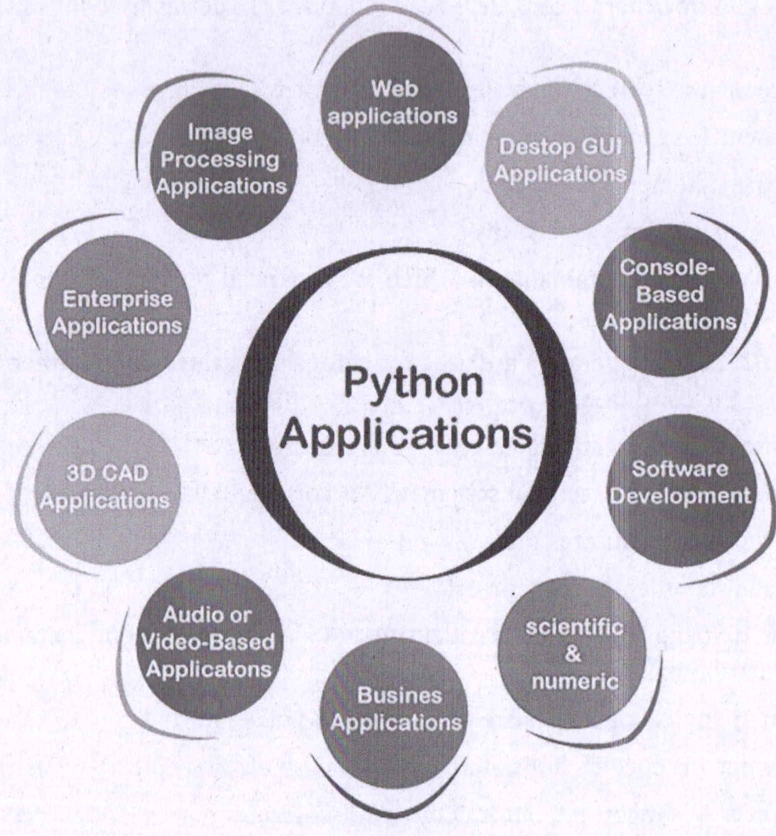

Figure 9.5

ANSWERS									
1. (c)	2. (a)	3. (c)	4. (b)	5. (c)	6. (d)	7. (a)	8. (c)	9. (a)	10. (c)

9.2.7 Competency-Based Questions

1. Suppose Iqbal is using a coding language that has the following features:

   i. It is a case-sensitive language.

   ii. Learning and using this language is easy.

   iii. It is portable, and its codes are short.

   iv. It is Interpreted, interactive, and OOP language.

   v. It is a very simple high-level language with a vast library of add-on modules.

This coding language is:

a) Java b) Maya c) C++ d) Python

2. Suppose Anjana is using a process that has the following steps:

   i. Define the inputs

   ii. Define the variables

   iii. Outline the algorithm's operations

   iv. Output the results of the operations

Which of the following is associated with these steps?

a) Algorithm b) Decoding c) Flowchart d) Mentoring

3. Consider the following properties:

   i. It exhibits the Sequence of instructions/happenings in a single program.

   ii. It consists of standardized and acceptable symbols.

   iii. It has a clear start point and End/Finish point.

   iv. It exhibits the individual steps and their interconnections.

   v. It shows the logic of an algorithm from start to end.

   vi. It has short, clear, and readable statements written inside the symbols.

   The above statements refer to:

   a) Algorithm b) Flowchart

   c) Code d) Coding language

ANSWERS
1. (d) 2. (a) 3. (b)

9.2.8 VSA

1. What is a flowchart?

Ans. A flowchart is a programming tool that uses different symbols to design a solution to a problem.

2. Define a program.

Ans. A program is a collection of instructions used to perform a specific task when executed by a computer.

3. Which website is used for the installation of Python?

Ans. https://www.python.org

4. Which weblink is used for downloading Python documentation?

Ans. https://www.python.org/doc

5. Which operator is used to store the values in a list?

Ans. The values stored in a list may be accessed using the slice operator ([ ] and [:]) with indexes starting with 0 at the beginning of the List and working their way to end -1.

6. How many standard data types are used in Python?

Ans. Python has five standard data types.

7. Who designed the first flowchart?

Ans. John Von Neumann in 1945.

8. What does it mean that Python is interpreted?

Ans. Python is processed at runtime by the interpreter, and we do not need to compile our program before executing it.

9. How is python interactive?

Ans. We can actually work at Python prompt and interact with the interpreter directly to write our programs. That's why Python is interactive.

10. How is Python Object-Oriented Program (OOP)?

Ans. Since Python supports Object-Oriented style or technique programming that encapsulates code within objects and hence, it is an object-oriented program.

11. Why is Python platform Independent?

Ans. Python can be used across different platforms and technologies with the basic coding, and hence, it is platform-independent.

12. How are strings identified in Python?

Ans. Strings in Python are defined as a contiguous set of characters represented in the quotation marks.

13. What is exhibited by a plus (+) sign and asterisk (*) in Python?

Ans. The plus (+) sign exhibits the string concatenation operator, and the asterisk (*) shows the repetition operator.

14. How items/elements in a list are displayed?

Ans. A list contains items that are separated by commas and enclosed within square brackets ([]).

15. How many types of conversions are present in Python?

Ans. Python has two types of type conversion: Implicit Type Conversion and Explicit Type Conversion.

16. Define constants in Python.

Ans. A variable whose value cannot be changed even later on is called a 'Constant.'

17. What is considered a blueprint of a design?

Ans. A flowchart is considered as a blueprint of a design used for solving any specific problem.

18. What are Comparison operators?

Ans. Comparison operators are used for comparing values. It either returns True or False as per the condition.

19. How many Logical operators are used in Python?

Ans. Logical operators are three: and, or, not.

20. Define assignment operators.

Ans. Assignment operators are mainly used in Python to assign values to variables.

21. Define Notebook.

Ans. A notebook integrates code and its output into a single document that combines narrative text, visualisations, mathematical equations, and other rich media.

22. What is the meaning of the word 'algorithm'?

Ans. An algorithm means a procedure or a technique. An algorithm is a sequence of steps to solve a specific problem.

23. What do you mean by Sequence in programming?

Ans. In programming, Sequence means to place statements one after the other, and the execution takes place starting from top to bottom.

24. What is 'branching'?

Ans. In branch control, there will be a condition, and according to the condition, a decision of either TRUE or FALSE is evaluated. In the case of TRUE, one of the two options is mentioned, whereas, in the case of the FALSE condition, the other alternative is taken.

25. What do you mean by Loop in Python?

Ans. The Loop or Repetition allows the Statement (s) to be executed repeatedly based on certain loop conditions, e.g., WHILE, FOR loops.

26. Define the while loop in Python.

Ans. A 'while' statement allows you to repeatedly execute a block of statements till the condition is true. A while statement is also an example of a looping statement.

27. What is the Syntax of while Loop in Python?

Ans. while test_expression: statement (s)

28. How is test expression checked in while loop?

Ans. In a 'while' loop, test expression is checked in the first step. The body of the 'loop' is entered only when the test expression evaluates to be True. After each iteration, the test expression is checked again and again. This process continues until the test expression evaluates to False.

29. What is the main purpose of the python virtual environment?

Ans. The main purpose of the python virtual environment is to create an isolated environment for these projects. It means that each project may have its own dependencies, irrespective of what dependencies every other project has.

30. What is the main use of NLTK?

Ans. NLTK is another open-source Python module that has been developed for natural language processing and text analytics.

31. Mention two commonly used Python AI libraries.

Ans. AIMA, pyDatalog, Simple AI, Open CV, Easy AI, etc.

32. Which shape is used to exhibit page connector in a flow chart?

Ans. Circle

33. Which shape is used to represent the start and end of the flowchart?

Ans. Oval

34. What symbol is used to indicate the flow of logic by connecting symbols in a flow chart?

Ans. Flowline or arrow

35. Which shape is used for arithmetic operations and data manipulations in the flow chart?

Ans. Rectangle

36. Which geometric shape is used for input and output operation in a flowchart?

Ans. Parallelogram

37. What is often considered as a blueprint of a design used for solving a specific problem?

Ans. Flow chart

38. Which shape in a flowchart is used to represent the operation in which there are two/three alternatives, true and false, etc.?

Ans. Diamond

39. What is a python identifier?

Ans. A Python identifier is a name used to identify a variable, module, function, class, or other objects.

40. What may be the value of a python identifier?

Ans. An identifier starts with a letter A to Z or a to z or an underscore (followed by zero or more letters underscores and digits (0 to 9).

41. What are strings in Python?

Ans. Strings in Python are identified as a contiguous set of characters represented in the quotation marks.

42. Define Lists.

Ans. Lists are an important data type of Python. A List contains items which are separated by commas and enclosed within square brackets ([]).

43. Define comparison operators.

Ans. Comparison Operators (Relational Operator) compare the values on either side of them and decide the relation among them.

44. What are Membership Operators?

Ans. Python's membership operators test for membership in a sequence, like strings, lists, tuples, etc.

45. What do you mean by Identify Operators?

Ans. Identity operators compare the memory locations of two objects.

46. Define type conversion.

Ans. Type conversion is defined as the process of converting the value of one data type (integer, float, string, etc.) to another data type.

47. What is explicit type conversion?

Ans. In Explicit Type Conversion, users can convert the data type of an object to the required data type.

48. Which type of conversion in Python is called 'Type Casting'?

Ans. Explicit type conversion

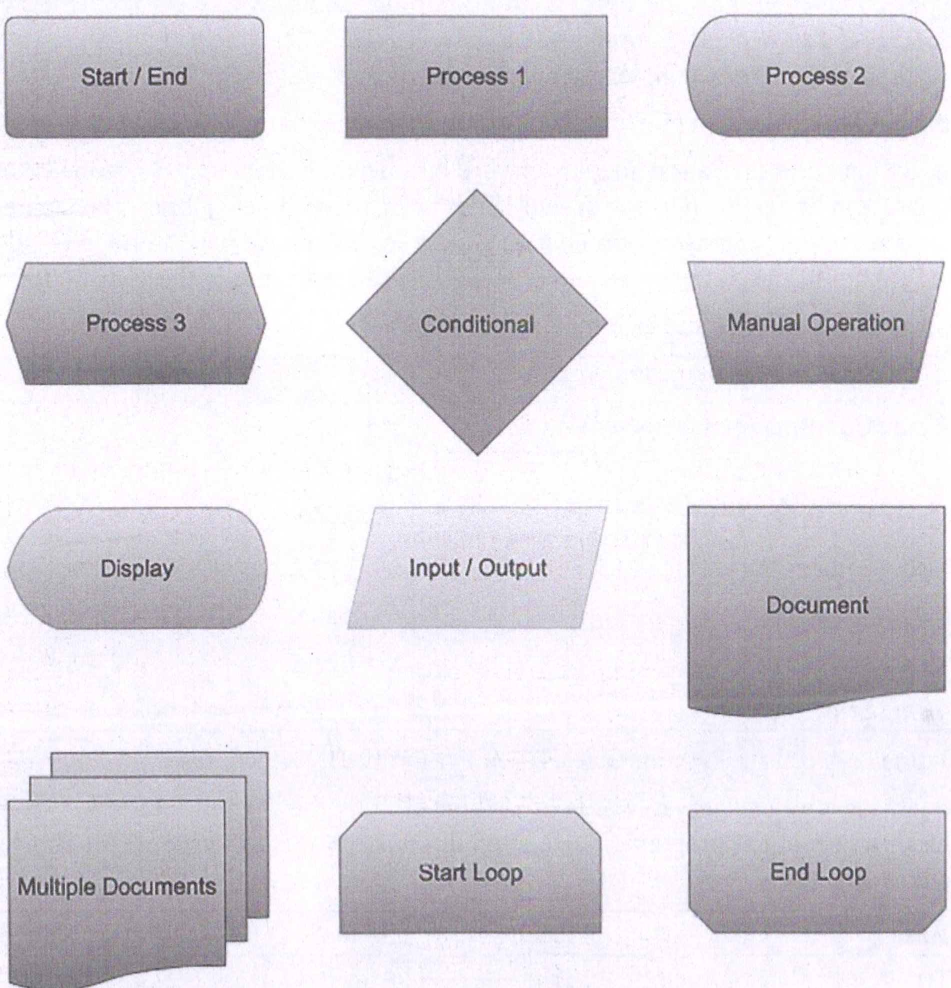

Figure 9.6: Flowchart symbols

9.2.9 Short Answer Type Questions

1. Enlist all the operators that are supported by Python.

Ans. Python language supports the operators: Arithmetic Operators, Comparison (Relational) Operators, Assignment Operators, Logical Operators, Bitwise Operators, Membership Operators, Identity Operators.

2. Explain script mode.

Ans. In script mode, the users type the Python program in a file and then use the interpreter to execute the content from the file. Working in interactive mode is easy and convenient for beginners and for testing small pieces of code, as users may test them immediately. But for coding more than a few lines, users should always save the code so that they may modify and reuse the code.

3. Define and illustrate Python Statements.

Ans. Statements are the instructions written in the source code for execution. There are various types of statements in the Python programming language, like Assignment statements, Conditional statements, Looping statements, etc. These statements help the user to get the required output. For example, n = 60 is an assignment statement.

4. Explain Multi-line statements in Python. Give suitable examples.

Ans. In Python, the end of a statement is marked by a newline character. However, Statements in Python can be extended to one or more lines using parentheses (), braces {}, square brackets [], semi-colon (;), continuation character slash (\). When we need to do long calculations and cannot fit these statements into one line, we can make use of these characters.

The various methods and examples are enlisted below:

Type of Multi-line Statement	Usage
Using Continuation Character (\) s	= 1 + 2 + 3 + \
	4 + 5 + 6 + \
Using Parentheses ()	7 + 8 + 9
Using Square Brackets []	n = (1 * 2 * 3 + 4 – 5)
	footballer = ['MESSI','NEYMAR', 'SUNIL']
Using braces {}	x = {2 + 3 + 4 + 5 + 6 + 7 + 8 }
Using Semicolons (;)	flag = 3; ropes = 4; pole = 5

5. Define keywords in Python. Give a list of Python (9.5.1) keywords.

Ans. Keywords are the reserved words in Python used by the Python interpreter to recognize the structure of the program. The List of all the keywords in Python 9.5.1 is given in the following Table:

False	Class	Finally	Is	return	None
Try	Continue	True	And	as	aasert
Break	Def	Del	Elif	else	except
For	From	Global	If	import	in
Nonlocal	Lambda	Not	Or	pass	raise
While	With	Yield			

6. What do you mean by identifiers? Explain the properties of Python identifiers.

Ans. An identifier is a user-defined name given to a variable, a function, a class, a module, or any other object under consideration. It becomes a programmable entity in Python- one with a name. Thus, it is a name given to the fundamental building blocks in a program.

Properties of Identifiers are as follows:

i. Python identifier can contain English alphabet letters in a small case (a-z), upper case (A-Z), digits (0-9), and underscore (_).

ii. Identifier names can't begin with a digit.

iii. Keywords cannot be used as identifiers.

iv. Python identifier can't contain only digits.

v. Special symbols, like !, @, #, $, %, ^, &, etc cannot be used in the identifier.

vi. The name of a Python identifier may start with an underscore.

vii. An identifier can be of any length.

7. Explain variables along with the examples.

Ans. A variable is a named location that is used to store data in the memory of the computer. It is like that variable as a container that holds data that can be changed later throughout programming. For example,

```
x = 42
y = 39
z = 71
```

These declarations make sure that the program reserves memory for three variables with the names x, y and z. The variable names stand for the memory location.

Some examples of variables are mentioned in the following table:

Task	Sample Code	Output
(i) Assigning a value to a variable	Website = "abc.com" print(Website)	abc.com
(ii) Changing value of a variable	Website = "xyz.com" print(Website) Website1 = "spr.in" print(Website1)	xyz.com spr.in
(iii) Assigning different values to different variables	a, b, c=5, 3, 2 print(a) print(b) print(c)	5 3 2
(iv) Assigning same value to different variable	x=y=z= "Shamima" print(x) print(y) print(z)	Shamima Shamima Shamima

8. Name the two main functions of NumPy.

Ans. (i) NumPy is a Python library that allows the user to handle multi-dimensional arrays and matrices.

(ii) It also offers multiple high-level mathematical functions to operate on these.

9. What are the rules and naming conventions for variables and constants in Python?

Ans. The following are the rules and naming conventions for variables and constants in Python:

i. Create a name that makes sense. Example: 'vowel' makes more sense than 'v.'

ii. Use camelCase notation to declare a variable. It starts with a lowercase letter. Example: myFriend

iii. Using capital letters were possible to declare a constant. For example PI

iv. Never use special symbols, like * , !, @, #, $, %, etc.

v. Constant and variable names should have a combination of letters in lowercase or uppercase or digits or an underscore (_).

10. Explain the steps used in writing algorithms.

Ans. The following steps are used in writing algorithms:

i. Define the inputs for the algorithm: Define the inputs required for the algorithm. Various algorithms take in data for processing. For example, while calculating the area of a circle, input will be the radius.

ii. Define the variables: Variables in an algorithm may be used by the user for more than one place, and hence, variables are to be defined. While calculating the area and circumference of a circle, the users need to define radius (variable).

iii. Outline the algorithm's operations: Outlining the operations of the algorithm is required to input variables for computation purposes. For example, to find the area of a circle, multiply the value of pie (3.14) with radius. Here, the radius is defined.

iv. Outline the results of the operations of the algorithm: Outline the result(s) of the operations of the algorithm. In the case of the area of a circle, the output will be the value stored in the variable AREA.

11. Write the characteristics of a flowchart.

Ans. A flowchart has the following characteristics:

i. It exhibits the Sequence of instructions/happenings in a single program.

ii. It consists of standardized and acceptable symbols.

iii. It has a clear start point and End/Finish point.

iv. It exhibits the individual steps and their interconnections.

v. It represents a workflow or process in a diagrammatic representation.

vi. It exhibits the control from one activity to the next one.

vii. It shows the logic of an algorithm from start to end.

viii. It has short, clear, and readable statements written inside the symbols.

12. Mention four applications in which Python is used.

Ans. Python is used for a large number of applications. Some of them are mentioned below:

i. Web and Internet Development
ii. Desktop GUI Applications
iii. Business Applications
iv. Software Development
v. Games and 3D Graphics
vi. Database Access

13. Mention different types of user's input (syntax and it's meaning) in Python.

Ans.

Syntax	Meaning
=input()	For string input
=int(input())	For integer input
=float(input())	For float (Real no.) input

14. Explain Implicit Type Conversion by giving an example.

Ans. In Implicit type conversion, Python converts one data type to another data type automatically. This process doesn't need any user involvement.

Example:

```
# Code to calculate the Simple_ Interest
principle_amount = 2000
roi = 3.5
time = 6
simple_interest = (principle_amount * roi * time)/100
print("datatype of principle amount : ", type(principle_amount))
print("datatype of rate of interest : ", type(roi))
print("value of simple interest : ", simple_interest)
print("datatype of simple interest : ", type(simple_interest))
```

When we run the above-mentioned program, the output we get is:

```
datatype of principle amount : <class 'int'>
datatype of rate of interest :  <class 'float'>
value of simple interest : 420
datatype of simple interest : <class 'float'>
```

15. Explain nested List with the help of an example.

Ans. A list may also have another list as an item. Such a List is called Nested List.

```
# nested list
learner marks = ["Samita Jain", "10-C", [ "Science",89]]
```

16. How do you access elements of a List?

Ans. A List is made up of various elements which need to be individually accessed on the basis of the application it is used for.

There are two ways to access an individual element of a list:

i. List Index

A list index is a position at which any element is present in the List. Index in the List starts from 0, so if a list has five elements, the Index will start from 0 and go on till 4. In order to access an element in a list, we need to use the index operator [].

ii. Negative Indexing

In Python, negative indexing for its sequences is allowed. The Index of -1 indicates the last item while -2 to the second last item, and so on.

17. Explain Slicing of a Python List.

Ans. In Python List, there are many ways to print the whole List having all the elements, but to print a specific range of elements from the List, we use the Slice operation. Slice operation is performed on the Lists with the use of a colon(:).

i. To print elements from beginning to a range, use [: Index].
ii. To print elements from the end, use [:-Index].
iii. To print elements from a specific index till the end, use [Index:].
iv. To print elements within a range, use [Start Index: End Index].
v. To print the full List with the use of slicing operation, use [:].
vi. While, to print the whole List in reverse order, use [::-1]. Pic

18. How many types of decision-making statements are used in Python?

Ans. Decision-making statements available in Python are:

i. if Statement
ii. if..else statements
iii. if-elif ladder

19. Draw a Python if Statement Flowchart.

Ans.

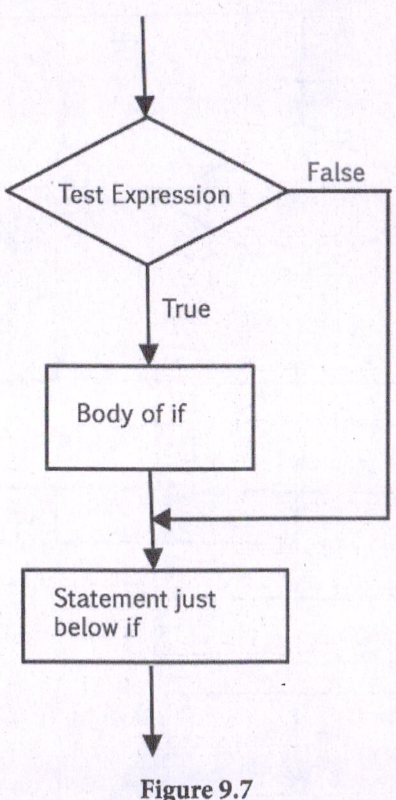

Figure 9.7

20. What is the syntax of the if…else statement?

Ans. Syntax of if...else

```
if test expression:
Body of if
else:
Body of else
```

The if..else Statement evaluates test expression. It will execute the body of 'if' only when the test condition is True.

When the condition is False, the body of else is executed. Indentation is used to separate the blocks.

21. Draw if…else statement flowchart.

Ans.

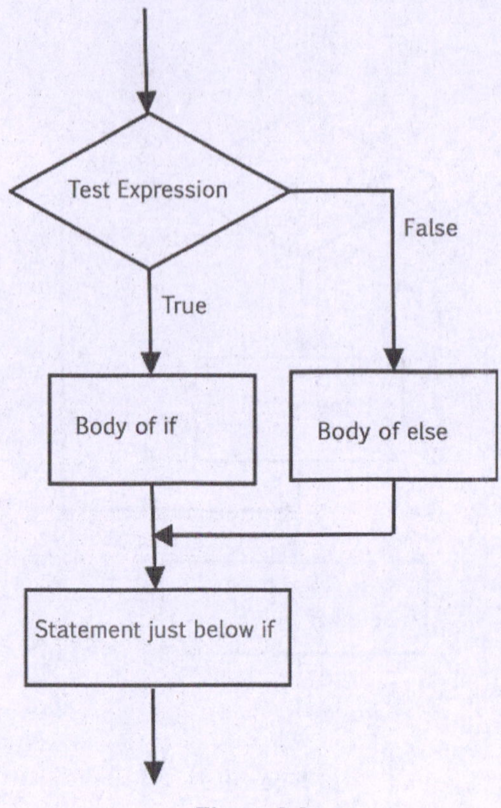

Figure 9.8

22. Write the syntax for Python if...elif...else Statement.

Ans. Syntax of if…Elif…else

```
if test expression:
Body of if
elif test expression:
Body of elif
else:
Body of else
```

The 'elif' is short for else if. It allows the user to check for multiple expressions.

When the condition for 'if' is False, it checks the condition of the next elif block and so on.

When all the conditions are False, the body of 'else' is executed.

Only one block among the several 'if…elif…else' blocks are executed as per the condition. The 'if' block can have only one 'else block. But it can have multiple elif blocks.

23. Draw if...elif...else statement flowchart.

Ans.

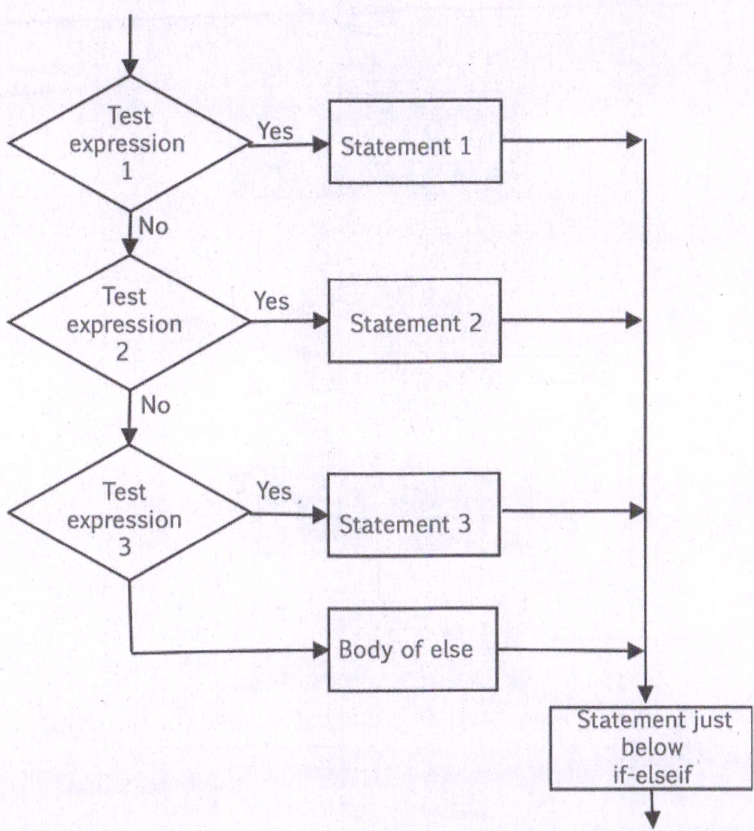

Figure 9.9

24. Write the syntax for a 'For' Loop.

Ans. The 'for' is a looping statement that iterates over a sequence of objects, i.e., go through each item in a sequence.

Syntax of For Loop

```
for val in Sequence:
Body of For
```

Here, Val is the variable that takes the value of the item inside the Sequence on each iteration.

Loop continues until the user reaches the last item in the Sequence. The body of the 'for' loop is separated from the rest of the code using indentation.

25. Draw the flowchart of the 'For' loop.

Ans.

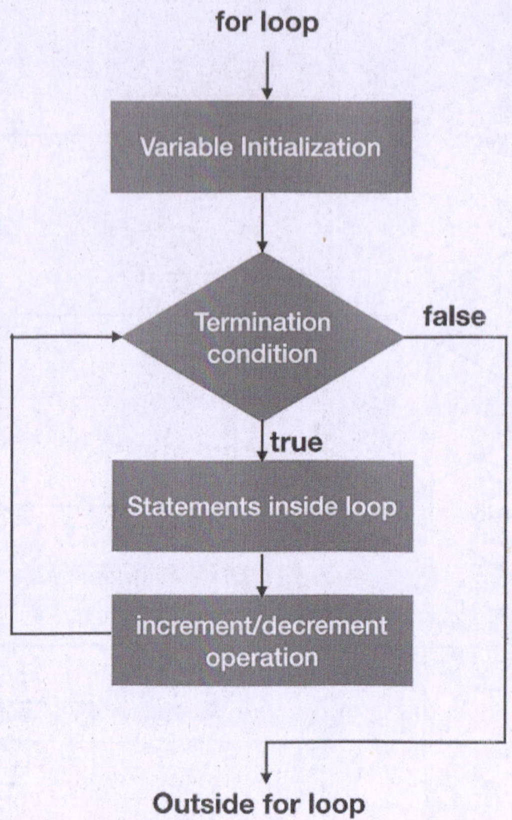

Figure 9.10: Flowchart of for Loop

26. What is the syntax for the 'while' Statement?

Ans. The 'while' statement allows the user to repeatedly execute a block of statements as long as a condition is to be True. A 'while' statement is an example of what is called a looping statement. A 'while' statement can have an optional 'else' clause.

Syntax of while Loop in Python

```
while test_expression:
Body of while
```

In a 'while' loop, test expression is checked in the first step. The body of the loop is entered when the test_expression evaluates to be True. After one iteration, the test expression is evaluated once again. This process continues until the test_expression is found to be False. In Python, the body of the 'while' loop is determined through indentation. The body starts with indentation, whereas the first unindented line marks the end. Python interprets any non-zero value as True. None and 0 are interpreted as False.

27. Draw the flowchart of the 'While' loop.

Ans. Flowchart of while Loop is below:

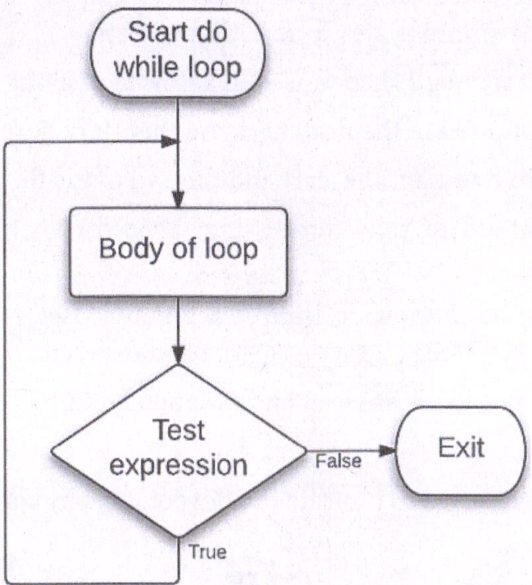

Figure 9.11

28. What do you mean by traversing a List in Python? Explain.

Ans. Traversing a list means going through all the elements from the beginning to the last element. To do this, use the index number/location number as seen in the previous example. When you specify the range, the first number specifies the starting index location, and the second number specifies that the List will be fetched one less than the second number. If the third number is not specified in the range using a colon, then by default, it is taken as +1. Otherwise, the third number is specified as the step statement, which means it will start fetching the List from the first number, and then the next element will be the location using the step statement.

9.3.10 Long Answer Type Questions

1. Enlist the main features of Python.

Ans. Python has the following features:

i. Python is a case-sensitive language because 'Coal' and 'coal' in Python are different.

ii. Learning and using Python is easy.

iii. Python codes are short.

iv. Python is portable.

v. Python programs are easily readable and understandable.

vi. Python is a very simple high-level language with a vast library of add-on modules.

vii. Python is Interpreted. It means that Python is processed at runtime by the interpreter. The user does not need to compile our program before executing it.

viii. Python is Interactive. The users can actually work at Python prompt and interact with the interpreter directly to write the programs.

ix. Python is Object-Oriented. Python supports Object-Oriented style or technique programming that encapsulates code within objects.

2. Explain the different standard shapes used in a flowchart along with their functions.

Ans. The standard symbols used in the flowchart and their functions are given below:

i. **Oval:** It is used to represent the start and the end of the flowchart.

ii. **Rectangle**: It is used to show processing; Used for arithmetic operations and data manipulations.

iii. **Diamond**: It is used to show decision-making. It is used to represent the operation in which there are two/three alternatives, true and false, etc.

iv. **Parallelogram:** it is used for input and output operation.

v. **Circle:** Page connector.

vi. **Arrows**: Flowline is used to indicate the flow of logic by connecting symbols.

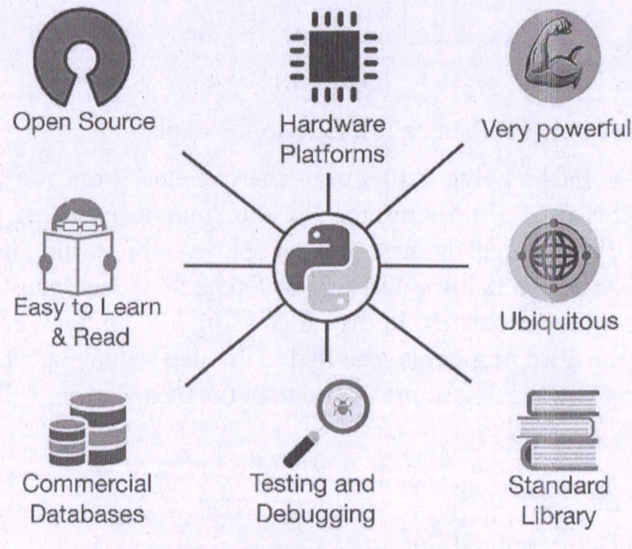

Figure 9.12

3. Mention four applications in which Python is used.

Ans. Python is used for a large number of applications. Some of them are mentioned below:

i. Web and Internet Development

ii. Desktop GUI Applications

iii. Business Applications

iv. Software Development

v. Games and 3D Graphics

vi. Database Access

4. Python has been gaining maximum popularity in recent times. Discuss the reasons behind it.

Ans. Python is gaining maximum popularity because of the following reasons:

i. **Less Code:** Python helps in the easy writing and execution of codes. Python has the ability to implement the same logic with about 1/5th of code as compared to other OOPs languages. Due to its interpreted approach, it enables check as the user code methodology.

ii. **Prebuilt Libraries**: Python contains a number of libraries for every need of AI projects. A few examples include NumPy for scientific computation, SciPy for advanced computing, and PyBrain for machine learning.

iii. **Support:** Python is an open-source resource with a great community. The host of resources available can get any developer up to speed in no time. Also, there is a huge community of active coders willing to help programmers in every stage of the developing cycle.

iv. **Platform Independence**: Python provides the flexibility to provide an API from an existing language which indeed provides extreme flexibility. It is also platform-independent. With just a few changes in codes, the user can get the app up and running in a new OS. This saves time for the developers in testing on different platforms and migrating code.

v. **Flexibility**: Flexibility is considered one of the core advantages of Python. With the option to choose between the OOPs approach and scripting, Python is suitable for every purpose. It works as a perfect backend and is also suitable for linking different data structures altogether. The option to check the validity of code in the IDLE is also a big plus point for developers who are struggling between different algorithms.

5. Explain Python Comments with the help of examples.

Ans. A comment is a text that doesn't affect the outcome of a code. It is just a piece of text to let someone know what the programmer has done in a program or what is being done in a block of code. In Python, the programmer uses the hash (#) symbol to start writing a comment.

(i) **Single Line Comments:** Python single-line comments start with a hashtag symbol with no white spaces (#) and may last till the end of the line. When the comment exceeds one line, then put a hashtag on the next line and continue the comment. Python's single-line comments are considered d useful for supplying short explanations for variables, function declarations, and expressions.

Example:

```
# This is a comment
# Print "ShailAnu" to console
print("ShailAnu ")
```

(ii) **Multi-Line Comments:** Python multi-line comments are pieces of text enclosed in a delimiter ("" "") on each end of the comment. Moreover, there should not be any white space between delimiter ("" ""). These comments are useful when the comment text does not fit into one line and needs to spread across lines. Multi-line comments or paragraphs serve as documentation for others reading the code.

Example:

```
"""
This is a multi-line comment in Python that
has several lines and describes SatyamAI.com
An AI Science portal for the whole world. It contains
well written, well thought
and well-explained articles on AI
and programming articles,
quizzes, worksheets, projects, and more.
...
"""
print("SatyamAI.com ")
```

6. Discuss different Datatypes in Python with the help of examples.

Ans. Because everything is an object in Python programming, data types are actually classes, and variables are instances (object) of these classes. There are various data types in Python. Some of the types are discussed below.

(i) **Python Numbers:** Number data type stores Numerical Values. These are of four different types:

(a) **Integer and Long Integer:** The range of an integer in Python can be from -2147483648 to 2147483647, and a long integer has an unlimited range subject to available memory.

Integers are the whole numbers containing + or – sign, like 1000, -99, 0, 17. While writing a large integer value, don't use commas to separate digits. Also, integers should not have leading zeros.

(b) **Float/Floating Point Number:** Float () is a built-in Python function that converts a number or a string into a float value and then returns the result. When it fails for any invalid input, then an appropriate exception occurs. Numbers with fractions or decimal points are called floating-point numbers. A floating-point number will consist of a sign (+,-) sequence of decimals digits and a dot, like 0.0, -21.9, 0.98333328, 15.2963, etc. Such numbers may also be used to represent a number in engineering/ scientific notation.

-2.0 x 105 will be represented as -2.0e5

2.0X10-5 will be 2.0E-5

(c) **Complex numbers**: A complex number is represented by the expression " x + yi. "

Python converts the real numbers (x and y) into a complex number by using the function complex(x,y), and the real part can be accessed using the function real(), and the imaginary part can be represented by an image().

(d) **None:** 'None' is a special data type with a single value, which is used to signify the absence of value/false in a situation.

(ii) **Sequence:** A sequence is an ordered collection of items indexed by positive integers. It is a combination of mutable and non-mutable data types. Three types of sequence data types available in Python are a) Strings, b) Lists c) Tuples.

(a) **String :** A string is defined as an ordered sequence of letters/characters. Strings are enclosed in single quotes (' ') or double (" "). The quotes are not part of a string, and they just tell the computer where the string constant begins and ends. They may have any character or sign, including space in them.

(b) **Lists :** The List is a sequence of values of any type. The values in a List are known as elements or items. These are indexed/ordered. The List is enclosed in square brackets. Example:

dob = [7,"January",1949]

(c) **Tuples**: A sequence of values of any type that are indexed by integers is called Tuples. They are immutable. Tuples are enclosed in ().

Example:

```
t = (3,'program',3.8) 5)
```

(iii) **Set:** A Set is a collection of unordered values, of any type, without any duplicate entry.

Example:

```
>>> a = {1,2,2,3,3,3} >>> a {1,2,3} 5)
```

(iv) **Mapping:** This data type is unordered. Dictionaries fall under Mappings. Dictionary contains an unordered collection of key-value pairs. It is used while dealing with a huge amount of data. Dictionaries are optimized for retrieving data. The key to retrieving the value should be known to the user. Python dictionaries are kept/defined within braces {} with each item being a pair in the form "key: value" while key and value can be of any type.

Example:

```
>>> d = {1:'Ajay','key':6}
>>> type(d)
  <class  'dict'>
```

7. Explain Python Operators.

Ans. Operators are special symbols that represent computation. They are applied to operand(s), which can be values or variables. Same operators can behave differently on different data types. Operators, when applied to operands, form an expression. Operators are categorized as Arithmetic, Relational, Logical, and Assignment. Value and variables, when used with the operator, are known as operands.

Arithmetic operators are enlisted in the following table:

Operator	Meaning	Expression	Result
+	Addition	15 + 20	35
-	Subtraction	35 - 10	25
*	Multiplication	30 * 15	450
/	Division	50 / 10	5.0
		1 / 2	0.5
//	Integer Division	24 // 10	2
		1 // 2	0
%	Remainder	45 % 10	5
**	Raised to power	4 ** 2	16

8. What are the methods for adding an element to a List?

Ans. We can add an element to any list using the following methods:

a) **Using append() method:** Elements may be added to the List by using the built-in append() function. One element at a time may be added to the List by using the append() method; for the Addition of a number of elements with the append() method, loops are used. Tuples are immutable, so they can be added to the List with the use of the append method. Additional Lists can also be added to the existing List with the use of the append() method.

b) **Using insert() Method:** Append() method only works for the Addition of elements at the end of the List; for the Addition of elements at the desired position, the insert() method is used. Unlike append(), which takes only one argument, the insert() method requires two arguments(position, value).

c) **Using extend() method:** Other than append() and insert() methods, extend() method is also there for the Addition of elements. This method is used to add many elements at the same time at the end of a List.

9. How can you remove elements from a List?

Ans. Elements from a list can be removed using two methods:

a) **Using remove() method:** Elements may be removed from a list using the built-in remove() function, but an Error arises when the element doesn't exist in the set. By this method, one element is removed at a time. For removing a range of elements, the iterator is used. The remove() method removes the specified item.

b) **Using pop() method:** The pop() function can also be used to remove and return an element from the set. By default, it removes the last element of the set. For removing an element from a specified position of the List, the Index of the element is passed as an argument to the pop() method.

10. Explain Explicit Type Conversion by giving an example.

Ans. In Explicit Type Conversion, the users convert the data type of an object to the required data type by using predefined functions, like int(), float(), str(), etc. Moreover, this type of conversion is known as typecasting because the user casts (changes) the data type of the objects.

Syntax:

```
(required_datatype)(expression)
```

Typecasting may be done by assigning the required data type function to the expression.
Example: Adding of string and an integer using explicit conversion

```
Birth_day = 21
Birth_month = "July"
print("data type of Birth_day before type casting :", type(Birth_day))
print("data type of Birth_month : ", type(Birth_month))
Birth_day = str(Birth_day)
print("data type of Birth_day after type casting :",type(Birth_day))
Birth_date = Birth_day + Birth_month
print("birth date of the student : ", Birth_day)
print("data type of Birth_date : ", type(Birth_date))
```

When we run the above-mentioned program, the output will be as follows:

```
data type of Birth_day before type casting: <class 'int' >
data type of Birth_month: <class 'str' >
data type of Birth_day after type casting: <class 'str' >
birth date of the student: ' 21 July '
data type of Birth_date: <class 'str' >
```

In the above program,

We add Birth_day and Birth_month variables.

We converted Birth_day from integer(lower) to string(higher) type using str() function to perform the addition.

We got the Birth_date value and data type to be a string.

11. How do you create a list in Python?

Ans. In the Python program, a list is created by placing all the items (elements) inside a square bracket [ ] and separated by commas. A-List can have any number of items, and they may be of different types (integer, float, string, etc.).

Example:

```
#empty list
empty_list = []
#list of integers
age = [13,19,11]
#list with mixed data types
candidate_height_weight = ["Kanshika", 5.2, 48]
```

Figure 9.13

9.2.11 HOTS Questions

1. How will you prove that Python is a case-sensitive programming language?

Ans. Python is a case-sensitive programming language because in Python, 'SUMER' and 'sumer' have different meanings.

2. How will you identify that an identifier is a language-defined special name?

Ans. When the identifier also ends with two trailing underscores, the identifier is a language-defined special name.

3. Which operator is used to store the values in a list?

Ans. The values stored in a list can be accessed using the slice operator ([ ] and [:]) with indexes starting at 0 at the beginning of the List and working their way to end -1.

4. Why is Python used for web programming?

Ans. Python is a scripting language, and hence, it can be used for web programming and for desktop applications (Blender 3D, or even for games).

9.3 PRACTICE QUESTIONS

1. Define and illustrate List in Python.
2. Define and illustrate loops.
3. What do you mean by Python nested if statements?
4. What are the main two types of Loops in Python?
5. What do you mean by 'strings' in Python.
6. Write the syntax of the 'for' loop.
7. Differentiate between 'for' loop and 'while' loop.

8. Why is a flowchart used?
9. What are the two kinds of Type conversion?
10. Write a program to find whether a number is prime or not using 'while loop.'
11. Discuss the main features of Python.

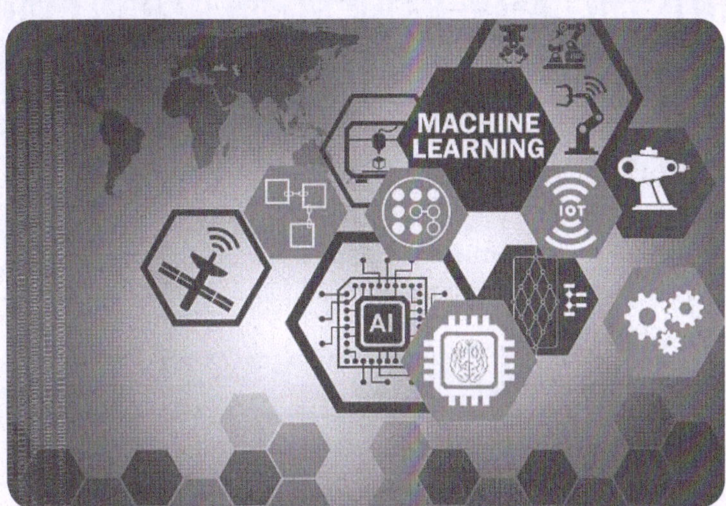

Figure 9.14

CBSE | DEPARTMENT OF SKILL EDUCATION

ARTIFICIAL INTELLIGENCE (SUBJECT CODE 417)

CLASS IX (SESSION 2021-2022)

BLUE-PRINT FOR SAMPLE QUESTION PAPER FOR TERM – 1

Max. Time Allowed: 1 Hour **Max. Marks: 25**

PART A - EMPLOYABILITY SKILLS (05 MARKS):

Unit No.	Name of The Unit	No. Of Questions (1 Mark Each)
1	Communication Skills-I	2
2	Self-Management Skills-I	2
3	Information and Communication Technology Skills-I	2
TOTAL QUESTIONS NO. OF QUESTIONS TO BE ANSWERED TOTAL MARKS	6 Questions Any 5 Questions 1 × 5 = 5 Marks	

PART B - SUBJECT SPECIFIC SKILLS (20 MARKS):

Unit No.	Name of The Unit	No. Of Questions (1 Mark Each)
1	Introduction to AI	13
2	AI Project Cycle	14
TOTAL QUESTIONS NO. OF QUESTIONS TO BE ANSWERED TOTAL MARKS	27 Questions 20 Questions 1 × 20 = 20 MARKS	

SOLVED CBSE SAMPLE QUESTION PAPER 2021 FOR TERM – 1

Max. Time Allowed: 1 Hour **Max. Marks: 25**

General Instructions:

1. Please read the instructions carefully
2. This Question Paper is divided into 03 sections, viz., Section A, Section B and Section C.
3. Section A is of 05 marks and has 06 questions on Employability Skills.
4. Section B is of 15 marks and has 20 questions on Subject specific Skills.
5. Section C is of 05 marks and has 07 competency-based questions.
6. Do as per the instructions given in the respective sections.
7. Marks allotted are mentioned against each section/question.
8. All questions must be attempted in the correct order

SECTION – A

Answer any 5 questions out of the given 6 questions on Employability Skills (1 × 5 = 5 marks)

1. Match the following.

Column A: Barriers	Column B: Examples
1. Language	A. Trying to read a book when somebody else is watching TV in the same room
2. Emotional	B. In some cultures, wearing shoes and walking inside the kitchen is considered rude and disrespectful
3. Environmental	C. Talking in Hindi when others know only Tamil
4. Cultural	D. Parent is not talking to the child

a) 1 -> D; 2 -> A; 3 -> C; 4 -> B
b) 1 -> C; 2 -> D; 3 -> A; 4 -> B
c) 1 -> C; 2 -> D; 3 -> B; 4 -> A
d) 1 -> C; 2 -> A; 3 -> D; 4 -> B

2. Which of these sentences use uppercase letters correctly?

a) I am Hungry.
b) Divya and Sunil are reading.
c) The bucket is full of water.
d) She lives in Delhi.

3. Niraj had difficulty in speaking English. He, therefore, avoided talking to his classmates. He believed that he can learn English by joining English speaking classes and in few days he was able to speak English fluently. Which of the following quality is he demonstrating?

a) Personal hygiene and grooming
b) Self-control
c) Self-confidence
d) Team work

4. What is the best way to start our day positively?
   a) Think about all your accomplishment so far and feel good about it.
   b) Think about all that can go wrong.
   c) Think about the difficult test you will face during the day.
   d) Think about the traffic on the road and feel stressed.
5. Put the following units of storage into the correct order, starting with the smallest unit first and going down to the largest unit:
   (a) Kilobyte (b) Byte (c) Megabyte (d) Terabyte (e) Gigabyte (f) Bit
   Give your answer from the following code:
   a) (f) -> (b) -> (a) -> (c) -> (d) -> (e)
   b) (f) -> (b) -> (a) -> (d) -> (e) -> (c)
   c) (f) -> (b) -> (a) -> (d) -> (c) -> (e)
   d) (f) -> (b) -> (a) -> (c) -> (e) -> (d)
6. Which one of the following statements is false?
   a) You need to create an account before you can send an e-mail.
   b) You do not need an Internet connection to use your Gmail account.
   c) You should sign out of your account when you are not using the computer.
   d) You must not share your password with others.

SECTION – B

Answer any 15 questions out of the given 20 questions **(1 × 15 = 15 marks)**

7. Statement1: AI is getting integrated into our lives seamlessly.
   Statement2: Often we do not even realize that we are using AI.
   a) Statement 2 is correct and Statement 1 is incorrect.
   b) Statement 1 is correct and Statement 2 is incorrect
   c) Both Statement1 and Statement2 are correct
   d) Both Statement1 and Statement2 are incorrect
8. IoT is abbreviated as
   a) Institute of Technology
   b) Internet of Things
   c) Index organised Table
   d) Inter-operability Test
9. Match column A with Column B.

Column A	Column B
1. Expert System	A. Simulate how a human would behave as a conversational partner
2. Chatbot	B. Uses knowledge stored in a knowledge base but requires the intervention of human expert
3. Digital Assistant	C. Autonomous vehicle
4. self-driving car	D. Works on various mobile platforms

a) 1 -> B; 2 -> A; 3 -> D; 4 -> C b) 1 -> A; 2 -> B; 3 -> C; 4 -> D

c) 1 -> D; 2 -> A; 3 -> B; 4 -> C d) 1 -> C; 2 -> A; 3 -> D; 4 -> B

10. An application lets you search what you see, get things done faster and understand the world around you – using just your camera or a photo. Which domain does this app belong to?

a) Natural Language Processing b) Data Sciences

c) Computer Vision d) Artificial Language Processing

11. A web-based software that is used to create interactive stories in Choose Your Own Adventure Format (CYOA) is

a) Chatbot b) Jupyter notebook

c) Internet explorer d) Inklewriter

12. Match the following.

Column A	Column B
1. Smart Mobility	i) Resources and Sustainability
2. Smart Environment	ii) Creativity and Social Capital
3. Smart People	iii) Infrastructure and Transport

a) 1 -> i) ; 2 -> ii) ; 3 -> iii) b) 1 -> ii) ; 2 -> iii) ; 3 -> i)

c) 1 -> iii) ; 2 -> i) ; 3 -> ii) d) 1 -> iii) ; 2 -> ii) ; 3 -> i)

13. Fill in the blanks with the correct answers given below:

The ________Sustainable Development Goals (SDGs) were launched at the United Nations Sustainable Development Summit in New York in the year ________, forming the ______ Agenda for Sustainable Development.

a) 17, 2015, 2030 b) 15 , 2010 , 2025

c) 17, 2010 , 2025 d) 15 , 2010 , 2030

14. 2.37 billion people are without food or unable to eat a healthy balanced diet on a regular basis. Which Sustainable Development Goal are we talking about?

a) No Poverty b) Zero hunger

c) Good health and well-being d) Decent work and economic growth

15. Statement 1: The drone technology help farmers spot intrusions, crop diseases, predict the amount of crop production, and saves time and avoids the difficulties of physical manual inspections.

Statement 2: The statement given above is an example of Natural Language Processing.

a) Both Statement1 and Statement2 are correct

b) Both Statement1 and Statement2 are incorrect

c) Statement 2 is correct and Statement 1 is incorrect.

d) Statement 1 is correct and Statement 2 is incorrect

16. When you search for 'Doctor' on a search website, the results for Doctor images might mostly come up as 'male'. Whereas for 'Nurse' most results would be 'female'. What does this depict?

a) Gender bias
b) Data Privacy
c) Poor training
d) Lack of access

17. Match column A with Column B

Column A	Column B
1. Problem Scoping	A. implement a suitable model that matches the requirements
2. Data Acquisition	B. interpret some useful information out of data
3. Data Exploration	C. collect data from reliable sources
4. Modelling	D. finalise the aim of the AI project

a) 1 -> B; 2 -> A; 3 -> D; 4 -> C
b) 1 -> D; 2 -> B; 3 -> C; 4 -> A
c) 1 -> D; 2 -> C; 3 -> B; 4 -> A
d) 1 -> C; 2 -> D; 3 -> A; 4 -> B

18. The 4 Ws of the 4W problem canvas are:

a) Who, What, Where and Why
b) Who, What, When and Why
c) Who, What, Where and When
d) Who, Where, When and Why

19. Statement 1: Where block helps you to focus on the context/situation/location of the problem.

Statement 2: What block helps you need to determine the nature of the problem.

a) Statement1 is correct and Statement2 is incorrect
b) Statement2 is correct and Statement1 is incorrect
c) Both Statement1 and Statement 2 are incorrect
d) Both Statement1 and Statement 2 are correct

20. __________ helps us to summarise all the key points into one single Template so that in future, whenever there is need to look back at the basis of the problem, we can take a look at the this and understand the key elements of it.

a) 4W Problem canvas
b) Problem Statement Template
c) Data Acquisition
d) Algorithm

21. Which of the following are valid sources for collecting data?

i) Announcements
ii) Surveys
iii) Web scraping
iv) Application Programming Interface

a) i) , ii) and iii)
b) i) , ii) and iv)
c) ii) , iii) and iv)
d) i) , iii) and iv)

22. Statement1 : The data with which the machine can be trained is the testing data

    Statement2 : The data with which the model is evaluated is the training data

    a) Statement1 is correct and Statement2 is incorrect
    b) Statement2 is correct and Statement1 is incorrect
    c) Both Statement1 and Statement 2 are correct
    d) Both Statement1 and Statement 2 are incorrect

23. Identify the correct representations in a system map
    a) Circles -> elements; arrowed lines -> relationship
    b) Squares -> elements ; dotted lines -> relationship
    c) Circles -> elements ; dotted lines -> relationship
    d) Squares -> elements ; arrowed lines -> relationship

24. Which of these is NOT used for visualisation in AI?

    a) Sketchy Graph   b) Scatter plot   c) Ruler   d) Bar chart

25. Which of the following is an example of rule- based approach?

    a) Pixel it activity   b) Decision trees
    c) Histogram   d) Illustration diagram

26. Which of the following is incorrect?
    a) In rule- based approach, the relationship or patterns in data are defined by the developer.
    b) Decision tree looks like an upside-down tree.
    c) Pixel It activity is an example of how computers see images, process them and classify them.
    d) In learning- based approach, the relationship or patterns in data are defined by the developer.

SECTION – C (COMPETENCY BASED QUESTIONS)

Answer any 5 questions out of the given 7 questions **(1 x 5 = 5 marks)**

27. With so many people using electricity on a daily basis—whether it is to charge their cell phones or to use their TV—a lot of cables (made of plastic) must be used. Plastic destroys our ecosystem, yet we continue to produce it. Indispensable as it may seem, it has an adverse effect on the environment. The manufacturing of plastic is not exactly eco-friendly. With a little help from modern technology Elif discovered a way to help curb our plastic problem. She used banana peels as the main ingredient to make bio-plastics.

    Which of the Sustainable Development Goal does this scenario relate to?

    a) Life on land
    b) Responsible consumption, and production
    c) Affordable and clean energy
    d) Sustainable cities and communities

28. Air pollution kills an estimated seven million people worldwide every year. WHO data shows that 9 out of 10 people breathe toxic air. From smog hanging over cities to smoke

inside the home, air pollution poses a major threat to human health and climate. The major pollution sources include vehicles, power generation, agriculture/ waste incineration, and industry. Harmful gases like SO2, NO2, CO are emitted directly into air because of pollution. Deploying an air quality index monitor is one way that would help to know the local air quality and take action to protect their health. Taking this as the problem, choose which of the following would be the ideal problem statement template.

a) Our WHO have a problem that people breathe toxic air when smog hangs over cities. An ideal solution would be to shut down industries and stop the movement of vehicles in major cities.

b) Our people have a problem that they die in accidents when more number of vehicles are used. An ideal solution would be to develop be to stop the movement of vehicles in major cities.

c) Our people have a problem that air pollution has damaging effects on human health when harmful gases like SO2, NO2, CO are emitted directly into air. An ideal solution would be to develop an air quality index monitor so that one can know the local air quality and take action to protect their health.

d) Our WHO have a problem that people die every year when there is an increase in the number of vehicles and industries. An ideal solution would be to make sure people stay indoors to protect their health.

29. While designing a surveillance system for the premises where a costly diamond was to be kept for exhibition, we do the following tasks.

a) Get photographs of all the authorised people.

b) Get photographs of all the unauthorised people.

c) Get photographs of the premises.

d) Get photographs of all the visitors.

Which stage of AI project cycle are we talking about?

a) Problem Scoping b) Data Exploration c) Modelling d) Data Acquisition

30. Match the best choice of graph for the data below.

1. Chart to show the number of students in a school over past 5 years.
2. Chart to show the temperature on each day of the week.
3. Chart to show percentage of each sale of ticket type at a concert.

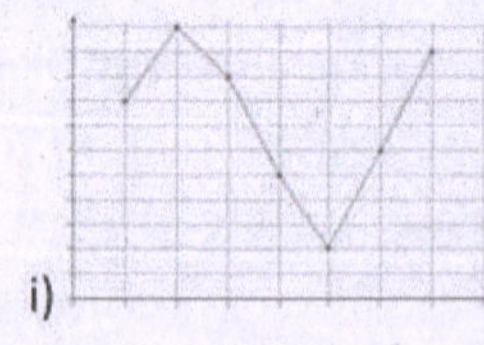

i)

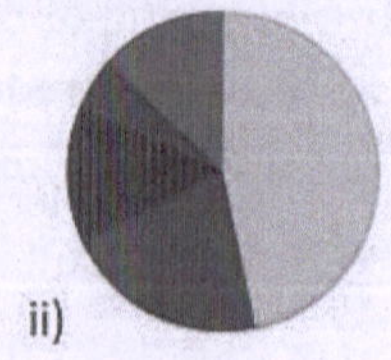

ii)

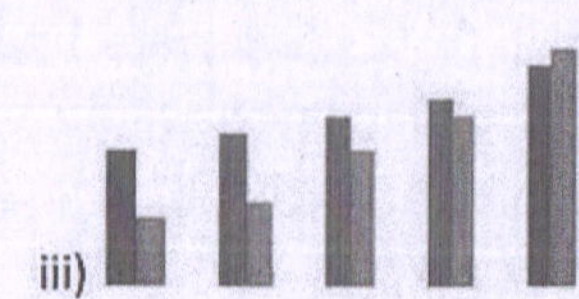

iii)

a) 1 -> i) ; 2 -> ii) ; 3 -> iii) b) 1 -> ii) ; 2 -> iii) ; 3 -> i)

c) 1 -> iii) ; 2 -> i) ; 3 -> ii) d) 1 -> iii) ; 2 -> ii) ; 3 -> i)

31. Information about three games are given below. Identify the game and the respective domain

1. The players of this game have to guess what the opponents will choose and make an appropriate shape to defeat them.

2. This is a simple twenty questions game in which the player can ask 20 Yes/No questions to identify the animal.
3. In this game, the computer asks the player to find the objects that match certain images within a time limit.

a) 1. Emoji Scavenger Hunt -> Computer vision; 2. Rock, Paper, Scissor -> Natural Language Processing; Mystery Animal -> Data Sciences

b) 1. Mystery Animal -> Data Sciences; 2. Emoji Scavenger Hunt -> Natural Language Processing; 3.Rock,Paper,Scissor -> Computer vision

c) 1. Rock, Paper, Scissor -> Data Sciences; 2. Emoji Scavenger Hunt -> Natural Language Processing; 3. Mystery Animal -> Computer vision

d) 1. Rock, Paper, Scissor -> Data Sciences; 2. Mystery Animal -> Natural Language Processing; 3.Emoji Scavenger Hunt -> Computer vision

32. Choose the AI applications among the ones given below:

i) Gmail uses Smart Compose feature can help you type emails faster as it offers suggestions for words and phrases as you type.

ii) Websites make use of a software that simulates human-like conversations with users via text messages on chat.

iii) Soap dispensers use infrared sensors with which when hands are placed in the proximity of the sensor, dispense the designated amount of soap.

iv) Face recognition technology that identifies and verifies a person using the person's facial features and automatically marks attendance.

a) i), ii) and iv) b) i), ii) and iii) c) ii), iii) and iv) d) i), iii) and iv)

33. Water availability is a major environmental problem in the world. We continue to flush billions of litres of treated fresh water down our toilets every day. Since 40% of the 6 billion people on earth use toilets, it is a lot of water. Rohit, an Indian embarked on a project to redesign the water closet / flush to reduce the consumption of water. He made this possible with a simple mechanism added to the conventional closet that creates a partial vacuum when the user pushes down the flush lever. He called it the Vacu-Flush.

Which of the Sustainable Development Goal does this scenario relate to?

a) Life on land

b) Responsible consumption, and production

c) Clean water and sanitation

d) Partnerships for goals

ANSWERS

1. (b)	2. (d)	3. (c)	4. (a)	5. (d)	6. (b)	7. (c)	8. (b)	9. (a)	10. (c)
11. (d)	12. (c)	13. (a)	14. (b)	15. (d)	16. (a)	17. (c)	18. (a)	19. (d)	20. (b)
21. (c)	22. (d)	23. (a)	24. (c)	25. (b)	26. (d)	27. (b)	28. (c)	29. (d)	30. (c)
31. (d)	32. (a)	33. (c)							

SOLVED CBSE SAMPLE QUESTION PAPER – 1
FOR TERM – 1

Max. Time Allowed: 1 Hour **Max. Marks: 25**

General Instructions:

1. Please read the instructions carefully
2. This Question Paper is divided into 03 sections, viz., Section A, Section B and Section C.
3. Section A is of 05 marks and has 06 questions on Employability Skills.
4. Section B is of 15 marks and has 20 questions on Subject specific Skills.
5. Section C is of 05 marks and has 07 competency-based questions.
6. Do as per the instructions given in the respective sections.
7. Marks allotted are mentioned against each section/question.
8. All questions must be attempted in the correct order

SECTION – A

Answer any 5 questions out of the given 6 questions on Employability Skills (1 × 5 = 5 marks)

1. Consider the following phrases:

   i. Plants need carbon dioxide and water.

   ii. Who ate the last samosa?

   iii. All passengers with valid tickets can board the flight no AIR 8401 now.

   iv. They are working since 7 am.

   v. Nithya Chandran has nice ideas.

   Examples of Noun phrases are:

   a) (i) (ii) only b) (iii) (iv) only

   c) (i) (ii) (iii) only d) (iii) (iv) (v) only

2. ______________ is a small electronic device that is used to move, select, and open items on the computer screen.

   a) Mouse b) Monitor c) Printer d) PD

3. Which of the following skills is more important than others in getting success in a professional career?

   a) Intelligence Quotient (IQ) b) Emotional and social skills

   c) Communication skills d) None of the above

4. Why should one prefer e-mails over other methods?

   a) To communicate with many people simultaneously.

   b) To talk to each other in real-time.

c) To keep a record of communication.

d) To share documents and files with one or more persons.

5. Which of the functions is not performed by an OS?

   a) It organises s the structure of the files and directories on a computer.

   b) It ruptures the software resources of the computer.

   c) It allows the user to create, copy, move, and delete files.

   d) It manages the computer memory and keeps track of memory space.

6. Statement 1: Stress may be defined as a reaction to any external stimuli that trigger changes in one's personality.

   Statement 2: The process of understanding a problem and finding a solution using a step-by-step method is called decision making skill.

   a) Statement 1 is correct, but statement 2 is incorrect.

   b) Statement 1 is incorrect but statement 2 is correct.

   c) Both the statements are correct.

   d) Both the statements are incorrect.

SECTION – B

Answer any 15 questions out of the given 20 questions **(1 × 15 = 15 marks)**

7. Which of the following products is not a part of Smart home?

   a) LED lights are controlled by using the smartphone.

   b) Turning lights and appliances at home on or off from the mobile device.

   c) Door locks and garage doors are controlled by using a smartphone.

   d) None of the above

8. ____________ intelligence is the ability to understand social situations and the behaviour of other people.

   a) Interpersonal b) Intrapersonal c) Musical d) Spatial

9. Which statements are part of AI Ethics?

   i. Financial investments in AI should be accompanied by funding for research on ensuring its beneficial use.

   ii. If an Al system causes harm, it should be possible to determine why.

   iii. A culture of cooperation, trust, and transparency must be raised among researchers and developers of AI.

   iv. Teams developing Al systems should actively cooperate to avoid money saving on safety standards.

   v. Al systems should be safe and secure throughout their operational lifetime.

   vi. The designers and makers of advanced AI systems are considered as the stakeholders in the moral implications of the use, misuse, and actions of these systems/devices, with a responsibility and opportunity to shape those implications.

vii. Highly autonomous AI systems should be designed so that their goals and behaviours can be assured to align with human values throughout the operation.

a) (ii) (iii) (iii)
b) (iv) (v) (vii)
c) (vi) (ii) (i)
d) All of the above

10. Statement 1: There are three types of Artificial Intelligence (AI): Artificial Narrow Intelligence (ANI) or weak AI, Artificial General Intelligence (AGI) or strong AI, and Artificial Superintelligence (ASI).

Statement 2: IBM's Deep Blue system defeated the World Chess Champion in 2017.

a) Statement 1 is correct, but statement 2 is incorrect.
b) Statement 1 is incorrect, but statement 2 is correct.
c) Both the statements are correct.
d) Both the statements are incorrect.

11. Match the items of column A and Column B

Column A	Column B
(i) Data visualisation tools	(a) Machine learns through experience
(ii) Modelling	(b) It helps in comprehending trends.
(iii) Deep Learning	(c) Pictorial Representation
(iv) Graphical tools	(d) most abundant approach

a) (i)-a , (ii)- d ,(iii)- b , (iv)-c
b) (i)-b , (ii)- d ,(iii)- a , (iv)-c
c) (i)-b , (ii)- a ,(iii)- d , (iv)-c
d) (i)-b , (ii)- d ,(iii)- c , (iv)-a

12. Assertion (A): AI is the term that is frequently applied to the project of developing systems endowed with the intellectual processes that are the characteristic of humans, such as the ability to reason, discover meaning, generalize or learn, from past experience.

Reason(R): The human-machine interface is also known as the man-machine interface (MMI), computer-human interface, or human-computer interface.

a) Both A and R are correct, and R is the correct reason for A.
b) Both A and R are correct, and R is not the correct reason for A.
c) A is correct, but R is incorrect.
d) A is incorrect but R is correct.

13. Which of the following will possess more cognitive capabilities than gifted human beings?

a) AGI
b) ANN
c) ASI
d) None of the above

14. Statement 1: Natural language processing does not uses different techniques like parsing techniques, text recognition, and part-of-speech tagging for implementation.

Statement 2: The range of NLP also includes generating sentences in natural languages by computers just like humans do.

a) Statement 1 is correct, but statement 2 is incorrect.

b) Statement 1 is incorrect, but statement 2 is correct.

c) Both the statements are correct.

d) Both the statements are incorrect.

15. The full form of NLP in relation to AI is:

a) Neural Learning Process
b) Neuro-Linguistic Processing
c) Natural Language Processing
d) Natural Logic Processing

16. Assertion (A): At the very core, CV means enabling computers to derive meaning from spoken or written text in natural language input.

Reason(R): AI is a field of study covering human behaviour, biology, psychology, language and linguistics.

a) Both A and R are correct, and R is the correct reason for A.

b) Both A and R are correct, and R is not the correct reason for A.

c) A is correct, but R is incorrect.

d) A is incorrect but R is correct.

17. Which of the following statements is INCORRECT?

a) Al systems should be designed and operated so that it is compatible with ideals of human dignity, freedoms, rights, and cultural diversity.

b) The usage of AI to personal data must not unreasonably limit people's real or alleged liberty.

c) Al technologies should benefit and empower high-powered people.

d) People should be given the right to access, manage, and control the data they generate, given Al systems' power to analyse and utilize that data.

18. Which of the following phases are included in the data analysis process?

i. Data Requirement Gathering

ii. Data Collection

iii. Data Cleaning

iv. Data Analysis

v. Data Interpretation

vi. Data Visualisation

a) (i)(ii)(iii)
b) (ii)(iii)(v) (vi)
c) (vi)(v)(iv) (iii)
d) (i)(ii)(iii) (iv) (v) (vi)

19. Which step of the AI Project is associated with data collected from different sources?

a) Project Scoping
b) Data Modelling
c) Data Exploration
d) Data Evaluation

20. ____________ provides a full-stack analytics platform, but its visualisation capabilities provide a simple-to-use drag and drop interface which creates charts and more complex graphics with a minimum of hassle.

a) Plotly b) Sisense c) Datawrapper d) Fusion chart

21. Statement 1: Clustering is the process of extracting useful and structured knowledge from unstructured documents to find useful associations and insights.

Statement 2: Text Analytics refers to the unsupervised learning algorithm that can cluster the unknown data according to the patterns or trends identified out of it.

a) Statement 1 is correct but statement 2 is incorrect.

b) Statement 1 is incorrect but statement 2 is correct.

c) Both the statements are correct.

d) Both the statements are incorrect.

22. In data visualisation, data is presented as:

a) Texts b) Maps

c) Pictorial/Graphs/ charts d) None of the above

23. Statement 1: While taking up any AI project in an enterprise, a scientific method is used that is known as the AI Project cycle.

Statement 2: The field of Deep Learning is used by many people and organisations in finding new ways to apply ML methods on their vast, complex, and expanding data sets.

a) Statement 1 is correct but statement 2 is incorrect.

b) Statement 1 is incorrect but statement 2 is correct.

c) Both the statements are correct.

d) Both the statements are incorrect.

24. Assertion (A): Fusion chart is a widely-used and JavaScript-based charting and visualisation package.

Reason (R): Fusion chart can produce 90 different types of charts and integrates with a large number of platforms and frameworks.

a) Both A and R are correct and R is the correct reason for A.

b) Both A and R are correct and R is not the correct reason for A.

c) A is correct but R is incorrect.

d) A is incorrect but R is correct.

25. Which of the following is a disadvantage of decision trees?

a) They are resistant to outliers.

b) They can handle only one type of data.

c) Adding new features is easy.

d) They provide strategic answers to uncertain situations.

26. Assertion (A): Classification is defined as the process of finding a model/ function for distinguishing the data into continuous real values in place classes.

    Reason (R): In classification, data is categorized under different labels based on some parameters mentioned in the input.

    a) Both A and R are correct and R is the correct reason for A.

    b) Both A and R are correct and R is not the correct reason for A.

    c) A is correct but R is incorrect.

    d) A is incorrect but R is correct.

SECTION – C (COMPETENCY BASED QUESTIONS)

Answer any 5 questions out of the given 7 questions **(1 × 5 = 5 marks)**

27. Suppose Kundan was suffering from a genetic disorder. He wants the personalized medical care to treat the disease or disorder that is caused due to gene mutations and that is achieved by understanding the genetic blueprint of the patient. Doctor asked him for the analysis to identify the order of nucleotides. This process is called:

    a) Genome sequencing b) DNA analysis

    c) DNA blue print d) None of the above

28. Suppose Atharv has purchased a house in Galaxy Wonderland Apartments in a city called PSK204. The house has the following features:

    i. Cameras will track the home's exterior even in the dark black outside.

    ii. A thermostat (controlling the temperature of AC or fridge) can be controlled from the bed, the airport, anywhere by his smartphone.

    iii. LED lights in the home can be switched on or off by using the smartphone.

    iv. Motion sensors are used to send an alert when there's motion around the house and to differentiate between pets and burglars.

    v. Turning lights and appliances at home on or off from the mobile device.

    vi. Door locks and garage doors can be opened automatically by using smartphone.

    vii. Setting Auto alerts from the security system to go to your smartphone.

    The city under reference is called:

    a) Electronic City b) Noble City c) Smart City d) Future City

29. . Which of the following sources is not used for data acquisition?

    a) API b) Survey

    c) DPI d) System map

30. Which of the following data visualisation tools does use integration with analytics-oriented programming languages, like Python, R, Matlab, etc.?

    a) Datawrapper b) Fusion charts

    c) QlikView d) Plotly

31. Suppose Shrikant is using an AI-enabled device for controlling his home from remote. Which of the following about the drawbacks of AI is correct?

    a) Unlimited Ability
    b) Can't Handle Emergency Situation
    c) Easy code
    d) Low cost

32. Suppose Sagar prepared a document having the following details:

    i. Project's purpose, vision, and mission
    ii. Measurable objectives and success criteria
    iii. Elaborated project description, conditions, and risks
    iv. Name and authority of the project sponsor
    v. Concerned stakeholders

    What is this document called?

    a) Project cycle
    b) Project charter
    c) Stakeholders' charter
    d) Project file

33. Suppose Neelima is preparing a Decision Tree, where she will show each:

    a) Internal node as a test on an attribute
    b) Branch as an outcome of the test
    c) Leaf node as a class label
    d) All of the above

ANSWERS									
1. (c)	2. (a)	3. (b)	4. (d)	5. (b)	6. (d)	7. (d)	8. (a)	9. (d)	10. (a)
11. (b)	12. (b)	13. (c)	14. (b)	15. (c)	16. (d)	17. (c)	18. (d)	19. (c)	20. (b)
21. (d)	22. (c)	23. (a)	24. (a)	25. (b)	26. (d)	27. (a)	28. (c)	29. (c)	30. (d)
31. (b)	32. (b)	33. (d)							

SOLVED SAMPLE QUESTION PAPER – 2
FOR TERM – 1

Max. Time Allowed: 1 Hour **Max. Marks: 25**

General Instructions:

1. Please read the instructions carefully
2. This Question Paper is divided into 03 sections, viz., Section A, Section B and Section C.
3. Section A is of 05 marks and has 06 questions on Employability Skills.
4. Section B is of 15 marks and has 20 questions on Subject specific Skills.
5. Section C is of 05 marks and has 07 competency-based questions.
6. Do as per the instructions given in the respective sections.
7. Marks allotted are mentioned against each section/question.
8. All questions must be attempted in the correct order

SECTION – A

Answer any 5 questions out of the given 6 questions on Employability Skills (1 × 5 = 5 marks)

1. Which of the following is mismatched?
   a) Message: It is the information that the sender wishes to send.
   b) Decoding: This is the method of how the sender chooses to bring the message into a form appropriate for posting it.
   c) Channel: This means the medium by which the message is sent.
   d) Feedback: The receiver's response to the message.
2. Consider the following examples of sentences:
   i. Chandrika sings a beautiful bhajan.
   ii. Go there.
   iii. Where are you moving to?
   iv. Subhash Chandra Bose is known as Netaji.
   v. Don't pack up that item.
   vi. Ahmedabad is famous for Sabarmati ashram.

   Examples of imperative sentences are:

   a) (i) (ii) only b) (iii) (iv) only c) (ii) (v) only d) (iii) (vi) only
3. Assertion (A): Software is a set of computer programs that perform a particular task.

   Reason(R): The operating system is a master control program that runs the computer.

   a) Both A and R are correct, and R is the correct reason for A.
   b) Both A and R are correct, and R is not the correct reason for A.

c) A is correct but R is incorrect.

d) A is incorrect but R is correct.

4. Consider the following examples and choose the examples of strengths.

I. I am good at creative articles and stories.

II. I have a fear of the water.

III. I play cricket very well.

IV. I am good at speaking Hindi and Marathi.

V. I find it challenging to solve Maths problems.

VI. I am good at writing in Marathi.

a) (ii) (iiii) (iv) b) (iv) (v) (vi) c) (iii) (iv) (vi) d) All of them

5. Which shortcut key is used to cut/delete a file?

a) Ctrl + w b) Ctrl + c c) Ctrl + d d) Ctrl + x

6. Suppose Nikita Sharma works hard to get the 'Best Anchor' award at the annual sports day function. What type of motivation is this?

a) Internal b) External

c) Both internal and external d) None of the above

SECTION – B

Answer any 15 questions out of the given 20 questions (1 × 15 = 15 marks)

7. Which of the following statements is correct?

a) The economic prosperity created by AI can be shared among all countries for the benefit of the world.

b) The power granted by control of highly advanced AI systems should respect and improve, rather than disrupt, the social and civic processes on which the health of society depends.

c) The arms race, particularly in lethal autonomous weapons, should be minimized and ultimately avoided by the governments.

d) All the above

8. ______________ is the term that is frequently applied to the project of developing systems endowed with the intellectual processes that are the characteristic of humans, such as the ability to reason, discover meaning, generalize or learn, from past experience.

a) Neural Network b) Intelligence

c) Artificial Intelligence d) Creativity

9. Which of the following dimension is a core element of sustainable development?

a) Social inclusion b) Economic growth

c) Environmental protection d) None of these

10. Which of the following pairs of subject and domain is/are incorrect?
    i. Computer Science: Building computers
    ii. Mathematics: Algorithms, computability, proof, methods of representation, tractability and decidability
    iii. Neuro-Science: How the basic information processing units, i.e., neurons Process Information
    iv. Statistics: Grammar, syntax, knowledge representations
    v. Linguistics: Learning from data, uncertainty/ certainty of modelling
    vi. Economics: Rational economic agents, the usefulness of data & models, decision Theory
    vii. Cognitive Sciences: Processes and things in nature, interpretation of different Phenomena & their impact

    a) (i) (ii)
    b) (iv) (v)
    c) (vi) (vii)
    d) All of the above

11. What is the art of the study of algorithms that learn from examples and experience known as?
    a) Deep Learning
    b) Machine Learning
    c) Supervised Learning
    d) PBL

12. Statement 1: AI can be defined as a form of intelligence, a type of technology, and a field of study, which is used for making intelligent machines including robots. The AI theory and development of computer systems are capable to perform tasks that generally require human intelligence.

    Statement 2: Computer vision is defined as a field of artificial intelligence that trains computers to interpret and understand the visual world.

    a) Statement 1 is correct, but statement 2 is incorrect.
    b) Statement 1 is incorrect, but statement 2 is correct.
    c) Both the statements are correct.
    d) Both the statements are incorrect.

13. Match the following:

Column A	**Column B**
(i) Data Acquisition	(a) Accurate, reliable, and correct
(ii) Raw facts	(b) Factors associated with problem
(iii) Data Features	(c) Data
(iv) Testing data	(d) Collection of Data

    a) (i)- d, (ii)-c ,(iii)-b , (iv)- a .
    b) (i)- a, (ii)-b ,(iii) c , (iv)- d .
    c) (i)- d, (ii)-c ,(iii)-a , (iv)-b .
    d) (i)- c, (ii)-d ,(iii)-b , (iv)- a .

14. Statement 1: Machine learning is not related of getting computers to act without being explicitly programmed. Arthur Samuel prepared the first computer learning application in 1952.

    Statement 2: Oxford University students in 1979 invent the self-navigating Stanford Cart.

    a) Statement 1 is correct, but statement 2 is incorrect.

    b) Statement 1 is incorrect, but statement 2 is correct.

    c) Both the statements are correct.

    d) Both the statements are incorrect.

15. Which part is not a framework part of Smart city?

    a) Smart Governance b) Smart Environment

    c) Smart Economy d) Smart Transport

16. Assertion (A): A biased person favours one side or issue over another.

    Reason(R): Biased means having a preference for one thing over another and the bias can also be present in Artificial Intelligence.

    a) Both A and R are correct, and R is the correct reason for A.

    b) Both A and R are correct, and R is not the correct reason for A.

    c) A is correct, but R is incorrect.

    d) A is incorrect but R is correct.

17. Which of the following statements are related to Data visualisation?

    i. It clarifies which factors influence customer behaviour.

    ii. It identifies areas that need attention or improvement.

    iii. It predicts sales volumes.

    iv. It helps human beings understand which products to place where.

    v. It helps to manipulate data.

    a) (i) (ii) (iii) b) (iii) (v)

    c) (ii) (iii) (iv) d) (i) (ii) (iii) (v)

18. Statement 1: The training data need not be reliable, authentic, and accurate for the AI machine to work efficiently.

    Statement 2: A technique in which a computer program extracts data from human-readable output coming from another program, is termed as data modelling.

    a) Statement 1 is correct but statement 2 is incorrect.

    b) Statement 1 is incorrect but statement 2 is correct.

    c) Both the statements are correct.

    d) Both the statements are incorrect.

19. Which of the following tools is regarded as 'the grandmaster of data visualisation software?

    a) Tableau b) QlikView c) Fusion charts d) High charts

20. Which technique is used in which a computer program extracts data from a human-readable output from another program?
    a) Data scraping
    b) Data acquisition
    c) Data modeling
    d) Vector mechanics
21. Which language/script is used in creating Fusion charts?
    a) C++
    b) Java
    c) Python
    d) All of the above
22. Assertion (A): Artificial intelligence (AI) is defined as the ability of a digital computer and/ computer-controlled robot to perform tasks, that are generally associated with intelligent humans.

    Reason(R): The intended purpose of AI is to make an intelligent machine that initially thinks as good as a human being.
    a) Both A and R are correct, and R is the correct reason for A.
    b) Both A and R are correct, and R is not the correct reason for A.
    c) A is correct, but R is incorrect.
    d) A is incorrect but R is correct.
23. Statement 1: The Artificial Intelligent project cycle describes all steps required to convert a real-life problem or a challenge into a computer-based Al model.

    Statement 2: AI Modelling refers to developing algorithms or AI models which can be trained to get intelligent output, i.e., writing codes to make a machine artificially intelligent.
    a) Statement 1 is correct but statement 2 is incorrect.
    b) Statement 1 is incorrect but statement 2 is correct.
    c) Both the statements are correct.
    d) Both the statements are incorrect.
24. Assertion (A): A regression problem arises when the output variable is a category.

    Reason (R): Datawrapper is a popular choice among media organisations that frequently use it to create charts and present statistics for media coverage.
    a) Both A and R are correct and R is the correct reason for A.
    b) Both A and R are correct and R is not the correct reason for A.
    c) A is correct but R is incorrect.
    d) A is incorrect but R is correct.
25. Which of the following statements is INCORRECT?
    a) The numerical data is the data where data points are exact numbers.
    b) A technique in which a computer program extracts data from a human-readable output from another program is termed data modeling.
    c) The time-series data is a sequence of numbers collected at regular intervals over some time.
    d) Data is the foundational element that makes AI so powerful.

26. Assertion (A): High chart is often chosen for a fast and flexible solution.

    Reason (R): With a minimum need for specialist data and visualisation training, high chart can be put to work.

    a) Both A and R are correct and R is the correct reason for A.
    b) Both A and R are correct and R is not the correct reason for A.
    c) A is correct but R is incorrect.
    d) A is incorrect but R is correct.

SECTION – C (COMPETENCY BASED QUESTIONS)

Answer any 5 questions out of the given 7 questions **(1 × 5 = 5 marks)**

27. Suppose Sugandha is using an AI technique that finds wide applications in email classifying into "Social", "Personal" and "Promotional" categories, image recognition, face recognition, and text recognition systems. The fundamental of this technique/device is to create parameters that draw the line between doing different objects classifying them into two classes. She is using:

    a) Vector Analysis
    b) Data Analysis
    c) Support Map
    d) Vector Machines or Support Vector

28. Which type of problems are solved by using Vector machines?

    a) Classification problems
    b) Regression problems
    c) Typical problems
    d) None of the above

29. A company has the following data. Identify the time series data out of it.

    i. Server metrics,
    ii. Application performance monitoring,
    iii. Network data, Sensor data,
    iv. Economic indicators
    v. Clicks on social sites

    a) (i) (ii) (iii)
    b) (iii) (v)
    c) (iv) (v)
    d) (i) (ii) (iii) (iv) (v)

30. Which of the following statements is INCORRECT?

    a) Al systems should be designed and operated so that it is compatible with ideals of human dignity, freedoms, rights, and cultural diversity.
    b) The usage of AI to personal data must not unreasonably limit people's real or alleged liberty.
    c) Al technologies should benefit and empower high-powered people.
    d) People should be given the right to access, manage, and control the data they generate, given Al systems' power to analyse and utilize that data.

31. Suppose Matin is using a visualisation package having the following properties:

    i. It is a widely-used visualisation package.
    ii. It has JavaScript-based charting.

iii. It can produce 90 different types of charts.

iv. It can be integrated with a large number of platforms and frameworks.

What is used by him?

a) Plotly b) Sisense c) Fusion chart d) Datawrapper

32. Suppose James is using a visualisation tool that enables more complex and sophisticated visualisations due to the use of its integration with analytics-oriented programming languages, like Python, R, Matlab, etc and it is built using JavaScript. He is using:

a) Plotly b) Sisense c) Datawrapper d) Fusion chart

33. Which of the following features is NOT associated with ANN?

a) Neural networks are able to automatically extract features without input from the coder/programmer.

b) Every artificial neural network (ANN) is controlled by the human brain.

c) The neural network system is modeled on the human brain.

d) Every neural network node is essentially a machine learning algorithm.

ANSWERS									
1. (b)	2. (c)	3. (b)	4. (c)	5. (d)	6. (a)	7. (d)	8. (c)	9. (c)	10. (b)
11. (a)	12. (c)	13. (a)	14. (d)	15. (d)	16. (a)	17. (c)	18. (d)	19. (a)	20. (a)
21. (b)	22. (b)	23. (c)	24. (d)	25. (b)	26. (a)	27. (d)	28. (a)	29. (d)	30. (c)
31. (c)	32. (a)	33. (b)							

CBSE | DEPARTMENT OF SKILL EDUCATION

ARTIFICIAL INTELLIGENCE (SUBJECT CODE 417)

CLASS IX (SESSION 2021-2022)

BLUE-PRINT FOR SAMPLE QUESTION PAPER FOR TERM – 2

Max. Time Allowed: 1 Hour **Max. Marks: 25**

PART A - EMPLOYABILITY SKILLS (05 MARKS):

Unit No.	Name of The Unit	No. of Questions (1 Mark Each)
1	Entrepreneurial Skills-I	3
2	Green Management Skills-I	3
TOTAL QUESTIONS NO. OF QUESTIONS TO BE ANSWERED TOTAL MARKS	6 Questions Any 5 Questions 1 × 5 = 5 Marks	

PART B - SUBJECT SPECIFIC SKILLS (20 MARKS):

Unit No.	Name of The Unit	No. of Questions (1 Mark Each)
1	Neural Network	7
2	Python Basic	20
TOTAL QUESTIONS NO. OF QUESTIONS TO BE ANSWERED TOTAL MARKS	27 Questions 20 Questions 1 × 20 = 20 MARKS	

SOLVED CBSE SAMPLE QUESTION PAPER – 1 FOR TERM – 2

Max. Time Allowed: 1 Hour **Max. Marks: 25**

General Instructions:

1. Please read the instructions carefully
2. This Question Paper is divided into 03 sections, viz., Section A, Section B and Section C.
3. Section A is of 05 marks and has 06 questions on Employability Skills.
4. Section B is of 15 marks and has 20 questions on Subject specific Skills.
5. Section C is of 05 marks and has 07 competency-based questions.
6. Do as per the instructions given in the respective sections.
7. Marks allotted are mentioned against each section/question.
8. All questions must be attempted in the correct order

SECTION – A

Answer any 5 questions out of the given 6 questions on Employability Skills (1 × 5 = 5 marks)

1. Which of the following options is the correct set of tasks of an entrepreneur?
   i. Owning the full income/profit
   ii. Creating a New Method, Idea, or Product
   iii. Making Effective Decisions
   iv. Managing the Business
   v. Taking Risk
   vi. Distributing the dividend
   a) (i) (ii) (iii) (iv) (v) b) (ii) (iii) (iv) (v) (vi)
   c) (i) (iii) (iv) (v) (vi) d) All of the above
2. Which of the following abilities refers to the ability of an entrepreneur to bring out the new ways to run a business?
   a) Creativity b) Hard work
   c) Patience d) Self-motivation
3. Which pair is mismatched?
   a) Tilak Mehta - Papers N Parcels
   b) Advait Thakur- Piramal Enterprises Ltd
   c) Farhad Acidwala - Rockstar Media.
   d) Sunil Mittal - Bharti Enterprises

4. Which of the following options describe a green economy correctly?

   A green economy ______________.

   a) uses less resources
   b) uses more resources
   c) wastes less items
   d) wastes more items

5. Which of the following statements are related to sustainable development?

   i. Use of digital media instead of paper
   ii. Deforestation
   iii. Use of energy-saving devices like LED.
   iv. Use of drip irrigation
   v. The practice of crop rotation

   a) (ii) (iii) (iv)
   b) (ii)(iii)(iv)(v)
   c) (iii) (iv) (v)
   d) All of these

6. Which of the following is not included in the components of a 'Green Economy'?

   a) Renewable energy
   b) Sustainable transport
   c) Green Building
   d) Ethics and transparency

SECTION – B

Answer any 15 questions out of the given 20 questions **(1 × 15 = 15 marks)**

7. Which type of AI Learning is associated with the following features?

   i. It helps in finding which situation needs an action.
   ii. It helps in discovering the action that yields the highest reward over a longer period.
   iii. It provides the learning agent with a reward function.
   iv. It allows to figure out the best method for obtaining large rewards.

   a) Supervised Learning
   b) Unsupervised Learning
   c) Semi-supervised Learning
   d) Reinforcement Learning

8. Match the items of column A and Column B

Column A	**Column B**
(i) Input Layer	(a) Axon
(ii) Hidden layer	(b) Dendrites
(iii) Output Layer	(c) Synapse
(iv) Interconnections	(d) responsible for processing

   a) (i)-a , (ii)- d ,(iii)- b , (iv)-c
   b) (i)-b , (ii)- d ,(iii)- a , (iv)-c
   c) (i)-d , (ii)- b ,(iii)- a , (iv)-c
   d) (i)-b , (ii)- d ,(iii)- c , (iv)-a ,

9. Which one of the following examples is not related to SL?

   a) Classifying the patients whether a patient is suffering from a particular disease or not.
   b) Predicting weather

c) Classifying the received emails whether an email is a spam or not.

d) Predicting house/property price or stock market price

10. Statement 1: Clustering is the task of dividing the data points into a number of groups such that data points in the same groups are more similar to other data points in the same group and dissimilar to the data points in other groups.

    Statement 2: Regression tree (e.g. Random forest) and linear regression are the examples of clustering algorithms.

    a) Statement 1 is correct but statement 2 is incorrect.

    b) Statement 1 is incorrect but statement 2 is correct.

    c) Both the statements are correct.

    d) Both the statements are incorrect.

11. Assertion (A): Clustering is the task of dividing the data points into a number of groups such that data points in the same groups are more similar to other data points in the same group and dissimilar to the data points in other groups.

    Reason (R): Clustering is basically a collection of objects on the basis of similarity and dissimilarity between them.

    a) Both A and R are correct and R is the correct reason for A.

    b) Both A and R are correct and R is not the correct reason for A.

    c) A is correct but R is incorrect.

    d) A is incorrect but R is correct.

12. Which application does not use python?

    a) Database Access b) Network Programming

    c) 2D Graphics d) Desktop Applications

13. Which platform can be used to run Python?

    a) Windows b) macOS, c) Linux d) All of these

14. All other identifiers except ____________ start with a lowercase letter.

    a) Class names b) Private identifier

    c) Complex number d) None of the above

15. A complex number consisting of an ordered pair of real floating-point numbers is denoted by x +yi, where x and y are the real numbers. What is 'i' in it?

    a) Identifier b) Imaginary unit

    c) Both a and b d) None of the above

16. Which of the following statements about Python is correct?

    a) It is a high level and interpreted programming language.

    b) It is a highly useful language focused on rapid application development (RAD), and don't repeat yourself (DRY).

c) It works perfectly to connect existing components together.

d) All the above

17. What is the output of sum(mylist), if mylist= [2,3,5,9]?

a) Displays an error | b) 4
c) 19 | d) 21

18. What is the output of min(mylist), if mylist%=[303, 4313, 363, 3313, 404]?

a) 3313 b) 4313 c) 303 d) 404

19. The process where a set of instructions are repeated in a sequence a number of times until and unless a condition is met, is known as:

a) Iteration
b) Sequential
c) Looping
d) Idealization

20. Match the items of column A and column B correctly.

Column A	Column B
(i) count()	(a) Delete the given element from the list
(ii) index()	(b) To create an empty list
(iii) remove()	(c) To return the number of times an element is found in the list
(iv) list()	(d) To return the index location of the element in the list

a) (i)-d, (ii)-c (iii)-a (iv)-b
b) (i)-c, (ii)-d (iii)-a (iv)-b
c) (i)-c, (ii)-d (iii)-b (iv)-a
d) (i)-b, (ii)-d (iii)-a (iv)-c

21. Assertion (A): In Lists, their elements and size can be changed while the tuples cannot be updated.

Reason (R): The elements in a List are separated by semi colon.

a) Both A and R are correct and R is the correct reason for A.

b) Both A and R are correct and R is not the correct reason for A.

c) A is correct but R is incorrect.

d) A is incorrect but R is correct.

22. Assertion (A): A package is a program of Python modules containing an additional application environment.

Reason (R): Lists are enclosed in square bracket.

a) Both A and R are correct and R is the correct reason for A.

b) Both A and R are correct and R is not the correct reason for A.

c) A is correct but R is incorrect.

d) A is incorrect but R is correct.

23. Statement 1: The Loop or Repetition allows the statement(s) to be executed repeatedly based on certain loop conditions.

    Statement 2: A 'for' statement allows you to repeatedly execute a block of statements till the condition is true.

    a) Statement 1 is correct but statement 2 is incorrect.

    b) Statement 1 is incorrect but statement 2 is correct.

    c) Both the statements are correct.

    d) Both the statements are incorrect.

24. Statement 1: A notebook integrates code and its output into a single document that combines narrative text, visualisations, mathematical equations, and other rich media.

    Statement 2: All other identifiers except class names start with a lowercase letter.

    a) Statement 1 is correct but statement 2 is incorrect.

    b) Statement 1 is incorrect but statement 2 is correct.

    c) Both the statements are correct.

    d) Both the statements are incorrect.

25. ____________ are also known as iteration or iterative statements.

    a) Codes b) Loops

    c) Histogram d) None of the above

26. Which of the following statements is INCORRECT?

    a) In a List, the elements and size can be changed.

    b) Flow chart makes program or system maintenance easier.

    c) Class names start with lowercase letters.

    d) A List contains items that are separated by commas and enclosed within square brackets ([]).

SECTION – C (COMPETENCY BASED QUESTIONS)

Answer any 5 questions out of the given 7 questions **(1 × 5 = 5 marks)**

27. Suppose 'Jhoom AI Creations & Solutions' is using the following applications:

    i. computer vision, & speech recognition,

    ii. machine translation, & social network filtering,

    iii. playing board, & video games,

    iv. medical diagnosis.

    Artificial neural networks (ANNs) have been used in:

    a) (i) only b) (i) (ii) only

    c) (iii) (iv) only d) (i) (ii) (iii) (iv) only

28. Suppose Leena wants to employ NN to analyse data, image processing, natural language processing, and some other kinds of cognitive tasks. Which of the following will be employed by her?

    a) ANN b) BNN
    c) CNN d) None of the above

29. Suppose Iqbal is using a coding language that has the following features:

    i. It is a case-sensitive language.
    ii. Learning and using this language is easy.
    iii. It is portable and its codes are short.
    iv. It is Interpreted, interactive and OOP language.
    v. It is a very simple high-level language with a vast library of add-on modules.

    This coding language is:

    a) Java b) Maya c) C++ d) Python

30. Suppose Anjana is using a process that has the following steps:

    i. Define the inputs
    ii. Define the variables
    iii. Outline the algorithm's operations
    iv. Output the results of the operations

    Which of the following is associated with these steps?

    a) Algorithm b) Decoding c) Flowchart d) Mentoring

31. Consider the following properties:

    i. It exhibits the Sequence of instructions/happenings in a single program.
    ii. It consists of standardized and acceptable symbols.
    iii. It has a clear start point and End/Finish point.
    iv. It exhibits the individual steps and their interconnections.
    v. It shows the logic of an algorithm from start to end.
    vi. It has short, clear, and readable statements written inside the symbols.

    The above statements refer to:

    a) Algorithm b) Flowchart
    c) Code d) Coding language

32. Consider the following reasons for the selection of Python for AI Projects and choose the correct set.

    i. A great library ecosystem
    ii. Flexibility
    iii. A low entry barrier

iv. Platform independence

v. Readability

vi. Good visualisation options

vii. Community support

a) (i) (ii) (iii) (iv)

b) (ii) (iii) (vi) (vii)

c) (iii) (iv) (v) (vi)

d) All the above

33. Which of the following statements is correct?

a) Python is case-sensitive when dealing with identifiers.

b) Python is machine-dependent when dealing with identifiers.

c) Python is not case-sensitive when dealing with identifiers.

d) None of these

ANSWERS									
1. (b)	2. (a)	3. (b)	4. (c)	5. (c)	6. (d)	7. (d)	8. (b)	9. (b)	10. (a)
11. (c)	12. (c)	13. (d)	14. (a)	15. (b)	16. (d)	17. (c)	18. (c)	19. (a)	20. (b)
21. (c)	22. (d)	23. (a)	24. (c)	25. (b)	26. (c)	27. (d)	28. (c)	29. (d)	30. (a)
31. (b)	32. (d)	33. (a)							

UNSOLVED SAMPLE QUESTION PAPER – 1
FOR TERM – 1

Max. Time Allowed: 1 Hour **Max. Marks: 25**

General Instructions:

1. Please read the instructions carefully
2. This Question Paper is divided into 03 sections, viz., Section A, Section B and Section C.
3. Section A is of 05 marks and has 06 questions on Employability Skills.
4. Section B is of 15 marks and has 20 questions on Subject specific Skills.
5. Section C is of 05 marks and has 07 competency-based questions.
6. Do as per the instructions given in the respective sections.
7. Marks allotted are mentioned against each section/question.
8. All questions must be attempted in the correct order

SECTION – A

Answer any 5 questions out of the given 6 questions on Employability Skills (1 × 5 = 5 marks)

1. Match the following.

Column A (Type of sentence)	Column B (Example)
i. Assertive	(a) Sugandha is not studying well.
ii. Interrogative	(b) Wow! You have done well.
iii. Exclamatory	(c) Rakesh is eating an apple.
iv. Negative	(d) Who is going to address the meeting?

a) i-(d), ii-(c), iii- (b), iv- (a) b) i-(c), ii-(d), iii- (b), iv- (a)ytr[po
c) i-(a), ii-(d), iii- (b), iv- (c) d) i-(c), ii-(b), iii- (d), iv- (a)

2. When we communicate verbally, we should use _______.

(a) difficult words (b) simple words (c) confusing words (d) abbreviations

3. Consider the following examples and choose the examples of strengths.

I. I am good at creative articles and stories.
II. I have a fear of the water.
III. I play cricket very well.
IV. I am good at speaking Hindi and Marathi.
V. I find it challenging to solve Maths problems.
VI. I am good at writing in Marathi.

a) (ii) (iiii) (iv) b) (iv) (v) (vi) c) (iii) (iv) (vi) d) All of them

4. Suppose Gauransh studies in class IX and he is aware of his personality, including his strengths, weaknesses, thoughts, beliefs, emotions, and motivations. Which of the following skills does he possess?

   a) Communication skills
   b) Empathy
   c) Self-awareness
   d) Critical Thinking

5. Which of the following extensions is a valid file extension for a picture file?

   a) .jpg
   b) .doc
   c) .text
   d) .txt

6. Statement 1: An operating system is the second program that gets loaded into computer memory.

   Statement 2: Antivirus software is a computer program designed to identify, prevent, and remove viruses from a computer.

   a) Statement 1 is correct but statement 2 is incorrect.
   b) Statement 1 is incorrect but statement 2 is correct.
   c) Both the statements are correct.
   d) Both the statements are incorrect.

SECTION – B

Answer any 15 questions out of the given 20 questions **(1 × 15 = 15 marks)**

7. What is the art of the study of algorithms that learn from examples and experience known as?

   a) Deep Learning
   b) Machine Learning
   c) Supervised Learning
   d) PBL

8. ____________ is the ability of machines to perform cognitive tasks, which a human brain can do, like thinking, perceiving, learning, problem-solving, decision making, etc. It is called:

   a) Supervised Learning
   b) ANN
   c) Artificial Intelligence
   d) CNN

9. Assertion (A): One of the key features that distinguish humans from other living things in the world is intelligence.

   Reason(R): Intelligence is the ability to understand, apply knowledge, and improve skills.

   a) Both A and R are correct, and R is the correct reason for A.
   b) Both A and R are correct, and R is not the correct reason for A.
   c) A is correct, but R is incorrect.
   d) A is incorrect but R is correct.

10. Match the following.

Column A (Bank)	**Column B (Digital Assistant)**
(i) Bank of America	(a) Aida
(ii) HSBC Hong Kong	(b) SIA
(iii) SEB Sweden	(c) Erica
(iv) SBI India	(d) Amy

a) (i)-c (ii) b (iii) a (iv) d
b) (i)-a (ii) d (iii) c (iv) b
c) (i)-c (ii) d (iii) a (iv) b
d) (i)-b (ii) d (iii) a (iv) c

11. Statement 1: Natural language processing does not uses different techniques like parsing techniques, text recognition, and part-of-speech tagging for implementation.

Statement 2: The range of NLP also includes generating sentences in natural languages by computers just like humans do.

a) Statement 1 is correct, but statement 2 is incorrect.
b) Statement 1 is incorrect, but statement 2 is correct.
c) Both the statements are correct.
d) Both the statements are incorrect.

12. Which robot became a Saudi Arabian citizen, the first robot to become a citizen of any country in the world?

a) Robot Shalu
b) Robot George
c) Robot Manav
d) Robot Sophia

13. Assertion (A): 'The goal of AI is to develop machines that behave as though they were intelligent.'

Reason(R): In 1985, John McCarthy, one of the pioneers of AI, was the first to define the goal of artificial intelligence.

a) Both A and R are correct, and R is the correct reason for A.
b) Both A and R are correct, and R is not the correct reason for A.
c) A is correct, but R is incorrect.
d) A is incorrect but R is correct.

14. Which of the following companies is considered a giant player in the field of data?

a) Google
b) Facebook
c) Amazon
d) All the above

15. Statement 1: The main three domains of AI are Data, Computer Vision (CV), and Natural Language Processing (NLP).

Statement 2: Smart estimation of unknown values by using the given series of past data is termed as Long Term Short Memory (LTSM) that is used in Recurrent Neural Networks (RNN).

a) Statement 1 is correct, but statement 2 is incorrect.

b) Statement 1 is incorrect, but statement 2 is correct.

c) Both the statements are correct.

d) Both the statements are incorrect.

16. Which of the following statements id INCORRECT?

a) Artificial Intelligence means a human-made interface with the power to reason and integrate knowledge.

b) Semantic analysis is a common method of processing meaning from natural language.

c) AI machines also keep updating their knowledge to optimize its output.

d) Alan Turing in 1950 created the Turing Test to determine the intelligence of a computer.

17. Which of the following is NOT time-series data?

a) Weather records b) Economic indicators

c) Patient health evolution metrics d) None of the above

18. ____________ Is a tool that has a tree-like structure of decisions and their possible outcomes.

a) Neural network b) Decision tree

c) Fusion Chart d) Bar Graph

19. Statement 1: Problem scoping is a skill where the learners need to focus on the relevant details related to the problem.

Statement 2: The Training data must not be relevant and authentic for the better efficiency of an AI project.

a) Statement 1 is correct but statement 2 is incorrect.

b) Statement 1 is incorrect but statement 2 is correct.

c) Both the statements are correct.

d) Both the statements are incorrect.

20. Which of the following type of problems are solved by using a decision tree?

a) Classification problems b) Regression problems

c) Both (a) and (b) d) None of the above

21. Assertion (A): The decision tree is the most potent and accessible tool for classification and prediction.

Reason (R): A Decision tree is a flowchart like a tree structure, where each internal node denotes a test on an attribute, each branch represents an outcome of the test, and each leaf node (terminal node) holds a class label.

a) Both A and R are correct and R is the correct reason for A.

b) Both A and R are correct and R is not the correct reason for A.

c) A is correct but R is incorrect.

d) A is incorrect but R is correct.

22. Statement 1: Data Analytics is the process of extracting useful and structured knowledge from unstructured documents to find useful associations and insights.

    Statement 2: AI models can be classified either on Rule-based or learning-based approaches.

    a) Statement 1 is correct but statement 2 is incorrect.
    b) Statement 1 is incorrect but statement 2 is correct.
    c) Both the statements are correct.
    d) Both the statements are incorrect.

23. Match the following.

Column A	**Column B**
(i) Simulation	(a) An interactive tool
(ii) LOOPY	(b) Factors associated with problem
(iii) Data Features	(c) Designing a model of a real system
(iv) Testing data	(d) Accurate, reliable, and correct

    a) (i)-a (ii)-c , (iii)-b , (iv)- d
    b) (i)-b (ii)-a , (iii)-c , (iv)- d
    c) (i)-d (ii)-a , (iii)-b , (iv)- c
    d) (i)-c (ii)-a , (iii)-b , (iv)- d

24. Which of the following is NOT a type of data analysis?

    a) Predictive Analysis
    b) Prescriptive Analysis
    c) Statical Analysis
    d) Diagnostic Analysis

25. Assertion (A): Plotly enables more complex and sophisticated visualisations due to the use of its integration with analytics-oriented programming languages, like Python, R, Matlab, etc. It is built using JavaScript.

    Reason (R): Transponders used in AI-enabled machines convert real-world phenomena like temperature, force, movement to voltage or current, etc., into signals.

    a) Both A and R are correct and R is the correct reason for A.
    b) Both A and R are correct and R is not the correct reason for A.
    c) A is correct but R is incorrect.
    d) A is incorrect but R is correct.

26. Which of the true statements?

    i. Sensors used in AI-enabled machines convert real-world phenomena like temperature, force, movement to voltage or current, etc., into signals.
    ii. Decision tree learning is the technique used for supervised classification learning.
    iii. A regression problem arises when the output variable is a category.
    iv. Data modelling is the third stage in the AI project cycle.
    v. The data is labelled when entered into the model in a learning-based approach.

a) Only (i)
b) Only (i) (ii)
c) Only (i) (ii) (iii)
d) All are True

SECTION – C (COMPETENCY BASED QUESTIONS)

Answer any 5 questions out of the given 7 questions **(1 × 5 = 5 marks)**

27. Assume that you have owned a house with the following features:

i. Turning lights and appliances at home on or off from the mobile device.

ii. Cameras will track the home's exterior even in the dark black outside.

iii. A thermostat (controlling the temperature of AC or fridge) can be controlled from the bed, the airport, anywhere by his smartphone.

iv. Setting Auto alerts from the security system to go to your smartphone.

v. LED lights in the home can be switched on or off by using the smartphone.

vi. Motion sensors are used to send an alert when there's motion around the house and to differentiate between pets and burglars.

vii. Door locks and garage doors can be opened automatically by using smartphone.

This type of houses will be available in:

a) Electronic City
b) Future City
c) Noble City
d) Smart City

28. Suppose Imran is using an AI technique that finds wide applications in email classifying into "Social", "Personal" and "Promotional" categories, image recognition, face recognition, and text recognition systems. The fundamental of this technique/device is to create parameters that draw the line between doing different objects classifying them into two classes. He is basically using:

a) Data Analysis
b) Vector Machines/ Support Vector
c) Vector Analysis
d) Support Map

29. Suppose Prof RS Patel is working in Jyoti Data Analytics and using data analysis. Which of the following phases are included in the data analysis process?

i. Data Analysis

ii. Data Requirement Gathering

iii. Data Collection

iv. Data Cleaning

v. Data Interpretation

vi. Data Visualisation

a) (i)(ii)(iii)
b) (vi)(v)(iv) (iii)
c) (ii)(iii)(v) (vi)
d) All of these

30. Suppose Nutan Parihar has to solve different types of problems while working in a company providing AI solutions to their clients. She is using Vector mechanics. Which type of problems are solved by using Vector machines?

    a) Typical problems
    b) Classification problems
    c) Regression problems
    d) Both b and c

31. Suppose Tina is working on an AI project and wants to prepare the project charter. Which of the following details will be included in this document?

    i. Project's purpose, vision, and mission
    ii. Measurable objectives and success criteria
    iii. Elaborated project description, conditions, and risks
    iv. Name and authority of the project sponsor
    v. Concerned stakeholders
    vi. Govt agencies working on that area

    a) (i) (ii) (iii)
    b) (i) (ii) (iii) (iv)
    c) (i) (ii) (iii) (iv) (v)
    d) (i) (ii) (iii) (iv) (v) (vi)

32. Suppose Vivek Verma, CMD, YetBut Financial Advisors is using a Decision Tree. What will he show in it?

    a) Leaf node as a class label
    b) Internal node as a test on an attribute
    c) Branch as an outcome of the test
    d) All of the above

33. Suppose Jevelson is working as Design Director in JanMan AI solutions and is using a visualisation package with the following properties:

    i. It has JavaScript-based charting.
    ii. It is a widely-used visualisation package.
    iii. It can produce 90 different types of charts.
    iv. It can be integrated with a large number of platforms and frameworks.

    What is used by him?

    a) Fusion chart
    b) Plotly
    c) SiSense
    d) Datawrapper

UNSOLVED SAMPLE QUESTION PAPER – 2
FOR TERM – 2

Max. Time Allowed: 1 Hour **Max. Marks: 25**

General Instructions:

1. Please read the instructions carefully
2. This Question Paper is divided into 03 sections, viz., Section A, Section B and Section C.
3. Section A is of 05 marks and has 06 questions on Employability Skills.
4. Section B is of 15 marks and has 20 questions on Subject specific Skills.
5. Section C is of 05 marks and has 07 competency-based questions.
6. Do as per the instructions given in the respective sections.
7. Marks allotted are mentioned against each section/question.
8. All questions must be attempted in the correct order

SECTION – A

Answer any 5 questions out of the given 6 questions on Employability Skills (1 × 5 = 5 marks)

1. Anand Mohan runs a Fresh Vegetable shop. A customer comes to his shop and starts shouting at him. He does not get angry, but he listens to what his customer is saying. He is:

   a) Confident b) Creative c) Hardworking d) Patient

2. Arman has a Cold Storage to keep the produce of farmers and employs more than 25 persons. He pays his employees on the 7th of every month. He:

   a) Do nothing special. b) Takes risk

   c) Manages the business d) Creates a new product

3. Study the following statements to choose the correct set of myths about entrepreneurs.

   i. A person who has a big business is an entrepreneur.

   ii. Entrepreneurs are not in the industry for the money.

   iii. Entrepreneurs take lots of risks.

   iv. An entrepreneur cannot borrow from banks.

   v. A new business always flourishes.

   vi. One must be young and restless to be an entrepreneur.

   a) (ii) (iii) (iv) b) (iii) (iv) (v) (vi)

   c) (i) (iii) (iv) (v) (vi) d) (i) (ii) (iii) (iv) (v) (vi)

4. Which of the following is not included in India's Eight-Point Intended Nationally Determined Contribution towards Green economy?

   a) To put forward and propagating a healthy and sustainable way of living based on traditions and values of conservation and moderation

b) To adopt a climate-friendly and cleaner path than the one followed hitherto by others at a corresponding level of economic development.

c) To reduce the emissions intensity

d) None of the above

5. Which of the following features is not related with Green Economy?

a) The transition from fossil fuels to renewable energy is the base of green economy.

b) There are weak links between conserving nature and reducing poverty.

c) The green energy promotes the steps required to avoid irreversible climate change.

d) Re-focusing of the development model at the global level with increasing weight of economic sectors based on energy and the environment.

6. ____________ economy must be not only efficient but also fair. Fairness implies recognising global and country-level equity dimensions, particularly in assuring a just transition to an economy that is low-carbon, resource-efficient, and socially inclusive.

a) Green b) Capitalist c) Mixed d) Traditional

SECTION – B

Answer any 15 questions out of the given 20 questions (1 × 15 = 15 marks)

7. Which app is used to convert the handmade drawing into HTML code?

a) SketchCode b) QuickDraw c) LearnDraw d) Vinci code

8. Which of the following is an application of Artificial Neural Network (ANN)?

i. Optimisation of logistics for transportation networks,

ii. Medical and disease diagnosis,

iii. Character and voice recognition (natural language processing),

iv. Targeted marketing,

v. Robotic control systems.

vi. For financial predictions for stock prices, currency, futures options, bankruptcy, bond ratings, etc.

vii. Drones

a) (ii) (iii) (iv) b) (iv) (v) (vii)

c) (vii) (vi) (v) (iv) (iii) d) (i) (ii) (iii) (iv) (v) (vi)

9. Assertion (A): Python is platform-independent.

Reason (R): Python can be used across different platforms and technologies with the basic coding.

a) Both A and R are correct and R is the correct reason for A.

b) Both A and R are correct and R is not the correct reason for A.

c) A is correct but R is incorrect.

d) A is incorrect but R is correct.

10. Which of the following is NOT an application of ANN?
    a) Ecosystem evaluation, medical imaging
    b) Forecasting of Electrical load and energy demand, identification of compounds
    c) Outdoor games for children, wood cutting industries
    d) Process and quality control in industries, facial recognition

11. Statement 1: A neural network is a computational data model that is capable to capture and represent the complex input/output relationships.

    Statement 2: Classification is basically a collection of objects on the basis of similarity and dissimilarity between them.
    a) Statement 1 is correct but statement 2 is incorrect.
    b) Statement 1 is incorrect but statement 2 is correct.
    c) Both the statements are correct.
    d) Both the statements are incorrect.

12. A diagrammatic/graphical representation of sequence of steps to solve a problem is known as ____________.

    a) Flowchart b) SiSence c) Histogram d) Pie chart

13. Which statement about the flow chart is NOT TRUE?
    a) The flow chart shows the logic of a program in a simple way.
    b) The flow chart makes program or system maintenance easier.
    c) The flow chart is an easy and efficient tool to analyse a problem.
    d) It is difficult to convert the flow chart into any programming language code.

14. Assertion (A): Self-learning resulting from experience can occur within networks, which can derive conclusions from a complex and seemingly unrelated set of information.

    Reason (R): Neural networks are not helpful in solving complex problems in real-life situations.
    a) Both A and R are correct and R is the correct reason for A.
    b) Both A and R are correct and R is not the correct reason for A.
    c) A is correct but R is incorrect.
    d) A is incorrect but R is correct.

15. What is a graphical representation of a sequence of steps to solve a problem known as?

    a) Vector analysis b) Venn diagram
    c) Flow chart d) Pie chart

16. Which geometrical shape is used in a flowchart to represent the operations having two/three alternatives, true and false, etc.?

    a) Square b) Diamond c) Triangle d) Rectangle

17. Statement 1: The plus (+) sign is defined as the string repetition operator, and the asterisk (*) is the concatenation operator.

    Statement 2: A flowchart is considered as a blueprint of a design used for solving any specific problem.

    a) Statement 1 is correct but statement 2 is incorrect.

    b) Statement 1 is incorrect but statement 2 is correct.

    c) Both the statements are correct.

    d) Both the statements are incorrect.

18. Due to which property is Python one of the fastest-growing programming languages?

    a) Ease of Learning
    b) Scalability
    c) Adaptability
    d) All the above

19. What is the other name for 'Iterative statements' in Python?

    a) Loops b) Lists c) Operators d) Strings

20. Match the items of column A and column B correctly.

Column A	Column B
(i) len()	(a) To create an empty list
(ii) append()	(b) To calculate the number of elements in list
(iii) list()	(c) To add an element at the desired index
(iv)d. insert()	(d) mylist.append(20)

    a) (i). –c, (ii).- d,(iii).- a,(iv).-b.
    b) (i). – b, (ii).- d,(iii).- a,(iv).- c.
    c) (i). – b, (ii).- d,(iii).- c,(iv).- a.
    d) (i). – b, (ii).- c,(iii).- a,(iv).-d.

21. Which geometrical shape is used to represent the start and the end in a flowchart?

    a) Triangle
    b) Oval
    c) Diamond
    d) Square

22. Which function is used to convert a string of digits into an integer?

    a) int() b) conv() c) string() d) str()

23. All control flow statements in Python start with:

    a) Colon (:)
    b) Semicolon (;)
    c) Hash sign (#)
    d) Full Stop (.)

24. Assertion (A): A flowchart is a programming tool that uses different symbols to design a solution to a problem.

    Reason (R): A program is a collection of instructions used to perform a specific task when executed by a computer.

    a) Both A and R are correct and R is the correct reason for A.

    b) Both A and R are correct and R is not the correct reason for A.

c) A is correct but R is incorrect.

d) A is incorrect but R is correct.

25. Statement 1: Python does not allow punctuation/special characters such as @, $, and % within identifiers.

    Statement 2: A variable whose value cannot be changed even later on is called a 'Constant.'

    a) Statement 1 is correct but statement 2 is incorrect.
    b) Statement 1 is incorrect but statement 2 is correct.
    c) Both the statements are correct.
    d) Both the statements are incorrect.

26. Which of the following statements is INCORRECT?

    a) Starting an identifier with a single leading underscore indicates that the identifier is private.
    b) When the identifier also ends with two trailing underscores, then the identifier is a language defined special name.
    c) It is difficult to convert the flowchart into any programming language code.
    d) The elements in a List can be changed. It shows that a list is mutable.

SECTION – C (COMPETENCY BASED QUESTIONS)

Answer any 5 questions out of the given 7 questions **(1 × 5 = 5 marks)**

27. Suppose Ankita is working with Shikha AI Modelling Services and is considering the following applications:

    i. Robotics for industrial automation.
    ii. Business strategy planning
    iii. Machine learning and data processing
    iv. In creating training systems that provide custom instruction and materials according to the requirement of learners.
    v. Aircraft control and robot motion control

    These applications are associated with:

    a) Reinforcement Learning
    b) Unsupervised Learning
    c) Supervised Learning
    d) None of the above

28. Suppose Manoj Talukdar is using a process that models a function through which the data is predicted in discrete class labels. The algorithms involve decision tree, logistic regression, etc. and predicts unordered data. It is evaluated by measuring accuracy.

    He is using:

    a) Regression
    b) Classification
    c) Clustering
    d) CNN

29. Consider the following reasons for the selection of Python for AI Projects and choose the correct set.

    i. A great library ecosystem

    ii. Flexibility

    iii. A low entry barrier

    iv. Platform independence

    v. Readability

    vi. Good visualisation options

    vii. Community support

    a) (ii) (iii) (iv) b) (iii) (vi) (vii) c) (iv) (v) (vi) d) All the above

30. Which statement about the flow chart is NOT TRUE?

    a) The flow chart makes program or system maintenance easier.

    b) The flow chart shows the logic of a program in a simple way.

    c) The flow chart is an easy and efficient tool to analyse a problem.

    d) It is difficult to convert the flow chart into any programming language code.

31. Suppose M Radha Krishanan is working in Southern AI Visualisation Council. He is considering the following statements about flowchart and choose the correct set.

    i. It exhibits the individual steps and their interconnections.

    ii. It represents a workflow or process in a diagrammatic representation.

    iii. It exhibits the sequence of instructions/happenings in a single program.

    iv. It does not show the logic of an algorithm from start to end.

    v. It consists of standardised and acceptable symbols.

    vi. It has no clear start point and End/Finish point.

    vii. It exhibits the control from one activity to the next one.

    a) (i) (ii) (iii) (iv) b) (iii) (iv) (v) (vi)

    c) (i) (ii) (iii) (v) (vii) d) (i) (ii) (iii) (iv) (vi)

32. Which of the following statements are correct?

    i. Python does allow punctuation/special characters such as @, $, and % within identifiers.

    ii. The flow chart shows the logic of a program in a simple way.

    iii. Lists are an important data type of Python.

    iv. Python has three types of type conversion.

    v. A diagrammatic/graphical representation of a sequence of steps to solve a problem is known as a flowchart.

    vi. Starting an identifier with a single leading underscore indicates that the identifier is private.

a) (i) (ii) (iii) (iv)
b) (iii) (iv) (v) (vi)
c) (ii) (iii) (v) (vi)
d) (i) (ii) (iii) (vi)

33. Suppose Sujata Menon wants to create a flowchart by using various geometrical shapes. Which of the following pairs (shape and description) is/are INCORRECT?

i. Oval: Page connector.

ii. Rectangle: It is used to show processing; Used for arithmetic operations and data manipulations.

iii. Diamond: It is used to show decision-making. It is used to represent the operation in which there are two/three alternatives, true and false, etc.

iv. Parallelogram: it is used for input and output operation.

v. Circle: It is used to represent the start and the end of the flowchart.

vi. Arrows: Flowline is used to indicate the flow of logic by connecting symbols.

a) (i) (ii) only
b) (i) (v) only
c) (iv) (v) only
d) (ii) (v) (vi) only

ACKNOWLEDGEMENTS AND REFERENCES
(Pictures/Figures/Photographs)

1.1 https://www.nextpit.com/best-books-about-artificial-intelligence

1.2 https://depositphotos.com/115101916/stock-photo-speak-less-listen-more-placard.html

1.3 https://www.educba.com/types-of-communication/

1.5 https://kingz0925.blogspot.com/2013/04/visual-communication-classs-publication.html

1.6 http://www.authorstream.com/Presentation/zulualien-638417-interpersonal-communication/

1.7 Communication in Healthcare - Physiopedia (physio-pedia.com)

1.8 https://www.usa.edu/blog/communication-in-nursing/

1.9 https://www.publicdomainpictures.net/en/view-image.php?image=221463&picture=feedback

1.10 https://newsmoor.com/communication-interaction-sharing-exchanging-information-message-opinion-and-imparting/journalism/

1.12 https://courses.lumenlearning.com/wmopen-organizationalbehavior/chapter/key-components-of-communication/

1.13 https://www.open.edu/openlearn/mod/oucontent/view.php?id=98509§ion=_unit2.5

1.14 https://www.slideshare.net/saikrishna758/paragraph-130626023636phpapp01

1.15 http://cygnet-infotech.blogspot.com/2013/06/8-must-have-features-in-your-intranet.html

2.1 https://www.nhs.us/students/futuready/self-management/

2.2 https://startupanz.com/importance-passion-goal-setting-2021/

2.4 https://stockfresh.com/image/6814671/strategy-tactics-plan-action-arrow-signs-achieve-goal-3d

2.5 https://www.marketing91.com/strategy-definition/

2.6 https://www.cuinsight.com/credit-unions-jump-to-help-members-during-leap-year.html

2.7 https://intentionalbygrace.com/

2.8 https://capazin.com/how-to-develop-a-winning-team-spirit/

3.1 https://news.samsung.com/global/samsung-electronics-sweeps-coveted-global-ai-awards

3.2 https://securityvaultsystems.com/ict/

3.3 https://www.quora.com/What-is-output-devices

3.4 http://dovemediaworks.net/the-different-types-of-social-media/

3.5 http://infozilla.blogspot.com/2011/02/

3.6 https://www.mobilitaria.com/parts-of-android-mobile-phones/

3.7 https://www.freepressjournal.in/tech/move-over-sophia-meet-shalu-indias-first-social-humanoid-robot

3.8 https://www.gizmoarc.com/most-popular-internet-browsers-from-2003-to-2020/

3.9 https://www.slideshare.net/Lito4174/smartphone-and-its-features

3.10 https://cornerstoneinternationalcollege.blogspot.com/2017/07/the-benefits-of-e-learning-cornerstone-international-college.html

4.1 https://techcrunch.com/2016/06/30/the-golden-age-of-american-entrepreneurship/

4.2 https://insight.kellogg.northwestern.edu/article/how-to-foster-entrepreneurship-in-emerging-markets

4.3 https://incparadise.net/introduction-entrepreneurship-development/

4.4 https://marketbusinessnews.com/successful-entrepreneurs/186269/

4.6 https://egov.eletsonline.com/2015/10/govt-ropes-in-isobar-with-negp-for-digital-india/

4.7 https://www.midgetherald.com/top-10-young-indian-entrepreneurs-2021/

4.8 https://electricalstudyportal.blogspot.com/2015/08/what-is-digital-india-campaign-impact.html

4.9 https://www.youtube.com/watch?v=a6LlqmKwYtQ

4.10 https://www.bms.co.in/what-is-the-meaning-of-entrepreneurship-2/

5.1 https://ied.eu/project-updates/green-skills-and-innovation-for-inclusive-growth/

5.2 https://blog.global.fujitsu.com/fgb/2018-08-01/exploring-the-challenges-to-and-solutions-for-achieving-the-sdgs/

5.3 https://www.utkaltoday.com/green-skill-development-program-india/

5.4 http://www.irishenvironment.com/iepedia/green-economy/

5.5 https://www.researchgate.net/figure/Green-economy-and-linkage-with-various-factors_fig1_325346331

5.6 https://www.green.it/litalia-unita-green-economy/

5.7 https://en.wikipedia.org/wiki/Green_economy

5.8 https://www.researchgate.net/figure/A-sustainable-development-has-to-involve-economy-social-community-and-environment_fig5_271766042

5.9 https://nyec.org/green_economy/green-economy-chart/

5.10 http://greenshootmedia.com/product/2015-water-conservation

5.11 https://www.world-energy.org/article/4553.html

5.13 https://gopinathpaper.com/2018/01/14/reduce-reuse-recycle/

5.14 https://www.worldatlas.com/articles/10-biggest-conservation-success-stories-2019.html

6.1 https://www.vecteezy.com/vector-art/622564-ai-concept

6.2 https://krishnakitchen.org/barmah/application-of-expert-system-in-artificial-intelligence.php

6.3 https://thevrio.com/2019/02/01/intelligence-is-not-uni-dimensional/

6.4 https://www.gadgetbridge.com/news/rashmi-the-first-humanoid-robot-made-by-a-software-engineer-based-out-of-ranchi-is-now-a-rj/

6.5 https://history-computer.com/arthur-samuel-biography-history-and-inventions/

6.6 https://www.heheltd.com/creating-a-chatbot-that-gets-smarter-over-time/

6.7 https://www.fiverr.com/categories/programming-tech/programming-services

6.8 https://createdigital.org.au/sophia-humanoid-robot-world-talking/

6.9 https://centurymedia360.com/artificial-intelligence/

6.10 https://venturebeat.com/2020/03/19/bnh-ai-is-a-new-law-firm-focusing-only-on-ai/?via=indexdotco

6.11 https://www.cittimagazine.co.uk/news/funding-investment/connexin-secures-80m-investment-to-develop-uk-smart-city-technologies.html

6.12 https://deana.ai/blog/what-is-an-artificial-intelligence-ai-personal-assistant.html

7.1 https://usmsystems.com/how-artificial-intelligence-ai-will-renovate-traditional-hiring-process/

7.2 https://brainly.in/question/30202383

7.3 https://visualisingadvocacy.org/resources/tools/datawrapper/

7.4 https://www.betterbuys.com/bi/reviews/sisense-business-intelligence/

7.5 https://blog.eduonix.com/software-development/convolutional-neural-networks-image-processing/

7.6 https://workhorseconsulting.net/data-analyst-process/

7.7 https://www.quora.com/What-are-the-steps-of-a-data-analysis-process

7.8 https://plotlygraphs.medium.com/what-scientists-engineers-teachers-and-journalists-say-about-plotly-c175199c5453

7.9 https://www.vebuso.com/2020/01/decision-tree-intuition-from-concept-to-application/
https://www.vebuso.com/2020/01/decision-tree-intuition-from-concept-to-application/

7.10 https://intellyticshub.com/tableau.html

7.11 https://www.analyticsvidhya.com/learning-paths-data-science-business-analytics-business-intelligence-big-data/qlikview-learning-path/

7.12 https://venngage.com/blog/data-visualization/

7.13 https://www.justinmind.com/blog/8-data-visualization-tools-for-ux-designers-visualize-insights-prototype-better-products/

7.14 https://www.betterbuys.com/bi/reviews/sisense-business-intelligence/

7.15 https://www.ebuyer.com/blog/2017/09/the-lords-and-artificial-intelligence/robot-thinking/

8.1 http://brainstormingbox.org/a-beginners-guide-to-neural-networks/

8.2 https://futurism.com/the-byte/human-brain-neural-network

8.3 https://www.practicalai.io/implementing-classification-using-logistic-regression-in-ruby/

8.4 https://towardsai.net/p/data-science/linear-regression-basics-for-absolute-beginners

8.5 http://alexhwilliams.info/itsneuronalblog/2015/10/01/clustering2/

8.6 https://www.quytech.com/blog/top-5-deep-learning-frameworks/

8.7 https://www.istockphoto.com/vector/deep-learning-infographic-as-vector-illustration-gm578558042-99435745

8.8 https://www.shutterstock.com/video/clip-27028492-neurons-brain-loop-3d-animation-neural-network

8.9 https://www.sitepoint.com/keras-digit-recognition-tutorial/

8.10 https://www.infoworld.com/article/3564164/kaggle-where-data-scientists-learn-and-compete.html

8.11 https://royaljay.com/healthcare/neural-networks-in-healthcare/

8.12 https://www.digitaltrends.com/cool-tech/what-is-an-artificial-neural-network/

9.1 https://logos-download.com/9988-python-logo-download.html

9.2 https://www.benchteq.com/top-10-features-of-python-you-need-to-know/

9.3 https://medium.com/the-andela-way/the-rise-of-modern-programming-languages-c923a2b914fc

9.5 https://www.javatpoint.com/python-applications

9.6 https://cacoo.com/resources/flowchart-guide/

9.7 https://www.geeksforgeeks.org/python-if-else/

9.8 https://www.w3programmers.com/php-if-if-else-statement/

9.9 https://www.geeksforgeeks.org/python-if-else/

9.10 https://www.journaldev.com/16450/java-for-loop

9.11 http://codepanel.blogspot.com/2013/07/do-while-loop-syntax.html

9.12 https://www.atnyla.com/tutorial/python-features/11/603

9.13 https://railsware.com/blog/python-for-machine-learning-indexing-and-slicing-for-lists-tuples-strings-and-other-sequential-types/